In Its Corporate Capacity:
The Seminary of Montreal as a
Business Institution, 1816–1876

The Seminary of Montreal – a French, male religious community – had crucial functions in pre-industrial Montreal. Since the 1660s the seminary, which was both seigneur of the island of Montreal and its titular parish priest, had been an integral part of the seigneurial, clerical, and merchant élite dominating Montreal. Early in the nineteenth century the seminary came under increasing attack from new forces in Montreal society, particularly the emerging industrial bourgeoisie, which resented the seminary's seigneurial expropriations.

The collapse of the rebellions of 1837–8 ended two decades of crisis for the seminary and assured its survival. Although seigneurialism on the island of Montreal was gradually dismembered, the seminary's corporate powers, its right of recruitment, and its income were guaranteed. At the same time, the seminary's growing social and ideological functions in industrial society insured its protection by an appreciative bourgeoisie.

In Its Corporate Capacity compares the seminary's pre-industrial forms of income to its new capitalist revenues from land sales, subdivision developments, bonds, and *rentier* income from office, warehousing, and urban-housing properties. As its income changed, management of the seminary took new forms. The business office expanded from a single priest/manager into a professionalized operation which included an accountant, architect, surveyor, clerk, and several notaries and lawyers. The seminary's banking and record-keeping operations were also brought into line with modern business practice. Given its new revenues, corporate powers, and social mandate from the state, the seminary was able to play a central role in the development of popular schools in Montreal, in financing and directing social institutions like hospitals, workshops, and hospices and — through the pulpit, newspapers, libraries, and national societies – in legitimizing the changing class structure of industrializing Montreal.

Brian Young, who teaches history at McGill University, is also the author of *George-Etienne Cartier: Montreal Bourgeois*.

In Its Corporate Capacity

The Seminary of Montreal as a Business Institution, 1816–1876

BRIAN YOUNG

McGill-Queen's University Press
Kingston and Montreal

©McGill-Queen's University Press 1986
ISBN 0-7735-0554-7

Legal deposit 2nd quarter 1986
Bibliothèque nationale du Québec

Printed in Canada

This book has been published with the help of a grant
from the Social Science Federation of Canada, using
funds provided by the Social Sciences and Humanities
Research Council of Canada.

Canadian Cataloguing in Publication Data

Young, Brian J., 1940–
    In its corporate capacity
    Bibliography: p.
    Includes index.
    ISBN 0-7735-0554-7
    1. Grand-Séminaire de Saint-Sulpice – History.
    2. Seigniorial tenure – Quebec (Province) –
    Montréal (Region) – History. * 3. Business enter-
    prises – (Quebec (Province) – Montréal (Region) –
    History. I. Title.
    HC118.M6Y68 1986   338.7'61333322'0971427   C86-093325-3

The cover illustration is based on a watercolour of the
Old Seminary, Montreal, by H. Bunnett, 1888, in the
McCord Museum, McGill University, Montreal.

To R.R.

The concluding request of the Seminary, respectfully presented to the well-meaning advocates of the Indians, is to pause a little, lest, by proceeding further, they should, though unwittingly, be assailing the very basis of all regularly organized human society, and of natural justice – the rights of property.

(Sulpician pamphlet, 1876)

Contents

Figures

Tables

Appendixes

Introduction

Nineteenth-century Canadian historiography over-emphasizes the staple, politics, ethnicity, nation-building, "last spikes," and progress. Canadian business history, strongly influenced by Alfred Chandler and the *Business History Review*, often concentrates on the innovative and the entrepreneurial.[1] In the broad brush strokes of cod, the St Lawrence River, railway builders, and upwardly mobile immigrants with which we have drawn our economic and business history, essential indicators of social relations such as debt, law, institutions, and the power of the landed proprietor have become secondary or, worse, have been delegated to what one historian calls "the stuff of romantic melodrama."[2]

To understand how the business institution central to this book functioned, contract, property condition, privilege, or class cannot be marginalized as incidental thorns on the road to material success or nationhood. This institution, in its first century and a half in Canada, lived on seigneurial income expropriated from rural and urban *censitaires*. Over the nineteenth century the company's business operations were transformed into capitalist forms. This history concentrates then on one institution's adjustment to fundamental change in its property relations and the implications for one company of the transition from feudalism to industrial capitalism.

This perspective coincides with important themes in European history: the Counter-Reformation, seigneurialism, institutionalization, church-state relations, industrialization, revolution, and the rise of the bourgeoisie. It is in pre-revolution France that the company has its roots and from which it assumed the structure, constitution, and ideological reflexes that still govern it today. The subject is old, Catholic, and French – and yet central to the urbanization and industrialization experience of Canada's most important nineteenth-century city. Instead of a "visible hand," this study emphasizes institutional persistence, changing class relations, and the power of property in Canadian history.

Since the seventeenth century the Séminaire de Saint-Sulpice de Montréal has had its Canadian headquarters on Notre-Dame Street in central Montreal. In 1840 the all male company had twenty-four members in Canada, over three-quarters of whom were born in France. The Sulpicians abandoned their families and personal independence to live by the constitution of a Roman Catholic religious community. Their business officers – some Sulpician and some lay – fulfilled various accounting, notarial, managerial, and clerking tasks in the seminary office. Instead of the entrepreneurial clichés of the cigar, the handshake, and the private railway car, our "heroes" moved in the quiet and often anonymous world of desks, vaults, refectories, and registry offices. The tools of their trade were the wax seal, the survey, the *Coutume de Paris*, the mortgage, the bond coupon, and, above all, the contract; behind their paper, particularly after 1840, was the coercive power of the state.

The Séminaire de Saint-Sulpice was founded in seventeenth-century Paris to train a reformed Roman Catholic clergy. Powerful and aristocratic, the company participated in the founding of Montreal in the 1640s, became perpetual rectors of the parish of Montreal, and acquired the seigneuries of Montreal, Two Mountains, and Saint-Sulpice. Perennially Gallican, the seminary was always characterized by a political suppleness that allowed it to prosper on two continents despite French monarchical crises, the British conquest of Canada, the French Revolution, and the Napoleonic upheavals. This political machiavellianism contrasted sharply with the seminary's moral and social rigidity, its vigorous training of priests, its strict attitude to nuns and other female occupation-groups, and its disciplining of popular classes – useful institutional characteristics in the unstable social environment of nineteenth-century Montreal. The seminary had four civil functions: direction of its seigneuries, the operation of its Indian mission, the provision of various social and educational services in Montreal, and the secular functions of the Lower-Canadian priest. By the early nineteenth century it had over 3,000 *censitaires* on its three seigneuries, and the city of Montreal was within the seminary's parish and seigneury.

The use of the term "feudalism" in nineteenth-century Lower Canada must be explained. For historians like Maurice Dobb, Kohachiro Takahashi, and Guy Bois, the term implies a mode of production in which the landlord lived off the peasant surplus; these dues might be paid in direct labour, kind, or cash. This expropriation, the root of social relationships in feudal society, was assured by supporting judicial and political structures. The work of historians like Louise Dechêne emphasizes the dynamism and rigour of seigneurialism in New France, and several recent studies suggest that seigneurialism became even more exploitive and authoritarian after the conquest.[3] Taken from this perspective, feudalism seems a particularly apt term to describe the seminary's property and social relations, the forms of its income before 1840, and, in a large sense, its historic comportment in the Montreal region from the 1640s into the nineteenth century. The first chapters describe the seminary's business operations in an environment of feudal relations and as a company whose primary income came from seigneurial levies collected from the holders of its ceded lands (*censitaires*).

Historians of the transition from feudalism to industrial capitalism emphasize the new mode of production with its changes in the form of work, its new technologies, its expanding market economy, and its evolving forms of capital. This process was accompanied by modernization of the state and by a bourgeois ideology that gave prominence to parliamentary institutions, individualism, and freedom of property. It also led to the formation of new social groups and a polarization of class tensions of which the rebellions of 1837--8 were a prominent manifestation. One important element in the transformation of land and labour into commodities was the change in land tenure from a seigneurial to a freehold condition.[4] It was this factor, the pressure on its seigneurial privileges, that marked the seminary's passage across the transition most immediately and most profoundly.

The seminary's history suggests strongly the quarter from which originated the attacks on its feudal property relations and explains the choice of 1816 as one perimeter of this study. Until the early nineteenth century – and under both French and British colonial regimes – the seminary coexisted nicely with the Montreal élite, a group dominated by merchants. The fact that there was no contradiction between feudalism and commercial capitalism in post-conquest Montreal surprised historian Donald Creighton but the phenomenon had its counterpart in feudal Japan, France, and England.[5] In the post-conquest period, Montreal merchants cemented this alliance by marrying into seigneurial families or other forms of gentrification, by themselves buying seigneuries, or by borrowing seigneurial capital.[6] By the early years of the nineteenth century, however, some artisans and merchants were making the transition to an industrial mode of production. Seigneurialism itself, it must be emphasized, was not incompatible with this form of production as evidenced by the industrial operations of seigneurs at Lavaltrie,

Terrebonne, and Beauharnois. Nor was the seminary hostile to industrial development. At Lac Oureau on the Saint-Sulpice seigneury, the seminary had leased sites on which had been built by 1845 a carding mill, flour mill, tannery, two sawmills, and an oat-grinding mill in addition to the banal mill. And the seminary's large, institutional construction projects, such as Notre-Dame Church (1824–9), were important in encouraging the accumulation of capital and the passage of masons, carpenters, and joiners from an artisanal to industrial mode.[7]

But industrial producers and large capitalist landowners objected vigorously to the impediment that the seminary's seigneurial privileges represented for their milling, manufacturing, and land-speculation projects in the immediate Montreal area. Resentful of the seminary's use of feudal instruments to obstruct what Harry Braverman describes as "the clearing of the market place" and what Albert Soboul calls the "autonomy of capitalist production," they sniped at the seminary's milling privileges, at its application of the mutation levy (*lods et ventes*) on suburban and urban land improvements, at its control over waterways and power sites, and at its domain which straddled and blocked potential industrialization along the Lachine Canal.[8]

The battle lines were formally drawn in 1816 when the seminary was forced to initiate a lawsuit against a Scottish-born miller, William Fleming. In flagrant violation of the seigneur's milling monopoly or *banalité* and in direct competition with a nearby banal mill recently rebuilt by the seminary, Fleming bought land near Lachine and constructed a stone windmill that utilized improved grindstones and other new technology. In his first year of operation Fleming ground only rice and barley but in March 1816 he began grinding the wheat of local farmers. Fleming's mill threatened the seigneur's investment, short-circuited the feudal relationship between seigneur and *censitaire*, and upset traditional town-country relations.

When accused in 1816 of "disturbing, molesting and disquieting" the seigneur "in open, quiet, peaceable and lawful possession and enjoyment" of a milling right which the seminary had exercised at Lachine since the seventeenth century, Fleming refused to demolish his mill and expressed willingness to appeal to the highest English courts for judgment against the seminary's monopoly. Hiring prominent lawyers, he attacked the seminary's corporate titles and its very right to hold property. Eight years later, largely because of the seminary's successful stalling tactics, the case was still dragging in Canadian appeal courts. The Fleming mill remained standing, and seminary opponents stepped up their demands in the 1820s for the dismantling of the "monkish institution" and its feudal properties which were "shackling and obstructing" industry.[9]

Fearful for its very existence, the seminary backed off consistently in the two decades before the rebellions of 1837–8. Confiding to the Colonial Office that "feudal rights are always odious," the superior of the seminary negotiated to cede the company's seigneurial lands in return for a cash indemnity.[10] With its property titles in doubt, the institution bought land in the name of individual Sulpicians, only transferring it to the seminary's name after confirmation of its corporate powers in 1840.

The Fleming case symbolizes the crisis of one feudal institution in the face of emerging industrial producers. As seigneur of the island of Montreal, the seminary was on the front line. At the same time, the increasing complexity of economic activities in Montreal was lessening the significance of the traditional alliance between seigneur and merchant. Benefiting from the seminary's weakened position and its reluctance to use the courts to assure its feudal property rights, many Montreal *censitaires* refused to pay *lods et ventes* in the decades before 1837–8.

Industrial producers were not alone in resisting seigneurial levies. The peasantry poached, cheated, concealed their property mutations, switched to crops not subject to seigneurial levies, milled at non-banal mills, and otherwise avoided payment of their seigneurial dues; hundreds accumulated interest-free seigneurial debts with the seminary.[11] Nor could the seminary count on support from other groups in the popular classes or from francophone professionals. Admittedly, conservative leaders like Louis-Joseph Papineau did cap more radical elements and supported the seminary by integrating seigneurialism, Roman Catholicism, and the Lower-Canadian civil law tradition to the "nation." Some *patriote* leaders had attended the Sulpician college and others benefited from seigneurialism through their professional fees; Papineau himself was a seigneur. But the more popular, industrial, and revolutionary elements turned on the feudal and pro-British seminary. Democratic, anti-monopolistic, and often anti-clerical, they attacked clerical power in education and the seminary's attempts to settle its property and corporate difficulties through private negotiations with the Colonial Office. Their position was made clear in the 1838 Proclamation of Independence for Lower Canada which demanded the immediate and outright abolition of feudal tenure and the annulment of all seigneurial debts.[12]

The Ordinance of 1840 permitted *censitaires* to transform their properties into freehold tenure by the capitalization of their ground rents (*cens et rentes, lods et ventes*); the seminary could not refuse a legitimate request for commutation. The ordinance also ended the mortmain restriction on the alienation of seminary land and forced it to sell the Saint-Gabriel domain along the Lachine Canal. At the same time as it reduced the seminary's importance in property relations in Montreal, the ordinance confirmed the seminary's corporate status, enabling it to enforce seigneurial levies and to collect seigneurial arrears.

From 1840 to 1859 the seminary's social relations reflected the existence in Lower Canada of seigneurial and freehold property regimes. Few rural *censitaires* had the means to commute their lands, thus leaving the seminary an important seigneurial force in the countryside. This persistence of feudal power was increased under the terms of the Ordinance of 1840 by the formalization of seigneurial debts in the form of interest-bearing, alienable contracts. In Montreal, large numbers of *censitaires* with a surplus opted to commute, thus removing their properties from the sphere of seigneurial levies.

The fattening of seminary coffers with new forms of income from commutations and land sales did not escape the attention of Montrealers looking for capital for their industrial projects. By 1849 the seminary had been dragooned into becoming, along with the British American Land Company, the largest private Canadian investor in the Grand Trunk Railway. Between 1876 and 1909 it invested in ten transportation companies and fifteen other industrial companies; in 1915 its portfolio of municipal bonds was over $1.2 million.

These deepening capitalist property relations were accompanied by the delegation to the seminary of new supportive functions in the ideological and social sectors. Its expanding cash income, its structure, and its two centuries of mission and parish experience made it a useful vehicle for legitimation, social order, and ethnic harmony in industrializing Montreal. After 1837 the seminary had an expanding planning, financial, and management function in the Roman Catholic institutional sector. It structured churches, newspapers, a reading-room, libraries, and popular, secondary, and theological school facilities, as well as a variety of welfare, national, and self-help organizations.

The choice of 1876 as the terminal date of this study makes sense from the standpoint of both historical conjuncture and seminary records. A six-decade period permits placing the institutional experience against relatively long-term economic and social change. The Ordinance of 1840 – the crucial political act for the seminary – comes in the centre of the period, thus facilitating examination of the seminary's feudal and capitalist property relations. The changes instituted by the ordinance coincided with an acceleration of the industrialization process in Montreal: enlargement of the Lachine Canal, construction of railways, introduction of the factory system. In this regime the seminary assumed the functions of a deposit bank, mortgage lender, and important urban *rentier*. Treating land and labour as disposable commodities, it sold off seigneurial debts and developed suburban subdivisions on its domains. By the 1870s industrial capitalism had reached a new stage. The stock market, new corporate forms, transcontinental corporations, changing technology, and the bureaucratization and professionalization of business organizations forced further changes in seminary business operations. The seminary's growing marginalization from direct economic influence was accentuated in 1876 when the Canadian government paid off the debt it had assumed for rural *lods et ventes*. The 1870s also marked the end of a business era for the seminary. Two procurators, Joseph Comte and Jacques-Victor Arraud, ran the business office from 1823 to 1876. Comte's organization, managerial stamp, and many of the accounting records begun in the 1820s terminated with Arraud's transfer to other duties.

Given this concentration on the institution, its business management and its property relations, there is little treatment of production and distribution in the countryside, of the agricultural "crisis" in the early nineteenth century, or of changes in food production. Nor, given the institutional focus, is there systematic attention to the popular classes. And although it might have been expected in this study of a religious community, theological questions and the internecine struggle between the seminary and bishop of Montreal have been subordinated; they are amply treated in the works of Lucien Lemieux, Léon Pouliot, Robert Rumilly, Richard Chabot, Nadia Eid, Gilles Chaussé, Marcel Lajeunesse, Louis Rousseau, and James Lambert.[13]

Two technical explanations are necessary. The first draft of this text left quotes in their original language, usually French. In response to suggestions of both the publisher and evaluators of the manuscript, I have translated all quotes into English. The variety of currencies used across the period posed recurring problems. Leaving "kind" aside, three currencies were common in seminary accounts in the period 1816–80. Until 1840 the seminary kept its books in *livres tournois*, referred to in legal documents as *livres anciens cours*. In 1840–1 most business office accounts were converted to Halifax currency and then in 1862 to dollars. Throughout the period, however, seigneurial collections continued to be conducted in *livres tournois* with the transactions being converted to Halifax currency or dollars in the seminary's account-books. Throughout the text, the currency used reflects that of the document. For purposes of comparison, however, in appendixes eleven and fourteen figures have been converted to dollars using the rate of exchange found in seminary records (six *livres tournois* equals one dollar; one £ Halifax currency equals ~~one dollar).¹⁴~~ four dollars).[14]

This study is based on two main sources – notarial acts in the Archives nationales du Québec à Montréal and the seminary's own collection of business records. These were supplemented with research in the seminary mother house in Paris, the collection of seminary documents in the Bibliothèque nationale du Québec in Montreal and various government and published documents.

Notarial records are a rich source of business history in Quebec, and some 6,700 acts dealing with the seminary were examined. All acts deposited by their five Montreal notaries between 1836 and 1880 were read systematically. There were, however, certain difficulties. It was not possible to examine seminary notarial documents deposited in jurisdictions other than Montreal and, despite the thoroughness of the Montreal business office, there are gaps in the materials deposited in Montreal. Commutations for a three-year period were not found, nor was it possible to track down systematically acts written by Montreal notaries who did not work in the seminary business office. This, however, represented only a very small percentage of seminary business.

Early in the research a decision was made to analyse commutations systematically, and in the summer of 1980 Hélène Paré began examining the commutation contracts. She devised the *fiches* on which the 3,165 commutations were analysed and read the first third of the acts. Peter Gossage finished compiling the commutations in the summer of 1981. Both worked under the aegis of the Montreal Business History Project.

The seminary's two vaults of records are a magnificent collection that includes minute books, a full range of correspondence, printed materials, and 525 volumes of accounting records. The documents were approached systematically, working backward from the summary accounts into the detailed registers of commutations, rents, land sales, and so on. There are some difficulties with the inventory descriptions, and there is important unindexed material in the archives, particularly dealing with surveyors' reports, auction accounts, land sales, and the disposition of land-sale revenues.[15] Nor, given the mixed organization of seminary archival materials by nominative and subject classifications, was it always possible to locate the relevant business correspondence. Finally, the sheer volume of materials was overwhelming. As at the notarial archives, I was aided at the seminary by a research assistant sponsored by the Montreal Business History Project, and Peter Orr had the pleasure of a summer spent examining account books in the confines of a religious community.

My project would have been impossible without the cooperation of seminary archivist Bruno Harel. Père Harel combined a generosity with the documents under his responsibility with an ample measure of Sulpician discretion as to my own work and interpretation. I am grateful to him.

Research for this book was facilitated by a leave fellowship of the Social Sciences and Humanities Research Council of Canada and by a research grant from the Faculty of Graduate Studies and Research of McGill University.

I owe particular thanks to several friends in the Montreal Business History Project, particularly Alan Stewart, Mary Anne Poutanen, Jane Greenlaw, and Gilles Lauzon. Robert Sweeny had a central influence on the project's formulation of the *problématique* of the transition. The reader should consult his doctoral thesis – presented as this text was in proofs – and his four papers collected as *Protesting History*.[16] He and Richard Rice read my first draft and responded with suggestions that amounted to short manuscripts. Although the final version has been marked by this collective effort, responsibility for the text remains entirely my own.

In Its Corporate Capacity

CHAPTER ONE

Holy Housekeeping: The Company and Business Management

... hope which is rooted in peace, consummate charity, profound humility, invincible patience, prompt obedience, perfect chastity, a true simplicity of spirit, a long tradition of keeping silent, perfect modesty, rare simplicity in life, morals and dress, a universal mortification.

Sulpician characteristics as given by a Sulpician, 1964[1]

Even though there is no danger on those lands for which there are debts, we have to press them in order that interest doesn't accumulate ... As soon as the harvest is in, squeeze the good Simon Paré ... You see that we have many arrears on our sales and that we need to keep our eyes open ... Renew his warning, so that he does not fall asleep.

Sulpician business manager to agent at Two Mountains seigneury, 1861[2]

THE COMPANY

The Séminaire de Saint-Sulpice in Paris, mother house of the seminary of Montreal, was one manifestation of the Catholic Counter-Reformation. The Council of Trent had called for renewed emphasis on the sacraments, increased piety among the laity, and a revitalization of religious orders and the European priesthood. In response to the council's appeal for rigorous theological colleges, Jean-Jacques Olier established the Séminaire de Saint-Sulpice. Son of the intendant for Lyons, tonsured at age eleven, and trained by the Jesuits and François de Sales, Olier was a priest of status and wealth. In 1641 he founded the seminary in the left-bank suburb of Saint-Germain and the following year accepted the charge of the local parish of Saint-Sulpice. This union of parish and seminary in the person of the superior became a Sulpician tenet and was repeated in Montreal. Since the seminary depended on the abbé of Saint-

Germain, Olier claimed independence from diocesan jurisdiction, another characteristic imitated in Montreal.[3]

Olier's intention was to create a small company of secular priests but, pressured to train clergy in other dioceses, the community expanded, and by Olier's death in 1657 four Sulpician seminaries had been established outside Paris. A formal and secret constitution was drawn up in 1659, in 1708 the statutes of the Compagnie de Saint-Sulpice were registered, and five years later it received its letters patent.[4] By the French Revolution the Sulpicians directed twenty-three theological colleges (Grands Séminaires) throughout France and eleven preparatory colleges (Petits Séminaires). In the eighteenth century their seminaries produced two hundred bishops, and after 1815 the Sulpicians dominated the French seminary system.[5]

In both their educational and their parish functions the Sulpicians reflected Counter-Reformation rigour. Known for strict entrance standards, the seminary sought mature, moral, and well-educated theological students. Olier personally weeded out the unsuitable or those seeking clerical sinecures and, obsessed with clerical decadence, exhorted the seminarian to exorcise the Adam in his body, "crucifying the flesh by poverty, suffering and mortification."[6]

Institutional isolation, a central element in Olier's training of priests, was part of the Council of Trent heritage. Olier's first seminarians lodged in the presbytery of Saint-Sulpice, but by 1650 a separate seminary building was completed. Surveillance of students was facilitated by a locked and guarded main door and an open central staircase to the upper floors – forms imitated in Sulpician seminaries at Issy, Viviers, and Montreal. Complementary to this physical structure was a rigid daily schedule that began with an hour of common prayer at 5:00 A.M., followed by mass, daily examinations, and instruction in tools of the clerical profession like catechism, confession, home visits, and the keeping of parish registers.[7] Except for the recreation period and the recitation of holy works during meals, silence was generally observed in the seminary. Routine, vigilance, and isolation enforced qualities that became synonymous with Sulpician seminaries: order, silence, exactitude, and calm.[8] To reduce moral slippage during individual outings or vacations, a country estate was acquired. Issy became the rural institutional setting for weekly group excursions and vacation retreats of Sulpicians in Paris.

If the Sulpicians' seminary was a model of seventeenth-century institutional order, their parish of Saint-Sulpice epitomized urban disorder and irreligiosity; witchcraft and superstition were important factors in local life, the annual two-month Saint-Germain fair was reputed for its excesses, the local cemetery was a skid-row hangout, prostitutes worked along the church wall, and in one week seventeen parishioners were killed in duels. Olier's approach to his parish was characterized by an emphasis on detailed information-gathering, by a pervasive attempt to control diverse social groups, and by his strict attitudes to women and sexuality. A priest was assigned to each of the parish's eight neighbourhoods, and at three-month intervals each submitted full reports on spiritual and temporal activities in his sector. In every street a devout layman was named to report on family life, poverty, and disorder. Time and the church clock assumed a new significance in the Sulpician parish: masses were held at fixed times and punctuality was enforced. To ensure that valets and domestics attended mass, tickets were distributed by their masters and collected at the church.[9]

Olier used various methods to subvert competing social and ideological forces in his parish. Meetings of schoolteachers were organized, a parish bookstore was opened, and bourgeois women were organized into charitable clubs presided over by Olier. To discourage duelling a society was established whose members vowed neither to duel nor to act as seconds. Local guilds and fraternal and worker associations had been known for their independence and the rowdiness of their festivals. Olier attacked their behaviour, organized common confessions, and converted their festivals into religious celebrations. The associations' welfare and educational functions were co-opted with the establishment of a used-clothing store and a school in which manual trades were taught. The catechism – always an important Sulpician tool for encouraging religiosity – was taught in religious-instruction classes organized for the young and aged. The cult of the Virgin Mary was an important tactic in attracting popular support; in his rounds among the poor the superior distributed alms from sacks emblazoned with the Virgin. Retreats were another method used to isolate and instruct women and youth. Protestants were perceived as a particular threat. Their meetings in the parish were broken up and death-bed conversions were attempted.

Olier improved the physical image of his church and clergy. The sanctuary was cleaned and redecorated with new religious ornaments. A sacristy was added, a wall was built around the cemetery, and two Swiss guards kept beggars away from the church doors. Emphasizing their insularity, Sulpician priests lived in community and, whatever their daytime parish function, returned to the institution at night. To further emphasize the gulf between the priest and civil society, proper clerical dress was obligatory. Sulpicians wore plain cassocks in public and were forbidden to enter church without their surplices.

The sexual mores of both his priests and his parishioners were of particular concern to Olier. After an initial period when female societies met in the seminary, women were banned. Sulpicians could receive women for short visits in the seminary's external parlour provided they were dressed in their cassocks and square caps. Displeased with the immodesty of the Parisian bourgeoisie, Olier refused the sacraments to women he considered improperly dressed. At the other end of the social scale, among women from the popular classes, he tried, with the help of magistrates, to incarcerate prostitutes in prison or in special hospices. Olier was a founder of the Maison d'Instruction, an institution where unemployed domestics, country girls, and reformed prostitutes learned sewing, embroidery, and domestic trades. Concubinage was attacked, marriage-counselling courses instituted, and beds distributed so that children could sleep separately. Midwives were taught special prayers to help women in childbirth accept their pain as "the punishment inflicted on sinners."[10]

Aspirants to the Sulpician company – as opposed to candidates for theological studies in the seminary – had to be priests and to have a dispensation from their bishop; lepers, the feeble-minded, eunuchs, the dishonourable, and those with foul breath were excluded.[11] Olier recruited wealthy individuals, thus reducing financial dependence on the parish. After discreet inquiries into the priest's background and approval by the Consulting Council, the candidate was approached by the superior who explained the company's rules. The aspirant then entered the Solitude, a one-year program that emphasized the rosary, prayers, meditation, Sulpician rituals, and the study of holy works and Olier's writings. Sulpicians did not take vows of poverty. They retained ownership of their individual property and, using wills, disposed freely of their wealth. Nor were Sulpicians bound to the community since they did not take vows of perpetuity. For example a Sulpician who accepted a bishopric could resign from the company.[12]

What characteristics can we anticipate the Sulpicians of Paris to transmit to their Montreal colony? Founded to train a reformed priesthood, the Séminaire de Saint-Sulpice was an élite religious community which emphasized its independence from the jurisdiction of the diocese and financial support by the parish. Its constitution and house rules developed in an institutional framework of self-sufficiency and self-regulation; the community had a tradition of vigilancy protecting its privacy from both the crown and the public. Choosing its members from among the sons of judges, officers, surgeons, and small landowners, the community was reputed for its wealth, its organizational skills, and its Gallicanism. Disinclined to

either Jansenism or ultramontanism, the Sulpicians were accom-
modating to French civil power. At the level of their Parisian parish,
they imposed moral reform, social conservatism, and a strong Catholic institutional presence.

Sulpician interest in Montreal dates from the city's origins in the
1640s. Olier was active in the founding of a pious organization, the
Société de Notre-Dame de Montréal, which was granted two seigneuries by the Company of New France: the 211,600-acre island
of Montreal and a 84,672-acre seigneury on the St Lawrence River
twelve kilometres downstream from Montreal (fig. 1). Founded to
convert Indians and to provide schools and hospitals for both col-
onists and the indigenous population, the Société de Notre-Dame
ceded its possessions to the Séminaire de Saint-Sulpice in 1663. The
new seigneur assumed the society's missionary and social obligations
and its debts. In 1677 the crown ratified this transfer and in 1717
granted the seminary a third seigneury at the Lake of Two Mountains.[13]

Four Sulpicians arrived in Canada in 1657 and by 1700 their
number had increased to twenty-one. These early Sulpicians put
their Montreal seigneury in order, enforced their feudal prerogatives, established a fort and Indian mission, supervised construction
of the parish church, and replaced the first seminary with the present
impressive building. In the last decades of the French regime, the
community grew from twenty-nine members in 1720 to forty-five in
1755 (fig. 2). The Seven Years' War and British conquest – although
not determinant factors for the seminary – did reduce the community in Canada to the level of its 1720 membership. In the uncertain period between the conquest and the end of the French
Revolution, the company dwindled to ten members. The arrival of
French *émigré* priests and the reluctant acceptance of Canadian-born
priests helped the community rebuild slowly in the early nineteenth
century. Of the twenty priests who became Sulpicians in Montreal
between 1796 and 1828, nine were French and eight were Canadian,
one was American, one Irish, and one English.[14]

Given the centrality of the transition to industrial capitalism for
the institution's changing social role, sources of wealth, and legal
status, the explosion of membership in the nineteenth century is not
surprising. The seminary's expansion was related to a new mode of
production, to renewed corporate status, to changing social relations,
and to the resulting demographic and class transformations. From
twenty members in 1840, the company increased to fifty-four in
1860, sixty-three in 1880, and seventy-four by 1900. Conforming to
the broader pattern of Quebec religious communities, growth is

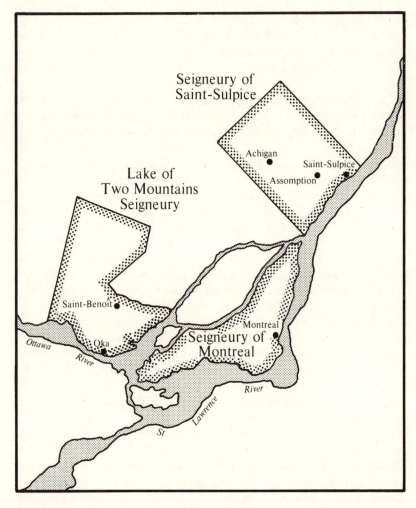

FIGURE 1
Seigneuries of the Seminary of Montreal, 1840

attributable to the increasing admission of Canadian born. From 25 per cent in 1840, the Canadian born increased to 53 per cent of the membership in 1900.

The first Sulpicians in Montreal lodged in the Hôtel-Dieu hospital but, as in Paris, priority was quickly given to living in a separate community. Their first residence on Saint-Paul Street was replaced in 1685 by the building that forms the core of the present seminary on Notre-Dame; significant additions were made in 1704, 1711, 1850, and 1910.[15] Sitting next to its parish church, the seminary

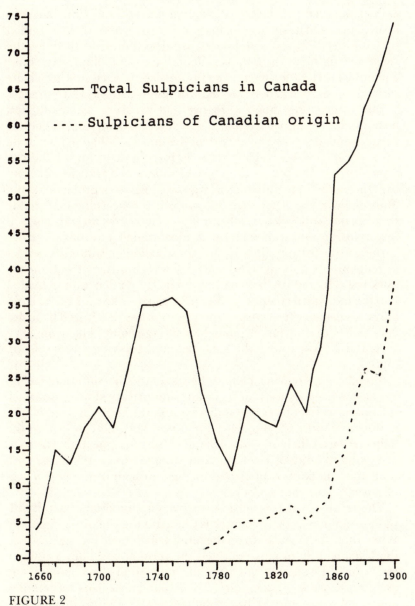

FIGURE 2

Sulpicians in Canada, 1657–1900
Source: Unpublished charts of Bruno Harel, archivist of the ASSM.

exudes material well-being, conventual privacy, and Christian self-assuredness. On its six-acre lot in the centre of Montreal, surrounded by bank head-offices, warehouses, theatres, and discothèques, the seminary still surprises with its maleness, its tranquillity, its verdure; a handbell is rung for meals, aged priests are pushed in wheelchairs through the garden, a porter scrutinizes visitors at the locked entrance.

The three-storey stone residence had a bakery, tailor's atelier, business office, infirmary, parlour, exercise room, 10,000-volume library, and chapel. The three sub-basements contained separate wine, meat, and vegetable cellars. Before construction of the city waterworks, water was assured by a basement well and run-off from the church roof. Heating such a large building was a problem during Montreal winters. After years of complaints concerning inadequate heat on the upper floors, a central heating system was installed in the 1850s; in one winter its furnace consumed 110 tons of coal.[16] To help in the battle against fire and constipation – traditional enemies in religious institutions – the seminary was constructed with metre-thick firewalls and latrines on every floor. Upper floors were divided into the individual chambers of each Sulpician. The rank of the curé, business manager (*procurator*), and superior was recognized by main-floor suites that included individual sitting-rooms. The seminary's most lavish rooms were the suite reserved for visits of the bishop (fig. 3).

Stretching a city block behind the seminary, the Sulpician garden has always been famous for its beauty and privacy. The walled park still boasts its fruit trees and walkways, but the large carriage-house, icehouse, woodshed, the court for *boules*, and the café where the Sulpicians took their after-dinner coffee have disappeared. The seminary's large outdoor clock on Notre Dame Street still exists, and, until the Anglicans added one to their cathedral in 1814, it was Montreal's only public clock.[17]

The residence at Issy outside Paris was an important part of Sulpician tradition as their country retreat and the site of the Solitude. When their Indian mission on the Mountain domain burned in 1694, the Canadian Sulpicians relocated the mission and built a country estate on the ruins. A thirty-minute hike from the seminary, the estate was used by generations of priests and collegians for Sunday-afternoon tea, nature walks, or billiards. The site was divided into two sections – the enclosed country estate and, to the west, pastures, fields, woodlots, and a quarry that were leased or worked by seminary employees.[18] Within the high stone walls that fronted on what is now Sherbrooke Street, the estate consisted of a twelve-acre apple, peach, pear, and plum orchard, a four-acre vineyard, vegetable gardens,

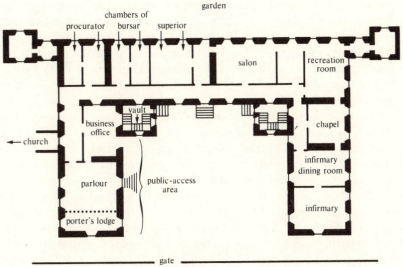

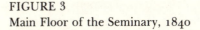

FIGURE 3
Main Floor of the Seminary, 1840

and a meadow. Buildings on the estate included a cider-press, coach-house, greenhouse, caretaker's house, chapel, and the Sulpician's three-story residence, Le Château. With its statue and water-jet fountain, the garden recalled Versailles for some visitors.[19]

Governors, military officers, and dignitaries, invited to join the priests and their students for Sunday visits, all agreed on the estate's charm:

a beautiful view of the basin of the St. Lawrence, which, on a fine day, shows its river gliding on with broad tranquil surface, peacefully to the sea, and exhibits the gardens, woods, and orchards, which cover the country with a fertile and smiling landscape. The grounds are large and well planted; and the rude gaze of the multitude is shut out by a high wall, which extends half round the farm itself. Here the good fathers come for a few days at a time, and in turns, to recruit exhausted nature, and spend their hours in exercise and reading. Fine old fellows! We need not envy them; but rather hope that all men may some day have as many of the means of quiet and simple happiness to resort to.[20]

The administration of the seminary of Montreal was modelled on the Parisian mother house. The company was directed by a superior, the four-man Consulting Council, and the Assembly of Twelve Assistants. Titular head of the seminary after its separation from the French mother house in 1764, the superior, during his five-year renewable term, was to act like a father and was to be respected with the "submission that well-bred children owe their father."[21] Seminary minutes make clear that real decision-making power in the nineteenth century was invested in the Consulting Council. Members were named for life and met regularly – usually in the superior's sitting-room or the Bishop's salon – and voted on policies, inspected all accounts, and assigned the duties (fig. 4). The Assembly of Twelve Assistants had a less-active role, meeting only for extremely important business or to elect the superior, a member of the Consulting Council, or one of its own members.[22]

The community's daily needs were assured by the bursar. His records detail the purchase of firewood, the house's substantial washing and bleaching, expenses for clerical gowns, books, dishes, linen, dentists, drugs, postage stamps, tobacco, razors, and stationery (table 1). He paid for voyages of the Sulpicians, furnished the country house, ordered books for the library, and subscribed to fifteen newspapers for the parlour.[23] The bursar's incidental expenses included a tooth-puller, a chamois shirt, a weigh scale, a trip to Baltimore, 350 visiting cards, "comb and shaving cream," "cabs pour les messieurs." The community's fetish for precision and comfort was evident; a fine watch was provided to each Sulpician, and seventy-four pairs of black silk and wool socks were ordered every year from Paris. Certain items, such as extra-heavy coats for winter cemetery duty, were held in common.[24] As the seminary's parish expanded, so did its transportation fleet. Painted in the Sulpician colours of green and red, the company's livery in 1846 included seven summer carriages, four sleighs, and five or six horses. With the advent of public transportation in the 1880s, livery costs were supplemented by the purchase of transit passes. When urban growth forced some priests to be absent from the seminary at noon while on their rounds, hot lunches were contracted in individual homes.[25]

Since the company largely replaced the family for its members, special attention was paid to important events in the Sulpicians' individual lives. Meat courses and desserts were doubled on birthdays and, when a Sulpician was near death, all members gathered at his bedside to share his agony. Sick and aged members received special care. One deranged Sulpician was placed in the Sisters of Providence asylum; another Sulpician was sent to New York for an operation. A doctor was kept on retainer, a male nurse was on permanent duty and special-care nurses were hired as required. The seminary infirmary had a dining room and special bath, and was adjacent to the

Assembly of 12 Assistants	Superior	Consulting Council
-members named for life by vote of assembly -meets once or twice a year for extraordinary business -presided over by superior -elects superior and members of Consulting Council	-elected to five-year renewable term by Assembly -no financial independence except small alms account -must consult Consulting Council and follow its advice	-four members -elected for life by Assembly of 12 -meets regularly and makes decisions by majority vote -appoints all officers except superior -inspects accounts -superior presides but must follow its advice

Officers

-appointed annually by Consulting Council
-submit annual reports to Consulting Council

Procurator	Curé	Bursar	Faculty	Missionaries	Almsman	Chaplains
-administers business affairs -receives seigneurial and investment revenues -keeps books, documents and contracts -submits annual report	-responsible for parish	-administers house	-teach and adminster Collège de Montréal and Grand Séminaire	-serve at Lake of Two Mountains Indian mission	-distributes alms	-service religious com-munities, hospitals, prisons

FIGURE 4
Administrative Structure of Seminary in the Nineteenth Century

chapel. The very ill were cared for by nuns in a room reserved for Sulpicians in the Grey Nuns hospital, and it is here that many Sulpicians died. Members of the company are buried in their private crypt under the chapel of the Grand Séminaire.

A large institution consisting of several domains, estates, manorhouses, a college, and seminary in which the inhabitants did not perform domestic, agricultural, or artisanal duties required a large staff for cooking, nursing, and gatekeeping. Early Sulpicians brought

TABLE 1
House Operating Expenses, 1864 (dollars)

Expense	Cost ($)
Salaries	
doctor, vicar, dentist	490
14 non-resident, household employees	1,536
Food	
bread	442
meat	2,212
wine and beer	454
other	2,520
Livery (carriages, horses, feed)	1,989
Travel	1,212
Post Office	212
Books and newspapers	666
Vestments and other sacristy items	5,980
Laundry and bleaching	1,225
Maintenance	
taxes	640
insurance	36
water	273
lighting	182
heat	453
repairs	741
Purchase of linen, furniture, utensils	1,026
Communion wine and bread	288
Other	237

Note: Resident in seminary: 39 priests, 2 students, 1 lay professor.
  Resident figures taken from 1861 census, individual returns for
  seminary.
Source: ASSM, arm. 2, vol. 25.

their own servants from France, and in 1657 the five Sulpicians in
Montreal had thirty-two domestics.[26] By 1840 the seminary hired all
of its staff locally, and its permanent employees varied from thirteen
to sixteen, not counting professionals, the foreman and other domain employees, workers at the Indian mission, Collège de Montréal,
or Grand Séminaire, part-time carters, copyists, gardeners, wood-
cutters, or student-readers, or the wives of employees hired for occasional cooking or sewing. The seminary kept careful employee
records that noted the employee's birthday, place of birth, marital
status, and salary. Employees had the right to the same food as the
Sulpicians except they were served leftover meat from the previous
day. They had tea at breakfast and lunch and cider on feast days.[27]
A glass of rum was served on Sunday mornings and after heavy

labour such as dismantling stoves, picking apples, or ditching. Stacking firewood, a particularly onerous task, was rewarded with a double tot of rum. The superior's saint's day was marked with a full bottle of wine for the cook and one third of a bottle for other employees.

The Sulpicians seem to have begun shaving themselves after 1839 when their full-time barber, Amable Dorval, "having become incapable of shaving," was given six month's severance pay and was not replaced. From 1832 to 1845 the seminary had an Italian cook and until 1849 employed a full-time baker. In 1849 the baker and Italian cook (total salaries £4 10s. a month) were replaced by two sisters who apparently did all the cooking for £2 17s. 6p. a month. This sexual differentiation in pay is apparent from other employee records; male domestics were generally paid £1 5s. to £1 10s. a month, female employees (usually cooks or seamstresses) were paid 17s. 6p. to £1 7s. In 1853, for example, Caroline Gauthier was paid £1 2s. 6p. for months when she cooked and 17s. 6p. a month when she worked as a seamstress. A year later Gauthier, aged thirty-four, was lodged by the Grey Nuns where her room and board was paid by the seminary in return for a salary reduction to 10s. a month. As compensation for "the modesty of their wages," women employees, unlike their male counterparts, were provided with soap to wash themselves.[28] Salary differences were sometimes seasonal as well as sexual. The first gardener, for example, was paid £2 5s. a month in the growing season and £1 10s. a month in the winter.

Ensuring privacy in the midst of neighbours, servants, parishioners, students, and business-office traffic was always a matter of careful attention. As late as 1850, leases for seminary-owned houses backing on the garden contained written guarantees for Sulpician privacy: "it is expressly agreed between the said parties that the said lessee shall keep the openings in the rear of the said premises closed so as to have no view upon the seminary garden."[29] The locked entrance of the seminary was guarded round the clock by porters, special service passages were built into part of the seminary, and seminarians who stayed in Montreal during vacations were not allowed to lodge at the seminary. The tailor, distinguished by his salary as the most important employee from the popular classes, had his social relationship with the Sulpicians carefully defined in seminary minutes: "he will have no meals, afternoon teas, nor lunches at the seminary."[30] Aged employees who needed shelter posed another threat to the private life of the community. On one occasion a retired employee was refused permission to lodge in the seminary, but the Consulting Council agreed to help him find a room.[31]

A male religious community requires that its employees have special moral and behavioural attributes. Only marginally pleased with its employees, whom the superior described as "generally pious but slow on the job," the seminary used a bonus system to encourage obedience, work habits, and personal comportment.[32] The salary of Alexis Poitier, for example, was increased from £1 to £1 5s. a month if, according to instructions in the payroll book, he was "obedient and works assiduously." Damasse Caouet [sic] was paid £1 a month and received a bonus "relative to his obedience to the head cook." Cook Olivier Rousseau was criticized several times for lack of work discipline and was ordered to dress properly for morning prayers and not to leave work before 8:00 P.M.; to help Rousseau with yet another problem the bursar lent him an alarm clock. Remy Hudon combined a fondness for alcohol with an indifference to morning prayers. Half his salary was retained as a bonus to be received "if he is punctual in his duties especially attendance at prayers ... it is agreed that Remy Hudon will not touch a drop of strong drink even mixed with milk under penalty of immediate discharge."[33]

Women employees posed a particular problem for, although a cheap source of labour, their presence in a male religious community was unwelcome. The seminary's various rule books carefully restricted contact with female domestics, and by 1850 there was pressure to rid the seminary entirely of women workers. Sulpician sponsorship of the Petites Filles de Saint-Joseph represented a different tactic – that of using chaste women as labour. In 1857 Sulpician Antoine Mercier drew up rules for three penitent women hired to wash laundry at the Grand Séminaire. At first a secular organization of women who performed domestic duties in presbyteries and seminaries, the Petites Filles de Saint-Joseph developed into a religious community, and in 1897 its mother house was constructed on seminary land at the Mountain domain.[34]

Life within the walls of the seminary of Montreal was ordered and precise. Sulpicians arose at 4:00 A.M. for prayers and mass. Breakfast of bread, butter, and tea was, as were all meals, eaten in silence. After further prayers the members dispersed to their parish, teaching, or administrative assignments. At 11:00 A.M. they returned to the seminary for meditation. The noon meal of soup, potatoes, and two meat dishes was accompanied by the reading of holy works. Until 1849 after-dinner coffee was served in the garden or, during the winter, in the common-room: some Sulpicians smoked. After recitation of the breviary and rosary, members returned to their community duties until 6:00 P.M. Supper, again a base of potatoes and meat, was followed by evening prayers and bed. This routine was broken only on Sundays when Sulpicians went to the Mountain estate for dinner and afternoon recreation. Summer vacations were spent at the mission at Oka. After it burned in 1877, the seminary rented a house in Cacouna, the lower St Lawrence summer colony of Montreal's bourgeoisie.[35]

The internal regime of the seminary became more puritan after 1840. Dress regulations were tightened in 1841, and the Consulting Council decided that Sulpicians should no longer wear straw hats or pants. The ritual of coffee and conversation in the garden fell victim to this new severity. After 1849 coffee was taken in the refectory where the silence rule was observed and lingering was discouraged.[36] Sulpicians regularly debated the problem of members forced to spend the night outside the seminary. Before 1851 all members, with the exception of Indian missionaries at The Lake of Two Mountains, returned to the community at night. Indeed, one Sulpician at Two Mountains felt threatened by his isolation from the community and asked colleagues for advice on avoiding contact with nuns in the mission church or garden. The reply from Montreal gives a strong sense of Sulpician puritanism:

It is quite proper that you not be alone with a nun in a walled garden but it does seem severe to prevent them from going there to pick flowers, especially when you are not there. It is quite proper that you not find yourself alone with them in the vestry. But I do not see why you do not want to confess children when nuns are present. It seems to me that the more people there are present, the less danger there is.[37]

Growing parish responsibilities and the establishment of new chapels forced the community to relax its night-time cloistering regulation. Parishioners complained of the long trip to the seminary for a priest in a night emergency and claimed that the dying were being denied attending priests. In 1851 two priests were allowed to sleep at St Patrick's.[38]

Like their Parisian counterparts, the Montreal Sulpicians had important civil responsibilities. In addition to being seigneurs and curés of Montreal, the Sulpicians in the seventeenth and eighteenth centuries served variously as missionaries, judges, soldiers, explorers, schoolteachers, social workers, supervisors of convents, almsmen, canal builders, urban planners, colonization agents, and entrepreneurs. There was a continuity in these functions – judicial excepted – across two centuries and in both the French and British colonial regimes.

Conversion of the Indians was part of the Seminary's original mandate in Montreal, and this missionary work continued into the twentieth century. To isolate Indians from urban life, the Sulpicians transferred their first mission on the outskirts of Montreal to Sault-au-Récollet on the far side of the island; after 1717 they built an Indian village at Oka. This mission formed part of the Two Mountains seigneury and, in addition to their parish and mission function, the Sulpicians retained control over housing, land concessions, milling, forest, and fishing privileges. These prerogatives were violently contested by the Indians at Oka in the nineteenth century.

As land proprietors, Indian advisers, and frequently the progeny of French noble families, the Sulpicians were actively interested in military affairs. The first significant fortifications in Montreal were built at the expense of a Sulpician priest.[39] Sulpician missionary Robert Gay personally led an Indian attack against the Iroquois in 1693, and, in the wars between France and Britain, several Sulpicians distinguished themselves organizing France's Indian allies. In fact the British put a price on the head of Sulpician François Piquet. After the conquest, the seminary was an indefatigable supporter of the British military in the American Revolution, the War of 1812, and the rebellions of 1837-8.[40]

Montreal and its suburbs formed a single parish until 1865. Independent rural parishes were formed around the island, but the parish of Montreal remained dependent upon the seminary (fig. 5). As titular curé its power over Canada's most important parish obliged the seminary to contend actively with secular conditions: the poor, immigration, housing, epidemics, and conditions of work. In its relations with the parish council or *fabrique* of Notre-Dame Church, the seminary was authoritative and patronizing. An early superior, Dollier de Casson, chose the site of the first permanent parish church, blessed the cornerstone, and contributed land and construction funds. Individual Sulpicians legated chapels, towers, and interior decorations. During the original construction of the present Notre-Dame Church (1823-9), addition of the towers (1840-3), and decoration of the interior (1870s), the seminary dominated all phases of construction, named the architects, and supervised the parish debt; it was the seminary business manager and not the churchwardens who controlled parish finances. The seminary bought the church organ, selected the paintings for the stations of the cross, built the bapistry, redecorated the choir stalls and altar, and, symbolically, contributed the largest bell in the belfry.[41]

Sulpician responsibilities as supervisors of religious communities, as social workers, and as educators expanded slowly in the New France period. They were occasional schoolmasters and the spiritual and economic advisers of the three most important female religious

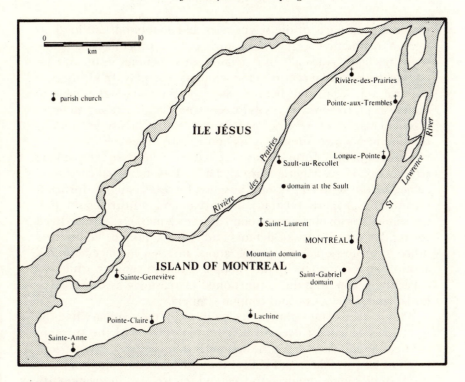

FIGURE 5
Island of Montreal, 1840
Source: from A. Jobin "Carte de l'Ile de Montréal, 1834."

communities in Montreal, the Sisters of Hôtel-Dieu (a hospital order), the Congregation of Notre Dame (a teaching order), and the
Grey Nuns (a charitable and hospital order). Late in the eighteenth
century they established the Collège de Montréal, a preparatory
school for priests and professionals. It was, however, after the rebellions of 1837–8 that their influence on schools, orphanages, hospices, and hospitals increased dramatically.

BUSINESS MANAGEMENT

Until the 1840s the seminary's business operations centred on its
seigneurial holdings. Its income, largely in the form of feudal expropriations and often given in kind, was paid to millers, rural notaries, or other agents around the three seigneuries. These officials
reported to the Sulpician business manager in Montreal, who supervised the delivery, sale, and storage of grains and the depositing
of monies in the seminary vault. Aided periodically by a notary, he

visited distant parts of the seigneuries, handled important local affairs, and updated seigneurial contracts. The procurator kept the seminary books – usually in the vault but sometimes in his room – and made an annual report to the seminary assembly. In its insecure political and legal state before 1837, the seminary was unable to impose its prerogatives across its three seigneuries. Increasing amounts of seigneurial dues were not paid in the pre-rebellion years and, by the seminary's own admission, its books were unreliable.

This seigneurial form of business activity, with its accompanying structures and managerial forms, changed as industrial capitalism subjected the seminary to new business forces. Changing forms of income and property relations, new urban and industrial land uses, the seminary's involvement in bond and stock markets, and the need for tighter surveillance of debtors and tenants pushed the business office to professionalism, specialization, and new management and accounting techniques. By the 1860s seminary managers, while still collecting seigneurial dues, functioned increasingly as urban landlords, land developers, and coupon clippers.

With its corporate right confirmed in 1840, the seminary had the legal force to collect overdue seigneurial debts, and the surge in debt-recognition acts are witness to the business office's new capacity to identify, formalize, and collect these debts. Commutation of its properties from seigneurial to freehold tenure – an innovation under the Ordinance of 1840 – provides another example of the expanding responsibilities of seminary business officers. In the decade after 1840, 1,181 commutations were signed; each commutation involved negotiations and land appraisals, the capitalization of certain seigneurial dues, and often systematic debt collection. Investment of the seminary's surplus in rental properties implied financial planning and new accounting techniques.

By the 1860s the seminary was developing industrial and residential subdivisions on the Saint-Gabriel domain and a bourgeois housing subdivision on the Mountain domain. It owned substantial commercial rental properties in the central business district, management of which was complicated by tenant demands for bank vaults, gas lighting, coal heating, and updated water and sanitary facilities. At the same time the business office was responsible for financing and constructing a series of major Catholic institutions.[42] Seminary managers learned to combine commercial and institutional uses. The mixing of land use was clear in the construction of the Cabinet de lecture in 1859. Located on prime commercial property on the corner of Saint-François-Xavier and Notre-Dame, the building housed the parish reading-room on the second floor and an 800-

seat auditorium on the third floor. Valuable rental space on the ground floor was reserved for retail or other commercial uses.

In this increasingly urban and capitalist environment, the seminary's business managers responded somewhat differently than managers in lay corporations. For a religious community, long-term economic stability was an act of faith. The seminary also had to weigh balance sheet considerations against political and public sensitivities about the role of Catholic institutions in the market-place. And the seminary was particularly cautious in taking action that might displease the large capitalist landowners or the industrial producers in Montreal. Seminary minutes show that the Sulpicians moved only slowly to sue hard-pressed millers: "because of the repulsiveness and costs which a court case entails, judicial means will be taken only as a last extremity after all possibility of a friendly solution and even pecuniary sacrifices will have been exhausted."[43] Nor did it press dozens of land speculators along the Lachine Canal who did not honour their purchases at the Saint-Gabriel land auctions. Seminary officials had to measure market factors against the religious community's collective conscience. Numerous concessions were made, for example, in the commutation evaluations for friendly institutions like the Anglican Cathedral, McGill University, and the convents of the Grey Nuns, the Sisters of Providence, and the Congregation of Notre Dame.[44] There was also a contradiction between Two Mountains as an Indian mission and the same property as a revenue resource for the seminary. Mission Indians were both parishioners and a source of labour to increase the value of the seigneurial domain.[45] The transformation of the seminary's business structure across these six decades of fundamental change in the mode of production is best treated in five components: consulting council, procurators, notaries, business office, lawyers.

Consulting Council

The seminary's four-member Consulting Council acted as a board of directors (see fig. 4). In normal conditions it met once or twice a month either in the superior's sitting room or the bishop's salon. Meetings began with prayer, a reading and approval of the previous minutes, and their signature by the four councillors. Council decisions were made by majority vote. Although the council treated all seminary affairs it took particular interest in business matters. Sulpician officers with financial responsibilities submitted annual reports in October and on at least two occasions in the nineteenth century were reprimanded for tardy and incomplete accounting records.[46] In 1874 a Sulpician was chastised for permitting an overrun of $4,953 in construction of the Cabinet de lecture: "the superior then made the observation that, conforming to the usual practice of the seminary, colleagues who are responsible for the construction of houses, churches or schools must submit plans and construction estimates to the Consulting Council before work is undertaken."[47] It was the council that in 1857 decided to borrow construction funds rather than exhausting its cash reserve. The business office regularly sought council approval for important expenses such as mill construction, purchase of a revenue property, or investment in municipal bonds. The most important financial decisions – major construction projects, terms of the seigneurial laws, purchase of the St Lawrence and Atlantic Railway bonds, and subdivision of the Saint-Gabriel domain – were forwarded to general assemblies of the whole community.[48]

The Consulting Council took responsibility for politically sensitive decisions. It authorized the procurator to proceed in certain law suits, twice urged him to be more vigorous in collecting overdue seigneurial rents, and in 1857 told him to be "very liberal" with a city proposition to build a market on seminary property. In 1847 the council approved subdivision plans for the Mountain domain.[49] The council did not hesitate to intervene in minor matters. It voted in 1875 to refuse a salary increase for office clerk Gustave Raymond, discussed construction plans for the seminary's proposed carriage-house, and, in another instance, decided to terminate the lease of the farmer on the Sault domain. The council acted as arbitrator between Sulpician officials transferring for example, mills from the jurisdiction of the bursar to the procurator. In 1874 it regulated a particularly testy dispute by refusing the bursar's request to appropriate the procurator's vault as a coal-bin.[50]

The Procurator

Day-to-day management of business affairs was delegated by the Consulting Council to the procurator or business manager. If the superior, curé and college principal played central roles in the spiritual, parish, and teaching life of the seminary, the procurator was the key official in the daily material life of the institution. He managed its investments, rental properties, and estates, and supervised its increasingly important office staff.[51] He received seminary revenues, kept a daily cash-book of all transactions, supervised the accounts of other Sulpician officers, and inspected and inventoried seminary properties. His annual financial report was submitted to the Consulting Council and was signed "seen and approved" by the superior.[52]

This control over finances gave the procurator a pervasive influence. At the end of good business years he approved expenses for mending, polishing, and repairing, and the bursar put in extra stocks of wine and beer; in the best financial years carriages, horses, and heating systems made their appearance.[53] Sulpicians had to turn to the procurator for travel expenses, personal loans, and capital for their projects. Financial transactions with Europe were difficult for individuals and represented a particular problem in a community with a large contingent of French priests. Dealing continuously with bills of exchange, European currencies, and international banks, the procurator paid colleagues' bills and forwarded money to Europe. His control over ordering the annual shipment of goods from Paris gave him special power. With his good graces a complete edition of the *Encyclopédie ecclésiastique* was imported for the missionary at the Lake of Two Mountains, and forty yards of fine European silk was presented to the Congregation of Notre Dame.[54] His functions gave him censorship power. With his 1846 European order for books on duelling, women in public life, usury, the death penalty, and penitentiaries, he included a letter asking the superior general in Paris to weed out "evil" or "insignificant" requests.[55]

The procurator had an important influence on the community at large. His pronouncement on the state of seminary finances was crucial for school and church construction. In 1845 Bishop Bourget and many Sulpicians were lobbying for increased seminary financial support for construction of St Patrick's Church. When an Irish Sulpician, Claude Fay, raised the question, the procurator exploded saying that the seminary's original agreement to contribute £625 had already escalated to £1,500.[56] His control over the seminary's seigneurial operation gave him influence on the agriculture practised on the domain. Go slowly, he advised a Sulpician colleague at the Two Mountains mission: "the Seminary certainly wants to promote the advancement of agriculture, but slowly and little by little, especially in the beginning for our funds are certainly low at the moment."[57] The procurator's familiarity with the seminary's financial dossiers made him an obvious choice to negotiate with government officials. He also had a public presence and accompanied the superior to an 1845 meeting to discuss financial aid for Quebec City fire victims.[58]

Finally, the procurator had financial powers over other Montreal religious organizations. He supervised the finances of the Grey Nuns and the Congregation of Notre Dame and handled certain of their financial transfers with Europe.[59] As treasurer of the *fabrique*, the procurator exercised financial control over the churchwardens, signing financial documents on their behalf and exercising a veto over *fabrique* expenses.[60] In 1876 the procurator was named treasurer of the Union des Prières, a burial society with an important capital reserve. His power was further increased because of legacies for Catholic charities and institutions that were administered by the seminary.[61]

The procurator's relationship to the Consulting Council was that of a manager to owners. He was usually a member of council himself, and his strong influence is clear from the minutes. In 1845 the procurator was the only member of council who favoured seminary participation in the municipal bond market. Despite the opposition of his three colleagues, the procurator was given freedom to decide whether to invest £2,000 in Montreal city bonds "after the fears of three councillors to this type of investment were pointed out to him." The boycotting of meetings by an angry and powerful procurator in the late 1840s rendered the council impotent and forced the calling of general assemblies.[62] The procurator's business dominated many council meetings, and by 1854 he was bunching his request into formal reports, many of which were rubber-stamped. In complicated technical questions such as land-sale negotiations and the Saint-Gabriel subdivision, the procurator – like a private company manager – had virtually a free hand. At times he used his financial expertise to exercise a near veto. In 1841, for example, the superior noted that, five years earlier, he had made a vow to contribute an expensive bell to the parish when the seminary's legal status was clarified by the crown: "on which the procurator declared that the seminary had in its vaults only enough for current expenses and owed 5,000 louis – on which a member concluded that the conscience of the conditional vow could remain quiet." This influence was often resented by colleagues on the council. One member quoted with disgust the superior's statement in a meeting: "I saw Monsieur Comte the procurator and he is resolved to act in such and such a manner: then all he has to do is ratify it."[63]

Unlike some religious institutions, the seminary named one of its own members as procurator. Although nominally filled in the Consulting Council's annual distribution of offices, the post was usually a career for a Sulpician priest. The average tenure of office in the nineteenth century was 19.6 years and many served first as assistant procurators. The careers of five procurators span the nineteenth century:

Joseph Borneuf   1798–1819

Jean-Baptiste Bédard   1819–1823
Joseph Comte   1823–1864
Jacques-Victor Arraud   1864–1876
Jean-Baptiste Larue   1876–1900[64]

This training and longevity was reinforced by a company tradition of careful notekeeping and *mémoires* which were bequeathed to successors. The Sulpician constitution of 1711 contains a detailed description of the procurator's duties: keeping registers, carrying a notebook to record transactions occurring outside the seminary, inventorying linen and dishes, budgeting for "bad years," and the necessity of avoiding compromising invitations or excessive eating or drinking in the homes of debtors. Particular instructions pertained to the vault, which was not to be located in the superior's apartment. Two keys – one entrusted to the superior – were necessary to open the room containing the vault and two keys to open the safe itself.[65] In 1721 a procurator left full instructions as to the organization of his books, contracts, survey maps, and accounts in the seminary vault: "As for papers, all those actively in use will be found in the procurator's cupboard arranged by order across three columns in thirty drawers, each of which is labelled. In the first five are (1) Titles and letters patent concerning ownership of the seigneuries of Montreal, St. Sulpice and Two Mountains. (2) Acquisition contracts (3) Legacies made to the seminary and foundations of which it is in charge."[66]

Nineteenth-century procurators were meticulous in leaving their successors detailed memoirs concerning post-office and registry-office hours, Bank of Montreal discount days, sitting days of the Montreal courts, methods of measuring cordwood, and the format of petitions to the government. Joseph Arraud kept a volume of newspaper clippings listing city land sales, street enlargements, and bankruptcies. A procurator who died in 1823 left a full collection of Italian and British bookkeeping manuals, while procurator Larue left a careful inventory of what he left in the manor-house vault at Assomption: "On my departure, January 19, 1889, I left in the vault – pencils, pens, folders, erasers, blank debt-recognition forms ... a little more than two packages of envelopes."[67]

One of the most important legacies of a procurator was his personal evaluation of debtors, and seminary ledgers contain hundreds of pencilled notations as to the reliability, health, or family situation of tenants and *censitaires*: "poor," "can pay," "old soldier," "promises much, pays nothing," "insane," "each year he brings $5," "squeeze," "old man, useless, wait for the succession," "negligent and very hard up," "English, Protestant," "sailor, absent," "sister-in-law of the minister."[68] One procurator drew up an evaluation code for *censitaires* – apparently secret and for use in office records – that he left in an 1852 volume of instructions on the seminary's seigneurial rights:

F	very rich	X/	rocky land
I	comfortable	U	negligent
-ε	broke	Ɛ	unknown
I-ε	has some wealth but is broke	O/	arrears from 10 to 700 french livres
ठ	very poor	b/	arrears over 700 french livres
+	poor		
⊃x	bad land	+ᶜ	pays nothing
⟊	virtuous man	v	owes nothing
ȼ	punctual, pays well	A	*cens et rentes* paid for year[69]

Jean-Baptiste Bédard was a retiring, meticulous procurator whose hobbies were map-making, physics, and watch-making. Concerned with organization, the conversion of currency, and modern accounting he trained his heir, Joseph Comte (1793–1864), who was in turn assisted by his successor. The most important nineteenth-century procurator, Comte was a product of that slice of the Montreal artisanry that made the transition from tradesman to important contractor. Comte was one of four sons of a master carpenter in the Saint-Laurent suburb; his brother Louis-Pascal became an influential building contractor who received important seminary contracts for projects including Notre-Dame Church.[70] First attracting attention as a pupil in the seminary's elementary school, Joseph Comte attended the Collège de Montréal with Sulpician patronage where he was a strong student in mathematics. He took the cassock in 1812, was ordained a priest in 1817, and became a Sulpician a year later. He taught rhetoric for a short period but found his real profession when he was named to the seminary business office as assistant procurator. In 1823 he became procurator, a post he held until his death forty-one years later.[71]

Comte trained himself in property law and, according to an obituary, was regularly consulted by commercial lawyers. This legal expertise was particularly useful in the pre-rebellion years when the seminary was battling to maintain its corporate and property rights. Comte played an important role in the seminary's negotiations with British officials in the 1820s and 1830s. It was Comte who led the successful battle to exempt the seminary from the government's seigneurial bill of 1854. He warned government officials of the seminary's important social role, predicted "destruction" of the Indian mission if the seminary was not protected financially, and insisted that the Ordinance of 1840 was a "treaty."[72] In 1859 it was Comte who prepared the seminary's position on seigneurial indemnities, clauses of which were included in the final abolition bill.

A one-man office for the first decade and head of an office staff of two notaries, an accountant, and two clerks when he died, Comte was the quintessential clergyman / manager. Forceful, hard-working, parsimonious, and authoritative, he brought missionary zeal to his profession. His correspondence with colleagues in Paris and Baltimore gave him expert knowledge of exchange rates and conditions in European capitals. He personally negotiated leases, received angry neighbours, and handled detailed dossiers, such as correspondence concerning broken fences along the Lachine Canal and complaints to the city over the seminary's water bill.[73] Aware of the importance of administrative continuity, he pasted instructions for his successors on the inside covers of his ledgers. Considered a "dictator" by some of his colleagues, Comte himself understood the managerial function and did not expect to be loved: "to try and please everyone is a difficult thing."[74]

No manager in the Chandler model was more diligent than Joseph Comte. His bedroom adjoined the business office, and it was perhaps lack of exercise that led to his suffering from swelling in the legs. Comte followed Sulpician regulations to the letter, insisting on being present for all daily prayer sessions, and after becoming a Sulpician he refused to eat in secular surroundings – even at his aunt's! His major non-business-office activity was giving Sunday catechism lessons to young girls.[75]

Never office-bound, Comte tramped subdivision sites with his surveyor, visited his mills regularly, and travelled to Quebec City for negotiations with government officials. For years he made annual inspection visits to the Two Mountains and Saint-Sulpice seigneuries where the habitants knew him as "notre seigneur." Comte's service to the seminary continued even after his death. A lifelong land speculator and investor on his own account Comte left all his property to the seminary and set up a scholarship fund for needy theology students at the Grand Séminaire.[76]

The Notary

Although the Sulpicians always retained decision-making power for themselves, the notary, at least until the 1870s, was the key lay professional in administering that power. Religious institutions and seigneurs had traditionally delegated important powers to their notaries; indeed, an historic function of the rural notary was to act as a social and financial bridge between members of rural society and external institutions such as an absentee seigneur. In the early seventeenth century around Lyons, France, the notary acted as *receveur* and judicial official for the seigneur, collecting seigneurial dues and the tithe and organizing the seigneurial court.[77] In the urban life of the Low Countries, Italy, Spain, Scandinavia, France, and Quebec, the notary was an important business force. By 1840 the seminary had three centuries' experience in utilizing notaries for both seigneurial and urban services. Within a few years of their installation in Montreal in the seventeenth century, the seminary was, for example, systematically notarizing its land concessions and important business dealings.[78] In the early nineteenth century, the seminary patronized several of the most prominent members of the Montreal notariat – Théodore Doucet, Frederick Griffin, Étienne Guy – but it was only in 1841 that it employed a full-time notary, Patrice Lacombe.[79]

Raised on one of the seminary's seigneuries, Lacombe exemplifies the social bridging performed by the notary between the lay public and a religious institution. A merchant's son, Lacombe was born on the Two Mountains seigneury, studied at the seminary's Collège de Montréal, and was admitted to the notariat in 1830.[80]

Lacombe began writing acts for the seminary in 1835 but for a few years retained a significant private practice. Like many Quebec notaries in the period, he may have found the profession overcrowded. In 1842 twenty-six notaries were practising in Montreal and, including acts for the seminary, Lacombe averaged only 74 acts a year between 1835 and 1840. After 1841 he worked full time in the seminary business office, remaining chief notary until his death in 1863. In seminary employment he almost doubled his output, averaging 129 acts a year between 1841 and 1863.[81]

By 1842 growth in seminary business warranted the employment of a second notary, Henri Valotte, who worked in the business office until his death in 1847. Like Lacombe, Valotte may have had slim pickings before joining the seminary staff. He completed a total of only 79 acts in his two years of private practice, 1840–2. In the seminary's employ he averaged 114 acts a year. While senior notary Lacombe specialized in commutations, Valotte handled other Sulpician business, particularly debt-recognition acts for seigneurial arrears. Valotte travelled on seminary business to the seigneurial villages, acted as Lacombe's second notarial signator, and represented the seminary at bankruptcy hearings.[82]

For four years after Valotte's death, Lacombe remained the sole full-time notary, and it was only in 1851 that Édouard Lafleur was hired as a seminary notary, a post he held until his death in 1897. A more worldly notary than his colleague Lacombe, Lafleur's diverse *rentier* and land-speculation activities gave him common ground with many in Montreal's business community, and his wife was the daughter of banker Benjamin Holmes.[83] It was Lafleur who acted as notary in most of the seminary's mid-century subdivision projects and leases. Lafleur succeeded Lacombe as chief notary and averaged the same annual number of acts (129) as his predecessor.[84] The business office employed three other notaries in the period before 1876. Édouard Moreau worked for the seminary from 1863 until 1867 when he moved to Quebec City. Beginning in 1872 Joseph Bonin prepared a large number of contracts for the business office. When he transferred his practice to Assomption in 1876, he was replaced by Jean-Baptiste Bonin.[85]

In addition to its Montreal staff, the seminary hired rural notaries to manage local seigneurial business. As well as handling collections, these notaries performed general legal, accounting, and administrative functions. They supervised property evaluations and land sales and kept the local account-books. They were important purchasers of the seminary's bad debts and useful informants; if the curé knew the spiritual life of his parishioners, the notary was well placed to know their financial condition.[86]

Notaries were important figures in the local bourgeoisie and, through their marriages and family links, the seminary's notaries may have provided family connection to philanthropic, credit, and property allies which a celibate community could not otherwise have. The family ties of the seminary's professionals to the Masson family is striking. A powerful merchant and seigneurial family, the Massons were close friends of Superior Quiblier and a source of loans for the seminary (see chapter 5). Its surveyor, H.M. Perrault, married a Masson and the daughter of its notary, André Jobin, was married to Damasse Masson. The mother of notary Joseph Belle, co-signer of many seminary acts, was a Masson.

As agent for much of its Two Mountains business, the seminary in 1842 hired Jean-Joseph Girouard, a prominent notary in the village of Saint-Benoît. Before the rebellions of 1837–8, Girouard – an important *patriote* – had competed for local power against the Sulpician missionary at Two Mountains. During the rebellions his house and office were pillaged by British forces and Girouard, arrested en route to the United States, spent eight months in jail. By the early 1840s the situation at Saint-Benoît was symbolic of the changing relationship among professionals, the clergy, and seigneurs. Girouard had re-established his notarial practice and was authorized by the seminary to collect debts, to sign seigneurial contracts, and to give promissory notes and official receipts. In 1846 his power of attorney was extended to include the right to initiate law suits and hire lawyers.[87] Girouard was replaced as agent in 1849 by his nephew and associate, Félix-Hyacinthe Lemaire. For thirty years Lemaire was paid a £125 annual retainer to act as the seminary's agent. In 1880 Lemaire was replaced by H. Massé and an agency, "Agence de la Seigneurie du Lac des Deux Montagnes." Although Lemaire's most important function was the collection of seigneurial dues, he also supervised the local miller and verified his books, represented the seminary in various law suits, and paid its local municipal taxes, crier and bailiff charges, registry fees, and parish tithes. At the end of each fiscal year the notary forwarded his own accounts for inspection and payment by the Montreal business office.[88]

For its rural business on the island of Montreal, the seminary hired André Jobin. A graduate of the Collège de Montréal, Jobin was a well-placed Montreal notary who moved to Sainte-Geneviève in 1834. He was a member of the provincial assembly for Montreal, 1835–8, 1843–51, a director of the Montreal City and District Savings Bank, and first president of the Montreal Board of Notaries. Between 1837 and 1840 Jobin wrote fifteen acts for the seminary, in 1839 he accompanied the procurator on his annual visit to the Saint-Sulpice seigneury, and in the peak debt-recognition period, 1841–3, he was placed on a seminary retainer of £200 a year.[89]

Less is known of the notarial operation at the Saint-Sulpice seigneury. Local notaries were hired for less important acts, and large transactions were contracted in the annual January visit from Montreal of the notary and procurator. A more structured system was instituted in the late 1860s. From 1868 to 1871 Ferdinand Faure was hired to provide notarial services for one month every year. In 1875 Joseph Bonin, who had acted for the seminary in Montreal, opened an office in Assomption.[90]

Notaries in the seminary's employ were normally paid £700 to £800 a year. At the end of his career Lacombe was receiving £800, and after 1876 Lafleur was paid £1000. In addition to their retainers, notaries received supplementary fees. Lacombe, for example, received one half of the service fee on a commutation – a substantial amount in good years.[91] Each of the notaries also maintained small private practices. Lacombe averaged twenty-four non-Sulpician acts a year; Édouard Lafleur, forty-two. Although for deathbed wills and other special circumstances they did make "house calls," they generally received their private clients in the seminary business office.

Indeed, a sizeable percentage of their non-Sulpician business consisted of work for fellow office employees. Almost all of Lacombe's non-Sulpician business after 1852 was in leases and land sales for his colleague Édouard Lafleur. For his part, Lafleur handled many of the private land sales of H.M. Perrault, the seminary's surveyor.

The Business Office

Until 1841 the business office corresponded to the person of the procurator himself. Without full-time office staff, he administered the seminary's affairs personally, kept the books, and hired notaries and copyists as required. *Censitaires*, tenants, or other debtors who came to make a payment and found the procurator absent simply left. At least until the 1820s the procurator kept the day-book – the volume in which he entered all transactions – in his own room.[92]

The changing volume and form of their business after 1840 forced the Sulpicians to introduce new administrative procedures. Official agents were named in Quebec City and Toronto to receive funds and government interest, and local notaries were given increased managerial responsibilities. In 1841 employment of a full-time notary signalled the professionalization of the business office. Two years later a second notary and a clerk were added. The functions of the two notaries were divided with the senior notary specializing in commutations. The responsibilities of the clerk, Frederick Glack-meyer, included correspondence, certain rural collections, inspection of mill accounts at Saint-Sulpice, and representation of the seminary in bankruptcy court.[93]

Before 1860 the seminary's business organization had few characteristics of modern business management. The procurator remained a dominant force with employees having limited independence of operation. His agent in Two Mountains could accept seigneurial payment in kind – a cow or bushels of potatoes, for example – but was not sure if he was authorized to accept payment in butter. "Do you accept it?" he wrote the procurator.[94] The business office continued to function on the basis of personal contact and, like a family enterprise, the seminary personalized its relations with faithful senior employees, most of whom spent their careers in the seminary's service. It offered loans and other "in-house" benefits to its employees plus the special circumstances of working for an institution that administered the sacraments. The seminary loaned money to one notary (Valotte), sold speculative land to another (Lafleur), and arranged special terms for purchase of a house lot on the Mountain domain for its accountant's son. It arranged the splendid funeral for its lawyer George-Étienne Cartier despite his quarrel with the bishop and his questionable family circumstances.[95]

The deaths of procurator Comte and notary Lacombe in the early 1860s facilitated the transition from a generalist business operation to a more structured, professional, and depersonalized management. The new procurator, Jacques-Victor Arraud, was a socially active priest whose special interest was female reform institutions. Less authoritarian than his predecessor, he seems to have been less interested in business and to have permitted more power to the office professionals. In 1861 a second clerk was hired and, significantly, a lay accountant. By 1880 the office had five permanent employees and a payroll ten times higher than in 1840. Accountant George Marler assumed much of the responsibility for the financial administration of the seminary and his annual salary of $1,236 (1862) distinguished him as the highest-paid office employee.[96] He increasingly represented the seminary in seigneurial inspections or in negotiations with government officials. In March 1865, for example, Marler travelled on Sulpician business to the west end of the island of Montreal; a month later he was in Assomption and in May he went to Quebec City.

The business office – referred to as the "Hôtel Seigneurial" in some documents – was located in the seminary in a section adjacent to Notre-Dame Church. With its flow of visitors, cash, and documents it formed, along with the parlour and porter's lodge, a zone external to the cloistered part of the seminary, where priests could meet their parishioners, *censitaires*, clients, and professional advisers. From the street one passed through the seminary's walled courtyard and, with the porter's approval, entered the parlour. The door leading from the parlour to the business office was equipped with a sliding peephole. The office had two other doors, one of which gave access to the interior of the seminary and to the procurator's private chambers immediately across the hall. Basement vaults for the storage of documents and money were accessible by stairs leading from the office's third door.[97]

The business office was renowned for its darkness and busyness, as clerks, copyists, messengers, and clients revolved around the two desks reserved for the procurator and chief notary. In the 1840s the office's oil lamps burned all day; these were replaced by gas lamps later in the century. Candles were used for trips to the vault. Office hours are not known, but the staff apparently continued work during the procurator's absences for the Sulpicians' daily religious exercises.

On rural inspection visits, the procurator's office hours were three hours in the morning and the same in the afternoon.[98]

Acts drawn up by seminary notaries in Montreal were, with few exceptions, settled in the business office. Here, the procurator and the client – the latter usually unaccompanied and on very foreign turf – signed the contracts in the presence of the notary. Important acts were also signed by the superior. The settlement of a land dispute with Jean-Baptiste Chevalier illustrates the signing procedure. The quarrel between the Chevalier family and the seminary dated from 1804. A settlement was finally reached, and in October 1847 Chevalier and his eight children – all illiterate – crowded into the business office and, after hearing the document read aloud by the notary, placed their marks.[99]

Collecting information and transacting business in remote parts of the three seigneuries was always difficult. Rural notaries sent full particulars on debtors and consulted head office on minute matters. At Two Mountains the Sulpician in charge of the mission devoted every Wednesday and Thursday to inspecting the mills, farms, and forests in his charge and received precise head-office instructions concerning the establishment of a brick factory, the treatment of Indians, transportation costs, and the exchange value of goods paid in kind.[100] Communication was difficult, especially before the expansion of post-office, telegraph, and rail services after 1860. To deliver letters and documents the procurator despatched messengers, one of the seminary's carters, or, for important matters, one of his own clerks. A combination of carters and St Lawrence steamboats were utilized for transport to the Saint-Sulpice seigneury.

In pre-industrial communities, village criers played an important communications role, and their fees appear regularly in the office expense ledgers. Criers read the seigneur's commutation, debtrecognition, and land sale announcements on the church steps after Sunday mass in villages around the seminary's three seigneuries. Pierre Dubreuil was paid fifteen shillings for announcements he made in Pointe-aux-Trembles and Stanislas David was paid twelve shillings for "five proclamations and distribution of announcements."[101] To warn debtors directly, to deliver documents, or to explain legal procedures, clerks were sent around the island of Montreal. A normal circuit took eight days with stops in Sainte-Geneviève, Pointe-Claire, Lachine, Saint-Laurent, Rivière-des-Prairies, Pointe-aux-Trembles and Longue-Pointe. Accompanied by a driver, clerk Frederick Glackmeyer made this circuit three times in 1847–8 delivering warnings concerning overdue seigneurial debts.

Inspections were an important head-office function and every winter the procurator and chief notary made official visits to the two seigneuries off the island of Montreal. Their visits were formally announced by the bailiff or village crier:

Sir, I ask you to make the following announcement in the usual manner on the doorstep of the church in St. Sulpice village: "All tenants of the St. Sulpice seigneury are notified that M. Bédard, priest and procurator of the seminary of Montreal, will be at the large mill of Achigan, Tuesday morning January 9, 1821 and will stay until Tuesday evening January 23, to receive old and new *lods*, the rent and arrears due to the seminary of Montreal, and to read and validate acquisition contracts."[102]

At Two Mountains, the procurator lodged in the mill at Belle-Rivière or with his Sulpician colleagues in the presbytery at Oka. On the Saint-Sulpice seigneury he stayed at the seminary manor-house in the village of Assomption. Destroyed by fire and rebuilt in 1877, the new manor-house had nine bedrooms, indoor toilets, and a waiting-room, office, and apartment for the procurator. Further in his rounds on the Saint-Sulpice seigneury, the procurator stayed in an apartment reserved for his use in the mill at Achigan.[103]

During these annual tours the notary drew up contracts, issued receipts, and settled the rare demand from rural *censitaires* for the commutation of their land into freehold tenure. While the notary handled legal matters, the procurator verified seigneurial account-books, inspected the mills, and resolved local problems. At Achigan in January 1848, for example, procurator Comte and notary Lacombe met with farmer Jacques Piquet to formalize Piquet's right of passage on seminary land. Since 1799 Piquet, whose farm adjoined the seminary domain, had benefited from holes in their common fence and driven his animals across the domain. Piquet had further encroached upon the seigneur's property rights by digging his well on domain land. On this occasion the two parties agreed that the present situation would continue with the seminary's "tolerance" but that its rights were in no way prejudiced.[104]

Lawyers

Defendant in court against Montreal millers and Oka Indians, plaintiff against myriad seigneurial debtors, party to thousands of contracts, and participant in complicated land transactions with city and government, the seminary was an important employer of lawyers. Threatened in the early nineteenth century, it twice consulted Parisian lawyers, and in Montreal it employed prominent anglophone lawyers like William Walker, Stephen Sewell, and James Stuart. In the 1820s and 1830s Michael O'Sullivan, a well-known Tory, was hired to defend the seminary's point of view. By the 1850s the seminary was employing Montreal's most prominent Bleu and Rouge law firms. Bleu lawyers acted as a bridge for the seminary to both government and industrial capitalists. Louis-Hippolyte La Fontaine and his partner Joseph-Amable Berthelot advised the seminary on its seigneurial claims against the government for Lachine Canal lands. By the 1850s La Fontaine's place in the law firm and in the party had been taken by George-Étienne Cartier. As attorney general, Cartier was in charge of the seigneurial-tenure dossier. Cartier, like O'Sullivan, La Fontaine, and Dorion, was a graduate of the Collège de Montréal and a lifelong friend of the seminary. The superior was particularly pleased in 1859 to settle the seigneurial question privately with Cartier "without intervention from commissioners, without a land survey and without subsequent investigation."[105] In the 1860s Attorney General Cartier was hired to give a legal opinion on the division of the parish of Montreal; his partner handled the seminary's investment in the North Shore Railway. Cartier's special retainer of $1,000 in 1871 far exceeded that paid to other seminary lawyers.[106]

If the seminary turned to Bleu lawyers for political and liaison work, Rouge firms were employed for day-to-day actions. Côme-Séraphin Cherrier and his partner Antoine-Aimé Dorion were hired in 167 cases over a nine-year period, 1854–62, and successive Dorion firms were used in the 1860s and early 1870s (table 2).[107] For suits on their seigneuries at the Lake of Two Mountains and Saint-Sulpice, the seminary hired local lawyers. In 1873 the seminary made an arrangement with lawyer L.L. Corbeil for the collection of small rural debts on the island of Montreal. Corbeil had the right to one-quarter of the proceeds and periodically he attempted collections across the island. As with Cherrier-Dorion, Corbeil was given the property titles and debt-recognition contracts which he kept in his office. Between September 1875 and May 1876, he collected $2,179.00 from 182 individuals. Average payment was under $12.00 and varied from $0.50 to $38.00. In December 1876 Corbeil devoted a month to seminary seigneurial debts, making 210 collections at an average of $10.65. By 1878 collections had become even more difficult and the seminary began paying Corbeil $1.50 for accounts on which he collected nothing. In the period December 1878 to February 1880 he made 48 collections but had no success with 353 accounts.[108]

This mid-nineteenth-century professionalization and bureaucratization of seminary management reflected the development of mod-

TABLE 2
Seminary Lawyers, 1816–76

Lawyer	Date of Service	Type of Case	Fee
James Stuart	1810s	law suits	
Stephen Sewell	1820s	law suits	
William Walker			
Michael O'Sullivan	1820s	jurisdictional struggle with Bishop Lartique	
	1830s	negotiations with British officials	
Louis-Hippolyte La Fontaine & J.A. Berthelot	1840s	consulted on seigneurial rights vs. government	$668 (1841–8)
George-Étienne Cartier, J.A. Berthelot & (later) François Pominville	1850s–1873	consulted on division of parish, appeal to Rome, some railway investments	$4000 (1871)
Côme-Séraphin Cherrier (partner of A.A. Dorion)	1854–62	minor law suits	
Dorion, Dorion & Geoffrion	1863–7	minor law suits	$999 (1863–7)
Geoffrion, Rinfret, Archambault & Dorion		minor law suits	
J.C.C. Abbott	1868	special consultation	$140
Siméon Lesage	1859	acts for seminary at seigneury of Saint-Sulpice	
Wilfrid Prevost	1876	handled case vs. Iroquois	
L.L. Corbeil	1873–85	debt collection in rural parts of island	25% commission

ern business administrative structures. While the Consulting Council continued to operate as an active board of directors, the generalist functions of the procurator and notary were increasingly divided among specialists like the architect, accountant, investment officer, or salesman. Management through third-party lay professionals did correspond to the end of the personal regime of procurator Comte, but the process was much more than one of personnel or style. Like investment outside the seigneurial framework or the sale of bad seigneurial debts, it reflected fundamental change in social and property relations. Seminary minutes, correspondence, account-books, and contracts show management giving a new orientation to time, interest and efficiency. The spatial dimension of the seminary's business activities was also changing as seigneurial income gave way to increasingly urban and capitalist revenues like subdivision sales, office rents, and stocks and bonds. Seminary activity in these spheres was related to the transition of its property rights from feudal to . capitalist forms.

CHAPTER TWO

Political Relations of the Seminary in the Transition

The importance of the law in the historical interpretation of a society, is that it names, it qualifies, and puts in a hierarchy every separation between the action of the individual and the fundamental principal of this society. Before the decisions of the Rhenish Diet, one could pick up deadwood; after the decisions, one stole it. An article of law transforms a "citizen" into a "thief."   Pierre Vilar[1]

The bourgeoisie, wherever it has got the upper hand, has put an end to all feudal, patriarchal, idyllic relations ...   Marx and Engels[2]

The seminary of Montreal was, by the end of the French period, the colony's largest male religious community, and, with 250,191 acres, the third largest landholder among religious institutions. With their instinct for privacy, separateness, independence, and conservative management, the Sulpicians developed structures attuned to pre-industrial Quebec society. Their institutional and economic power brought a certain political power; parish, mission, and seigneury represented significant *ancien régime* infrastructures and, in a colonial community without a single printing press, the seminary was a strong Gallican and conservative ideological force. The French crown recognized the seminary's legal status, subsidized it, and reinforced its tithing and seigneurial privileges.[3]

We have already noted the seminary's vulnerability in the period between the conquest and the rebellions of 1837–8. First, the seminary's nebulous legal position under British rule rendered it timorous in defending its feudal property rights. This legal uncertainty intensified in the 1820s with the deepening social and political crisis in which pressure from the popular classes, professionals, and Canadian clergy delayed any private settlement between the crown and

a Roman Catholic seigneurial institution. The second and fundamental element in this conjuncture – and central to the crisis of 1837
– was the transition to capitalism. This complex process threatened
feudal relations and incomes of the seminary in both Montreal and
the countryside. This chapter's theme is the political resolution of
this dialectic between emerging industrial capitalism and the tenacity
of a feudal institution.

The British conquest might have jeopardized the seminary's existence in Canada. The very epitome of what was Catholic, French,
and *ancien régime*, the seminary had never had a French-Canadian
member, four Sulpicians had served in the war as chaplains for
France's Indian allies, and, when Wolfe took Quebec, Bishop Pont-
briand took refuge in the seminary of Montreal, dying there in 1760.
But British rule was far from disastrous and neither penury nor a
real restriction of power followed the British flag. In the eighty-year
period after 1760, the seminary continued to exercise its seigneurial
powers; it collected increasing revenues, and it maintained its social
role. The conquest did, however, initiate a lengthy period of inse-
curity in which the seminary was permitted an ill-defined and semi-
official continuation of its pre-conquest rights while not being granted
the legal arms to enforce effectively its property rights. This legal
limbo, which intensified after 1816, was only resolved with the crushing of the rebellions and state affirmation in the Ordinance of 1840
of the seminary's corporate rights.[4]

By the peace terms of 1763 French subjects had eighteen months
to liquidate their Canadian holdings and return to France. Not a
single Sulpician took up the offer and every member of the company
in Canada swore allegiance to Britain. Even before peace was signed,
the seminary showed its colours in offering a Te Deum for George
III's marriage and prayers when an heir was born. The company's
determination to remain in British North America was given legal
form in 1764 when – in response to British qualms over a Canadian
religious community being directed from France – ownership of the
Séminaire de Montréal was transferred from the Parisian mother
house to the twenty-seven Sulpicians in Canada. The seminary, Superior Montgolfier wrote Governor Murray in 1766, is "entirely subject to the British government."[5] Under these conditions, the Colonial
Office allowed the seminary to retain its property but with the prov-
isos that it remain strictly independent and that it admit no new
French members. Official tolerance of Catholicism as evidenced by
the Quebec Act of 1774 was extended to the Séminaire de Montréal
and the Séminaire de Québec in 1786 by Colonial Office instructions
which permitted the two communities to recruit members locally and

to educate priests. The seminary's particular claims to its seigneuries seemed enhanced in 1781 when the Sulpicians were permitted to swear fealty and homage to the British crown.[6]

Survival of the conquest subjected the seminary, however, to the important ambiguities in British policy concerning Roman Catholicism, seigneurialism, Quebec civil law and other *ancien régime* institutions. Transfer of ownership in 1764 of the company's Canadian holdings from the Parisian mother house to the Sulpicians residing in Montreal was an attempt to assure corporate independence for the seminary of Montreal, a status which would entitle it to full property rights in Canada and in particular, the right to collect seigneurial dues. But the legality of this transfer, the validity of the seminary's corporate titles, and the applicability of its property rights were regularly challenged – first in 1774 and 1789 by British officials and then in the 1790s by Indians at the Two Mountains mission. A third, and again inconclusive, challenge came from a group of Montreal *censitaires* who in 1795 contested the seminary's right to collect seigneurial dues. The seminary defended itself as best it could, preparing a seven-page memorandum summarizing its corporate status. In 1797 it consulted French lawyers about the implications of the peace agreement of 1763, the validity of the seminary's letters patent, and the legality of the separation between the Paris and Montreal sections of the company.[7]

As noted in chapter one, the seminary's ability to recruit priests from France was jeopardized by this uncertain legal status. And although aging and isolated from France, the Sulpicians remained unenthusiastic about admitting Canadians to their company. For their part, British officials did not – with the exception of émigré priests from the French Revolution – facilitate the immigration of French Sulpicians. Two Sulpicians who arrived from France without British permission in 1783 were deported, and in 1816, 1826, and 1831 the Colonial Office refused to approve the entry of French Sulpicians to teach at the Collège de Montréal. Worse, each request to admit French priests exposed the seminary to examination of its corporate status and property rights by the Colonial Office.[8]

By 1790 the seminary had declined to ten members in Montreal, had entrusted much of its business affairs to a notary, and was considering abandoning its seigneurial holdings or bequeathing the community's wealth to the church wardens of Notre-Dame Church. This stagnation was halted by the French Revolution, a phenomenon described by a Sulpician superior as "the saviour" of the seminary.[9] As well as doubling the Montreal community with the arrival of eleven émigré priests, the Revolution emphasized the common interests in Lower Canada of the crown and the Roman Catholic Church. It renewed Sulpician inspiration in their Canadian mission and revitalized their Gallicanism, their conservatism, and their loyalty to the British crown. In the early 1800s the seminary rebounded in size and income and with growing seigneurial revenues built a new college to educate the local male and Catholic élite.

In both the French and British regimes, the seminary and its seigneuries existed nicely alongside Montreal's large merchants. Its mission, college, and parish functions were quite complementary to the needs of colonial merchants. With their income coming from exchange across time and space of Canadian and European commodities, commercial capitalists in the post-conquest period had, in the words of Donald Creighton, "not the smallest objection to feudal tenure."[10] Wealthy merchants bought seigneuries and married into seigneurial families. The seminary cemented its alliance by lending part of its surplus wealth to merchants in return for mortgages.[11]

Early nineteenth-century pressures on the seminary did not come then from commercial capitalists but as part of the complex transition to industrial capitalism; it is for this reason that the 1816 attack on its milling privilege is crucial in the history of the seminary. For if international merchants accepted feudal institutions, emerging industrial producers who depended on local production and markets contested seigneurialism.

The seminary had exercised a banal or seigneurial milling monopoly at Lachine since 1673. With the rebuilding of its hydraulic mill in 1792, construction of a dike to ensure consistent water-power, the leasing of the mill to the experienced miller Joseph Barbeau, and investment in the all-season road between Lachine and Montreal, the Sulpician mill at Lachine became an increasingly important source of flour for Montreal bakers and, by the early 1800s, was the most profitable seminary mill.[12]

William Fleming's construction of a mill at Lachine in the period 1814–16 struck not only at the seminary's milling revenues but at the whole structure of feudal relations in the Montreal countryside. Fleming built his windmill of stone and utilized smaller grindstones than those used locally for flour milling. His neighbours, who had seen only seigneurial mills, were impressed by Fleming's technology. Jean-Baptiste Parent, a Lachine resident for twenty years, testified that he had "never seen such an operation," particularly the cleaning process and the installation of the grindstones vertically "like wheels on a coach."[13] In 1816 Fleming began grinding wheat and quickly attracted local farmers who were delighted to avoid the banal levy. The seminary, which had assiduously avoided the courts for years for fear of a challenge to its property rights, had no option but to sue the intruding miller: "Our *censitaires* have gone running en masse to the new mill and no longer frequent the seigneur's banal mill. Enemies of the seminary of Montreal, who have long disputed its rights indirectly, are using Fleming to attack the seminary's very existence."[14]

Rather than base his defence on banal privilege, Fleming challenged the "pretended Seigniory" to prove that it was a legal corporation entitled to hold property. Employing both Parisian lawyers and the former solicitor general of Lower Canada, the seminary drew on French cases of 1558 and 1675 in which seigneurs had utilized banal monopoly to have wine presses, bread ovens, and mills demolished.[15] In Quebec, appeal courts as recently as 1774 had forced *censitaires* to bring their grain to the banal mill and had ordered the demolition of non-banal mills. There were other means that helped the seminary to win its case in the lower courts and to block the case in appeal in 1824–6. It argued that Fleming, a *censitaire* of the seminary, could not force the seigneur to produce his titles; this was a prerogative of the crown. The seminary did in fact produce letters patent of 1677 and various decrees and court judgments from before and after the conquest attesting to its status as a perpetual community.

The fact that the Fleming case tarried in the courts for a decade only led to more diversified attacks against the seminary. Its banal monopoly had grated potential millers since the seventeenth century, but in the political conjuncture of the 1820s challenges were more dangerous. Transportation improvements encouraged the construction of flour mills in Montreal for the export trade, but these mills, like Fleming's, would invariably attract local production and thereby violate banal monopoly. In 1825 the seminary blocked construction in the Récollets suburb of a steam-driven flour mill that might divert *censitaires'* grain from the seminary's two banal windmills in neighbouring Sainte-Anne. Angry mill developers complained about the "insufficiency" of seminary mills and charged that "there is not a mill belonging to the seminary that can manufacture a barrel of flour fit for exportation."[16] Other mills, perhaps to serve breweries, were built in Montreal, and by 1831 the important Ogilvie steam mill was in operation in east-end Montreal.

This conflict with millers, it must be emphasized, centred on the banal monopoly and the seminary's seigneurial right to expropriate surplus local production rather than seminary opposition to technological improvement or industrial production. For throughout the first three decades of the nineteenth century the seminary encouraged brick and nail manufacturing, a forge, and saw and carding mills at hydraulic sites across its three seigneuries. And Corinne Beutler has shown how the seminary's own flour mills used the latest industrial milling techniques.[17]

Faced with dangerous attacks from millers, the seminary opted to alienate its banal monopoly by giving long-term leases or selling its Montreal-area mills. In the period 1767–1800 the seminary was associated with fourteen mills across its seigneuries. But it built its last mill on the island of Montreal in 1800 and by 1840 had leased or sold all its mills except two grist mills at the Two Mountains seigneury and two on the Saint-Sulpice seigneury.[18]

This distancing of the seminary from a feudal relationship by transferring its banal privilege to mill lessees or purchasers was more difficult to achieve in other seigneurial contexts. The Sulpician farm domain at Saint-Gabriel, for example, lay across the proposed route of the Lachine Canal at an important lock, water-power, and docking site. The result was an acute, four-decade conflict between seigneurial property privilege and the exigencies of transportation and industrial development. An early version of the 1819 Lachine Canal Bill forbade canal proprietors from entering on fenced seminary property without written permission. In striking out this clause, the Legislative Council raised the spectre of the seminary's property rights: "we have no evidence of the legal existence of a corporate body called the Seminary of St. Sulpice."[19] Important contractors, land developers, and industrial producers like Thomas Phillips, Stanley Bagg, and John Redpath were among the canal's promoters and by the 1830s they were pressing to remove the domain from a seigneurial jurisdiction. The seminary readily admitted that the Saint-Gabriel domain was impolitic but its integration into a capitalist land market begged more global questions of the seminary's property relations. Would the seminary, for example, be permitted to cede property on freehold tenure conditions?

In the city itself, the seminary's substantial properties, along with those of other Catholic institutions, were depicted as retarding public improvements such as street repairs, water supply, market construction, and harbour development. While these criticisms mounted after 1825, there was increasing recognition of the seminary's social-control value. Catholicism and capitalism were not incompatible but religious institutions, as import-export merchant Thomas Cringan expressed it, must not block commercial and industrial sites:

The exercise of devotion need not be rendered injurious to the interests of trade and navigation. Those who are religiously inclined may pass their lives as usefully and happily, and edify and improve their fellow-creatures by their piety and precepts as greatly, if they be one or more furlongs from a navigable channel as if they occupied a nearer and more obstructive position.

But for the erection of warehouses, the establishment of wharfs, and other facilities of commerce, a location at the water's edge, and at the head of navigation, may be indispensably necessary.[20]

The seminary would be forced to cede domain and milling privileges that were incompatible with industrial capitalist use. There was, however, yet another seigneurial levy, vital to seigneurial income but anathema to large real-estate owners in Montreal and its suburbs. *Lods et ventes* were a mutation levy of 5 to $6^1/_4$ per cent on land transfers except those among family members. Determined by market value (usually the sale price), *lods et ventes* represented a levy not only on land and the accumulated work thereon, but on capital invested in buildings or other improvements. This assumed new significance with urbanization, industrialization, and rising land prices. In 1832, for example, when the city of Montreal sold land on the old commons to the Department of Public Works for transportation improvements, the seminary claimed *lods et ventes* of £3,492.[21]

By the mid 1820s large property holders were attacking *lods et ventes* as nothing more than "punishment for having had the interest and enterprise to build" and as a tax paid to "foreign men." To emphasize their incompatibility, capitalist enterprise was juxtaposed with the seminary's feudal spirit; if the property holder "possesses a mill site or a piece of land useful for a manufactory, he cannot profit from it ... every progressive improvement in this country is paralyzed."[22]

Judge Samuel Gale was the most vociferous in challenging the seminary's right to collect *lods et ventes*. From an important loyalist and south-shore landowning family, Gale had property in Montreal evaluated at £2,250 in 1825 and he commuted £19,165 worth of property between 1840 and 1860.[23] Petitioning the crown in 1826, Gale described his motives as "not private interests but the public good" and noted that other large property holders such as John Molson were considering similar applications. In order to be discharged from his status as a "vassal of monks," Gale asked for the right to pay *lods et ventes* from two land transactions directly to the crown in return for their commutation into free tenure. Pleading under terms of the Land Tenure Act of 1822 Gale offered, if the crown preferred, to test the seminary's property and seigneurial rights in the courts.[24]

Gale does not seem to have appealed to the courts but during the 1830s property holders fought the *lods et ventes* privilege by appearing before legislative commissions, by forming protest committees, by editorials, petitions and delegations to Britain – and by simply refusing to pay them. The commutation file and other records of the Montreal Business History Project have been used to establish the occupations and landed property of thirty-eight individuals, who, by construction of mills, testimony, letters, petitions or committee membership between 1816 and 1840, can be identified as publicly attacking the seminary's seigneurial privileges (see appendix 1). Three characteristics mark them. With the exception of steam-mill applicant Joseph Leduc, all have English names, and most can be presumed to be Protestant. Secondly, almost all can be identified in notarial records as large real-estate owners and many have a significant concentration of their property in the suburbs. Of twenty-seven who appear in the commutation file for the period before 1880, seven had property worth over £10,000, nine had £5,000 to £10,000 worth, and seven had £1,500 to £5,000.[25] The large number of landowners who quickly commutated properties into freehold land tenure after the Ordinance of 1840 attests to their surplus of capital and their anticipation of rising property values in Montreal and the suburbs.

The group's third characteristic is its members' involvement in major construction projects, particularly the Lachine Canal, and various steam, gas, tramway, and rail enterprises. Many are industrial producers; two are tallow and candle manufacturers and others are in food production such as milling, brewing, distilling, and sugar. Several are involved with banking, in the Bank of Montreal and particularly the newly founded City Bank. These producers' sensitivity to land prices, local markets, and regional supplies of labour, water-power, and raw materials – factors all directly affected by feudal relations – put them in the forefront of opposition to the seminary.

What role did other social classes play in the transition of the seminary's feudal privileges? Given the bias of the seminary's own archives, peasant reaction to seigneurialism has to be drawn largely from other sources. Before the revision of its property regime in 1840, the seminary appears isolated from its rural *censitaires* who functioned as small independent producers. Seminary records make clear that in the years before 1823 its bookkeeping was inadequate and its business manager aged; except for the posting of a Sulpician to the Indian mission, the understaffed seminary relied on country notaries, millers, and merchants for collection and local accounting. In his yearly inspection visits, the business manager could only treat the most important matters, such as auditing books and updating contracts. The local economy was affected by seigneurial privileges such as fishing, milling, and river tolls but, since these were often leased, the procurator was sometimes reduced to giving suggestions to local officials. Early in the century, for example, a procurator urged millers to keep peasants from seeing the stocks of grain in seminary mills since "that encourages them to make remarks against the seigneur."[26] The ineffectiveness of the seigneur's control over *censitaires* in the decades before the rebellions was evident when the superior admitted to British officials that its land registry and debt volumes were not up to date and that a large number of land transfers remained hidden from the seminary even years after transactions had taken place.[27]

The seminary's ability to enforce its seigneurial powers in the countryside was further weakened by deteriorating relations with other elements of the local élite. In the deepening struggle between seminary and episcopacy, parish clergy usually sided with the bishop. In any case, the seminary had little confidence in the power of the pulpit over the peasantry: "Excited men," the superior told the governor in 1811, "don't hear the voice of religion ... And it is only in the pulpit that they listen to us ... outside of Church they view us as ordinary men."[28] At the same time, francophone professionals competed with the clergy for control of the school and *fabrique*. They objected to the seminary's outspokenness on the *fabrique* question as well as to its cosiness with the Colonial Office and many of the important anglophone merchants.

The seminary's administration of its seigneuries – described in chapter three – can be summarized as one of patience and caution. There is some evidence that at least in part of the seigneury of Saint-Sulpice there was little "complaint of any abuse of power on the part of the Seigneurs" and that *lods et ventes*, at least in the opinion of one *censitaire*, were more onerous on large capitalist landowners than on the peasantry whose property was exempt from *lods* in the normal passage of family succession.[29] Although it is not clear if the seminary imitated other seigneurs in keeping unconceded lands off the market, its few new concessions did not include increased seigneurial levies.[30] And, fearful of the repercussions of the courts or other recourses to state enforcement of its property rights, it allowed interest-free seigneurial debts to accumulate across its seigneuries.

Because of inadequate documentation, peasant reaction can only be suggested hesitantly, but there seems to have been less overt opposition than on volatile seigneuries like Beauharnois.[31] Instead of appeals to the legislature, the seminary's rural *censitaires* adjusted their resistance to their seigneur's particular predicament and, in the face of an insecure and often absent seigneur, we see wood cut on the domain, land sales hidden, endebted concessions abandoned, milling at non-banal mills, non-banal crops such as peas grown, or seigneurial dues paid in inferior grains. Poaching in seigneurial fishing waters was a practice that the seminary found almost impossible to stop: "Near the mill [Gros Sault] there is a well-known fishing hole for shad. It has been difficult for the seminary to benefit on any sustained basis and will be for some time to come until old customs are destroyed."[32] Above all, the peasantry – like urban *censitaires* – stopped paying seigneurial dues. On the Saint-Sulpice seigneury over two-thirds of the *censitaires* were in arrears to the seminary![33]

The growth in the number of francophone professionals and their rancour to the Catholic clergy has been well documented. In twenty years, between 1791 and 1810, the number of francophone notaries in Quebec doubled and that of francophone lawyers tripled. By 1820, there were more professionals in Quebec than priests, with the Montreal region particularly slow in the production of priests. By 1830 there were 1,834 Roman Catholics per priest in Lower Canada as compared to 750 per priest in 1780. In addition to challenging Catholic ideology, many professionals sought power in the clerical domains of the *fabrique* and local education.[34]

Conservative, aristocratic, French, anti-nationalist, and the richest clerical force in Montreal, the seminary became an important target of the professionals. Its superior doubled as vicar-general of Montreal, a position that gave him important ideological responsibilities across the diocese. In 1822 Superior Roux entered the debate over the control of local schools by publishing the *Traité des fabriques*, a handbook for parish priests to combat the ascendancy of professionals in church councils and school boards.[35] Sulpician correspondence with Paris emphasizes their suspicion of professionals. Fearing revolution in Canada years before the rebellions, the superior wrote to the mother house that "it is time to organize ourselves before the nationalist and liberal effervescence turns everyone's head. Already they are speaking out against the priests and episcopal authority in the legislative assembly."[36] And just months before the rebellions, another Sulpician commented that he was "fed up" and "disgusted": "the leaders of this country view us as public enemies because they know we do not favour their ... revolutionary ideals. The common people, taught or tricked by their masters see us only as ravenous foreigners who come here to nourish or fatten ourselves."[37]

Sulpicians were particularly shocked at the spread of revolutionary ideas among young professionals and students. One Sulpician teacher tried to avoid politics in his class but found it necessary to refute the "demagogues" who came to the school gates to gather petition signatures. In 1830, law and medical students scaled the wall of the Collège de Montréal and, joined by resident students, hanged a Sulpician teacher in effigy, wrote anti-Sulpician slogans on the wall, set a small fire, and left the revolutionary tricolour flag on the school flagpole.[38] On Bastille Day, 1835, the superior's bedroom window was smashed and a cloth depiction of the superior, lynched and adorned with the ears of an ass, was thrown into the seminary courtyard. During the rebellions of 1837–8 Sulpicians, fearful of *patriote* invasion of the seminary grounds, burned incriminating papers, particularly their correspondence with Catholic officials in Paris and the United States.[39]

This radicalism and strong anticlericalism towards the seminary was generally kept under control by conservative *patriote* leadership and separated from the frontal attack on the seminary's feudal privileges. Seigneurialism, for example, was not addressed in the Ninety-Two Resolutions (1834). Leaders like Augustin-Norbert Morin and Louis-Joseph Papineau led in insisting that seigneurialism was inextricably tied to French civil law and Quebec family and succession traditions. Papineau, in particular, argued that these national institutions had to be safeguarded from British officials and Montreal capitalists: "feudal tenure and its governing laws are only an infinite part of the civil laws which French Canadians want to conserve in their entirety along with their political importance."[40]

The confusion of class interest, nationalism, and old-boyism was clear in the activity of a special legislative committee formed in 1834 to inquire into rumoured plans to alienate seminary property. Two of the five committee members, Jean-Jacques Girouard and Elzéar Bédard, were important *patriotes* and former students at the Collège de Montréal. Both wrote privately to the superior assuring him of their affection and support.[41] The committee report criticized secret negotiations between the seminary and crown, urged participation of the assembly in any settlement, and, in an important concession to capitalists, foresaw the commutation within the city of seigneurial rights which "might be advantageous to the increase of commerce and industry of the City of Montreal." This was hedged however, by the insistence that any settlement be acceptable to the seminary and by recognition of its "uncontestable" property titles.[42]

These pre-1837 *patriote* statements recognizing the seminary's property rights and the distinction between capitalism in the city and seigneurialism in the countryside contrast sharply with the Proclamation of Independence of 1838 which called for the outright abolition of seigneurialism: "Seigneurial tenure is hereby abolished as if it had never existed in this country. Every person who bears arms or furnishes help to the Canadian people in its struggle for emancipation is discharged from all debts ... due to seigneurs for seigneurial arrears."[43]

The conjuncture after 1816 can thus be summarized as mounting capitalist pressure for release from feudal obligations, growing resistance among *censitaires* of all classes to the payment of certain seigneurial levies, and stiffening opposition by professionals and the local clergy to any secret agreement between crown and seminary. And if the seminary maintained a moderate profile in its relations with its rural *censitaires*, other seigneurs who were trying to maximize seigneurial expropriations endangered the political position of all seigneurs. Added to this were long-standing Sulpician fears of a testing of their property titles in the courts. As early as 1798 Attorney General Jonathan Sewell questioned the seminary's ability to defend its titles, and in 1810 Governor Craig reported that the seminary "drops all claims by which the discussion might be brought into court."[44] Forced to sue in 1816 to protect its banal prerogative, the seminary a decade later was stalling the case in Canadian courts to avoid appeal to Britain. When it became clear that the seminary did not have rigorous collection procedures, that it did not charge interest on seigneurial arrears, and that it refrained from court action against its seigneurial debtors, *censitaires* inevitably stopped paying. By 1833 *lods et ventes* totalling £14,000 were due on over half the lots in the City of Montreal and, although his books were unreliable, the superior estimated arrears of *lods et ventes* in the suburbs at £8,000 and at £12,000 for the rest of the island.[45]

Sulpician correspondence in the decades before 1837 makes clear that the seminary was prepared to make an accommodation in its seigneurial privileges in return for an indemnity that would ensure its survival. "Feudal levies are always odious," Superior Roux confided in 1819 to a British official who queried why the seminary did not pursue its seigneurial rights more vigorously.

We do not prosecute, Sir, because it would be odious for the [Sulpician] priests. And the population, accustomed to this attitude over the years, would rebel if we changed our approach ... In any case, would this money be more useful in our vaults than in the hands of merchants or artisans? By the present means, commerce is sparked and work compensated.[46]

The same desire to separate the seminary from seigneurialism was expressed by the Sulpician business manager nine years later. Joseph Comte was convinced that the seminary could not win the Fleming case in Canadian courts and that its feudal rights must ultimately be ceded: "Conserve the legal existence of the community and sufficient revenues to maintain our work – that is the essential. The rest can easily be sacrificed."[47]

In the unstable decades before 1837, seminary relations with British authorities were crucial. Sharing class association with most British governors, the seminary worked to ingratiate itself as an *ancien régime* institution valuable for perpetuating paternalistic and feudal values. Unfailing in its support of the crown, the military and social conservatism, the Sulpicians used important crises like the War of 1812 to demonstrate their loyalty. In 1812 the superior offered a Te Deum for the war effort against the United States and issued a mandement exhorting Montreal-area priests and the faithful to support the British war effort.[48] Embarrassed by the governor's complaints that it had not neutralized resistance to militia musters in Lachine, the seminary helped sponsor a corps of three hundred men who were sent to Châteauguay, dispatched two war chaplains, encouraged Indian support for the British at its Two Mountains mission, and contributed £500 at the outset of hostilities and £100 annually through the war.[49]

The seminary understood the political importance of close social relations with British officials. Using the fondness of the upper clergy and British administrators for rank, pomp, and the banquet circuit, the seminary chose school inspections, graduations, and award days as suitable occasions for merging military, clerical, and royal ceremonial traditions; in good weather British officers and their ladies joined the priests for Sunday tea at the Sulpician country estate. Lord Dalhousie, in accepting an 1826 Sulpician dinner invitation, suggested several navy captains as suitable table companions. During the delicately revived negotiations in 1831 over importing six French priests, Governor General Aylmer, his wife, and a party of ten dined with the Sulpicians. The superior reported to Paris that he "had done his best" to receive him royally and that he had in turn been twice invited to the governor's mansion. Aylmer visited the Sulpician Indian mission and, dropping the formality of secretaries, wrote Superior Quilbier a handwritten note in French. In 1839 Lord Durham was received at the Sulpician college with what the superior described as "royal pomp."[50]

Whatever their personal empathy for an established church and feudal institutions, British authorities could not ignore the social struggle and transition in Lower Canada which were accompanied by intensifying demands for democratic and capitalist structures. At intervals (1764, 1774, 1789, 1810, 1811), officials questioned the seminary's property titles, usually suggesting a settlement in which the Sulpicians would cede their seigneurial properties in return for an indemnity. We have noted how pressure to regulate the seigneurial question in the Montreal area increased steadily after 1816. During debate in 1819 on the Lachine Canal Bill and the status of seminary lands along the proposed route, legislative councillors challenged the seminary's very right to hold property. And the manifestations of millers and grain merchants opposed to the Sulpician banal monopoly had repercussions in the governor's office. In addition to the Fleming case, which the seminary had been forced to initiate and then stall, its banal rights were threatened by the important Montreal capitalist, Thomas Porteous, who built a flour mill on land granted for waterworks construction. This milling operation would utilize the steam pump when it was not pumping for the waterworks.[51] When the seminary called on Governor Richmond to confirm its property prerogatives, he refused, questioned the validity of the seminary's titles, and referred the whole matter to the Colonial Office.

As preparations were made for negotiations in London, the Sulpicians found their situation further complicated because of their increasingly Byzantine relations with the episcopal hierarchy. The seminary's envoy to London, newly appointed Bishop Jean-Jacques Lartigue, also represented the bishop of Quebec. The episcopal clergy opposed a private and unilateral settlement by the seminary in which the Catholic hierarchy was not consulted. Increasingly in the 1820s, they linked seigneurialism to French civil law and Catholicism as inalienable national institutions. Finally, they opposed the cession of seigneurial revenues in return for a simple indemnity to the seminary in its capacity as a distinct corporation. The episcopacy argued for a broader settlement which would ensure adequate income for the education and social services of the larger Catholic population.[52]

In the fall of 1819 a senior Sulpician was despatched from Paris to London. Jean-Baptiste Thavenet hired British lawyers, prepared and translated seminary documents, and oversaw Lartigue. The government apparently proposed life annuities (*rentes viagères*) to the Sulpicians in return for the cession of their feudal properties. The offer was refused but the precariousness of the seminary position was evident.[53]

This vulnerability increased through the 1820s. The proposed union of Upper and Lower Canada (1822), the Canada Tenures Act (1825), which permitted commutation into freehold land tenure under certain conditions, and yearly assaults on the Lower-Canadian mortgage and land-registry systems were indicators of increasing capitalist pressure in both Lower Canada and London. Specifically, the seminary was challenged by industrial millers who petitioned to build steam-powered mills and by large Montreal property holders who demanded that the crown commutate their lands. This was accompanied by the accelerating radicalization of francophone professionals and the deterioration of relations between the seminary and episcopacy into "a small war of the deaf."[54]

In 1826 Colonial Secretary Lord Bathurst denied the seminary permission to import six priests from France and instead instructed Governor Dalhousie to ascertain by legal proceedings "whether the ecclesiastics of the seminary are or are not a legal Corporation." His letter of refusal to Superior Roux again raised the double spectre of the seminary's weak property titles and its obstructive feudal privileges:

the concurrent opinions of all the successive law officers of the Crown who have been consulted upon these questions have declared that the Ecclesiastics of Montreal are not a legal corporation and are not the Proprietors of the Seigneury ... And even if the feudal tenures could with propriety be maintained in the remote agricultural districts it is indisputable that they must be destructive to the increase and wealth of a large commercial city.[55]

To avoid what business manager Comte called "the sad necessity of defending ourselves before the courts," Superior Roux left for England to negotiate with the Colonial Office.[56] Uncertain of the superior's intentions and apparently fearful that he would exchange the community's seigneurial rights for life annuities, the seminary's Consulting Council met in February 1827. It urged Roux to seek a settlement with the British government and to take recourse to the courts only if the Colonial Office tried to impose life annuities. The council forwarded three options as guidelines for Roux's negotiations.

1 Land might be commutated under terms of the Canada Tenures Act with up to half of the revenues being given to the government. This option was attractive because it would ease pressure on the seminary's feudal privileges while not significantly altering the status quo. The committee estimated that few *censitaires* would commutate in Montreal and "none at all in the countryside."

2 Alternatively, the Sulpicians might transfer to the crown the city and suburbs of Montreal with the seminary keeping its domains, college, and seminary grounds. This zone – in which feudal rights were most sharply contested – would be exchanged for a government indemnity which the seminary could invest in real estate. Even if the government refused an indemnity, the city and suburbs might be

ceded in return for the rights to collect commutation revenues in the rest of their seigneuries and to sell unconceded land under freehold-tenure conditions.

3 Finally, the seminary might cede its Montreal seigneury (and even all three seigneuries if necessary) keeping the Sault-au-Récollet domain for its firewood, a flour mill (preferably Sault-au-Récollet) for its bread supply, and the mill and domain at Two Mountains to provision its Indian mission. As compensation the seminary would receive five thousand to six thousand pounds sterling which it could invest as it wished. If this option was preferred by the Colonial Office, the Consulting Council emphasized to Roux the political significance of having seigneurial arrears reserved for the seminary. For the peasantry would be "in large part ruined if the government forced payment and we would be accused of having sold them to conserve ourselves."[57]

In a series of meetings between September and November 1827, Roux negotiated with Wilmot-Horton, under-secretary at the Colonial Office. In a tentative agreement, Roux accepted to cede seigneurial rights on the seminary's three seigneuries in return for a new corporate charter and an annual and perpetual indemnity equal to seigneurial revenues transferred to the government. In a clause which clearly identified the seminary's collection difficulties, the indemnity was to be calculated upon an average of the previous seven years' revenues: "the sum to be estimated is not the amount actually paid to the seminary, but the amount which might have been legally claimed and could without harshness and without departing from the usual practice of other seigneurs have been exacted."[58]

The agreement was never presented for ratification to either the Lower-Canadian assembly or Parliament. In the conjuncture of the pre-rebellion years it became clear that a settlement needed not only to satisfy the seminary, crown, and capitalists but would demand concurrence of the varied *patriote* and episcopal constituencies. And frequent references to the dangers of ruining the peasantry suggest the seminary's fears from this quarter. These forces were clearly evident when news of the agreement reached Montreal. Despite rumours that Superior Roux would not return to Canada if his settlement was disavowed and the urging of acceptance by seminary lawyers, Sulpicians in Montreal perceived the potential political repercussions. The seminary business manager pointed out that the Roux agreement might render the community "odious" to nationalists who saw the dismantling of seigneurialism as the first step in reform of the Quebec civil law tradition. Nor would the seminary, with new forms of revenue and dependence on the state, have "the same influence on the peasantry and would as a result no longer have the same wealth nor usefulness to the government."[59]

The agreement did provoke "fear and apprehension" across Lower Canada. The bishops met and protested formally to the governor. Their protest described the agreement as illegal since mortmain institutions like the seminary could not alienate their lands. Interpreting it as a prelude for cessions by other religious communities, the bishops emphasized that the seminary's resources must serve all Catholics.[60]

With the agreement a political embarrassment, the seminary stumbled for interim solutions. But in 1831 it was again refused permission by the Colonial Office to import French priests until its property titles and feudal status had been regulated. Colonial Secretary Goderich's instructions to Governor Aylmer suggested impatience and his determination to impose freehold tenure in the Montreal area whatever the feelings of the local populace: "It is an object of the highest importance to emancipate from the restrictions of the Feudal Law, a commercial city, enjoying natural advantages so extraordinary as are those of Montreal ... Nor am I shaken in this opinion by the statement that the inhabitants feel little solicitude on the subject. Supposing the assertion to be accurate, which I have considerable reason to doubt, nothing is more natural than that an advantage which has never been enjoyed should not be adequately appreciated ... This is one of those questions on which the general principle of commercial policy may be confidently opposed to individual opinions founded on local knowledge."[61]

The seminary however, had increasingly less manoeuvrability to negotiate a private settlement. In 1832 for example, Rome denied the seminary the right to negotiate without the consent of the bishop of Quebec. For his part, Bishop Panet used the rhetoric of the leader of a national church to isolate the seminary. He insisted, for example, that any deal between the crown and seminary be approved by the Lower-Canadian legislature. He urged the Sulpicians to recruit Canadians instead of French priests and to be more open in explaining the actual state of their seigneurial revenues. Reminding the seminary of its larger obligations to the Catholic population, the bishop linked a change in land tenure to the eventual usurpation of French civil law. He also worried that a settlement would lead to state participation in education. Finally, he raised the susceptibility of the seminary to resistance, noting that its *censitaires* might be "ruined" by state enforcement of *lods et ventes*.[62]

In 1834 Superior Quiblier appeared before a special committee of the House of Assembly examining the extinction of seigneurial rights. The five committee members, three of whom had been pupils at the Collège de Montréal, gave Quiblier a sympathetic hearing. He emphasized that the aborted agreement of 1826–7 had been intended to relieve the industry and trade of Montreal from the feudal burden. And the granting of new property titles to the seminary would have ensured perpetuation of a fundamental Canadian institution and its important social services.[63] The committee report reflected this dual aim of protecting the seminary while promoting capitalist property relations in Montreal. For this reason, and to regulate the difficulty of the alienation of property held in mortmain, religious communities and their *censitaires* must be permitted to extinguish seigneurial rights on the same basis as lay seigneurs or fiefholders. Commutations by religious communities should be approved by episcopal authorities but the committee agreed that religious communities be allowed to invest their commutation income in real estate. The report concluded with an important distinction between the needs of capitalist Montreal and those of pre-industrial regions of Quebec where seigneurialism could be left intact. The commutation provisions, it summarized, "would have the effect of removing gradually, quietly and without coercion, all the seigniorial dues and burdens which might be considered as tending to shackle trade, or to check the spirit of enterprise among capitalists in this Province, and would preserve those seigniorial rights only of which the agricultural population should not deem it advisable to relieve themselves by redeeming them, because in reality the greater portion of those rights form part of a system which experience has proved to have been of eminent advantage in the settlement of this Province, and against which its inhabitants have never remonstrated."[64] The committee's recommendations were lost in the escalation of the Ninety-Two Resolutions which soft-pedalled the seigneurial question. A seminary proposal to the Gosford Commission in 1836 was buried in the furor that followed the Russell Resolutions, the British government's response to the Ninety-Two Resolutions.

The rebellions of 1837–8 and the crushing of the national democratic movement in Lower Canada was a godsend for the seminary. Although the roles of various social groups in the rebellions need further analysis, the function of the seminary is clear. It had no sympathy whatever with the coalition of common people, peasantry, radical clergy, small manufacturers, and petite bourgeoisie who precipitated the rebellions. Identified with conservative, hierarchical, and antipopular forces, the seminary performed four specific services in the suppression of the rebellions. Its ideological role in support of the crown and military was a repeat of 1776, 1789, and 1812.

In contrast to the more ambiguous attitude of the bishop of Montreal and the Canadian clergy, the seminary solicited local enlistment and contributed funds to militia units.

Sulpicians offered important tactical support to the British military. In the attack on Saint-Eustache which culminated in the sacking of Saint-Benoît, a village on the Two Mountain seigneury, Superior Quiblier gave information, supplied an important map, and "pointed out the road by which [Colborne] could march on St. Eustache without impediment; and by doing which and not taking the direct road, which led thro' woods and other obstacles, as the rebels expected, all their plans were disconcerted."[65] Quiblier also acted as a mediator, meeting with Papineau and his wife and encouraging them to leave Montreal. Once the first phase of the rebellions had collapsed, Quiblier acted as an intermediary discussing the exile problem with the governor and carrying safe-conduct passes to *patriotes* in the United States. In 1840 the seminary distinguished itself by refusing to join with Bishop Lartigue and the rest of the Montreal clergy in petitioning Parliament against Durham's recommendations.[66]

The seminary's most important service to British authorities was its influence on the popular classes, particularly the Irish. The first Christian Brothers arrived in Montreal during the rebellions and were lodged in the seminary. A French teaching order, the Christian Brothers were sponsored by the Sulpicians to establish schools for males in Montreal's popular classes. The Sulpicians used their weight in the Irish community to discourage Irish support for the *patriotes*, blocking public meetings and giving prominence in the pulpit to the popular Irish Sulpician, Patrick Phelan. Lord Durham's report recognized this work with the Irish: "The endowments of the Catholic church, and the services of its numerous and zealous parochial clergy, have been of the greatest benefit to the large body of Catholic emigrants from Ireland, who have relied much on the charitable as well as religious aid which they have received from the priesthood. The priests have an almost unlimited influence over the lower classes of Irish; and this influence is said to have been very vigorously exerted last winter, when it was much needed, to secure the loyalty of a portion of the Irish during the troubles."[67]

Regulation of the seminary's corporate and seigneurial status came quickly in the authoritarian regime that followed suspension of the Lower Canadian constitution in November 1837. The popular, nationalist, and clerical elements, which had opposed seminary attempts over two decades to trade off seigneurial rights for a private indemnity, were silenced, jailed, exiled, or planning the second rebellions. British authorities were even "suspicious" of the loyalty of

Bishop Lartigue.[68] Under these conditions, the seminary was able to negotiate in confidence and privacy and to regulate its corporate and seigneurial problem by executive ordinance and imperial statute. The settlement with the seminary must be seen then as part of the larger transition in Lower-Canadian property relations in the years 1837–41 – a shift that included dispositions on clergy reserves and municipal institutions, establishment of a state system of land registry, application of public and individualistic hypothecary forms, and forced political integration with the capitalist land market of Upper Canada and non-seigneurial regions of Lower Canada.[69]

In August 1838, Lord Durham's office asked for a full account of the seminary's financial state and the social services it rendered. Superior Quiblier responded with an impressive list of the seminary's parish, Indian mission, hospital, orphanage, welfare, and educational contribution. He was unable, however, to provide exact accounts of seigneurial debts owed to the seminary explaining that it would take several notaries up to a year to bring seminary land registers to date. Many land transactions had been hidden from the seminary over past years and, according to the superior, peasants preferred open accounts in which debts were mixed with current seigneurial dues.

The first draft of what became an Ordinance of the Special Council was worked out in what Governor Colborne described as tripartite meetings with Charles Buller representing the crown, lawyer Michael O'Sullivan the seminary, and Adam Thom the *censitaires*. A violent Tory and francophobe, Thom certainly did not represent the interests of *censitaires* from social groups like the peasantry or artisanry. For their part, industrial capitalists and large property owners disavowed Thom as a defender of their interests. Thom had for example, opposed the nomination to the bench of Samuel Gale, one of the largest Montreal landowners and vocal opponent of the seminary.[70]

In October 1838 the draft was forwarded to the seminary for its comment. With their lawyers, Sulpician officials scrutinized each clause making marginal comments, noting where the phrasing was "long, loose, and diffuse" and where Buller was "wavering" and might be pushed. They focused in particular on Thom's insistence that the seminary be obliged to make regular financial reports to the crown. The seminary argued that it was a religious community and as such was subject only to periodic visits from the crown rather than strict financial accountability. Thom also worried about the substantial wealth that the seminary would collect from commutations, but the Sulpicians rejected his proposal that any income over £150,000 be ceded to the crown. With his revised draft and accompanied by the seminary's lawyer, Superior Quiblier met for eight consecutive days with Buller, and on 27 October an agreement was reached.[71]

With the House of Assembly suspended, the protocol was presented to the appointed Special Council. During presentation of three different drafts to the council, Quiblier was reported to have worked on revisions with officials in the governor's office on a daily basis for six weeks.[72] Just a week before council approval of the protocol, opposition from large landed proprietors suddenly materialized. Describing themselves as "a few *censitaires*," twenty-two large landowners met, disavowed Adam Thom as representing their interests, and demanded a ten-year instead of seven-year repayment period for seigneurial arrears, a reduction of the interest rate on arrears from 6 to 5 percent, the possibility of partial commutations of properties on which the commutated section was valued over £500, and the right to commutate large properties outside the city and suburbs on which substantial improvements had been made. In a meeting with seminary officials, the committee was rebuffed except for agreement that rural properties evaluated over £500 might be treated on the same basis as urban concessions; the seminary referred other criticisms to the Special Council. Unsympathetic to committee demands, the Special Council approved the protocol on 8 April, 1839.[73]

After referral to England, the protocol returned to the Special Council in June 1840 where, after final objections were "pulverized" by Governor Sydenham, it was approved by a vote of fourteen to two; the opponents were George Moffatt, an important import-export merchant and port-area landowner, and John Molson Jr, steamboat owner, brewer, and large landowner (see appendix 1). As in 1839 a committee of large landowners was formed. It protested the "notorious" exercise of pressure on Special Council members and with editorial support from the *Gazette* published a pamphlet protesting that the British government was treating them "like so many Russian serfs": "If the feudal yoke must be borne, let it, at all events, have the impress of Royalty, for, if serfs at all, the landed proprietors are the serfs of the Queen."[74] The seminary responded with its own eighty-page pamphlet in which it emphasized its social role on behalf of "the sick, the aged, the infirm, and the helpless, the destitute widow and the orphan." It defended its property titles with a lengthy paragraph for each of what it called the eleven Laws: Law of Honour, Law of Good Faith, Law of Preservation, Law of Succession, Law of Possession, Law of Deeds, French Law, Law of Trustees, Law of England, Law of Conquests, and Law of Natural Rights.[75]

The landowners' committee delegated two members to carry their petition of opposition to London. Parliament however, approved the ordinance even though the Duke of Wellington described it as a complete departure from the principles of the Reformation. Ecstatic, Superior Quiblier complimented Britain for "the most Catholic and Papist law that it had sanctioned in over three hundred years."[76] Quiblier's joy was well founded for the ordinance represented a new charter for the seminary. It confirmed its titles under British jurisdiction and facilitated collection of seigneurial arrears and many of its traditional feudal levies. At the same time, it ensured the seminary new capitalist forms of revenue and enlarged its social and ideological function in the industrial state.

The ordinance abruptly ended decades of resistance to the payment of seigneurial dues to the seminary. With new corporate status the seminary could begin exacting its seigneurial rights with the full force of the law. All *censitaires* – rural and urban – would now have their seigneurial debts notarized and would pay legal interest (6 per cent) on debts incurred after 1840 and on old seigneurial debts unpaid after the legal delay specified by the ordinance. Despite important modifications to mortgage and registry regulations, seigneurial debts continued to be secured by the seigneur's traditional hypothecary priority, a right which remained privileged over other mortgages. And, although the *banalité* had been largely alienated by the seminary, the seigneurial levies of the *cens et rentes* and *lods et ventes* continued in force unless the *censitaire* exercised his option of commutating his lands into freehold tenure. In short, over the next two decades the seminary's feudal powers in the countryside were reinforced by the state while the application of interest and the institution of vigorous collection methods would heighten the implications of peasant endebtment to the seminary.

While the ordinance facilitated the enforcement of the seminary's feudal levies in the countryside, it served at the same time to relieve capitalist pressure on the institution in two important ways. The seminary's Saint-Gabriel domain along the Lachine Canal would be sold under freehold tenure within twenty years. This process relieved the seminary from mortmain restriction on the alienation of seigneurial land, ended its confrontation with industrial developers along the canal, and allowed the seminary to enrich itself from industrial and residential subdivision sales. Secondly, the ordinance permitted *censitaires* on the seminary's seigneuries to commutate their lands into freehold tenure by the capitalization of their *cens et rentes* and one-time *lods et ventes* payments. Provided that seigneurial arrears were paid up, the seminary could not refuse a commutation request. The commutation procedure was, as we shall see in subsequent chapters, utilized in the first years almost exclusively by Montrealers who had a significant surplus.

The years 1838 to 1840 marked the watershed for the seminary in its relationship to the larger societal transition from feudalism to capitalism. The failure of the rebellions devastated its social opponents, inaugurated an authoritarian regime favourable to settlement with the seminary, and set the stage for coexistence with the emerging industrial bourgeoisie. The transition was also clear in clauses of the ordinance that directed the disposition of the seminary's revenues. Up to £30,000 could be invested in income-producing real estate in Canada and an unlimited amount in benevolent institutions. The balance of its capital could be invested in the public securities of Great Britain or its colonies. With its financial, organizational and legal bases assured, the seminary was equipped and backed by the state to perform greatly expanded social functions in industrial society.[77]

CHAPTER THREE

Seigneurialism on Seminary Lands

In Canada, the seigneur was not the oppressor of his people but rather their watchful guardian. He planned roads and other improvements, checked abuses, and enforced justice. At this side stood, usually, the priest ... Each village would thus usually have at least two men of some culture working together for its spiritual and temporal interests.   George Wrong, 1926[1]

It is clearly evident therefore that the seigneurial régime evolved ... This seigneury [Montreal] became rigid and encroaching and, on the whole, has little to begrudge to its French counterpart.   Louise Dechêne, 1974[2]

The procurator will, as already authorized, use his own discretion and wisdom in suing tardy payers who are capable of supporting the costs of a lawsuit.   Instruction of Seminary Consulting Council, 1846[3]

We have seen that the first four decades of the nineteenth century represented an extended period of crisis for the seminary. Its legal status remained uncertain while its ecclesiastical relations were characterized by the resentment of a strengthening Canadian-born clergy and a new Montreal episcopate. By the 1820s with their seigneurial base buffeted by popular, nationalist and capitalist forces, the Sulpicians came close to renouncing their seigneurial lands and privileges in return for an indemnity and recognition as an ecclesiastical corporation. The rebellions of 1837–8 stilled most of the seminary's opponents allowing it to negotiate a settlement with Special Council and Colonial Office officials. The resulting Ordinance of 1840 confirmed the seminary's corporate status, reinforced its social function, and assured its right of recruitment. The ordinance's economic clauses were aimed at reducing feudal influence on Sulpician lands subject to urban or industrial uses while confirming the seminary's seigneurial powers in other areas and ensuring it adequate revenues for an expanding social role in Montreal. The seminary's property relations can be described in an essentially seigneurial institutional context before the early 1840s and, after that, in an increasingly mixed seigneurial / freehold tenure framework. If we set aside the tithe which was minimally important in Sulpician finances, the seminary's seigneurial regime in the nineteenth century is best treated by dividing its lands into two categories: reserves and conceded lands.[4]

SEIGNEURIAL RESERVES

The reserve consisted of unconceded lands that remained under the seigneur's direct control: mill, fishing, docking and other water sites, institutional sites, forest, pasture, and farm domains. These lands provided the seminary with food, heat, building supplies, cash income, future concessions or sales, and mission, teaching, and recreational sites. At Two Mountains the reserve totalled one-sixth of the seigneury and included the large Indian mission, a smaller domain of some 800 acres at Sainte-Scholastique, three grain mills, a sawmill, and the manor-house (1846). The domain at the Saint-Sulpice seigneury was much smaller, consisting of three mills, a 45-acre farm, a 100-acre woodlot, manor-house, and the church and presbytery site at Saint-Sulpice. On the island of Montreal, the seminary sold off its small reserve parcels before 1841: the pasture lands at Lachine, all mill sites on the island, sites in Pointe-Claire and the Tanneries, the islets in the Rivières des Prairies. This left the seminary with three large rural estates on the island: the 300-acre Mountain domain, the 300-acre Saint-Gabriel domain along the Lachine Canal, and the 300-acre domain at Sault-aux-Récollets (see fig. 5).[5] In Montreal itself the seminary had retained the college and seminary grounds along with several school, warehouse, office, and residential sites.

Institutional use was an important function of the reserve. The Grand Séminaire, Collège de Montréal, and country retreat were built on the Mountain domain and a church, presbytery, school, and agricultural college were constructed on the reserve at the Indian mission. Reserve lands were sometimes ceded for institutional use by third parties. Land near the seminary's mill at Achigan was granted to the parish in 1853 and at Saint-Benoît a mill was torn down and the site leased to the Grey Nuns in 1861.[6]

A monopoly on milling the grain of their *censitaires* was a traditional right of Canadian seigneurs and, even if they had never enforced the *banalité* within the city limits of Montreal, mill sites had formed an important part of the seminary's reserve. The *banalité* gave the seigneur exclusive right to construct mills on the seigneury and obliged *censitaires* to utilize the seigneurial mill and to pay a levy of 1/14 of their unmilled grain. Between 1767 and 1840 the seminary was associated with fourteen mills, nine of which were on the island of Montreal.[7] The mill represented a major capital investment and occupied land sites that often had valuable fishing, bridge, navigation, timber-slide, and water-power possibilities. Two of the seminary's mill sites on the island of Montreal took on special value because of canal construction while its mill sites at Saint-Sulpice were sought by industrial developers for their tanning, sawmill, and carding potential.

The seminary's attempt to protect its milling monopoly in the Fleming case was examined in chapter one. Although the seminary sold off most of its mills before 1841, land concession and sale contracts as late as 1856 included fines and grain confiscation for *censitaires* who contravened the *banalité*; the same contracts confirmed the seigneur's traditional right to repossess land for windmill, sawmill, or mill-stream construction.[8]

Fishing rights were another seigneurial privilege that can be included under reserves. Seminary contracts demonstrate that – at least in good fishing waters – the Sulpicians tried to enforce their seigneurial privilege of according fishing concessions. Gamekeeper "bonhomme Laurin" was paid six piastres a year (1804) to protect fishing waters around five of the seminary's islands in the Rivière des Prairies. Didier Jobert of Île de la Visitation fished under contract to the seminary. For seventy-two *livres tournois* a year he was allowed to keep all of the fish he caught in the first year of his contract (1808) and one quarter of the catch in subsequent years.[9] Two mill sale contracts in 1837 mention the cession of seigneurial fishing privileges to the purchaser. The sale of three mill sites on Rivière des Prairies included a clause committing the purchaser to respect the unwritten fishing lease accorded by the seminary to the curé of Saint-Philippe.

If fishing rights were of receding importance in the nineteenth century, other seigneurial water-site privileges had new value as hydraulic power assumed a broader significance. In 1843 the seminary invested in a carding mill at Two Mountains and in 1846 it negotiated the construction of hydraulic-powered industries on its Saint-Sulpice seigneury. The mixing of land use was most evident on the Montreal reserves. Beyond the orchard and fields of its Mountain domain, the seminary had an important quarry. On the Saint-Gabriel domain 120 cows were pastured beside a barge basin of the Lachine Canal (1825). Nearer the Montreal end of the domain was the field in which the immigrant sheds were built. The seminary owned a large warehouse just beyond the city limits and leased its mill site at the mouth of the Lachine Canal as a tobacco manufacture (1832).[10] On other parts of the reserve, merchant capitalism and signeurialism continued to coexist in traditional forms. Economic activity on the Lake of Two Mountains domain, for example, continued to centre on the Indian mission and fur trade. In 1836 the seminary still retained twelve to fifteen miles of forest and pasture as Indian hunting-grounds and as sources of wood and hay. A year later, the Hudson's Bay Company renewed the lease for its store site in Oka, an Indian village that held some 200 houses owned by the seminary. By 1862 the seminary had leased sixteen farms on the Two Mountains do-main, some for a fixed rent and others for half the produce.[11]

Production of food, fuel, and building materials were traditional functions of the reserve. Part of the banal expropriation had always been used for direct consumption by the seminary or its subsidiary institutions. In his "General Rules for the Operation of all Mills," Procurator Molin noted that "the seminary takes the flour which it needs, sometimes in one mill, sometimes in another, depending on the quality of the wheat and the state of the roads."[12] In the early nineteenth century the *banalité* collected at the important Lachine and Gros Sault mills was normally sold to bakers, merchants, or peasants. Flour for the seminary's bread and for inmates in the Hôtel-Dieu came from the two windmills in the Saint-Anne suburb. On the Mountain domain, mixed crops were produced including beeswax, honey, fruit, dairy products, cider, hay, oats, wheat, corn, nuts, pumpkins, cabbages, and potatoes. In 1847 a gardener spe-cializing in fruit trees was hired at the Mountain and was lodged in the house of tenant farmer Charles Marois. John Nicolson's main responsibilities were the apple orchard, market garden, and cider press. In 1850, for example, he delivered 100 gallons of cider and 23 quarts of apples to the seminary fruit cellar. Most of the Moun-tain's vegetable production was consumed in the Collège and Grand Séminaire while excess potatoes were sold to the Grey Nuns; in 1853 the farm produced 4,000 gallons of milk. Stone from the Mountain quarry was used in various Sulpician building projects.[13]

Until its subdivision and sale after 1845, the Saint-Gabriel domain was important for its pastures and its production of maple sugar and cedar fence posts. Its barberry was used to brew the Sulpicians' beer; its horses and employees hauled firewood from forest domains at Two Mountains, Saint-Sulpice, and Sault-au-Récollet to religious institutions in Montreal. On the Sault-au-Récollet domain only eighty acres had been cleared by 1846 and as late as the 1860s firewood was still its major product. By the 1880s the farm had been cleared, ditched, and fenced; its livestock included a twenty-eight head dairy herd, thirteen horses, nineteen pigs, sixty hens, and assorted ducks, turkeys, calves, and a steer. With improvement of the farm, foreman Paul Deschamps was given a five-year lease but domain account books emphasize the condition of the seminary's tenant farmers: "Monsieur Deschamps owns nothing except a few household items."[14]

Although reserve lands were sometimes worked by the seminary's own employees, they were usually rented out. This rental could take the form of a verbal or private written contract, but increasingly in the nineteenth century the seminary utilized the notarized lease. For the landlord, this form of contract had the advantage of being prepared by his notary; it was a witnessed document, and in disputes the lease facilitated recourse to the state. Twenty rural leases for the period 1839–76 were found in the notarial and seminary archives and summaries of many earlier contracts are contained in the seminary's account books.[15]

Although most of the seminary's urban leases were contracted on printed forms, leases for rural properties were normally handwritten by the notarial clerk. Some included special clauses in the landlord's favour, such as exemption from docking tolls or the right of passage across leased land.[16] The procurator negotiated most leases on the seminary's behalf, approved repairs and, increasingly after 1850, encouraged formal bookkeeping on leased properties. Capital expenditures on the reserve went to the Consulting Council for approval. The procurator also referred to the Council for decisions on unprofitable properties or unsatisfactory tenants. The former were sold; the leases of the latter terminated.[17]

The seminary's rural leases varied in length from a few months up to ten years, but most were for a period of one to five years. This allowed the seminary to adjust use of its reserve lands to market conditions. In changed economic circumstances a forest warden might be replaced by farmers who cleared the land.[18] The length of a rural lease had special significance in zones subject to industrial or urban development. The seminary held periodic land sales in the 1840s and 1850s on reserve lands along the Lachine Canal. Farm tenants on these properties were restricted to using the land as pasture, and some were given six-month leases that included conditions for early eviction if the lands were sold. Carter Michael Hennessy, for example, was granted a one-year lease with the proviso that the Sulpicians could repossess "as they may think proper."[19]

Forms of payment for reserve land varied. Fishermen who contracted for seigneurial waters normally paid one-quarter of their catch to the seminary. Contracts with millers were more complicated and included specific clauses for employee and road-maintenance costs, payment of the tithe to the local parish, and the use of arable land, pastures, or woodlots on the mill site. Millers normally returned one quarter of the wheat *banalité* and one half of the charges on other grains. The seigneur had exclusive right to all waterpower sites, a prerogative that the seminary exercised as late as 1848.[20] This monopoly enabled the seminary to profit from a variety of industrial activities particularly the construction of tanneries and saw, carding, and woollen mills. At Two Mountains, the seminary was involved in three sawmill operations. It ran the first one itself (1781), leased a second sawmill site to a local notary (1791), and shared the profits equally with the sawyer at the third site. The tenant of a carding mill at Rivière du Nord paid £60 a year (1837).[21]

Farm contracts also took several forms. Some included payment in kind of a percentage of farm produce; others called for fixed rents in currency. Paschal Saint-Gebert, tenant on the important Sault-au-Récollet domain (1841), delivered one third of his grain, hay, and fruit production to the seminary in Montreal as well as three-quarters of the cash proceeds from his wood and animal sales. Tenant on an isolated farm on the Saint-Sulpice seigneury, Abraham Forest agreed to a rental (1839) of twenty bales of his best hay delivered each summer to the seminary's mill at Achigan. Lancelot Franklin rented pasture along the Lachine Canal for a fixed rent of £24 for an eight-month season (1844). Joseph Guilbault, two years in arrears for rent on his property on the Mountain domain, agreed to pay the £31 due either in plants or in fruit seedlings (1846).[22]

Rents and produce from reserve lands represented an increasingly smaller proportion of the seminary's income after 1840. In 1835 reserve revenues (land sales excluded) represented 9.3 per cent of the seminary's income, in 1845 it had dropped to 3.6 per cent, and by 1865 it was less than 1 per cent.[23] Business office and bursar accounts suggest, however, that the farms were consistently profitable. Although it is difficult to appropriate expenses, income in 1843 from the farms on the Mountain reserve was £138, the Saint-Gabriel domain had income of £274, the farm at Sault-au-Récollet £133, and the seminary garden £68. By 1867 important parts of the reserve had been sold, but cash rents from farms on the island brought $204 for the year and the sale of produce $679. After deduction of taxes, insurance, repairs, seed costs, some capital expenses (construction of a pig pen), and $33 worth of butter given to the procurator, farms on the island of Montreal showed a profit of $612. In 1862 farms on the domain at Two Mountains returned the seminary a profit of $2,106.[24]

Expropriation in the form of cash or produce never took priority over the maintenance of the natural, invested, and work-acquired value of the seminary's reserve lands. Forests, river, pastures, farm buildings, and fences were recognized as valuable assets and along with the right to tap sugar maples, to cut trees, to collect deadwood, or to sell manure were carefully defined in seminary leases. Many farm tenants had warden responsibilities to protect the seigneur's fishing, forest, and agricultural preserves from timber scavengers, fish poachers, and picnickers. The lease (1864) of Jean-Baptiste Pilon, tenant farmer at Sault-au-Récollet, was typical. Provided that he gave a full account to seminary authorities, Pilon could collect deadwood to heat his own house. He did not, however, have the right to cut live trees. This was a prerogative of the seminary which assumed the cutting and hauling costs and kept three-quarters of the proceeds. Pilon was also forbidden to sell manure produced on his farm; all animal wastes were to be used to fertilize the land.[25]

Two volumes of wardens' reports and timber-cutting permits granted at Two Mountains (1868–1903) attest to the importance given to forest reserves. Seminary wardens patrolled domain forests marking trees for cutting, fining scavengers, and watching for fires. Warden Moyse Labrosse noted that he had restricted the collection of deadwood to an eight-day period (July 1867) and that he had allowed the bailiff Brazeau to cut one tree. Another warden reported that he had granted permission to one resident to collect deadwood and standing bushes for construction of a fish trap. In return for eight pairs of turkeys, Léandre Boisseau was permitted to cut twenty cords of firewood, most of it on his own farm. His permit did not permit the cutting of wood suitable for sawing into lumber. Wardens were particularly vigilant to prevent the burning of brush without permission, perhaps because it indicated illegal cutting or because of the danger of fire: "The German will no longer put a foot on the domain – on account of wood burned by the Bay." By 1848 scavenging by mission Indians had assumed such proportions that the seminary decided to take legal action against Indians who collected or sold deadwood from the domain without permission.[26]

In addition to the inherent value of its reserve, the seminary improved its properties, an investment it protected by obliging lessees to maintain its buildings, implements, and cultivated fields. This concern is most obvious in the instructions given to millers who had responsibility for the capital-intensive mills, but most tenants had responsibility for fences on their land, some pastured seminary live-stock, and others repaired bridges and roads.[27] A twenty-eight clause, handwritten lease (1886) for the Lorette farm on the Sault-au-Récollet domain illustrates tenant responsibility for the landlord's investment. Tenant Paul Deschamps was to maintain farm equipment in good condition and was forbidden to lend implements or farm vehicles. He could not sell animals without permission, was to ensure their winter feed, and was obliged to replace animals that died through his negligence. Deschamps was also responsible for third-party dam-age to the farm's woodlots and, in his own name, was to sue indi-viduals who damaged seminary property. Veterinary, fertilizer, and crop-insurance costs were shared equally by landlord and tenant. Deschamps' farm was located beyond the northern outskirts of Mon-treal and his lease included a clause obliging him to prevent dancing and picnics: "The lessee promises not to tolerate dancing or any other disorder in his house. In addition he will not permit the farm or woodlot to become a *rendezvous de plaisir* nor allow any picnic – even for a charitable cause."[28]

The seminary reserve was also enriched by the labour of its ten-ants. Unlike ceded lands, which remained in the possession of the *censitaire* and his heirs, rented lands reverted to the landlord; ac-cumulated work by tenants such as clearing, ditching, and the con-struction of immovables was inevitably inherited by the seminary.[29] The work of Louise Tremblay suggests that as early as the seven-teenth and eighteenth centuries the Sulpicians understood the value of the labour power added to seminary reserves by Indians, first at the Montreal mission, then at Sault-au-Récollet, and finally at the Two Mountains seigneury.[30] The seminary's nineteenth-century ru-ral leases sometimes took the tenant's labour into account in deter-mining rents. Farmer Gervais Descary was given a nine-year lease (1851) on land at the Coteau Saint-Pierre. In addition to a rent of half his hay production, Descary was to clear the remaining woods on his land and to have it in pasture within five years. Michel Cadire was granted a three-year lease (1839) for land he was to clear and fence. Exempt from rent in the first year, Cadire was to deliver fifty bales of his best hay to the seminary's mill in the following two years. Other leases stated explicitly that all improvements became the prop-erty of the landlord.[31]

The seigneur had a much more direct influence on his reserve lands than on ceded land. Indeed, the effective exploitation of the seigneurial reserve implied strong supervision and the implemen-tation of formal accounting procedures by tenants and farm em-ployees. Taking again an example from the Sault-au-Récollet domain, it is clear that the landlord had the right to intervene directly in the running of the farm. By the terms of his lease, farmer Jean-Baptiste Pilon was to accept all "direction" which the seminary might give him and was to obtain written authorization before undertaking work which might incur expense for the landlord.[32] To ensure their reliability, some lessees were obliged to have their leases co-signed by guarantors. In almost all seminary rural leases, subletting was forbidden and, at least as early as 1801, inspection clauses appeared in leases. Farmer Boyer who leased part of the Mountain domain was forbidden to harvest any crop before its evaluation by a seminary official. The cutting of wood on seminary domains required close supervision. At Two Mountains, the seminary's forest wardens insisted that all wood cut for sale be transported to the commons for measurement and that cutting and docking fees be paid before the loading of barges. Animal and furniture inventories were standard in mid-century leases and in the same period a more rigorous attempt was made to enforce tenant bookkeeping and monthly returns. When leases were violated, the seminary's notaries were mobilized. For example, Edward Dunwoody, a tenant on the Saint-Gabriel domain, was sent a protest (1847) for allowing his cattle to destroy trees and to soil the ground around seminary buildings.[33]

CONCEDED LAND

Most of the seminary's seigneurial land was not kept as reserve but was ceded either as fiefs or as individual concessions. Some 14 fiefs were granted in the years 1658–80, of which 7 (Nazareth, Saint-Joseph, Saint-Augustin, Closse, Lagauchetière, Saint-Germain, and Morel) remained in 1836.[34] Most of the seigneury of Montreal was distributed to individual *censitaires*. In 1666–7 the seminary ordered a survey of the island, and around 1680 it began notarizing all concessions. By 1763 it had conceded 1,376 properties on the island outside the city and 478 within the City of Montreal; less than 3 per cent of the island remained as domain. In keeping with Canadian seigneurial practice, rural concessions made by the seminary were divided into narrow strips seven to ten times longer than wide. Depending on the terrain, individual grants varied from 40 to 120 *arpents* with a normal concession being some 60 *arpents*. *Censitaires* invariably built their homes along the front of their properties, giving a density on the island of some nine houses per kilometre. At the Saint-Sulpice seigneury some 600 concessions had been made by 1835 and at Two Mountains some 1,260.[35] For the period after 1835 only 14 concessions were found in the records of the seminary's notaries in Montreal – 3 in 1835, 1 in 1838, 4 in 1839, 1 in 1840, 4 in 1847, and 1 in 1855. Since most of these concessions were at Saint-Sulpice there may be others in the notarial archives of Saint-Jérôme. Most of the post-1835 concessions seem to have been granted in special circumstances: one property was ceded to the church wardens at Pointe-Claire, another to the seminary notary at Saint-Benoît, and a third to a bailiff at Saint-Sulpice. An 1835 concession was noted as being a "compensation," and the final concession found in research was made in fulfillment of a promise made by the seminary in 1826.[36]

Drawn up on forms printed in the 1820s, the post-1835 concessions contained many of the historic obligations of seigneurialism as known in New France and western Europe. Given the emphasis in much Canadian historiography on seigneurialism as a paternal system of watchful guardianship and of checking abuses, the actual concession-contract surprises by its one-sidedness and its long list of *censitaire* obligations.[37] Little protection for the *censitaire* can be found in the contract and, although he became a small independent farmer and master of his own production, the *censitaire*'s control over his land was far from absolute.

The *censitaire* contracted to pay seigneurial rents, milling fees, and mutation dues, to reside on the land for at least one year, and to keep the land under cultivation. Probably with a view to reducing fraud in property sales, the concession contract gave the seigneur first refusal (*droit de retrait*) at the sale price; this right of the seigneur took precedence over all buyers. Although seminary concession contracts in the nineteenth century contained this redemption clause, the seminary stated in 1840 that "it has never been customary" for it to exercise this privilege.[38] The conditional nature of the *censitaire*'s property tenure is reinforced by other terms in the contract. The seigneur had the right to take timber, stone, and sand from ceded lands for construction of a church, presbytery, mill, and manor-house. Concessions in the 1830s included the appropriation of these building materials for "other public works" and "even for the needs of their farms." Firewood was a resource of primary importance and the seigneur reserved the wood on one ceded *arpent* in twenty (i.e., 5 per cent of the ceded land) for his use. The seigneur could build roads of public utility across ceded lands. In none of these instances was he obliged to compensate the *censitaire*. The contract also gave the seigneur the right to expropriate water-access routes for construction of a church, presbytery, and mills. If he did so, he was to prorate the *cens et rentes* and to compensate the *censitaire* for clearing done on the expropriated land. Finally, the *censitaire* was obliged to labour on "public works." It is not clear if this clause was ever applied.

Certain concessions contained supplementary, handwritten conditions. Although the printed contract called for the mutual maintenance of common fences, Luc Poirier was obliged to assume "alone and at his expense" all costs of maintaining the fences, waterways, ditches, and the road between his land and the seigneur's domain.[39]

Before 1800, wheat was the main agricultural product on the seminary's seigneuries. Usually operated by its farmer-concessionaire who operated as an independent commodity producer, a typical Montreal-area farm had, in addition to its wheat fields, livestock, and fowl, a vegetable garden, and pastures; the climate made a woodlot essential for the production of heating fuel. By the 1830s wheat production in the Montreal area was plummeting. Fernand Ouellet terms the collapse as a "catastrophe"; John McCallum describes "periodic food shortages, declining living standards and mounting debt."[40] In Saint-Laurent, a northern parish on the seigneury of Montreal, wheat production dropped from 29,157 minots in 1831 to 3,414 in 1844. Further east on the seigneury at Rivière-des-Prairies, 1844 production was only 10 per cent of the 1831 level. Sulpicians coffers reflected this falling grain production. Seminary income from the sale of grains collected as seigneurial dues fell from 103,092 *livres tournois* in 1816 to 54,385 *livres tournois* in 1826 and to 27,299 in 1833.[41]

From the perspective of the seminary several observations can be made concerning the debate by Fernand Ouellet, John McCallum, and R.M. McInnis over the staple, ethnicity, and market demand as factors in falling wheat production.[42] As noted in chapter two, the seminary was wary in the application of its seigneurial prerogatives in the two decades before the rebellions. Sulpician fears of popular resistance, the courts, and certain urban and industrial capitalists were reflected in their private correspondence and their failure to collect certain seigneurial dues owed to them. In 1838 Superior Quiblier estimated that on the seigneury of Montreal outside the city and suburbs an annual average of £433 had not been paid over the past thirty years.[43] While we witness widespread indebtedness of the Montreal-area peasantry before 1840, it was only after this date that the seminary was able to exploit this phenomenon. Seigneurialism in a period of reduced agricultural surplus led to indebtedness, but the repercussions – rigorous collection, the application of interest, the vigorous use of state power, and the alienation of debts to third parties – were only fully felt by the seminary's *censitaires* after the Ordinance of 1840.

Still from the perspective of one Montreal-area seigneur, we can suggest two other hypotheses – the evasion of seigneurial dues and production of agricultural goods for the local market – as causes for the drop in wheat production. Seminary officials in the 1840s perceived that farmers in the parish of Montreal had stopped growing wheat in favour of producing hay and vegetables for the Montreal market. The full implications of this fodder and market-garden production for the local market need further examination. As well, a *censitaire* who grew other crops than grains was not subject to the seigneurial appropriation of part of his surplus in milling fees. The tithe represented yet another seigneurial factor since it was payable only on grain production. Tithe revenues for the parish of Montreal hardly totalled £100 in 1845 while at Two Mountains the tithe produced only £15 to £20 a year.[44]

Aside from the tithe, seigneurial dues consisted of the *cens et rentes, lods et ventes*, and the *banalité*. As already noted, the *censitaire* was obliged, for a payment of one-fourteenth of his harvest, to mill his grain at the seigneur's mill. The *cens et rentes* was an annual rent payment on the concession and was payable at the manor-house on Saint-Martin's Day (11 November). On rural concessions the *censitaire* paid half a minot of wheat and 10 *sols tournois* for every 20 *arpents*. This rate was levied on lots in the suburbs and city of Montreal which had been subdivided from rural concessions. Concessions originally conceded as urban lots in Montreal and the villages paid six *deniers tournois* for every thirty-six square feet (*toise quarrée*). According to seminary officials in 1836, these rates "with the exception of a very small number" had remained unchanged since 1671. Unlike other seigneurs, the seminary did not increase the *cens et rentes* in concessions made after 1820.[45]

Lods et ventes were a mutation levy applied when a concession changed hands other than by succession. In rural concessions 6.6 per cent of the price was charged, rising to $8^1/_2$ per cent if legal action was required to collect the levy. City and suburban lots valued under £500 paid 6.6 per cent while urban properties evaluated at over £500 were charged 5 per cent.[46]

THE COLLECTION OF SEIGNEURIAL ARREARS

The seminary's ability to collect seigneurial dues on its conceded lands was dramatically reinforced by the Ordinance of 1840 and other enactments of the Special Council. Historically, the seminary had been a patient creditor, allowing debts to accumulate and waiting to collect in propitious family or economic circumstances.[47] However, in the decades before 1837, this tradition of tardy payment to the seminary had ballooned into wholesale non-payment of seigneurial dues, sometimes the annual *cens et rentes* but more often the larger, lump-sum *lods et ventes*.

In Montreal it was public knowledge that certain seigneurial dues could be ignored. In 1838 the superior estimated overdue *lods* in the city and suburbs over the past thirty years at £31,000.[48] Turton Penn, a Bank of Montreal director, testified in 1835 that "the seminary was not in the habit of enforcing the collection of the *lods et ventes* ... and [they] do not bear interest." Brewer, banker, and steamboat owner, John Molson, was equally blunt: "I have always opposed the claims of the St. Sulpicians [sic] at Montreal and have never made any payments to them; but I believe my son has done so."[49] The seminary's arrears list was a Who's Who from all social ranks. Banker Jacob DeWitt owed *lods et ventes* of £600 on seven urban property transactions, one of which dated from 1810. Contractor John Redpath owed the seminary £100 in seigneurial dues for his estate. The illiterate widow of shoemaker Jean-Baptiste Thibault owed £33 for *lods* due in 1830. Even the parish priest of Saint-Laurent had seigneurial debts dating from 1827.[50]

The resistance of rural *censitaires* to seigneurial dues has already been noted. On the seigneury of Saint-Sulpice, seigneurial debts were owing on 484 of some 600 concessions while on the island of Montreal outside the city over 800 of the 1,376 concessions had unpaid debts.[51] In 1838, seminary authorities estimated unpaid *lods et ventes* on the island of Montreal outside the city and suburbs at £13,000. On its other two seigneuries, arrears of *lods et ventes* were put at a minimum of £12,700 in 1840.

A few seigneurial debtors did sign debt-recognition contracts before 1840. Forty-one of these *reconnaissance* acts – all from the period 1835–40 – were found in the records of the seminary's notary. These contracts confirm that, even after arrears of forty years, interest was not paid on seigneurial debts. Nor was payment encouraged by the collateral clause of the contract since, under the original concession contract, the seminary was already the privileged creditor holding a mortgage on the property. To this security, the debt-recognition contract added a pledge of "all the goods" of the debtor.[52]

In addition to being few in number in proportion to the number of debtors, the pre-1840 debt-recognition acts did not come from large propertyholders. When Ernest Idler, a Montreal butcher, bought a lot in the Saint-Laurent suburb, he "recognized" that he owed £17 to the seminary for the *lods et ventes* due on three sales of the property since 1810. A farmer in Pointe-Claire, Alexandre Brunet, recognized his *lods et ventes* debt of £2 and agreed to pay five piastres in three weeks time and the rest on demand. James Carswell, guardian of the four children of the deceased Montreal grocer James Birss, came to the seminary in 1834 and "recognized" accumulated Birss family seigneurial debts of 4,000 *livres tournois* which had accumulated since 1799.[53]

The Ordinance of 1840 abruptly ended resistance to the payment of seigneurial dues. All *censitaires* – rural and urban – were forced to pay their overdue seigneurial debts and, unless they commuted their lands into freehold tenure, to pay promptly ongoing seigneurial levies of the *cens et rentes* and *lods et ventes*. The renewed corporate status of the seminary enabled it to enforce fixed payment dates, to begin the levy of legal interest rates on overdue debts, and to exact its seigneurial property rights with the full force of the law.

Seigneurial debts owed to the seminary and the mortgages which secured them were to remain privileged over other liens on the property. Nor could a property be commutated into freehold tenure until seigneurial arrears had been discharged:

that the Right and Title of ... the Seminary of Saint Sulpice of Montreal [to its three seigneuries] ... and to all Seigniorial and Feudal Rights, Privileges, Dues and Duties ... and to all ... the Domains, Lands, Reservations, Buildings, Messuages, Tenements, and Hereditaments [therein] ... and to all Monies, Debts, Hypothèques, and other Real Securities, Arrears of Lods et Ventes, Cens et Rentes, and other Seigneurial Dues and Duties payable ... by Censitaires, Tenants and others ... [and] Goods, Chattels, and moveable Property whatsoever, now [or hereafter] due, owing, belong, or accrued to the ... Seminary ... are hereby confirmed and declared good, valid, and effectual in the Law ...

Nothing herein before contained [i.e. commutation clauses] shall ... discharge the [properties] from the Rights, Hypothèques, Privileges, Reservations and Demands of the [seminary] ... for the Security and Recovery of any Arrears of Seigneurial Dues ... or in anywise ... destroy, alter, or affect the Remedies and Recourse at Law which [the Seminary] ... might lawfully have had or have taken for the Recovery of the same ... [and] all and every the lawful Rights, Hypothèques, Privileges, Actions, Demands, Recourse, and Remedies in that Behalf [of the Seminary] ... are hereby saved and maintained.[54]

The Ordinance did place three restrictions on the seminary's collection of debts. On property in the city of Montreal with a value (including buildings) of more than £500 the seminary was not to collect more than 5 per cent of the property's value for each instance of unpaid, pre-1840 *lods et ventes*. Outside of Montreal the seminary was restricted to 6.6 per cent. Since these percentages were precisely the pre-1840 *lods et ventes* rates, these clauses apparently meant that the seminary was not permitted to add interest or surcharges to *lods et ventes* debts for the period before 1840. The second restriction limited the pre-1840 arrears that the seminary could collect to £53,700 of which £41,000 could come from the seigneury of Montreal and £12,700 from its other two seigneuries.

Finally, the ordinance obliged the seminary to differentiate between large and small *lods et ventes* debtors. On *lods et ventes* arrears of more than £41 the debtor could repay in equal annual instalments with the final payment before June 1847. The *lods et ventes* debtor who owed less than £41 had no statutory instalment privilege, a factor reflected in debt-recognition contracts.[55] While large debts were paid over several years, the seminary normally made small debts payable "on demand" with interest applicable after the demand date. In the 1840s some small debtors negotiated periods of grace – usually one year – after which interest was applied. Master shoemaker Joseph Leduc was given fourteen months to pay his *lods et ventes* arrears of £14 10s. Carter Narcisse Vinet arranged special terms for a five-year *lods et ventes* debt of 570 *livres tournois* on his Quebec suburb lot. Vinet was to pay 330 *livres* on demand and the rest in proportion as his children married or attained majority. The seminary was less generous with those who had resisted paying the annual *cens* as well as the *lods et ventes*. Saint-Laurent farmer Pierre Cousineau had not paid the *cens* for three years in addition to a *lods et ventes* debt. He was given until "next Friday" to pay notarial registration costs of 30s. and five weeks to pay his debt of 636 *livres tournois*.[56]

Other parts of the Ordinance of 1840 were reflected in the revised debt-recognition contracts drawn up and printed by the business office. The new contracts emphasized the strengthened legal and mortgage powers of the seminary. In its pre-1840 debt-recognition contracts the seminary described itself as "seigneurs of the island of Montreal"; on one of the new forms the title was expanded into "proprietory seigneurs in possession of fiefs and seigneuries." In a clear reference to the ordinance's reinforcement of the seigneur's first-mortgage privilege, the phrase "according to the law" was added to one of the mortgage clauses. A comparison of the security clauses emphasizes this.

Pre-1840 "Security" clause of *Reconnaissance* contract (the underlined words are handwritten on the forms):

Pour sûreté de quoi il a affecté et hypothéqué tous ses biens présents et à venir sans préjudice néanmoins à l'hypothèque déjà acquise par les dits

Seigneurs sur la dite terre pour le paiement des dits arrérages; à laquelle hypothèque le dit Mess. Sr. Procureur, agissant comme dit est, n'entend nullement déroger ni innover par ces présentes.[57]

Post-1840 "Security" clauses of two *Reconnaissance* contracts:

Pour sûreté de quoi, le dit emplacement continuera de demeurer spéciale-ment affecté et hypothéqué et, par privilège, selon la loi; à laquelle hypo-thèque spéciale et privilégiée les Sieurs Seigneurs n'entendent nullement déroger ni innover par ces présentes.[58]

En garantie du paiement de la présente reconnaissance, tant en principal qu'intérêt, l'héritage ci-dessus désigné demeurera spécialement affecté et hypothéqué aux dits sieurs seigneurs, qui réservent expressément et dans leur intégralité, tous les droits de préférences et privilèges qui leur sont acquis sur le dit héritage, sans aucune novation ni dérogation.[59]

The new role of interest was evident on the printed forms: one form stated that legal interest of 6 per cent was due on overdue accounts and extended the seminary's first-mortgage privilege to include interest debts as well as principal (appendix 2). Finally, one of the new forms obliged the debtor to pay the costs of registering the mortgage.

The ordinance's effect on seminary business procedures – the expansion and structuring of the business office after 1840, the revision of its reporting and accounting systems, the expanding no-tarial function – have been described in chapter two. The growth in the notarial staff from the occasional services of a notary in the early 1830s to three full-time notaries in 1842 needs re-emphasis however, since it witnesses the seminary's changing legal and prop-erty condition into forms in which pre-industrial family and com-munity relations had diminishing effect. The transformation of seminary lands into disposable commodities was particularly evident in the collection of seigneurial arrears, a process after 1840 which moulded the debtor-seigneur relationship into new, free-market re-lations. Under the terms of the ordinance a seigneurial debtor of the seminary was given a limited period of interest-free grace. If not settled after the agreed-upon delay, interest was applied and collec-tion procedures instituted. Fearful of using the law before 1840, the seminary now had state backing to enforce its property rights. By 1859, the Seminary was buying newspaper advertising space to pub-lish extracts of seigneurial law.[60]

The first step in the collection process was the compilation of exact accounts of seigneurial arrears and the notification to indebted *censitaires* of the application of the new law. Debtors were invited to acquit their arrears immediately or to arrange repayment in a formal debt contract. Warning forms printed by the Seminary emphasize its readiness to use the law to exact payment:

St.-Benoît,   187__
A

_____

Monsieur,
    Je suis chargé de vous notifier que le Séminaire de St.-Sulpice de Montréal exige le paiement immédiat de la somme de   que vous lui devez pour
                            et qu'à défaut par vous d'en faire le paiement
sous   de cette date, il sera adopté des procédés judiciaires contre vous.

                                    J'ai l'honneur d'être
                                    Votre humble serviteur, etc.
    N.B. – Ne négligez pas cet avis[61]

    In the eight-year period, 1834–41, before application of the ordinance, the seminary had averaged only seven debt-recognition contracts a year. This was dwarfed by hectic notarial activity after 1841; two Seminary notaries worked full-time writing debt-recognition contracts in 1842. On the two seigneuries of Saint-Sulpice and Montreal, 1,382 debt recognitions were signed in 1842, 107 in 1843, 14 in 1844, 84 in 1845, 36 in 1846, and 13 in 1847 (see fig. 6).
    To handle seigneurial debt-collection in the Montreal area, Henri Valotte was hired. Between May and December 1842 he drew up 130 debt-recognition contracts for debtors. On 24 September 1842, for example, Valotte drew up debt recognitions for two merchants. Jesse Thayer owed two *lods et ventes* debts dating from 1833 and 1835. Since his debt was over £41 Thayer had until 1847 to pay it off. He negotiated to pay the principal of £350 "at will" with interest starting in five years (1847). On the same day Samuel Hart settled his £125 *lods et ventes* debt agreeing to pay two-sevenths the following 1 July and the rest in five equal payments. In his next notarial act, written two days later, Valotte settled an 1832 *lods et ventes* debt with master carpenter Robert Robinson. With a debt under £41, Robinson could not claim the 1847 clause; he agreed to pay the £14 he owed the following May. All three paid registry fees.[62]
    Urban *reconnaissances* for seigneurial debts were often for substantial amounts and included complicated terms. For its rural debts

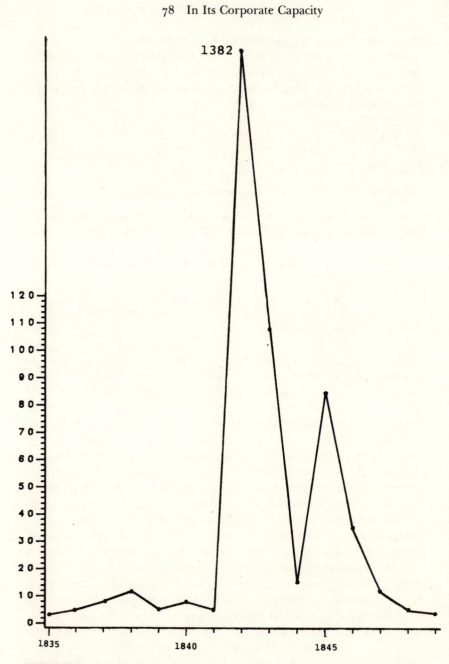

FIGURE 6

Debt-Recognition Contracts (*reconnaissances*) on the Seigneuries of
Montreal and Saint-Sulpice, 1835–49
Source: Appendix 2.

TABLE 3
Debt Recognitions Contracted by Notary André Jobin,
4 April 1842–24 June 1843

Date	Village	Seigneury	Number
1842			
4–23 April	Sainte-Geneviève	Montreal	82
26 April–2 May	Sainte-Anne	Montreal	38
3 May	Sainte-Geneviève	Montreal	1
4–27 May	Pointe-Claire	Montreal	97
27–28 May	Sainte-Geneviève	Montreal	9
30 May–11 June	Saint-Laurent	Montreal	62
15 June–11 Aug.	Saint-Sulpice	Saint-Sulpice	439
16–27 Aug.	Sainte-Geneviève	Montreal	10
29 Aug.–16 Sept.	Saint-Laurent	Montreal	110
17 Sept.	Pointe-Claire	Montreal	5
19–20 Sept.	Saint-Laurent	Montreal	13
21 Sept.–8 Oct.	Lachine	Montreal	65
14 Oct.	Pointe-Claire	Montreal	1
17 Oct.–9 Nov.	Sault-au-Récollet	Montreal	131
10–25 Nov.	Rivière-des-Prairies	Montreal	53
25 Nov.–14 Dec.	Pointe-aux-Trembles & Longue-Pointe	Montreal	123
1843			
3 Jan.	Sainte-Geneviève	Montreal	1
12–23 Jan.	Achigan	Saint-Sulpice	5
10 April	Sainte-Geneviève	Montreal	1
16–24 June	Saint-Sulpice	Saint-Sulpice	37

– usually simpler in format and for smaller sums – the seminary
hired André Jobin in April 1842. A well-known politician and prominent notary, Jobin began in his home village of Saint-Geneviève
where he wrote 82 debt recognitions in nineteen days. He then
worked his way twice around the villages on the island of Montreal
and the Saint-Sulpice seigneury (table 3). In fifteen months Jobin
wrote 1,283 debt-recognition contracts for the seminary.

This combination of the law and newly hired professionals quickly
dissipated the resistance which had characterized the payment of
seigneurial debts to the seminary before 1840. Seminary dossiers
show the forcefulness of the business office and the trepidation of
many *censitaires*. In the spring of 1842 debtors on the Two Mountains
seigneury delivered wheat, money and even old French currency to
the seminary's two notaries and miller; one *censitaire* arrived twice
in the same day with cash at notary Girouard's office. At Sainte-
Geneviève a debtor promised to make a payment in March 1855.

When he had not appeared by the twenty-seventh of the month he was sent a verbal warning and a notation was made in his account. In Lachine, Henri Pigeon was given a few days grace in order that he might sell a horse.[63]

Income from the collection of pre-1840 seigneurial debts was an important source of revenue in the first years after 1840. The £41,306 collected from 1841 to 1847 represented 20.5 per cent of seminary income for those years – strong evidence of the implications for the seminary of its new legal status and property relations.[64] After 1848 collections dropped off and 1850 was the last year that pre-1840 seigneurial-debt revenues amounted to more than 10 per cent of seminary income.

The seminary had several recourses if a debt-recognition contract was not honoured. In some cases it simply waited for better times. Farmer Jean-Baptiste Le Roux of Sainte-Geneviève went before notary Jobin in 1842 and recognized arrears of 1,421 *livres tournois*. Ten years later he appeared before notary Lacombe to recognize ongoing debts of 809 *livres*. The seminary often allowed the principal and interest to accumulate until there was a succession or sale. François Payment, a farmer at Sainte-Geneviève did not pay his *cens et rentes* for twenty-nine years. When he died in 1848 his heirs were obliged to pay the arrears plus the costs of collection. Pascal Persillier was a prominent miller at Sault-au-Récollet. Among his several debts when he died in 1859 was £218 owing to the seminary in seigneurial arrears. Rather than face a lawsuit, Persillier's heirs agreed to pay the debt over four years. If a debtor went bankrupt, seminary officials appeared at syndic meetings to ensure the seminary's seigneurial priority.[65]

In other instances in which the debtor refused to pay his seigneurial arrears and ignored official warnings, his dossier was forwarded to the seminary's lawyers, Dorion and Cherrier or, in the 1870s, L.L. Corbeil. Thomas O'Neil, whose seigneurial debts had accumulated for years, quickly paid off the £15 he owed when Cherrier initiated a lawsuit on behalf of the seminary. Cherrier handled dozens of cases such as that against Pierre Vendon, who in 1855 owed pre-1840 *lods et ventes* of 158 *livres tournois* for a lot in the village of Saint-Laurent plus 147 *livres* for thirteen years of back *cens et rentes*. Cherrier collected 144 *livres* immediately from Vendon and for the balance marked the account "wait till Christmas 1855."[66] Threat of a suit deterred others. In 1845 Daniel Gorrie sold a brewery site without paying off seigneurial debts owing on the property. Three years later he was in the seminary business office to arrange terms of paying his arrears and to avoid what his debt-contract described as "the expense of a lawsuit." The seminary was just as thorough in the countryside. On its Two Mountains seigneury for example, the seminary initiated thirty lawsuits in a two-month period, May–June 1847. Once court judgments had been won, it was the sheriff who collected on the seminary's behalf.[67]

Seigneurial arrears and the payment of current seigneurial dues made the seminary an important third party to land transactions. Even granting the widespread refusal to pay *lods et ventes* before 1840, the seminary was active. From 1820 to 1837 its lawyers filed protests an average of forty-one times a year.[68] The Ordinance of 1840 and Registry Act of 1841 greatly facilitated seminary collection procedures, and by 1841 it was systematically blocking the sale of land on which seigneurial dues were owing. When Montreal lawyer John Easton Mills bought a suburban lot from Abner Bagg, the seminary stopped the sale until Mills agreed to pay the seigneurial debts and the seminary's legal costs.[69] This third-party interest was also evident in certain lawsuits between individuals. Pierre Mireau had signed a seminary debt-recognition contract during notary Jobin's visit to Saint-Sulpice in 1842. Twenty years later his debt had increased through interest and unpaid *cens et rentes* to $167 – a sum that represented 20 to 25 per cent of the property's value. As a result the seminary was an active party in the lawsuit brought against Mireau by Pierre Venne and the subsequent auction of his land by the sheriff of Joliette.[70]

SALE OF DEBTS

By 1852 the seminary had collected £44,144 in arrears on the island of Montreal and £6,640 in arrears from its seigneuries at Saint-Sulpice and Lake of Two Mountains. Despite these impressive collections it was still owed £4,270 from debtors on the island of Montreal and £6,723 on its two other seigneuries.[71] Wringing these often-decades-old arrears from obstreperous or impoverished debtors led inevitably to high-profile suits, sheriff seizures, and bankruptcy hearings – all unattractive business climes for a publicity-sensitive religious institution. To avoid the bullying image concomitant with vigorous debt collection while maximizing its return on seigneurial arrears, the seminary sold difficult debts. This transfer (*transport*) – usually formalized in a notarized act – permitted the seminary to recuperate part or, in some cases, all of difficult debts.[72] For its part in the transfer contract (see appendix 4), the seminary conveyed to the purchaser all of its "rights, privileges and mortgages" on the property in question but accepted no further responsibility if the debt was uncollectable. Aside from guaranteeing the validity of the debt, the property title, and the mortgage, the seminary extricated itself from involvement in the collection process. The wholesale alienation of seigneurial debts emphasized the seminary's wish to distance itself from feudal modalities.

The price of seminary transfers of seigneurial debts could only be determined in seventeen of the ninety-two transfer contracts examined since most simply stated that the seminary was satisfied with "value received." In an indeterminable number of other cases transfers were not notarized. Of the seventeen contracts which are specific, the transfer price varied from 40 to 100 per cent of the value of the debt. Six debts were discounted and transferred at 40 to 60 per cent of their face value. These highly discounted debts were, with one exception all on the Saint-Sulpice seigneury, an apparent reflection of depressed land values in the region. For the transfer of a 100 *livres tournois.* debt on a village lot in Assomption, merchant Asprit Chaput paid only 50 *livres.* Eight years later the seminary was even more liberal in its transfer of the debt of the "absent from the province" farmer Jean-Baptiste Brien. His 455 *livres* debt for *cens et rentes* and *lods et ventes* on his Saint-Sulpice farm was transferred to Joseph Landry for 200 *livres.* Landry, a neighbour along the Saint George creek, could pay only 50 *livres* but gave the seminary a mortgage as guarantee that he would pay the balance without interest over three years. Significant discounts were also necessary at Two Mountains where a seigneurial debt of 1,304 *livres* was transferred to farmer Benjamin Dorion for 69 per cent of its face value in consideration of what the act described as "costs, risks and perils."[73]

Although the sample is small, it is apparent that most seigneurial debts on the island of Montreal sold for a higher percentage of their value than debts elsewhere and this percentage increased with proximity to Montreal. Higher land prices around Montreal presumably made ownership of the debt more valuable. The one exception found in our research was the $96 debt of voyageur Félix Cardinal of Sainte-Geneviève; it was transferred for 54 per cent of its face value in 1864. Closer to Montreal, a Lachine debt brought 64 per cent (1864) and a Pointe-Claire debt 82 per cent (1856).[74] In Montreal, the suburbs and the surrounding farm land, full payment of the seigneurial debt was the norm in transfers. Of seven Montreal-area transfers in which a sale price is mentioned, six were transferred for full face value. One transfer – the nine-year-old seigneurial debt of £285 owed on the Exchange Coffee House – was made for 87 per cent of the value of the debt, probably because of the complicated and bankrupt state of its owner John Donegani.[75] Donegani was an important Catholic philanthropist and former Montreal councilman, and his debt was an embarrassment to the seminary.

The transfer was used by the seminary in a variety of overdue debt circumstances. It was useful in dealing with debtors who had left their land. "Ex farmer and traveller" Jacques Lauzon had abandoned his Two Mountains land and was living in Saint-Jérôme in 1851. Since 1810 the annual *cens et rentes* on his property had been paid only twice. On two occasions in the 1840s Lauzon had sold his land; each time the seminary went to court and nullified the sale. In 1851 it transferred Lauzon's debt of 897 *livres* to the Saint-Eustache bailiff Joseph Dorion. Other *censitaires* disappeared from the region, their seigneurial debts partly or totally unpaid, and their dossier marked "absent" or "captain in the Indian department." The transfer was also a useful official means of transferring seigneurial debts to another member of the debtor's family.[76]

The seminary used the transfer to extricate itself from its creditor relationship with certain notaries, influential public figures, or prominent Catholic laymen. Sydney Bellingham, a newspaper publisher, railway entrepreneur and Ottawa Valley politician, had seigneurial arrears to the seminary of £197 on property he had bought in Montreal. This debt was judiciously transferred to a Montreal lawyer, William C. Meredith. In 1856 the business office discounted a second seigneurial debt of Joseph Donegani and sold it to Arthur Ross. It is not clear why the seminary transferred the seigneurial debts of Pierre Maynard, former parish priest at Saint-Benoît on the Two Mountains seigneury.[77]

The majority of seigneurial debtors were neither prominent nor absent. In most cases they still occupied their property but, for reasons that cannot be determined from the notarial documents, had not paid off their arrears. Until the mid-1860s the seminary transferred debts singly, and eighty-eight were found for the period 1835–64, thirteen predating 1840. The Montreal tinsmith William Roland was typical of a medium-sized urban debtor. In 1842 Roland signed a debt-recognition contract acknowledging £84 owing in *lods and ventes* and *cens et rentes* on his property in the Sainte-Marie suburb. Eleven years later, with the capital, seven years of *cens et rentes*, and £42 in interest unpaid, the seminary transferred the debt to lawyer John Rose for £134. The transfer of Robert Akins' debt on his Lachine farm seems representative of rural actions. Akins owed *lods et ventes* dating from 1809 and had lost a court case with the seminary. In July 1864, his debt of $502 was sold to Montreal banker Canfield Dorwin for $323.[78]

Although its seigneurial debtors came from all property-holding

TABLE 4
Professions of Purchasers of
Seigneurial Arrears, 1835–76

Farmer	16
Merchant/shopkeeper	14
Lawyer	13
Notary	12
Bourgeois	9
Bailiff	5
Doctor	3
Esquire/gentleman	3
Banker	2
Entrepreneur	1
Innkeeper	1
Navigator	1
Postmaster	1
Master builder	1
Master carpenter	1
Unknown	18
Total	101

Source: Transfers notarized by seminary notaries and deposited in ANQM.

social classes, the purchasers of the seminary's bad debts were, for the most part, members of the petite bourgeoisie and, more particularly, small merchants and local professionals. Of eighty-three buyers of transfers who can be identified, 40 per cent were professionals and another 14 per cent were merchants or shopkeepers (see table 4). These investors had an obvious preference for purchasing local debts. A doctor in Assomption, a Joliette merchant, a bailiff in Saint-Eustache, a Sainte-Geneviève notary, and a navigator from Pointe-Claire all bought debts on property near their own communities.[79] Farmers occasionally took transfers on local properties, often on the lands of family members. This investment in the known had a further dimension in the case of professionals, many of whom had worked for the seminary – often in debt collection – and had personal familiarity with the debt dossiers, local land values, and debtor stability. Two of the seminary's lawyers, Louis-H. La Fontaine and Joseph-Amable Berthelot, bought transfers as did seminary notaries Henri Valotte, André Jobin, and Édouard Moreau.[80]

This system of disposing of bad seigneurial debts by individual sales was drastically altered in 1866–7 when the seminary disposed of 484 separate *censitaire* debts in seven block sales (table 5). In April 1867 for example, the seminary – in an unregistered minute (*sous seing privé*) – transferred *en bloc* the debts of sixty-seven *censitaires* in the villages of Lachine, Sault-au-Récollet, and Saint-Michel. Totalling $3,237, the debts represented all overdue *lods et ventes, cens et rentes*, and interest due to November 1866 in the three villages. For an undisclosed sum they were transferred to the seminary's own notary, Édouard Moreau. In October 1867, Moreau left the seminary's employ to work in Quebec City and in turn sold the debts – again for an undisclosed amount – to two Montreal lawyers, Napoléon Beaudry and Ferdinand Corbeille. This sale necessitated proof of Moreau's legal possession of the debts and, as a result, in the registration of the transfer, the seminary officially acknowledged the deal made seven months earlier. In similar notarized sales the seminary sold off bad debts totalling $19,705 across its three seigneuries. In only one contract was the sale price mentioned. Bailiff Ludger Piquette appears to have paid $900 cash and $1,400 in promissory notes for bad debts totalling $3,000 on the Saint-Sulpice seigneury.[81]

Since these transfers were not mentioned in Consulting Council minutes it can be assumed that transfers were a business office decision. Less active in the daily business routine than his predecessor, procurator Arraud may have concluded that stubborn seigneurial arrears were best sold off in blocks.

What do these changes in the form of seigneurialism mean? We have observed the seminary carefully exploiting the natural resources of its reserve and, with hiring or lease contracts, utilizing labour in farming, guarding, hauling, fishing, or collecting duties. At the same time, the seminary tried to isolate its feudal relations from conflict with industrializing sectors; here their tactics form part of the political approach examined in chapter two. Active supporters of industrial production in several forms across their seigneuries, the seminary's defence of the banal obligation outside Montreal showed their concern to avoid confrontation with industrial producers: "This reserve denies nothing to commercial or industrial enterprises. It does not include any form of machines or establishment other than flour mills."[82] Its willingness to sell the Saint-Gabriel domain – albeit with maximum delay – is further evidence of this compromise.

The rapid evolution of the seminary's debt-collection system, its stricter accountability of human and natural resources, and its new alliance with the state demonstrate the effects of the aborted rebellions of 1837–8 on one institution. Paradoxically, the Ordinance of 1840 strengthened the seminary's seigneurial powers outside the Montreal region while – and this forms the subject of the subsequent chapter – alleviating the influence of feudal relations in industrial-

TABLE 5
Block Transfer of Bad Seigneurial Debts, 1866–7

Purchaser	Profession	No. of Debts Sold	Place	Amount ($)	Terms
Casimir-Fidèle Papineau	notary, Montreal	132	Montreal & suburbs	5,290	"valeurs reçues"
L.U. Fontaine	lawyer, Assomption	54	Saint-Sulpice seigneury	2,019	"considération et valeur"
Edmond Robillard	doctor, Montreal	65	Saint-Laurent	2,798	"valeurs reçues"
Edmond Robillard	doctor, Montreal	7	Sainte-Geneviève	171	unspecified
Ludger Piquette	bailiff, Saint-Sulpice seigneury	77	Saint-Sulpice seigneury	3,000	"considération"
Pierre Hudon & Jules Tremblay	merchant, shopkeeper, Sainte-Anne	82	Côte Saint-Léonard, Longue-Pointe	2,084	unspecified
Édouard Moreau	notary, Montreal (seminary employee 1863–7)	30	Sault-au-Récollet	1,278	unspecified
		13	Saint-Michel	1,540	unspecified
		24	Lachine	1,696	unspecified

Source: ANQM, Moreau, 1836, "transport," seminary to C.F. Papineau, 29 May 1866; Moreau, 1862, "transport," seminary to L.U. Fontaine, 27 June 1866; Moreau, 1872, "transport," seminary to Edmond Robillard, 11 July 1866, and 1888, seminary to Edmond Robillard, 29 Aug. 1866; Moreau, 1880, "transport," seminary to Ludger Piquette, 14 Aug. 1866; Moreau, 1941, "transport," seminary to Pierre Hudon & Jules Tremblay, 31 Dec. 1866; Lafleur, 2118, "transport," seminary to Édouard Moreau, 5 Oct. 1867.

izing parts of its seigneuries. There is ample evidence of the seminary's renewed strength. In 1864 for example, the seminary collected $19,106 in *lods et ventes* and *cens et rentes*. And throughout the century the institution fed and heated itself from seigneurial revenues, much of which was appropriated in kind. Still in 1864, reserve provisions with an estimated value of $9,977 were furnished to the bursar. In addition, the bursar disposed of garden produce worth $346 and received $442 from the sale of surplus firewood on the domain. We have already noted the increasingly efficient collection of seigneurial debts. In 1840 seigneurial debts owing to the seminary totalled £61,777; by 1852 these had been reduced to £10,993.[83]

Nor must the importance of this seigneurial income hide the accompanying shift in seminary business practice. Its use of the notary, a new legal discourse, and changing means of communication were facets of the institution's tightening grip over its constituency. While the seminary's debtor population largely owed its indebtedness to seigneurial arrears predating 1840, it was now subjected to a gamut of free-market conditions: interest payments, enforcement of collection by an expanding state administration, growing utilization of professionals, the alienation of seigneurial debts to third parties.

Finally, how does the seminary compare to other seigneurs? Indebtedness was common among the *censitaire* population in the early nineteenth century in communities around Montreal like Joliette, Saint-Ours, Sorel, and Noyan.[84] The seminary was perhaps less abrasive in exploiting seigneurial privilege (particularly before 1840) than the seigneurs of Lotbinière or Beauharnois.[85] The seminary, unlike other seigneurs, did not increase the *cens et rentes* nor ask for under-the-table payments when new concessions were made. It did not exercise the right of first refusal (*droit de retrait*) when property was sold and, since it held its land in mainmort, it could not follow the seigneurial practice of issuing new titles and recognizing seigneurial arrears at each mutation of the seigneury. The seminary's land concession policy is unclear and it is not known if the seminary imitated other seigneurs in holding unconceded land off the market until population pressure and improved economic conditions drove up land prices. Income from land sales before the 1850s was certainly not great; land sales totalled £2,645 in the period 1840–52, an average of £203 a year.[86] The right of the seminary's *censitaires* to commutate their lands into freehold tenure after 1840 did distinguish – at least until 1854 – Sulpician seigneuries from their Lower-Canadian counterparts and it is to this process that we must turn.

CHAPTER FOUR

Freedom of Property: The Commutation of Property Privilege from Seigneurial to Freehold Tenure

The economists have a peculiar way of proceeding. For them there are only two kinds of institutions, artificial and natural. The institutions of feudalism are artificial, those of the bourgeoisie natural.   Marx, 1847[1]

The meaning of property is not constant. The actual institution, and the way people see it, and hence the meaning they give to the word, all change over time. We shall see that they are changing now. The changes are related to changes in the purposes which society or the dominant classes in society expect the institution of property to serve.   C.B. Macpherson[2]

From its installation in Canada in the seventeenth century, the seminary's property relations had been determined within a seigneurial framework. During the first half of the nineteenth century much of the political and business history of the seminary turned on pressures for the transformation of these seigneurial property relations in the Montreal region. By 1816 the seminary perceived that its coexistence in pre-industrial society with international merchants no longer assured its protection. To avoid conflict with new social groups like the emerging industrial producers, the seminary accepted over the next decades the alienation of traditional seigneurial privileges like its mills and its Saint-Gabriel domain.

The central element in this transition for the seminary – an institution whose wealth was based on land – was the commutation of its three seigneuries into freehold tenure. Commutation was the process by which property was transformed from a feudal into a freehold condition. Through commutation, fixed seigneurial rents (cens et rentes) and casual dues (lods et ventes) were capitalized. This fundamental change in the property structure with its marginalization of the seminary from labour and land markets facilitated the expropriation of the surplus in new forms and the integration of seigneurial property into an increasingly uniform and pan-Canadian system of freehold property relations. In short, commutation must be seen not simply as a process of "anglicization" (although that was one possible result), but as part of the larger transition in Lower Canada from feudalism to industrial capitalism.[3]

Like all but two Quebec seigneurs, the seminary had not acted on the Canada Tenures Act of 1826, a measure which permitted seigneurs to commute their lands to freehold tenure.[4] The political means to achieve commutation on seminary lands grew out of the ruins of the rebellions of 1837–8. The seminary's seigneurial privileges were sharply challenged before 1836; after the rebellions, commutation, to borrow Albert Soboul's important expression, could be imposed "from above" without the concurrence of a local assembly and without the participation of the *censitaires*.[5] Even social groups like the large urban and suburban proprietors were obliged to protest the private arrangement worked out by seminary and crown.

The Ordinance of 1840 was a mixed blessing for the seminary. It did announce renewed wealth and security and new state endorsement of the Sulpicians' dramatically expanded ideological and social functions. At the same time, the transformation of property relations after 1840 signalled important slippage in the seminary's larger economic significance. From centre stage in the seigneurial mode, the seminary would be moved to the wings. Its declining influence on urban food producers such as bakers, its increasing reliance on professionals and specialists, its wholesale transfer of seigneurial arrears, its alienation of thousands of urban and rural seigneurial concessions, and assumption by the state of the bulk of rural commutation costs were all part of this process. From lord of the manorhouse with a direct influence on property relations, the seminary would become an anonymous coupon-clipper, a medium-sized player on a changing stage. Financial institutions, railways, and manufactures would rise past the seminary in their control of Montreal capital, labour, and political power.

The ordinance ended Sulpician voluntarism and set in motion what the act called "the gradual extinction" of seigneurialism on their lands (see appendix 5). The seminary could not refuse a legitimate demand from a *censitaire* requesting the commutation of his land. By capitalizing his seigneurial dues, the *censitaire* could convert his land to freehold tenure thus permitting its alienation and incorporation into the free market. Under the law of 1840, however, commutation was voluntary on the part of the *censitaire* and few properties outside the Montreal suburbs were commutated. This led to a deepening contradiction between Montreal with an increasing core of freehold property and its rural margins where seigneurial relations persisted.

The high-level and often secret negotiations that had preceded the Ordinance of 1840 were repeated in the 1850s. During assembly debate in 1854 over reform of seigneurial tenure throughout Lower Canada, the seminary insisted on its "total exemption." Its leadership equated the Ordinance of 1840 to a formal "treaty" between the state and the seminary and reminded the government of the institution's importance in industrializing Montreal.[6] Although the seminary was exempted from the seigneurial legislation of 1854, pressure for the application of freehold tenure to all of its lands increased through the 1850s with the general restructuring of Lower Canada's legal, social, and administrative institutions. As finally passed, the Seigneurial Act of 1859 legislated progressive, compulsory commutation on the seminary's seigneuries.

In negotiations preceding passage of this act, the seminary benefited greatly from its strengthening alliance with the national bourgeoisie and particularly from its privileged relationship to George-Étienne Cartier, government minister in charge of seigneurial reform. For a generation the seminary had employed the law firm in which Cartier, his friend Joseph-Amable Berthelot, and his mentor Louis-Hippolyte La Fontaine practised. Attorney General Cartier, a student in its college, a parishioner in its church, and a political ally in its struggle with the bishop, had a lifelong personal attachment to the seminary. He also had a clear understanding of the seminary's utility as an institution of legitimation.

Empathy with the seminary did not alter Cartier's opposition to seigneurialism. The national bourgeoisie, which he led in Montreal, was tied to railways and canal promoters and other industrial producers that favoured the transformation of seigneurialism. Distressed by the slow pace of commutations under the 1840 measures, Cartier complained that the process would take 200 years.[7] Over a period of years, Cartier encouraged the Sulpicians to consider an accelerated dismantling of their seigneurial holdings. He urged the seminary's business manager, "my dear Comte," to negotiate seriously; if concessions were not made, Cartier predicted "disagreeable agitation" for the seminary. He used his state power to make the transformation palatable for the Sulpicians. In determining state compensation for the seminary's *lods et ventes* revenues, he used calculations made by the seminary's own business office and forwarded government proposals for Sulpician comment.[8] Cartier's proposition was discussed by the Consulting Council and, in a rare meeting of its Assembly, seminary policy was settled. The Sulpicians agreed to reduce their demands for seigneurial compensation in return for greater freedom in the disposition of its capital and land:

The 28th of March 1859, the Assembly met again to examine government propositions for the purchase of seigneurial rights. The honourable Cartier took as base the figures of Monsieur Comte ... [Assembly suggests lower rate of capitalization than Cartier, and, in exchange] we ask for an extension in the time accorded to us for the sale of the St. Gabriel domain, the right to sell our properties at will either for cash or for quit rents, the right to invest privately the money from these sales, and the free disposition of our unconceded lands.[9]

Each of these terms appeared in the final bill worked out between the superior and Cartier. Superior Granet was particularly pleased that the seminary had settled the property tenure question privately with the government "without the intervention of commissioners, without land surveys and without any subsequent investigation."[10]

The main financial principle in the commutation process was the formation of a capital, interest on which equated the two main seigneurial rents previously levied on the property. By the Ordinance of 1840 this capital was paid by the *censitaire* at the time of the commutation or was taken back as a debt by the seminary. Two seigneurial dues were capitalized: the *cens et rentes* and the *lods et ventes*. Capitalization of the *cens et rentes* represented small sums from each property, but the accumulation of hundreds of these payments represented significant income for the seigneur. Merchant William Moodie's property at Longue-Pointe can serve as an example.[11] *Cens et rentes* on this property of six *arpents*, which included an ice-house, was capitalized at $3.33. Annual interest of 6.5 per cent on this principal was the equivalent of Moodie's annual *cens et rentes* of some $0.20.

Conversion of the *lods et ventes* into capital was a more financially significant and complicated transaction. Government and seminary officials agreed that the capital should represent one *lods et ventes* payment. This was rationalized on the calculation that *lods* were paid on an average of every fifteen to twenty years in the country (more often in the city) and on the fact that in fourteen years capital invested at 5 per cent reproduced itself. This emphasis on the capital and its return was reflected in the variables in the *lods* reimbursement legislation. For example, *censitaires* who commuted their lands after several years were obliged to pay a larger capital to compensate the seminary for lost interest. On properties outside the city of Montreal, the capital increased from 8.33 per cent of the property's value in the first seven years after 1840 to 10 per cent for seven to fourteen years, and to 12.5 per cent for a commutation thereafter.

Since urban property was sold more often, *lods* were more frequent in Montreal than in the countryside. This made commutation particularly appealing to the urban landowner who anticipated rising land prices and who had sufficient surplus to initiate the process. The ordinance differentiated between land within Montreal's city limits and land outside. The *lods* on city properties evaluated at over £100 were capitalized into sums that represented a smaller percentage of their value than those on rural properties. Large city landowners were also favoured over smaller city proprietors by the indexing of *lods* capitalizations in the city into three categories: properties evaluated under £100, properties at £100 to £500, properties over £500. The result was that small city proprietors and all rural property holders paid up to double the percentage of their larger urban counterparts. Master butcher Joseph Martin, for example, paid a 12.5 per cent commutation rate for his £80 property on Grand Street (1857) while in the same year Simon Valdis paid 6.25 per cent on his £1,200 property in the Saint-Marie suburb.[12]

Even without a sale almost all evaluations were settled by mutual agreement between the seminary and demander. Before 1849 only twenty-one property evaluations went to arbitration, and none did after 1849 (see appendix 6). After 1870 the phrase "settled by mutual agreement" was printed on the commutation form. The high percentage of amicable settlements appears to represent temperate evaluations by seminary officials and its *rapprochement* with urban landowners. The seminary's land assessor was John Ostell, an influential architect, contractor, and door and sash manufacturer. Ostell worked closely with business manager Comte, himself no stranger to the real-estate market. Their experience and class association with important land proprietors facilitated amicable settlement of evaluations and perhaps discouraged small landowners from entering costly arbitrations. Although a quantitative analysis of the relationship between commutation evaluations and actual market prices was not possible, sampling indicates equality among similar-sized properties. The Saint-Alexandre Street property of merchant William Pawson for example was evaluated on the same assessment base as banker James Ferrier's property further up the block.[13]

Stronger evidence of the seminary's moderation is provided by the dozens of contracts marked "price reduced" or "reduced claim." Grocer Jane Scanlan's commutation (1864) on her Vitre Street property was reduced by over 50 per cent to $31.05; baker Joachim

Telmosse's property evaluation (1865) was reduced $100.00. In other commutations the seminary offered interest-free loans or delayed interest payments.[14] The reduction of property evaluations is particularly noticeable with railways. Between 1847 and 1849 the Montreal and Lachine Railway paid £10,676 for ninety-five properties forming its right of way from Montreal to Lachine. Referring in the commutation contract to a "special agreement," the seminary reduced the property evaluation to £9,000.[15] Favouritism to railways was confirmed in the commutation of the Montreal and Bytown Railway. In this instance, instead of lowering the property evaluation, the commutation was reduced 25 per cent from £200 to £150 in order, in the words of the agreement, to "promote public ventures."[16]

Although commutations were normally handled entirely by the business office, commutation terms of certain "friendly" religious, social, and educational institutions were determined by the Consulting Council. The Congregation of Notre Dame and the Grey Nuns, two female orders patronized and confessed by the Sulpicians, performed essential institutional functions under seminary direction. Reduction of their commutation took several forms. The Consulting Council lowered commutations on the mother house properties of the two convents as well as on that of the Soeurs du Bon Pasteur. The seminary also reduced the commutation on the Grey Nuns orphanage and agreed to use interest paid by the nuns to support orphans. When the Congregation of Notre Dame sold part of their Villa Maria estate on the western outskirts of Montreal the Consulting Council cut its commutation in half. A male teaching order, the Oblates, had one-quarter of their seigneurial arrears written off by the seminary as part of their commutation settlement.[17] If aid to these religious institutions was perhaps normal, the favourable commutation terms offered by the seminary to its long-time antagonist, the bishop of Montreal, is surprising. In the midst of appeals to Rome and the particularly bitter struggle over the division of the parish of Montreal, the seminary reduced the commutation evaluation of the bishop's properties to £1,068.[18] Nor, despite the supposedly heated ethnic and religious debate of the 1850s, were the seminary's Protestant counterparts excluded. The Anglicans of Montreal, faced with reconstruction of their burnt cathedral, were granted favourable conditions as was McGill University.[19]

Of the few commutations that went to arbitration, many involved widows, institutions, or government bodies in which responsible officials seem to have preferred third-party evaluations. The city, for example, asked for arbitration in the assessment of its lands on the old commons of Montreal between the river and Nazareth fief.[20] A few individuals resorted to arbitration. The seminary and farmer Toussaint Martin of Côte-Saint-Luc could not agree on his land evaluation and went to arbitration. John Donegani was a large property holder known for his contentiousness.[21] Evaluation of his property on Saint-Pierre Street went to arbitration. His arbiter, merchant Hosea Smith, evaluated the property at £1,500. John Ostell, the seminary's representative estimated it at £1,875. Obliged by arbitration rules to name a third umpire, the two arbiters named wholesale merchant Benjamin Brewster who agreed with the seminary's assessment.[22]

A total of 3,165 commutations were examined for the period 1840–80. Notarial records for the years 1866–72 may be incomplete and have been left in tentative fashion on figure 7.[23] Seminary notaries drew up the commutation contracts; all forms and handwritten inscriptions were in French (unlike leases which were usually written in the language of the lessee) and the completed contracts were signed by the demander, two seminary officials (superior and procurator), and two notaries.

From our perspective of an institutional study it has proven difficult to explain the frequency of commutations. Effective analysis must account for factors as diverse as the stimulus of the legislation itself, the social composition of demanders and the dynamics of individual classes, the price of credit, various factors in the land market, general economic conditions, and – since the transmission of property to heirs was a favoured occasion for commutation – death rates. Certain patterns do emerge. Peaks in 1841–5 and 1859–60 are clearly tied to the inauguration of the measures of 1840 and 1859. Prosperity in the years 1850–3 and during the American Civil War are reflected in a rise in commutations while depressions after 1854 and 1873 correspond to sharp downturns in commutations. This is seen by comparing Gerald Tulchinsky's chart of ocean ships arriving at Montreal from 1835 to 1858 or Hamelin and Roby's description of economic conditions to figure 7.[24] But these general comparisons cloud factors of space, time, and class. For example, large urban and suburban landholders are concentrated in the first hump of commutations, 1841–5, while in the period 1859–60 there is a predominance of artisans and petits bourgeois from the suburbs of Sainte-Anne and Sainte-Marie.

The demander of a commutation had two options in paying off his capital; immediate payment or constitution of a debt payable to the seminary. In 83 per cent of the commutations in the years 1840–5, and in 82.5 per cent in the period 1855–9, the capital was paid off at the signing of the contract. Part payment does not seem to

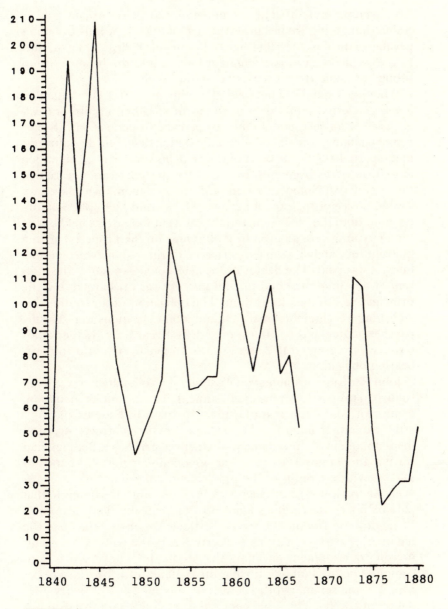

FIGURE 7
Commutations Notarized by the Seminary of Montreal, 1840–80

have been permitted.[25] The commutation capital was usually paid in cash although in rare instances the seminary took promissory notes payable to third parties. Pharmacist Romuald Trudeau, for example, paid £57 of his £120 commutation in cash and the balance with a promissory note from Charles-Séraphin Rodier.[26]

When the capital was not paid off at the time of the commutation, it was converted into a debt in the form of either a quitrent (*rente constituée*) or an obligation. In the first period of commutations, 1840–5, 124 obligations were signed for commutation debts and 21 quitrents; in the period 1855–9 all but 1 of the 55 debts which can be identified as to form were obligations. By the 1870s quitrents were so rare that the seminary printed two standard commutation forms: one included a receipt for capital paid off; the second established an obligation. Both the obligation and the quitrent were debts held by the seminary and were secured by a mortgage on the property. With a quitrent the capital became a permanent principal on which annual interest was paid. The debtor or his heirs could extinguish the quitrent at any time provided that all interest was discharged and the principal paid in one lump sum. The obligation was a contract establishing a term debt. Small commutation obligations were usually payable on demand or after a one- or two-year term. Larger landowners were granted five-, six-, or, exceptionally, ten-year interest-bearing obligations.[27]

John Redpath's commutation illustrates the commutation of a large suburban property and the establishment of a quitrent. Stonemason, contractor, and sugar manufacturer, Redpath had suburban properties extending along Sherbrooke and Dorchester streets. A prominent opponent of the seminary's seigneurial privileges, Redpath had travelled to London to represent opponents of the Ordinance of 1840.[28] Within months of the proclamation of the ordinance, however, Redpath was in the seminary business office to commute that part of his estate running from his home on the flank of Mount Royal down to Dorchester Street. Between Mountain Street and the Simon McTavish estate, this property was in the path of bourgeois housing development, meaning that Redpath had every reason to commute before building further on the land or before land prices rose. He and seminary officials agreed amicably on a property evaluation of £4,000. The 5 per cent *lods* capitalization on this sum was £200 and £2 10s. represented the capitalization of the annual *cens et rentes* of 3s. The total commutation of £202 10s. was formed into a quitrent on which the annual "perpetual" interest was £12. After paying interest for only eighteen months Redpath extinguished his quitrent.[29]

Stanley Bagg's commutation illustrates an agreement which was linked to both the payment of seigneurial arrears and to a property sale (see appendix 7). In 1816 Bagg had bought a McGill Street lot some 35 feet wide and 110 feet deep. *Lods et ventes* totalling £50 from this purchase and from a previous mutation of the property in 1815 had never been paid. In his commutation agreement, Bagg agreed to pay this debt in two instalments, £25 on 1 May 1845 and the second half a year later. By the terms of the ordinance these seigneurial arrears were interest free if paid on time. In 1844 Bagg and the seminary agreed amicably on a property evaluation of £3,000. His *lods* were capitalized at 5 per cent into a sum of £150 and the annual *cens et rentes* of 3 *deniers tournois* capitalized into a sum of 2*s*. Bagg opted to form the commutation capital into a quitrent on which annual 5 per cent interest was £9. As security the seminary extended mortgage rights it already held on the property for seigneurial arrears. Three days after commuting his property, Bagg sold it. This sale meant that the seminary – instead of dealing with Bagg, a well-known Montreal contractor, landowner, and merchant – became creditor of an absentee proprietor, for the new owner, the Reverend Thomas Rattray, soon moved to Toronto and neglected both his seigneurial arrears and interest on his quitrent. After a suit by the seminary, Rattray forwarded £50 in seigneurial arrears, £18 for two years' interest, plus £2 2*s*. for the seminary's court costs.[30]

Even if a full prosopography of large property commutators must await full studies of the transition, of land values, and of sources of bourgeois wealth, we can, by utilizing the commutation file, go beyond simple instancing. What relationship, for example, did the large property holders who dominate the commutation file have to the Montreal business community? To answer this partially, a nominative comparison was made between the file and business figures named in Gerald Tulchinsky's *River Barons*. Of the 181 important Montreal business figures named by Tulchinsky for the period 1837–53, 80 appear in commutation records as having commuted property before December 1845. In commutations over the next fourteen years, 1845–59, an additional 20 businessmen from Tulchinsky's study appear.

This enthusiasm to commute on the part of "large" property holders (defined here as those with property evaluated at over £500) can be further documented.[31] Over four decades, 1840–80, there were only four years (1850, 1851, 1852, 1861) when properties evaluated at over £500 did not represent at least 30 per cent of total commutations; over the four decades, these "large" properties represent 47 per cent of the total number of commutations. And there is an important bunching of large commutations in the years following the Ordinance of 1840. From July 1840 to December 1845 property evaluated at £959,436 was commuted, an average commutation evaluation of £1,051.[32]

If we turn to the "very large" property-holders (those with property evaluations over £5,000) we find that John Redpath's eagerness to commute was imitated by his peers. In the six months following the ordinance, he was joined in the seminary office by "very large" property holders Peter McGill, Olivier Berthelet, James Ferrier, and Hubert Paré. Twenty-nine of the thirty-two "very large" property holders (institutions excepted) commuted properties in the five years following the ordinance (appendix 8).

This predominance of very large proprietors was predictable. Large property holders had led the pre-1840 agitation against seigneurial levies in the Montreal area and not surprisingly they used the ordinance to free their property from feudal obligations. It must be re-emphasized that commutation was voluntary before 1860; initiation of the process implied either a surplus in hand to pay off the capitalized seigneurial dues or anticipation of an adequate surplus to maintain quitrent or obligation payments. Since the commutation – or at least the major part by which *lods* were capitalized – was settled in reference to the market value of property, speculators, developers, and other large landowners in the city and suburbs clearly perceived that it was in their interest to commute before land prices rose and before subdividing or making building improvements. In short, commutators came from social groups with a surplus and from areas in which rising land prices were anticipated.

Within the rubric of "very large" proprietors, several different categories of landowners can be isolated. For example, with his flamboyant land speculations, John Donegani stood in contrast to his more discreet landowning peers. A rentier and land developer, Donegani made up to sixty land transactions a year in the mid-1840s. He commuted a £3,000 property in the central business district in April 1842 and a month later commuted seventeen properties evaluated at £11,000. Donegani, unlike more conservative landowners, operated on credit and to pay seigneurial arrears and commutations on his properties he took a £650 obligation with the seminary. In 1843, 1845, 1846, and 1848 he added to his commuted properties, which by 1848 had a total evaluation of £26,570. His bankruptcy in 1850 is a major reason for the appearance of his primary creditor, the Banque du Peuple, in commutation records. Other large land developers included Judge Samuel Gale (property evaluations of £15,165) and James Ferrier (£13,553). At the opposite end of the scale from the extravagant Donegani was Catholic philanthropist Olivier Berthelet. Moving cautiously and utilizing small commutations and cash settlements, Berthelot came before the seminary notary thirteen times between 1840 and 1859, commuting properties with evaluations as low as £23.

Nineteenth-century commercial fortunes are readily identifiable in commutation property evaluations. Among the largest merchant / land proprietors were Joseph Masson (evaluation of £15,540), Peter McGill (£11,430), George Moffatt (£7,850), Hubert Paré (£7,585), and Samuel Gerrard (£5,950). The landed wealth of merchants with developing interests in production can also be identified. Shipper and steamship owner John Torrance (£17,136) and hardware merchant and shovel, scythe, and nail manufacturer John Frothingham (£9,500) had increasingly important industrial interests, as did Hugh Allan. The latter had accumulated landed property evaluated at £6,018 by 1845 and at £11,018 by 1857.

By mid-century some of the largest landed proprietors were from the production sector. The brewing, foundry, and steamship-owning Molsons, for example, had the largest landed fortune of any family in the commutation file. The property of just two Molsons, William and John Sr, totalled £43,296. Seven other brewers – William Dow, Miles Williams, Thomas Dawes, James Powley Dawes, Daniel Gorrie, Johnston Thomas, and Henry Phillips – commuted properties evaluated at over £500. Miller William Watson, a partner in the Watson-Ogilvie mill at the Saint-Gabriel locks (1836), commuted property evaluated at £6,785. Other important Lachine Canal millers were Alexander Ogilvie (£480) and William Parkyn (£1,860). In addition to their hardware and iron interests, Frothingham and William Workman (£3,750) had a steam elevator and corn mill. Lachine Canal proprietors are underrepresented in the commutation file since their land was bought in freehold tenure from the seminary or government (see chapter six).[33] Even so, many Lachine Canal industrial producers appear as large commutators for land held elsewhere in Montreal: rope and plaster manufacturer John Converse (£550), oil and drug miller William Lyman (£1,390), door and sash manufacturer John Ostell (£879), and nail manufacturer Thomas Peck (£1,000).

The property evaluations of commutators describing themselves as artisans suggest that some in this social group utilized the new mode of production to become important owners of real property. Tailor Benaiah Gibb is a good example. As work done by Mary Anne Poutanen and the Montreal Business History Project has shown, Gibb and Company were, as early as the 1820s, among Montreal's most important tailoring firm as evidenced by the number of their apprentices, the size of their credit, and their ability to absorb major losses.[34] Besides clothing production, Benaiah Gibb had important retail, rentier, and railway interests and by 1847 had commuted property evaluated at £5,890. Tailor William Adams (£650), bakers Walter Benny (£5,650) and Théodore Paré (£864), and shoemaker Edward Thompson (£1,500) were among other commutators who defined themselves as artisans and who accumulated significant landed wealth. Three master butchers – Ernest Idler (£2,405), Joseph Frederick Hetz (£1,400), and Gotlieb Reinhart (£2,405) – had properties evaluated at over £500.

The construction trades provide dramatic examples of the transition. While many masons, carpenters, and joiners slipped from artisanry into wage labour, others accumulated fortunes in the large transportation and institutional construction projects that characterized Montreal as it industrialized. Master mason Louis Comte, for example, was brother of the seminary's business manager and prominent contractor in Sulpician building projects. By 1856 he had commuted property evaluated at £2,050. Carpenters Allen Robinson (£1,500) and John Whitlaw (£1,300) were important proprietors in the Saint-Laurent suburb. Perhaps the best-known artisan was stonemason John Redpath whose contracting fortune facilitated his entry into industrial production like sawmilling and sugar refining; by 1845 "esquire" Redpath had commuted properties evaluated at £12,030.

This linkage between commutation and capital becomes even clearer when we examine small (property evaluations of less than £100) and medium (£100–£499) commutations. Of course we find in these categories many of the same "merchant," "bourgeois," "esquire," or "gentleman" professions that dominated the large property categories. Many of the commutations, such as those of Berthelet, represent small land transactions by large proprietors. However, small and medium commutations were made by large numbers of commutators who declared petty bourgeois (grocer, bookseller, auctioneer, postmaster, tobacconist) and intellectual (medicine, dentistry, architecture, bookkeeping, pharmacy, law, teaching, surveying, theology) occupations.

It is more difficult to deal precisely with commutation among the popular classes particularly in the complexity of the transition in mid-nineteenth-century Montreal. As noted, a few artisans became important industrial producers, accumulating significant capital and appearing in commutation records as large landed proprietors. A larger number of mid-century artisans appear to have become neither industrial producers nor unskilled wage labourers and, pre-

sumably through the practice of their trade in its traditional form
or employment as a skilled wage labourer, accumulated sufficient
surplus to become modest urban proprietors and, further, to commute. The long list of commutators in this category include comb
makers, candle makers, cord makers, bookbinders, clock makers,
gardeners, tanners, and growing numbers of machinists and engineers. Beyond this upper strata of the popular classes commutation
hardly penetrated. There is, for example, little representation from
unskilled occupations, an absence we can presume indicates both
lack of proprietorship and lack of a surplus to commute. Only 29
of the 1,891 commutators in the years 1840–59 declared a profession
classifiable as unskilled.[35] Table 6 also suggests that our unskilled
category may be even further separated from commuting elements.
We include bronze worker and copper worker even though Craven
and Traves suggest that the latter may have been a skilled occupation
much in demand in Grand Trunk shops. Our category of unskilled
workers also includes William Ransom whose own definition of his
occupation evolved from "labourer" to "milkman," to "milk-seller,"
and finally in 1863 to "milk merchant," a progression strongly
suggestive of mobility out of the popular classes.[36] George Harrison
twice declared his profession as labourer although the value and
number of his three commutations imply a distancing from his peers.
Including Harrison and Ransom, the total property evaluation of
the unskilled was £4,069 or an average evaluation of £140. The
concentration of these unskilled proprietors in the suburbs of Sainte-
Anne, Sainte-Marie and, after 1859, Pointe Saint-Charles corre-
sponds to popular residential areas.

Yet another striking feature of commutation on the seminary's
three seigneuries was its concentration in Montreal and its suburbs.
In twenty years, 1840–59, only 18 of 600 concessions were commuted
on the Saint-Sulpice seigneury and 9 of 1,260 at Two Mountains
(see appendix 6). Of these 27 commutators over half can be identified; 8 were proprietors of water-power sites with tanning, carding,
grain or saw milling potential. Other commutators listed their professions as watchmaker (2), bourgeois, merchant, priest, doctor, and
agent.

Commutation is more difficult to evaluate in rural parts of the
island of Montreal because of the increasing variety of land uses.
Railways and the Lachine Canal were changing the temporal and
spatial dimensions of the western part of the island and urban forms
were developing along Côte-des-Neiges, Côte-Sainte-Catherine and
St Lawrence Street. Important capitalists were building estates near
Lachine and along the river east of Montreal; industrial sites in the

TABLE 6
Commutators Declaring an Unskilled Occupation, 1840–59

Year	Commutator	Occupation	Location	Property Evaluation (£)
1841	Samuel Ralston	messenger	Saint-Laurent	107
	Charles Tuggey and Thomas Cooke[1]	store watchman; engagé	Saint-Laurent	50
1842	James Brogan	labourer	Sainte-Anne	54
	Augustin Gadouri	labourer	Saint-Laurent	120
	William Frankish Ransom	labourer	Sainte-Anne	225
	James Bourke	labourer	Saint-Laurent	185
1844	William Gregg	labourer	Sainte-Marie	110
	Robert Dalgleish	office watchman	Sainte-Marie	93
	George Harrison	labourer	Sainte-Anne	600[2]
1845	George Harrison	labourer	Sainte-Anne	144
	Thomas Williams	labourer	Lachine	132
	William F. Ransom	milkman	Sainte-Marie	201
1846	James Simpson	letter carrier	Sainte-Marie	250
	William Ransom	milk seller	Sainte-Marie	110
1847	George Grant	toll collector	Sainte-Marie	216
1848	William Ransom	milk seller	Sainte-Marie	110
1851	Thomas McDowell	labourer	Sainte-Marie	90
1852	James Close	bronze worker	Côte-des-Neiges	300
	Arsène Chapleau	servant	Sainte-Marie	100
	Robert Hall	labourer	Sainte-Anne	45
1855	François-Xavier Gareau	labourer	Saint-Antoine	200
	William Stuppell	labourer	Sainte-Marie	180
1858	Peter Sharples	railway mailman	Pointe Saint-Charles	80
	James Richard Ashcroft	copper worker	Pointe Saint-Charles	80
	— Leclerc	labourer	Sault-au-Récollet	16
1859	John Hays	labourer	Pointe Saint-Charles	64
	John Shotten	labourer	Pointe Saint-Charles	64
	William Leonard	labourer	Sainte-Anne	63
	George Stewart	labourer	Pointe Saint-Charles	80

1. Joint commutation
2. Two properties commuted

villages of Côte-des-Neiges and Sault-au-Récollet were of increasing significance. Another difficulty lies in the evaluation of the profession of "cultivateur" listed on commutation contracts – or on census returns.[37] Retired farmers commuting urban properties, gentlemen farmers, and peasants all had recourse to the term.

Despite these ambiguities over land use and occupational classifications, it is clear that few peasants commuted their land. Of 3,395 properties on the island of Montreal outside the city and parish of Montreal, only 239 had been commuted by 1858.[38] Twenty-seven were from one commutator, the Grand Trunk Railway. At the western tip of the island in the parish of Sainte-Anne not a single commutation was made aside from those of the Grand Trunk. At the other end of the island in the parish of Pointe-aux-Trembles, 21 properties had been commuted by 1859, 5 of them in the village of Pointe-aux-Trembles. The presence of the ubiquitous John Redpath as commutator of a £750 Pointe-aux-Trembles property suggests changing land use.[39] In the back-river parish of Rivière-des-Prairies a single property had been commuted.

The majority of commutations occurred on properties closer to Montreal with the parish of Lachine and Saint-Laurent accounting for half the rural commutations on the island of Montreal (table 7). In Lachine, commutators included well-known Montrealers such as brewer William Dow, Sir George Simpson of the Hudson's Bay Company, forwarder John Young, and miller Archibald Ogilvie. In Saint-Laurent parish, commutated properties were concentrated in the village of Saint-Laurent and along Côte-Saint-Laurent rather than along the more remote Côte-Vertu. Taking rural commutators for the whole island that can be identified, anglophone names outnumbered francophones eighty-one to forty-nine.

Indebtedness and the lack of a surplus are obvious explanations for the peasantry's few commutations. Seminary notaries were moving efficiently across the côtes and villages collecting thousands of pounds in seigneurial arrears, notarizing hundreds of debt-recognition contracts of those unable to pay, and selling off overdue debt contracts. This is strong evidence that the peasantry were not among those social groups enjoying a surplus.[40] From their pre-industrial perspective and with what John McCallum describes as an "indisputable preference for the seigneurial system," the formation of additional debts in the form of a commutation obligation was not an interesting proposition; *lods et ventes* were not paid on successions and formation of a debt to the seminary tied the peasant to the market system, the payment of interest, and the production of cash crops.[41] Peasant suspicions of the transformation of their land into freehold tenure was part of a larger resistance that reaches back to burnt villages and the issues of 1837–8 to their evasion of seigneurial

TABLE 7

Commutations on the Island of Montreal
Excluding City and Parish, pre-1859

Parish	Number
Sainte-Anne	22[1]
Pointe-Claire	17[2]
Sainte-Geneviève	3
Lachine	62
Saint-Laurent	60
Sault-au-Récollet	31
Longue-Pointe	22
Rivière-des-Prairies	1
Pointe-aux-Trembles	21

Note: There were 3,395 properties on the island
excluding the city and parish.

1 All commuted by Grand Trunk Railway
2 Five commuted by Grand Trunk Railway

dues by transferring to crops not subject to seigneurial levies, and
forward to the imposition of strengthened and centralized judicial,
educational, and municipal institutions. The abrupt end to the evasion of seigneurial dues, changing registry law, and compulsory education were part of a fundamental restructuring of Quebec society.
Freehold tenure was integral to this transition and, if the peasantry
would not undertake it voluntarily at its own cost, the state would
impose it.

By the mid-1850s the seigneuries of the seminary were divided in
land tenure. Land commutated into freehold tenure stretched out
from Montreal into the suburbs, along the Grand Trunk and Montreal and Lachine railway lines, and skipped to waterfront estates
and water-power sites across the three seigneuries. On one hand
were the commutators with a surplus to invest in anticipation of
accumulation in a free labour and land-market system. On the other
hand were those without a surplus, wage labourers, the propertyless,
and the peasantry. Peasant resistance to changing the landholding
structures and institutions of a pre-industrial society was weakened
after 1840. Their seigneur was not an absentee landlord or anglophone merchant such as Edward Ellice or Robert Christie but the
most important Catholic religious community in Montreal; this complicated the linking of land reform and nationalism. And important
elements in the local bourgeoisie who had played crucial leadership
roles in 1837 resurfaced in the seminary camp in the 1840s. Notaries
Félix Lemaire and Jean-Jacques Girouard, important rebel leaders

in the Two Mountains seigneury, later worked for the seminary collecting seigneurial arrears and administering seigneurial mills and domains; notary André Jobin of Sainte-Geneviève had the same evolution.[42] This co-opting of leaders was nowhere more evident than in the case of George-Étienne Cartier. Montreal agitator and gun-runner at Saint-Denis, Cartier acted as middleman for the seminary in the 1850s explaining the inevitability of commutation to Sulpician authorities and working out details of a new settlement. Symbolically, the Seigneurial Act of 1859 corresponded to the opening of the Grand Trunk's Victoria Bridge; both were stage-managed by Cartier.

By the Seigneurial Act of 1859 the state assumed responsibility for the *lods et ventes* capitalization for all seminary *censitaires* outside the city and parish of Montreal. The seminary accepted a government indemnity (later established at $336,917) on which the government paid 6 per cent interest in the early years. This left *censitaires* outside the city and parish with responsibility only for commuting their *cens et rentes*. However, even with this relatively small payment, few peasants acted to release their property from seigneurial obligations.

Within the city and parish of Montreal, commutations theoretically became more systematic. Commutation became obligatory when a property was sold and within twenty years of a succession; corporate bodies had to commute their properties within twenty years. Although some two-thirds of the commutations formed part of an acquisition in the period immediately following passage of the act, this percentage steadily dropped (appendix 6). One author suggests that it was seminary policy to postpone legally due commutations with a view to allowing land values to increase, but this cannot be determined from seminary minutes or the commutation file. There is in fact some evidence to the contrary. Shopkeeper F.X. Deladurantaye, for example, inherited a Sainte-Marie suburb lot in 1879 on which a commutation settlement had been pending since its purchase five years earlier. The seminary sent Deladurantaye a summons inviting him to name an arbiter and threatening a lawsuit if terms of the act of 1859 were not fulfilled.[43]

The commutation file for the two decades after 1859 confirms the profile suggested for the earlier period. Few are the examples such as labourer André Brunet who in March 1880 commuted his property on St Lawrence Boulevard in Côte-Saint-Louis. Twenty feet wide and eighty feet deep, the property, which included a house, was evaluated amicably at $800 in 1880. An obligation of $66.67 was established, representing a 12 per cent capitalization of the property's value. Brunet agreed to pay interest on this amount from the previous 1 May and gave the seminary a first mortgage.[44] Most commutations, however, remained a preserve of the skilled worker or bourgeoisie. For example, many of the larger commutations were the settlement of estates such as that of Judge Hippolyte Guy.[45]

Certain features of commutation as it related to the seminary's client population can be summarized before turning to its effects on the institution's own balance sheet. We have noted an important corelation between capital and commutation. The extinction of seigneurial dues before 1859 was restricted to proprietors with a surplus and was an option with particular appeal to large urban and suburban proprietors. Many of the largest commutators were familiar commercial capitalists who were joined by large proprietors whose wealth was based in production rather than exchange. Indeed, production seems a major spark of commutation both in the origins of the legislation and in the subsequent pattern of commutation; railway lines, manufactures, water-power sites, and industrial neighbourhoods give a certain shape to the commutation file. Some artisans, developing intellectual and management professions, and the petty bourgeoisie also figure strongly in commutations. Wage labour is virtually absent from the commutation file suggesting a widening gap in the property relations of labour and capital. Even after 1859 and the restriction of voluntarism for urban commutators, the profile remains valid.

The factor of time gave further leverage to the proprietor with capital. The proprietor with a surplus in hand could commute in the years immediately after 1840, paying off the commutation in cash; the landholder who could at least anticipate a surplus could take a commutation debt with the seminary. In both cases the commutation was paid on the basis of property values in the 1840s and could be recuperated from subsequent rents or sales. An urban *censitaire* who waited until 1880 to commute paid seigneurial dues over the intervening decades and his property evaluation took into account building improvements and increased land values.

The sharp town-country division in commutations before 1859 needs re-emphasis. Aside from water-power sites, certain properties of the local bourgeoisie, and the estates of urban capitalists, commutation was ignored by the seminary's rural *censitaires*. Like poorer urban proprietors, many peasants were already indebted to the seigneur for seigneurial arrears. The failure to commute – what Cartier called a lack of motivation on the part of the peasantry – led the state to assume the capitalization of rural *lods et ventes*. This major expense emphasized the state's determination to transform the feudal landholding system.[46]

CHAPTER FIVE

From Seigneur to Capitalist: The Balance Sheet

For capitalism the land was a factor of production and a commodity peculiar only by its immobility and limited quantity ... The rural world as a whole was a market, a source of labour, and a source of capital. In so far as its obstinate traditionalism prevented it from doing what political economy required, it had to be made to.   E.J. Hobsbawm[1]

Sir:
Presuming that the multiplicity of your engagements has prevented you from returning as you promised to the procure of the Seminary of Montreal the last time you were in town for the purpose of terminating the settlement of your account of Lods et ventes due to the said Seminary. I am instructed to state that the Seminary being under the obligation towards the government of procuring a statement of all their arrears on Lods et ventes due them up to the 9th June 1840, request me to send you another copy of said account which you have here annexed together with such explanations that you may require in the same and beg to observe that this done in conformity to the disposition of the ordinance of the Special Council ...
Seminary clerk to Thomas McKay, March 1842[2]

The seminary's roots as a seigneurial institution and the process by which its seigneurial lands could be commuted into freehold tenure have been recurrent themes in previous chapters. The role of the state in this changing property regime has also been emphasized. The acts of 1840 and 1859 provided the ideological and procedural framework for the seminary's evolving property privileges and gave it the legal force to impose its prerogatives. In addition to this legal and physical support, the state after 1859 intervened directly, assuming the major part of the capitalization of rural seigneurial dues.

The Ordinance of 1840 assured the seminary important revenues but also orchestrated their disposition. Any Sulpician temptation to invest entirely in real property was blocked by law; the seminary was forced to direct much of its new revenues to government securities many of which were transportation subsidies (see appendix 9). From a seigneurial institution in 1819, the seminary by 1880 had become an important coupon-clipper, urban landlord, and subdivision developer.

The first financial effect to be noted in the seminary balance sheet after 1840 was that the institution – as figure 8 makes evident – did not suffer from the changes made to its seigneurial privileges. Revenues in the 1840s averaged four times higher than average annual income in the 1830s; by the 1860s annual income was some seven times higher than in the 1830s. Some caution is necessary because of the presence of "one-time" land-sale, commutation income, and government indemnity. However, the one-time effect of these revenues was offset by their investment in forms that provided ongoing income to replace lost seigneurial dues.

Seminary accounts show that the law of 1840 did not immediately weaken seigneurial income. Except for the loss of *banalités* resulting from the sale of mills, seigneurial revenues held up in the 1840s and 1850s. Domain income peaked in the 1850s and only declined after 1864. *Lods et ventes* and *cens et rentes* – the most important seigneurial revenues – remained strong into the 1860s. Seigneurial income from this source in the period 1841–9 was 67 per cent of levels in the 1830s. These high returns, despite the removal of commuted properties from the seigneurial rolls, probably represent more vigorous collection methods under the Ordinance of 1840. They also reflect a general rise in urban land values since all post-1859 *lods et ventes*, and 1860 was the year of greatest seigneurial income, came from the city and parish of Montreal (figure 9).

In the 1830s, land formed the essence of the seminary's wealth and its revenues consisted largely of seigneurial levies. Although a small percentage of its income came from mills and domains, the seminary's major income – some 80 per cent in the 1830s – was paid in the form of *cens et rentes* and *lods et ventes*. The representation of 1834 on figure 10 demonstrates the dependence on seigneurial levies in the 1830s.

The persistence of seigneurial revenues must not, however, obscure the evolution of seminary income from seigneurial into capitalist forms of revenue. Dependent on seigneurial income in the 1830s, the seminary after 1840 began receiving new forms of revenue. The rapid transformation of seminary income can be seen in the decline of current seigneurial revenues from 91.1 per cent in

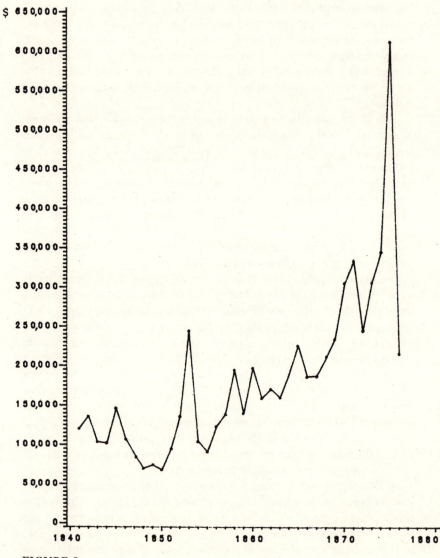

FIGURE 8
Total Seminary Income, 1841–76 (dollars)
Source: Appendix 11.

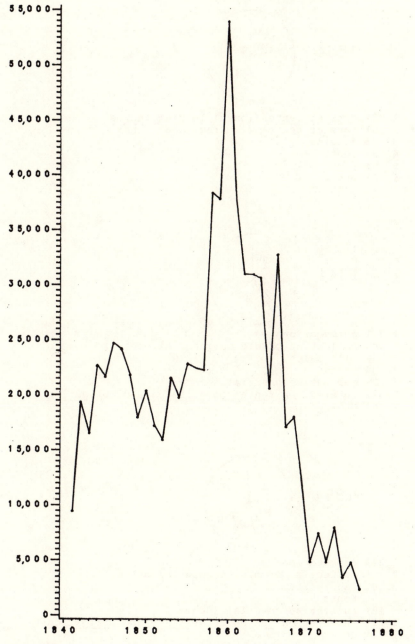

FIGURE 9

Income from Seigneurial Sources, 1841–76 (dollars)

Source: Appendix 11.

Note: Seigneurial sources of income include *cents et rentes, lods et ventes* domains, mills.

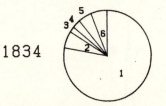

1834

1 78% cens et rentes (cash) lods et ventes
2   6% cens et rentes (in kind) and tithes[1]
3   2% domains
4   3% rents
5   5% flour mills
6   6% other

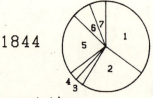

1844

1 35% commutations
2 24% collection of old seigneurial debts
3   3% mill sales
4   3% rents
5 22% current seigneurial income
6   7% interest on rentes constituées and obligations
7   6% other

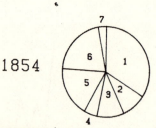

1854

1 34% commutations
2   9% collection of old seigneurial debts
3 10% land sales
4   5% rents
5 18% current seigneurial income
6 21% interest on rentes constituées and obligations
7   3% other

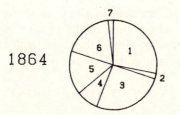

1864

1 28% commutations & government seigneurial indemnity
2 2% collection of old seigneurial debts
3 26% land sales
4 8% rents
5 16% current seigneurial income
6 18% interest on rentes constituées and obligations
7 2% other

1874

1 34% commutations
2 3% collection of old seigneurial debts
3 17% land sales
4 5% rents
5 1% current seigneurial income
6 13% interest on rentes constituées and obligations
7 27% borrowed capital

FIGURE 10
Sources of Seminary Income, 1834–74
Sources: ASSM, arm. 2, vol. 24; arm. 2, vol. 225: arm. 2, vol. 157; arm. 3, vol. 402. See appendix
11 for summary of figures.

1 The 1833 figures were used since mill and cens et rentes (in kind) were lumped together in
the 1834 figures.

1834, to 22 per cent in 1844, 18 per cent in 1854, 16 per cent in 1864, and 1 per cent in 1874. These new forms of income were from commutations, urban land sales, debt collection, urban rents, and interest from bonds, mortgages, and other securities.

COLLECTION OF SEIGNEURIAL DEBTS

The collection of pre-1840 seigneurial debts forms a passage between seigneurial and capitalist income. Incurred – sometimes generations earlier – by the non-payment of seigneurial dues, these interest-free debts languished until 1840. Under the Ordinance of 1840 the seminary assigned debt-collection to newly hired professionals. Seminary notaries and lawyers organized the formal recognition of debts, applied interest, renewed mortgages that now guaranteed the payment of interest as well as the principal, and initiated judicial procedures against the recalcitrant. The transferring of overdue seigneurial debts to third parties symbolized new relationships between seigneur and *censitaire*. In the first years after 1840, income from the collection of seigneurial debts represented the seminary's second most important form of income. In five years, 1841–5, debts amounting to £33,930 were collected – 22 per cent of the seminary's income for these years (see appendix 11).

COMMUTATION INCOME

Commutation income immediately became the seminary's most important form of revenue. Seigneurial dues were extinguished by a commutation payment which the seminary could use to invest within the guidelines of 1840. In the first year of commutations, it represented 42 per cent of seminary income, a percentage below which it did not fall in the following thirty-five years; commutation income formed 42 per cent of seminary revenues in 1844, 55 per cent in 1854, 46 per cent in 1864, and 47 per cent in 1874.

Commutation income took four forms: principal paid off at the time of commutation; payment of principal on commutations contracted in earlier years and formed into *rentes constituées* or *obligations*; interest paid on these debts; and interest and principal paid by the government under the Seigneurial Act of 1859. Most commutators paid off the principal at the signing, and for the period 1841–76 the seminary received $997,932 in this form. Another $297,027 was received as payment for anterior commutations, that is, as the principal of *rentes constituées* and *obligations*. The new significance of interest in seminary finances is evidenced in the commutation accounts. $1,020,204 was paid in interest on commutation debts before 1877. To this must be added interest paid by the government as the capitalization of *lods et ventes* for the seigneuries of Saint-Sulpice and Two Mountains and the rural parts of the seigneury of Montreal. For fifteen years, from 1860 to 1874, the seminary received annual 6 per cent interest from the government (appendix 11). In 1875 the government paid off the principal of $336,719. For the thirty-five year period 1841–76, the seminary received $1,631,678 in payment of capital and $1,323,234 as interest, a total of $2,954,912.

It is important to note the changing form of commutation income. Before 1859, commutation income came largely in the form of payment of principal; interest on commutation debts represented only 34 per cent of commutation income from 1841 to 1859. After 1859 interest payments became increasingly important, forming 64 per cent of commutation income in the 1860s. This reflected the growing payment of commutations by the assumption of a debt and the government's payment of interest to the seminary after 1860.

URBAN RENTS

The seminary's nineteenth-century activities as an urban *rentier* were characterized by a growing investment in rental stock that ranged from apartments and suburban single-family dwellings, to offices, stores, and warehouses. In the first decades of the century it rented six buildings, all of them on property near the seminary grounds. Its tenants included the government, a notary, a tailor, two British officers, and several widows, including the mother of Bishop Lartigue.[3] Rental income was £25 in 1795, £163 in 1815, and £137 in 1825. Average rental income for the 1830s was £172 (appendix 10). Rental income rose dramatically in the 1840s to an average annual net income for the decade of £1,104, remained steady in the 1850s, and rose sharply again in the 1860s and 1870s (fig. 11). Average annual rental income of $17,826 for the period 1870–6 was twenty-five times higher than annual rental revenues in the 1830s. This sharp rise corresponded to the overall increase in seminary revenues, and from 1830 to 1876 rents remained at between 3 and 8 per cent of seminary income (appendix 11). The growth in rental income represented both increased investment and rising rents. On most seminary properties, rents rose moderately in the 1840s and stagnated and often dropped in the period 1849–52. Alfred Pinsoneault's rent on a three-storey building on St James Street, for example, was reduced 20 per cent in 1849, the last year of his five-year lease, "as a consequence of the business depression."[4] Thereafter rents rose sharply, with rents in the 1860s being two to three times higher than those of the 1840s.

Seminary accounts show a cautious but growing investment in urban rental properties. The seminary spent £2,470 to construct a rental building in 1836–7 and two years later installed water and gas in another property.[5] In 1842 the seminary bought two fire-damaged houses on Saint-François-Xavier Street. Rebuilt in 1843 for £500 they were rented as offices. Later in the year, the seminary added a storey to a commercial building further up the same street. In 1851 an additional storey was built on two disaffected school buildings on Notre-Dame Street for, although the seminary had to borrow funds for construction "we will," in the language of the minutes, "be able to draw considerable rent."[6] This lack of investment capital characterized the seminary's rental operations throughout the 1850s. During the depression of 1857 the seminary, "in light of the difficulty in finding loans," refused to renovate offices for its tenant, the Montreal Telegraph Company. Instead, the business office proposed that the telegraph company undertake the renovations itself in return for reduced rent.[7] The same year the seminary sold office-site space over its ice-house which fronted on the choice Saint-François-Xavier Street. The upper-storey, twenty-foot-wide site was sold to the seminary's own architects, Ostell and Perrault, for £500 and 10 per cent of rent revenues. A condition of the sale was that the building have no opening at the rear which faced the seminary garden.[8]

By 1849 the seminary had sixteen tenants with leases and an indeterminate number of tenants – usually widows or single young women – who occupied rooms on the top floors of seminary rental buildings. At 63 Saint-François-Xavier, for example, the top floor of the four-storey building was rented to "several poor tenants from whom Sister Chèvrefils collects rents totalizing $8 a month."[9] The seminary's largest tenants were Frothingham and Workman, the city's leading hardware merchants and manufacturers, who rented a large building behind the seminary garden. Their annual rent dropped from £150 in their 1845 lease to £130 in a two-year lease signed in 1850. In 1853 a nine-year lease at £415 was signed.[10] In the 1840s the seminary's four buildings on Saint-François-Xavier were rented mainly as stores and offices. Further up the block, the old registry office on the corner of Saint-François-Xavier and Notre-Dame was rented successively by Peter McGill, the City and District Savings Bank, and the Trust and Loan Company. Rent on the building rose from £65 in 1847 to £200 in 1860. Next door the seminary rented a wine and grocery shop to W.L. Macfarlane for £65 (1845);

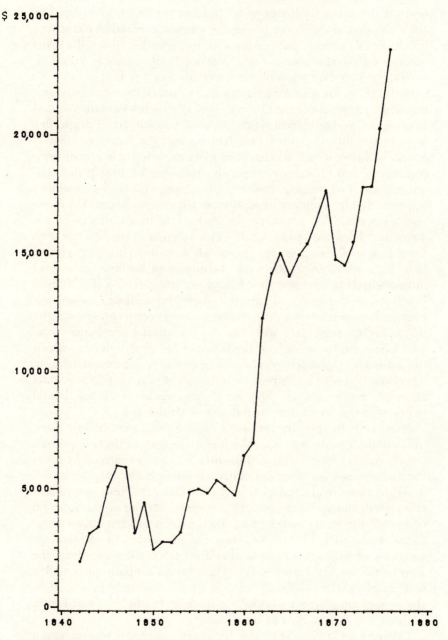

FIGURE 11

Net Rental Income from Urban Properties, 1842–76 (dollars)

Source: ASSM, arm. 2, vol. 24; arm. 2, vol. 157; arm. 3, vol. 402.

Note: Net calculated by deducting operating expenses and repairs; depreciation not included.

rent on the property dropped to £50 in 1851 but rose to £300 in 1861. Further along Notre-Dame, the seminary rented its old school buildings as three shops to a bookbinder, jeweller, and tailor. Another disaffected school on St Lawrence Boulevard was leased to carriage maker Louis-Joseph Gauthier for £34 a year.

In the 1860s the seminary vigorously expanded its *rentier* activities, utilizing its right under the Ordinance of 1840 to invest up to £30,000 in revenue-producing real estate. Most of its commercial properties were in the financial district on Notre-Dame, St James and Saint-François-Xavier streets and its office space attracted banks, insurance companies, and brokerage firms. The insistence of these prime tenants on modern heating, lighting, plumbing, and storage facilities was reflected in seminary expenditures for cesspools, coal furnaces, and sidewalks. The seminary installed a safe in the offices of the Trust and Loan Company, a telegraph antenna in the bell tower of Saint-Jacques Church, and expensive glass windows in offices rented in its library building.[11] Railways, the improved Lachine Canal, and industrialization imposed new wholesale, storage, and distribution functions on the west end, an area where the seminary owned important commercial sites. The modern business enterprise – with its managers, professionals, and sales and accounting personnel – created a demand for suburban, single-family housing, a need to which the seminary responded by subdividing part of its Mountain domain. The Civil War also had a positive influence on the seminary's rental accounts. From 1862 to 1867 the Collège de Montréal was leased ($4,800) to the crown for the lodging of British troops.[12]

From 1861 to 1863 the seminary spent $5,685 remodelling three office buildings. By the 1870s the former tenants of these buildings, largely individual notaries and doctors, had been replaced by firms like the Aetna Insurance Company, accountant Douglas Battersby, and the commercial notaries, Stuart and Marler.[13] These renovations completed, the seminary bought a commercial site at the junction of Wellington Street and the Lachine Canal on which it built a warehouse. Constructed in 1863–4 with a house added in 1867–8 at a total cost of $10,000 for the land and $9,316 for the buildings, the warehouse was first leased to Jane Oliver and Company and by 1875 to G.F. Hart. Hart's annual lease of $1,300 was only exceeded by the $4,000 annual rent paid by the Bank of Hochelaga, and Frothingham and Workman's $1,900 lease.[14]

Between 1866 and 1875 the seminary instigated several major renovation projects. At a cost of $19,305, five new stores were constructed in existing rental properties on Saint-François-Xavier Street. From 1870 to 1875 the seminary built the Cabinet de lecture on the corner of Notre-Dame and Saint-François-Xavier streets. Although primarily a reading-room, three offices in the building were rented, one to a real-estate agency. The same institutional / revenue land-use was applied on the Bonsecours church site purchased by the seminary in 1869. As well as the church itself, the site included five stores which the seminary maintained and rented.[15] To improve its property on the choice corner of St James and Saint-François-Xavier, the seminary spent $1,200 to break the lease of the Trust and Loan Company and a further $2,652 in construction. The foundations of another building were raised ($1,867) and the Bank of Hochelaga premises completely remodelled ($23,107). After renovations, the bank paid annual rent of $4,000, the second-floor tenants, the Hamilton Powder Company, paid $700, and lawyers Carter and McGibbon paid $300 for their third-floor offices. In 1876 the seminary gutted and began reconstruction of the building occupied by brokers Burland and Lafricain at 115 Saint-François-Xavier; this three-year project cost $26,194. Further down the block at number 79 the seminary invested $2,150 in renovating the Dominion Telegraph Building.[16]

Two residential rental projects were undertaken by the seminary in the 1870s. Although it sold most of the lots on its Mountain subdivision (chapter six), the seminary built, at a cost of $72,000, fourteen single-family houses on Baile, Saint-Marc, and Saint-Mathieu streets.[17] Completed in 1876, the six larger homes were rented for between $450 and $548 a year to tenants who included a bank cashier, a ship broker, and a widow. Tenants in the eight smaller houses – a leather merchant, chemist, engineer, book and produce broker – paid $280 to $320. In 1865 the seminary paid $13,872 for twenty-eight building lots comprising a city block surrounded by Napoléon, Roy, Cadieux, and Pantaléon streets. The purchase was made for construction of school, parish, and social services, but in 1879 the seminary used a corner of the property to construct five rental houses. Built at a total cost of $6,501, each of the single-family houses was rented for $144 a year; tenants gave their occupations as travelling salesman, insurance agent, real-estate agent, house painter, and widow.[18]

In the late 1870s the seminary had some twenty-nine commercial rental properties in the financial district around the seminary, five stores in the block around the Bonsecours Church, nineteen houses on the Mountain domain and on Cadieux Street, a warehouse at the Wellington Bridge, and a house rented at 1142 Sherbrooke Street. In addition the seminary had rented its manor-house in the village of Assomption, a wooden house in the village of Saint-Gabriel, and four vacant lots in Montreal. Some 116 leases were counted on urban properties for the period 1875–82. Of commercial tenants whose business can be identified, eleven were insurance companies (including Aetna Life Insurance Company, British American Insurance Company, and Sovereign Assurance Company), eight were stockbrokers, seven lawyers, four notaries, four merchant / importers, three restaurants, two banks (Bank of Hochelaga, Banque Nationale), two real-estate companies, two accountants, two watch makers, one telegraph company (Dominion Telegraph), one newspaper store, one tailor, one agent, and one architect. The seminary's net rental income was $23,667 in 1876, $25,369 in 1890, and $50,976 in 1915.[19]

BOND AND STOCK INCOME

Disposition of its sharply increasing income was a recurring concern of both the Consulting Council and the business office. Real property was a traditional investment for a religious corporation, but the seminary was restricted by law to £30,000 of new investment in revenue-producing real property. Further, with a view to more anonymous and profitable investments, the Consulting Council decided in 1841 that the seminary should look to "a public enterprise like the port, a canal or a railway ... as a less odious and more advantageous form of investment than having houses in the city."[20]

In the 1840s this investment policy took the form of both short-term loans and the purchase of public debentures for the construction of harbour, road, water, and market facilities. By 1848 the seminary held Montreal Harbour and Welland Canal bonds, had lent £900 to the Montreal waterworks, made a cash advance of £165 against future taxes to the City of Montreal for surfacing the street in front of the seminary, bought City of Montreal bonds worth £7,567 for road, market, and aqueduct construction, and purchased road-construction bonds worth £7,000 from the Corporation des chemins de Québec and the Corporation of Chambly (table 8). The seminary added to its portfolio of City of Montreal bonds in 1853, 1860, 1867, 1872, and 1875. In the 1870s this predilection for the issues of public bodies accelerated with the purchase of bonds from the Quebec Government, the City of Sorel, the Montreal Catholic School Commission, and the City of Trois-Rivières. Between 1882 and 1909 the seminary bought the bonds of thirty-eight municipalities ranging from Quebec to British Columbia (appendix 12). The value of its "municipal" portfolio rose from $87,266 in 1880 to $241,904 in 1883 and $1,272,072 in 1915.[21] These municipal issues were usually floated to raise capital for local improvements and transportation projects.

The Trois-Rivières issue, for example, was used for local harbour and railway construction, as was the Montreal bond issue of 1872.[22] Investment capital was also drawn from the bursar's funds, the Union des Prières treasury, and the private – and often substantial – funds of individual Sulpicians. Certain reimbursements were transferred directly into capital expenditures. A $24,000 reimbursement of City of Montreal bonds, for example, was used to pay off promissory notes given to Grand Trunk officers.[23]

By the mid 1840s the seminary's coffers and its purchase of the debentures of public bodies attracted the attention of Montrealers promoting a trunk line linking Montreal to its western hinterland and to an ice-free port at Portland, Maine. But the Sulpicians were reluctant to invest directly in railway issues. In 1846 the seminary declined to buy shares in the St Lawrence and Atlantic Railway pleading that under the terms of the Ordinance of 1840 it could not invest directly in railways.[24] This led to pressures to change the law and in 1849 the provincial assembly removed legal obstacles to direct investment by religious corporations in transportation projects.

This changed legal situation coincided with what the seminary perceived as a very dangerous political and social climate: the rebellion losses bill, the annexation movement, the burning of the parliament in Montreal, the stoning of the governor general, and the need to have Sulpicians staying up all night through the summer to protect their buildings from arsonists. "We are on a volcano which smoked all summer, which slowed down a little, but which is now on the point of exploding with fury."[25] Pressed by promoters, the government, city officials, the bishop, and the clergy to give evidence of civic support by investing in the railway, the Sulpicians – their fear of isolation revived – felt they could not refuse without being depicted, as the procurator reported to Paris, as "people opposed to the well-being of the city who want to take out every advantage, [and have] the growth of their properties without risking anything, without contributing to change ... If we refuse, who knows if our institutions, schools, churches will meet the same fate as parliament, Doneganas Hotel, the Hotel Nelson, etc? It is a most distressing condition."[26]

In September 1849 the seminary made a last attempt to rebuff the railway promoters, pointing out that its funds were "firmly" invested and that it had refused similar requests for financing from Toronto and Quebec City entrepreneurs.[27] But even while protesting, the Sulpicians in the privacy of their correspondence with Paris were reporting the inevitable. In October 1849 they agreed to co-sign and guarantee £25,000 of the railway's debentures on condition

TABLE 8

Interest-bearing Bonds and Stocks Held by Seminary, 1841–76

Year	Institution	Amount ($)
1841	Montreal Harbour bonds	6,666
1842	City of Montreal bonds¹	12,852
1843	City of Montreal bonds¹	268
1844	City of Montreal bonds¹	8,672
1845	City of Montreal bonds¹	8,075
	Corporation of Chambly bonds	12,000
	Corporation des chemins de Québec	16,000
1846	City of Montreal (aqueduct)	400
1847	Province of Canada debentures	5,533
1848	Welland Canal bonds	466
1849	Grand Trunk Railway debentures	100,000
	Quebec City fire bonds	1,200
1851	Montreal Harbour bonds²	12,000
1852	Industry to Rawdon Railway bonds	4,000
1853	City of Montreal bonds	400
1860	City of Montreal bonds	960
1865	Montreal Harbour bonds	2,000
1867	Mechanics Bank shares	1,000
	Jacques Cartier Bank shares	152
	City of Montreal bonds	19,580
1868	Merchants Bank shares	1,340
	_____"bonds"	4,000
1871	North Shore Railway bonds	500
1872	Quebec Government bonds	6,326
	City of Sorel bonds	10,580
	City of Montreal bonds	6,000
	Montreal Catholic School Commission bonds	10,000
1874	Gas Company bonds	8,183
1875	City of Montreal bonds	5,012
	City of Trois-Rivières bonds	30,400
	Montreal Harbour bonds	69,319
1876	Montreal to Carillon Navigation Co.	250

Source: ASSM, arm. 2, vol. 37; arm. 2, vol. 157; arm. 2, vol. 63.

Note: Interest-bearing loans to the *fabriques* of Montreal, Beauharnois, and Saint-Benoît have been excluded.

1 Bonds issued for roads and market construction and in payment for land bought by city from seminary

2 Bonds accepted by seminary as payment for land bought by Harbour Commission

that the City of Montreal make a municipal subscription of £100,000 to the railway. The British American Land Company – with holdings along the projected line in the Eastern Townships – matched the seminary's guarantee making these two landed proprietors the largest private backers in Canada's first major railway project. Each of the five debentures taken by the seminary had a face value of £5,000, bore 6 per cent interest, and matured between 1861 and 1865. The seminary's support for what became the Grand Trunk Railway was clearly inscribed on the debentures: "The payment of this debenture is guaranteed by the Ecclesiastics of the Seminary of St. Sulpice of Montreal." As security the seminary took a mortgage on the line between Longueuil and Saint-Hyacinthe. In addition to the annual interest of £1,500 the railway was to pay the seminary £375 in annual rent, this money being kept in a separate account until the capital was paid off.[28]

Given the seminary's changing position through the transition, this investment is highly significant. The leading seigneur in the Montreal area was using the surplus of its *censitaires* – with the state adding important muscle in its expropriation – to finance a major transportation system and industrial producer. The £25,000 is strong material evidence of the forcing of the seminary and its slippage towards adjunct status in industrial capitalist Montreal. We can anticipate that its ideological message, its institutional role, and its subdivision of the Saint-Gabriel domain will reflect this dependence.

During the 1850s the Grand Trunk kept up its annual interest payments to the seminary and even increased its indebtedness by purchasing Sulpician land with deferred payments. For their part, seminary officials expressed their misgivings only privately. Publicly, they echoed the virtues of economic development and in 1856 contributed £100 for the gala organized to celebrate completion of rail and water services into Montreal.[29] By 1860 the Grand Trunk's catastrophic financial situation was reflected in its Canadian payments. Only in 1861 did it pay off interest due to the seminary the previous September nor was it able to reimburse a principal of $10,857 due to the Grey Nuns for land purchases made in the 1850s. When the Grand Trunk did not pay principal due on the first seminary-guaranteed debenture, Sulpician officials wrote to the Grand Trunk, and in 1863 its notaries filed an official notification of Grand Trunk arrears.[30]

The Grand Trunk default and the subsequent failure of the seminary to take strong recourse to the law or state were added symptoms of Sulpician vulnerability. The Grand Trunk was a powerful industrial producer and Montreal employer, its shops were adjacent to the seminary's Saint-Gabriel subdivision, and its political friends were legion. As well, the railway had appropriated the status of a national enterprise. The activity of the railway's Montreal lawyer, George-Étienne Cartier, gives a measure of the complicity; he doubled as solicitor for both the railway and the seminary while in his political capacity he was attorney general for Canada East. In these circumstances, the seminary had apparently little choice but to continue supporting the railway. It quietly paid off the Grand Trunk's debt to the Grey Nuns on condition that the railway reimburse it within five years. This debt was finally settled sixteen years later when the Grand Trunk paid off land-purchase debts to the seminary of $28,420; the £25,000 guarantee of 1849 was carried forward on seminary books with the railway paying ongoing interest.[31]

The seminary was able to stave off other pressures for investment in private securities although in 1852 and 1871 it did increase its railway portfolio with small investments in the Industry to Rawdon Railway and the North Shore Railway – both of which crossed the Saint-Sulpice seigneury. The seminary also bought shares in three banks in the years 1867–8, but it was only after the chartering of the Montreal Stock Exchange in 1874 that the seminary moved enthusiastically into bond and stock markets. Between 1882 and 1909 it invested in ten transportation companies and fifteen other industrial companies (appendix 12).

MORTGAGES AND PRIVATE BANKING

As a landed proprietor and institutional creditor, the seminary was an interested party to the evolving mortgage system of Lower Canada. The mortgage – essentially the right of a creditor to the immovable property of the debtor – is closely linked to the form of property ownership, since to have debt secured on real property, the borrower must have absolute title and be able to assure the creditor's privilege to this security. Before 1840 the hypothecary system was general and secret; indeed every notarial act bore "a tacit general hypothec" binding the debtor's present and future goods.[32] The *Coutume de Paris* protected certain groups. Seigneurs, women, minor children, heirs, the crown, vendors, and architects / builders / workers were privileged creditors and could obstruct what one judge called "the authenticated claim of a more diligent creditor."[33] Although there were means of reinforcing real security by voluntary sheriff sales or the grafting of specific mortgages onto the general hypothecs, it was the Registry Ordinance of 1840 that ensured the security of specific mortgages. This law, like the Seigneurial Ordinance, was passed by the Special Council in the post-rebellion period and made four fundamental changes in mortgage practice. It made hypothecary agreements public by the establishment of registry offices, it abolished general hypothecs, it established a new order of privilege of mortgage agreements, and it reduced the special privileges of some creditors, particularly women.[34]

This registry law and the corporate powers granted to the seminary by the Ordinance of 1840 facilitated its collection of seigneurial arrears. In chapter three we noted how the seminary formalized hundreds of debt-recognition contracts in the 1840s. These debts, like the *rentes constituées* and obligations formed by commutators, were secured by specific, first mortgages. The seminary also took mortgages as security from public bodies. In 1859, for example, its loan of £25,000 to the City of Montreal was secured by a specific mortgage on the Bonsecours Market as well as insurance policies on city buildings.[35]

In the 1870s the seminary began to invest in rural mortgages. Concentrating on properties in parishes around Saint-Jean – some forty kilometres from Montreal and well away from its seigneuries – the seminary wrote the first mortgage of this series in 1871; by 1900 it had taken 125 mortgages in the area. The 22 mortgages written between 1871 and 1876 represented loans of $30,306 and had an average value of $1,378. Mortgages written between 1871 and 1874 bore 6 per cent interest. In 1873 parliament gave religious communities the right to charge 8 per cent and seminary mortgages quickly rose to that rate. Much as Weaver and Doucet found for Hamilton, interest rates dropped back to 6 per cent in the period 1881–97, and to 5 per cent in the period 1897–1917.[36]

This mortgage business, which corresponded to the sharp growth in Canada of building societies and mortgage-loan companies, emphasized that the seminary's financial operations were becoming more indirect and professional.[37] Its business office was increasingly an impersonal participant in the lending process. Written on land well away from the seminary's parish and seigneuries, the mortgages were drawn up and registered in Saint-Jean by two local notaries. Only occasionally was principal paid at the Montreal business office, and routine interest payments were always made in Saint-Jean. Instead of a reference from a local priest or a business office notation concerning the borrower's family or religious and financial status, formal guarantors were used; thirteen of the first twenty-two mortgages included guarantors. There was apparently a higher degree of default on these mortgages – at least during the depression years 1873–6 – than in other known examples. Four of the first twenty-two mortgage holders defaulted. Their land was seized and sold by the sheriff.[38]

As the seminary's business operations multiplied, it made increasing use of Canada's developing financial institutions. The Toronto

TABLE 9
Seminary Debts, 1826–55

Year	Lender	Profession	Amount (£)	Interest	Terms	Repaid
1826	Sisters of Hôtel-Dieu	religious institution	6,000	6%	perpetual	1879–80
1827	Congregation of Notre Dame	religious institution	2,208	none	on demand	1839–45
1833	Sisters of Hôtel-Dieu	religious institution	3,500	5%	perpetual	1880
1835	Sisters of Hôtel-Dieu	religious institution	3,300	5%	perpetual	1880
1835	Bishop of Montreal	religious institution	700	6%	perpetual	1844
1836	Sisters of Hôtel-Dieu	religious institution	2,340	5%	perpetual	1880
1837	Thomas Caldwell	merchant	300	4%	?	1837
1838	fabrique of Châteauguay	religious institution	350	4%	?	1840
1839	fabrique of Saint-Denis	religious institution	389	none	1 month notice	1844
1839	fabrique of Saint-Athanase	religious institution	150	none	1 month notice	1843
1839	Sisters of Hôtel-Dieu	religious institution	250	none	perpetual	1843
1839	Sisters of Hôtel-Dieu	religious institution	2,820	none	on demand	1842–3
1840	Edward Rogers	religious institution	150	none	1 year	1841
1841	Curé A. Dansereau	ecclesiastic	300	none	on demand	1842
1841	fabrique of Sainte-Geneviève	religious institution	774	none	on demand	1842
1845	George Gregory[1]		6,500	6%	1 year	1848–50
1850	Joseph Masson estate	merchant	4,000	6%	15 years	1852
1851	Joseph Masson estate	merchant	1,100	6%	15 years	1854
1852	Thomas Corcoran	merchant	1,850	6%	2 years	1854
1852	Eulalie & Alfred Chalifoux	tailors	130	5%	?	1853
1852	George Peck[2]		650	6%	?	?
1852	City and District Savings Bank	bank	1,000	6%	6 months (int. payable in advance)	?
1852	City and District Savings Bank	bank	500	6%	3 months	1853
1852	Widow Vallières		550	6%	1 year	1853
1855	James Brankin		1,545	6%	2 years	1856–7
1855	Bank of Montreal	bank	2,000	6%	3 months (renewable)	1858

Source: ASSM, arm. 2, vol. 264.
1 Loans taken as part of land purchase
2 $3,000 payable in 1848, $3,000 in 1849, and balance six months after Gregory's death

and London branches of the Bank of Montreal served as clearing-houses for its paper. In the 1840s government payments for its land purchases along the Lachine Canal were paid into the Toronto branch of the Bank of Montreal, and the seminary paid regular commissions to transfer these funds to Montreal.[39] The seminary also turned to the Bank of Montreal for short-term loans (table 9). In its real-estate operations, banks were among the seminary's most important tenants: in the 1870s the Bank of Hochelaga and the Banque Nationale rented two of the seminary's larger buildings.

The seminary's growing money revenues in the 1840s made it an important depositor, particularly at the Banque du Peuple and the Montreal City and District Savings Bank. In years when it had a cash surplus the seminary kept a substantial interest-bearing account at the Banque du Peuple, receiving £174 in interest for the period 1852–4.[40] Founded to collect savings from the popular classes for investment by its directors, the Montreal City and District Savings Bank had been encouraged by the Catholic hierarchy as a philanthropic organization. As part of its support, the seminary rented to it (for £150 a year) a three-storey building on St James Street, kept deposits in the bank, and in 1852 turned to it for two short-term loans.[41] By Confederation the seminary had begun taking shares and granting special loans to local banks. In 1871 it had interest-bearing accounts in four Montreal banks: the Banque du Peuple ($179 interest in 1871), Hugh Allan's Merchants Bank ($132), the troubled Jacques Cartier Bank ($856), and the Mechanics Bank ($346). It held stock in the last three banks and had invested $4,200 from its reserve in a 6 per cent note issued by the Banque du Peuple.[42]

The seminary's deposits and investments in local banks turned sour with the bank crisis of the late 1870s. At the Banque Ville-Marie it had to accept a six-month delay in withdrawing the $23,505 it had on deposit. As guarantee it was granted a mortgage on the bank's building on the corner of St James Street and St Lawrence Boulevard until it was reimbursed in December 1880.[43] The seminary was less successful in recovering its funds from the Mechanics Bank. By 1880 it was in litigation with the bank and apparently recovered only 50 per cent of its deposits of $12,451.[44]

With its increasing social investments and complex business operations, the seminary incurred periodic deficits. Between 1848 and 1876 it built twelve schools, undertook nine church, chapel, or church-decoration projects, as well as two residences for the teaching brothers, the Grand Séminaire, the new Collège de Montréal, and the Cabinet de lecture.[45] Seminary income from investments such as bonds often did not mature at propitious moments, while risk issues, such as that of the Grand Trunk, diverted funds available for social investments. Other important revenues, such as commutations, seigneurial arrears, and land sales, dried up during the depression of the late 1850s – the very period when social investment pressure on the seminary was strongest.

In this conjuncture, the seminary had to borrow, and in 1857 and 1858 the Consulting Council authorized the business office to contract debts.[46] The seminary had indebted itself in the past for major construction projects. In 1805 it had incurred a debt to build the Collège de Montréal, and from 1826 to 1839 it borrowed to construct the new Notre-Dame Church. The latter was financed with £18,210 borrowed from the Hôtel-Dieu nuns, most of which was not repaid until 1880. In the 1850s the seminary began borrowing regularly, first from local capitalists or banks, and then from small lenders who turned to the seminary to fulfil the deposit functions of a private bank.

The estate of Joseph Masson became the seminary's most important lay creditor in the 1850s. To pay off their 1845 debt on the purchase of the Gregory Farm, procurator Comte and superior Billaudèle met with Masson's executors and negotiated a fifteen-year loan of £4,000. In 1850 the seminary borrowed another £1,100 from the Masson estate to pay off a *fabrique* debt, in 1858 a further £4,000, and a final £1,000 in 1870. Other important sums were borrowed in the period 1850–70, from Thomas Corcoran (£3,350), the daughter of Quebec City merchant George Symes (£5,400), and Gaspard-Aimé Massue (£30,168).[47]

The late 1850s were years of furious institutional investment by the seminary. St Anne's, the second Irish church of Montreal, was opened in 1854. After the fire of 1852, Saint-Jacques Church was rebuilt, only to burn again in 1859; the new St Patrick's Church regularly filled with smoke for lack of an adequate chimney. The Grand Séminaire involved heavy expenses after construction began in 1855. Schools for the popular classes were needed in developing industrial suburbs; a Christian Brothers school was completed in the Sainte-Marie suburb in 1855, and a year later the procurator presented estimates of £2,500 for a girls' school in Sainte-Anne. Construction lumber for institutional projects cost £3,450 in the years 1859–60.[48]

These construction expenses, which seminary minutes described as "enormous," were not matched by increasing revenues, a situation that became even more critical when several anticipated large loans fell through. The Consulting Council discussed selling blocks of land at Saint-Gabriel, decided to put judicial pressure on seigneurial debtors, and ordered the business office not to invest in improvements to its office buildings. To raise cash, the mill at Achigan and the old orphanage site at the corner of St Lawrence and Sainte-Catherine were put on sale. In 1856 the seminary turned to another source of capital and in effect ran a small savings bank by accepting deposits – large and small – from the Catholic population of the Montreal region. Whereas large lenders were accompanied by notaries, insisted on fixed and high rates of interest, took mortgages as security, and even asked for interest in advance, deposits at the seminary were unnotarized and were guaranteed only by the good name of the institution.[49] For their part, depositors who entrusted their savings, trusts, or legacies at the seminary drew interest while serving Catholic social goals. From 1856 to 1876 the seminary took in 710 deposits; total deposits for the period were $814,540. Of 149 depositors who can be identified in the period 1860–71, 66 were women, 34 clergy, 14 merchants or shopkeepers, 12 religious or benevolent associations, 2 professionals, 14 artisans, 1 farmer, and 6 other members of the popular classes (guard, labourer, gardener, porter, 2 post-office workers).[50]

The clergy and Catholic associations were frequent depositors at the seminary. Of 21 depositors in 1857, 11 were priests or benevolent societies; in the 1870s the estates of several Sulpicians were deposited at the seminary. Dozens of rural priests and nuns made deposits. Curé Joseph Rémillard of Saint-Polycarpe, for example, made a deposit every year after 1871 and in 1880, the first year he made a withdrawal, his balance was $7,700. Several benevolent societies for the popular classes, founded and advised by the Sulpicians, kept their funds at the seminary. In 1857 the Société Saint-Antoine, a mutual-aid society for shoemakers, had 115 members and £150 on deposit at the seminary. Two other societies advised by Sulpician Eustache Picard, the Société Bienveillante de Bonsecours and the Société Saint-François-Xavier, kept deposits at the business office.[51]

Female depositors at the seminary came from all classes and some had sizeable accounts. In 1862, two women – Ann Symes and the widow of Henri Tugault – deposited a total of $22,650. Some female accounts had special conditions that suggest trust functions. Between 1872 and 1875, $18,856 were deposited to the account of widow Alexis Patenaude with the proviso that she be reimbursed within six months of the death of her father.

The seminary accepted both term and demand deposits. The usual interest on both was 6 per cent although after 1870 the seminary gave 5 per cent on an increasing number of deposits. At least one client, Ferdinand Paré, was offered 5 per cent on his demand deposits and 6 per cent on one-year term deposits. Occasional female depositors, certain benevolent associations, and many priests accepted 4 per cent on their deposits.

This savings-bank operation is yet another example of the seminary moving in tandem with urban and industrial society in the financial sector. By spreading a broader net that scooped up savings from friendly societies, rural parishes, the popular classes, and women from all classes, the seminary acted as intermediary and transfer agent. For on the debit side of its books, it was at the same time the largest private investor in Montreal in the Grand Trunk and the motor of social investment in the Catholic sector. The Sulpician fear of class conflict and revolution coincided with the anxiety of the bourgeoisie and led to the institutionalization and class legitimation described in chapter seven. For the seminary, the financial implications of this social investment were periodic indebtedness and close attention to expanding or new revenues in the form of urban rents, land subdivisions, stocks, bonds, mortgages, and other investment income, and certain operations of a private bank. Although seigneurial revenues were never neglected, new financial activities show a distancing from the social relations characteristic of feudal society toward the bureaucratized, professionalized, fungible, and more impersonal relations associated with a capitalist society.

CHAPTER SIX

Land Developers:
Subdivision on Two
Seigneurial Domains

... the modern right of land use, in comparison with the feudal right which preceded it, may be called an absolute right in two senses; it is a right to dispose of, or alienate, as well as to use; and it is a right which is not conditional on the owner's performance of any social function.

C.B. Macpherson, 1978[1]

We have seen that although most of its land on the island of Montreal was ceded in fiefs or concession lots, the seminary had retained three large domains for food, storage, wood, recreation, and its Indian mission. The 800-acre domain at Sault-au-Récollet on the north side of the island produced primarily firewood; peripheral to urban expansion it was still leased to a tenant farmer in 1880. This chapter treats the effects of industrialization and urbanization on the two domains closer to Montreal. The 300-acre Saint-Gabriel domain was located just west of the city on the flats between the St Lawrence River and the hill rising to the mountain (fig. 12). Straddling the Lachine Canal and choking potential development around an important lock and hydraulic-power site, the domain epitomized the incompatibility of feudal and industrial modes and was a perennial target of opponents of seigneurialism. Obliged by the Ordinance of 1840 to sell the Saint-Gabriel domain within twenty years, the seminary manoeuvred to exploit the domain's potential as subdivision sites for manufactures and popular housing. A different strategy was used in the 1860s to develop the southern part of the Mountain domain. Located on the plateau below Westmount this subdivision would serve another urban land use as prestigious residential lots for Montreal's expanding community of anglophone managers and professionals.

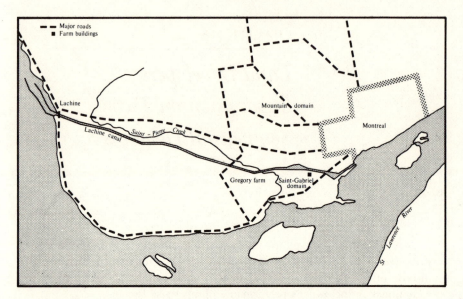

FIGURE 12
Southern Part of Island of Montreal, 1840

THE SAINT-GABRIEL DOMAIN: INDUSTRIAL SITES

Sulpician interest in constructing a bypass of the Lachine rapids dated from the seventeenth century. A canal from Lachine to Montreal would increase water volume in the Saint-Pierre creek permitting construction of water-mills to grind banal grain. It would also allow canoes loaded with fur-trade or military supplies to depart for the west directly from Montreal. Canal construction began in 1689 under Sulpician patronage using the labour of peasants conscripted for seigneurial arrears. Aborted because of Indian attacks and the difficulty of cutting through rock near Lachine, the project was revived eleven years later when the seminary signed a contract with engineer Gédéon de Catalogne. Financial difficulties and the death of its strongest Sulpician advocate, Superior Dollier de Casson, again brought work to a stop and for over a century various proposals to finish the canal remained dormant.[2] In 1821 the government assumed construction of the canal completing it four years later.

Land use on the Saint-Gabriel domain was not dramatically affected by canal construction in the 1820s. A kilometre beyond the urban conglomeration, the farm's pastures were fenced off from the canal. Its eight buildings were grouped along the Saint-Pierre creek and were maintained by two farm labourers and a part-time domestic. The domain showed a book profit from the leasing of pasture, the sale of farm produce, and the use of farm workers and horses to haul firewood.[3]

Enlargement of the Lachine Canal and the forced sale of the domain jeopardized these traditional land uses. Between 1843 and 1848 the canal's depth was doubled to three metres and larger turning and docking basins were added. Canal reconstruction included the addition of weirs and sluices to facilitate the utilization of excess water as hydraulic power. In 1846 and 1847 the government held auctions of hydraulic lots along the basin near the mouth of the canal and by 1856 twenty sites had been leased; flour milling and nail production were the dominant early industrial uses in this sector.[4] In 1851 John Young and Ira Gould signed a perpetual lease for five hydraulic lots which benefited from the eight and a half foot drop at the Saint-Gabriel locks. They in turn subdivided and by 1856 the seminary's farm domain was neighbour to some of Montreal's most important industries: Frederick Warren Harris's cotton mill, John Converse's rope factory, the Montreal India Rubber Company, foundries of the Redmond Brothers and William Bury, Thomas and Robert Scott's axes factory, Augustin Cantin's shipyard, and the door and sash factories of John Ostell and Thomas Shearer. By the mid-1850s some 2,000 workers laboured in canal-side foundries, flour mills, sawmills, engine works, shipyards, and shoe, drug, rope, cotton sack, paint, axe, nail, sewing machine, barrel, and door and sash manufactures.[5]

A persistent theme of this work has been the insistence that the seminary was not a reactionary institution committed to the defence of a feudal mode of production. Well before 1840 it accepted the inevitability of the cession of the Saint-Gabriel domain: its policy was to maximize returns from its alienation. This called for persistent, informed negotiations with both political leaders and public works officials, for the formulation of subdivision strategies, and for the utilization of professionals who could steer the seminary through the maelstrom of industrialization along the canal.

Although the turf was now industrial rather than seigneurial, the seminary – reinforced by renewed corporate rights and a stable of professionals – showed its usual scrupulosity in negotiations with canal officials. Its lawyers advised that the seminary had the right to exact seigneurial dues on canal land purchased by the government prior to 1840 and could insist that the government replace the seminary's bridge over the canal. To ensure subdivision under what its minutes described as "the most lucrative" conditions, the seminary

gave priority to road, bridge, docking, and hydraulic facilities along
the canal. Boat basins were choice factory sites and seminary officials
lobbied hard over their size and location. By 1845 issues such as
arbitration procedures, the ownership of dirt excavated from the
canal, flooding damages, fence replacement, the right to draw off
canal water, and land swaps had become so complicated that the
seminary business manager had opened a special "reminder" dossier.[6]

John Ostell was a particularly important official for the seminary
in its Saint-Gabriel business. Architect, surveyor, and brother-in-law
of the assistant commissioner of public works, Ostell was himself a
prominent Lachine Canal industrial developer until the bankruptcy
of his door and sash factory in 1863. He had other useful connec-
tions. He was an organizer of the city's major tramway company and
drew up both Montreal's first comprehensive city plan in 1840–1
and John Redpath's villa subdivision in 1842. Ostell received tenders
for the seminary, acted as their overseer on bridge and basin sites,
and represented them in land arbitration cases. In 1844 he surveyed
and laid out fences on seminary land that was rented as immigrant
sheds, a marshalling area, and temporary housing facility for
immigrants.[7]

In 1842 the business office instructed Ostell to divide that part of
the domain closest to Montreal into "town lots." Ostell worked on
the subdivision plan for over three years, laying out streets, placing
stakes, and numbering the lots. His plan contained 501 lots. On the
south side of the canal in the triangle formed by Wellington Street,
the canal, and the farm buildings, 133 lots were staked. The largest
part of the subdivision was on the north side of the canal where 368
lots were laid out with the choicest sites being along the boat basin
and canal (fig. 13).[8]

In 1845 the once-discreet seminary placed newspaper advertise-
ments announcing its first land sale for 10:00 A.M., 21 August in the
offices of its auctioneers Cuvillier and Sons. The seminary invited
prospective buyers of industrial, commercial, or residential lots to
visit the site or to examine Ostell's subdivision plan at the auctioneers.
Purchasers were required to make a 10 per cent down payment and
to pay survey and registry costs totalling 1 1/2 per cent of the purchase
price. The ads, which offered ten-year, 6 per cent seminary mortgages, lauded the industrial potential of domain land: "it is scarcely
necessary to notice the great increasing value of these lots, being
situate [sic] on immediate line of Lachine Canal and many of them
surrounding two of the largest and best basins."[9]

Despite anticipation of a canal bonanza and published reports that
the sale brought £68,565, actual results of the auction were chas-

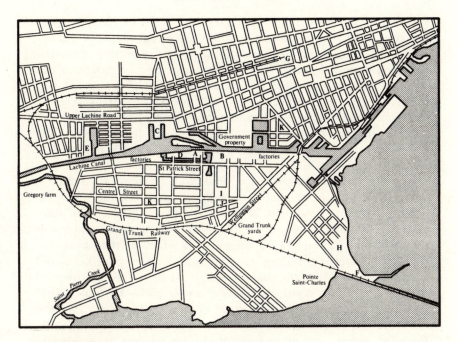

FIGURE 13
Saint-Gabriel Subdivision, 1872

Legend

A Saint-Gabriel locks
B Redpath sugar refinery
C Cantin shipyards
D Young-Gould-Ostell development
E John Young Property
F to Victoria Bridge

G railway station
H immigrant sheds
I market
J school
K church

tening for the seminary. Many bidders refused to honour their auction purchases, and four months after the sale only twenty-three of thirty-nine accepted bids had been confirmed by a down payment and the signing of a deed. Only 225 lots – less than half the subdivision – were finally sold and among the largest purchasers were the seminary's own employee John Ostell (£3,650) and its auctioneer Austin Cuvillier (£3,220). Faced by the refusal of many of the largest bidders to sign deeds, seminary notaries delivered warnings threatening legal action to sixteen delinquent purchasers including Canfield Dorwin (£5,975), Jacob DeWitt (£4,430), Austin Adam (£1,025), Donald Murray (£2,290), and Thomas Byrne (£1,320). These warnings brought little response; only one recipient, Charles Austin, came forward to sign his deeds.[10] Seminary accounts trace the disastrous sale results. In 1849 earlier sales figures of £37,695 were crossed out and replaced with £7,249 – much of which was in promissory notes. Despite substantial sheriff fees, collections in the next two years did not improve, and in 1851 the seminary wrote off £1,115 in bad promissory notes. Another indication of mediocre returns were the amounts the seminary transferred out of the Saint-Gabriel land-sale account. By 1851 the seminary had been able to divert only £2,844; £2,344 was used to purchase school sites, and £500 was placed in Chambly road bonds.[11]

Although it is unclear why the seminary's auction was character-ized by over-bidding and refusal to honour purchases, the late 1840s brought a general decline in land prices – a crisis reflected in Saint-Gabriel land values. John Tully, for example, bought several lots at the 1845 sale. Eleven years later, a lot for which he paid £510 was sold by the sheriff for £145, two lots for which he paid £550 sold for £360; Tully's total purchase of £1,636 in 1845 brought the sem-inary – after taxes, court, bailiff, and lawyer fees – £816 in 1856.[12] Several purchasers of Saint-Gabriel land went bankrupt and the seminary was forced to repossess or to purchase lots at sheriff sales. Foundry owner Scott Shaw had kept up his interest payments and had increased the original £450 value of his four lots by constructing buildings. At his bankruptcy sale in 1851, the seminary, in the ab-sence of other buyers, took his lots back as payment for £456 owing.[13]

Faced with a slumping market the seminary did not hold a public sale for eight years. In the interim it increased accessibility to its subdivision by building roads and bridges. It continued to move only slowly against delinquent purchasers. Where possible, the seminary seems to have avoided messy lawsuits against reneging purchasers, many of whom were important industrial neighbours and powerful political allies. Instead, quietly and several years later, it allowed purchasers to retrocede their land, permitting them to renounce any claim to ownership without payment of accumulated interest. Be-tween 1851 and 1856 eleven retrocessions occurred with most of the acts referring to the fact that the amounts due on the land were "much over its value." In 1856, for example, the heirs of Austin Cuvillier owed £3,260 in principal and £2,045 interest on the nine lots he had purchased in 1845. "In light of the depreciation of real-estate in this city," the seminary accepted the land back with the payment of £150 in damages.[14]

The most important seminary land transactions in the early 1850s occurred near the Saint-Gabriel locks where domain land became part of the land-assembly scheme organized by forwarder and soon-to-be commissioner of public works John Young, banker Jacob DeWitt, miller Ira Gould, and the seminary's dextrous employee John Ostell. In addition to leasing from the government "the entire surplus water" at the lock, their company, the Saint-Gabriel Hydraulic Company began buying up plots of seminary land at bargain prices in the years 1851–7. In 1851 they bought some fifteen acres in four parcels on both sides of the lock, paying, in what appears to have been a private sale, £150 an acre for the five-acre parcel on the south side of the lock.[15] Young and Gould took up two plots of land retroceded by bankrupt purchasers at the 1845 auction and in 1854 Young bought yet another canal lot plus thirteen acres further up the canal at the seminary-owned Gregory farm (fig. 13). Served by the canal, the Grand Trunk Railway, and the Upper Lachine Road, the latter purchase, for which Young paid £100 an acre, was subdivided into 122 building lots.[16]

Freehold tenure implied the virtually absolute right to dispose of land, and seminary involvement with industrial developers along the canal quickly became complicated with promoters engaging in a maze of exchanges and sales in which their domain holdings were divided and sold off. In particular, John Young – one of the seminary's largest debtors – edged towards bankruptcy. By 1864 only eight lots had been sold on his Gregory farm subdivision, and the seminary was forced to assume some of his mortgages and to ease his credit terms. Seven years later it repossessed the Gregory farm holdings of the bankrupt Young.[17]

The wearing of double hats, insider action, and conflicts of interest were endemic to purchasers of the seminary's industrial land and, more than entrepreneurial resourcefulness, represent part of the protective and exploitive action of the emerging industrial bourgeoisie. This larger class consciousness is clear in the action, for example, of John Redpath as factory employer, villa subdivision developer, Presbyterian official, and hospital, House of Industry, and temperance promoter. John Young's several caps as commission merchant, hydraulic-power entrepreneur, canal, rail, bridge, and telegraph promoter, Lachine Canal real-estate developer, commissioner of public works, harbour commissioner, and Board of Trade official represent facets of the behaviour of the industrial bourgeoisie at this stage of capitalist development, as do John Ostell's multiple functions as factory owner, church architect, land developer, and seminary agent.[18] George-Étienne Cartier's various services to the seminary and state represent an intellectual's contribution to the same pattern.

To the limit of their capital, other seminary employees and civil servants utilized their position to speculate on the subdivision. Seminary notary Édouard Lafleur bought a large lot from Ostell which he in turn subdivided and sold as three building lots three months later. The senior notary in the business office, Patrice Lacombe, bought three acres of land on Grand Trunk Street as did seminary surveyor H.M. Perrault. Perrault and Lacombe were allowed to waive an immediate down payment. Government engineer Robert Begly handled Public Works Department negotiations with the seminary and was himself a speculator who bought eight Saint-Gabriel lots at the inflated prices of the 1845 auction. Caught by the real-estate crisis and what he called his "imprudent" purchase, Begly – in the midst of delicate negotiations over the location of basins and bridges along the canal – was allowed by the seminary to retrocede his land without penalty.[19]

The limited returns from the auction of 1845 did not alter the seminary's legal obligation under the Ordinance of 1840 to sell the Saint-Gabriel domain before 1860, and in April 1853 it held a public sale, the first of twenty-four auctions between 1853 and 1866 (appendix 15). As in 1845 this auction attracted substantial capitalists and was dominated by manoeuvring of the Young-DeWitt-Ostell-Gould group around the Saint-Gabriel locks and by John Redpath's land assembly for his sugar refinery. Only two of twenty-four purchasers at the 1853 auction – a blacksmith and a shoemaker – can be identified as members of the popular classes and they made the only two purchases under £150.[20] After 1853 the number of buyers, their social class, and the size and cost of their land changed dramatically.

THE SAINT-GABRIEL DOMAIN: HOUSING-SITE SALES

By the mid-1850s the seminary's subdivision south of the canal was in the afternoon shadow of important new manufactures, like Redpath's seven-storey sugar refinery, and abutted the Grand Trunk yards. Given the emphasis on transportation in most Canadian railway histories, it is worth re-emphasizing the "industrial production" argument of Paul Craven and Tom Traves that railways, and the Grand Trunk in particular, "were Canada's first large-scale integrated industrial corporations."[21] The railway shops and canal-side factories had a broad range of industrial employees – labourers, foremen, ironworkers, rope makers, carpenters, mill workers, guards, paint-shop workers, bolt makers and copper-smiths – some of whom had the surplus to purchase cottage or duplex sites in nearby subdivisions like Saint-Gabriel, Pointe Saint-Charles (subdivided by the

Sisters of Hôtel-Dieu) or Sainte-Cunégonde (organized by Alexandre Delisle and hardware manufacturer William Workman).[22] The majority of workers presumably became boarders or tenants.

Buyers from the popular classes first appeared in number at the Saint-Gabriel auction of 1854; the 22 purchasers included 6 labourers, 5 carpenters, a dyer, and a bricklayer. In the twenty years 1854–74, Saint-Gabriel land was purchased by 439 individuals, the overwhelming majority of whom gave occupations that can be linked to nearby industrial work-sites. Ninety-eight purchasers – almost a quarter of the total – described themselves as "labourers"; 94 purchasers were unable to sign their deeds.[23] The Saint-Gabriel land account bulged with the income from these sales and formed an increasingly important percentage of seminary income. Between 1852 and 1859, £30,794 of land-sale income was diverted to various seminary projects and $227,324 was diverted during the period 1860–76.[24]

Through the 1850s sales continued to take the form of summer or autumn auctions in the downtown offices of Bernard and Company, auctioneers who had replaced Cuvillier and Sons. However, the changing social composition of the buyers and revised conditions of sale permitted to the seminary by the Act of 1859 led to new sales techniques. In 1861 the seminary again changed auctioneers and began holding its auctions in the schoolhouse on the subdivision site. But the land auction was apparently not an attractive sales environment for buyers unaccustomed to making major housing, financial, and family decisions under the auctioneer's hammer. The Act of 1859 allowed the seminary to dispose of the domain in private sales and soon afterwards the auction declined in importance; only four sales were made at the auctions of 1863 and 1866, the last held by the seminary (table 10). Private, on-site sales became the rule with the seminary's surveyor acting as salesman. He was paid to place pickets on available lots and to show potential buyers around the subdivision.[25]

In its auctions in 1853–4 the seminary demanded a 25 per cent down payment. This need for capital clearly discouraged buyers from the popular classes, and in 1856 the business office reduced down payments to 5 per cent with a £5 minimum payment. In 1857 it settled on a 10 per cent down payment, a percentage that remained in effect through the period. In certain cases the down payment was reduced or waived. Hyacinthe Allard, for example, was excused from a down payment on his $260 Saint-Henri Street lot but – unlike other purchasers – was obliged to construct a habitable dwelling within one year; if not constructed, his entire debt fell due. Carter Michael Hennessy was allowed to return with an additional $16 "next

TABLE 10
Private and Auction Sales on the Saint-Gabriel Domain, 1860–79

Year	Purchased in Private Sale	Purchased at Auction	Lots Sold	Total Sales ($)	Other
1860	9	–	11	4,868	includes lot sold to City for
1861	2	24	30	9,272	market ($1,200)
1862	8	14	28	6,784	
1863	29	3	40	16,590	includes four lots ($2,580) sold
1864	20	–	22	7,846	to Public Works for basin
1865	2	–	2	904	expansion
1866	7	1	9	5,420	
1867	3	–	3	1,150	
1868	6	–	9	17,350	includes $12,400 sale to wood
1869	4	–	5	2,940	merchant Michael Mullins
1870	14	–	21	10,280	
1871	28	–	31	14,358	
1872	34	–	38	27,600	includes $9,000 sale to wood
1873	52	–	64	32,975	merchant Isaac Plumb Wilson
1874	1	–	3	1,350	and Leonard Marler
1878	1	–	2	1,100	
1879	1	–	1	500	

Source: ANQM, Lafleur, and ASSM, unindexed, arm. 5, tir. 47, St. Gabriel, livre d'encan, no. 1, no. 2.
Note: The terms were 10% down; balance in equal payments over five years; interest (6%) from 1 October of year of purchase; auction purchasers to sign deeds within 24 hours; service charge of $10 for notarial, survey, and registry costs.

week," and milkman Alexander Henry was given one month to make his $60 down payment.[26]

To avoid any repetition of defaulted auction bids as in 1845 the seminary insisted after 1861 that deeds be signed within twenty-four hours of the auction. Private sales were formalized by an immediate down payment and deed signing. Laxity was further reduced by halving the mortgage term from ten to five years (1856). Finally, buyers from the popular classes made their down payments in cash, thus eliminating the problem of promissory notes or other potentially bad paper.

To exploit the housing potential of its land between the Grand Trunk shops and the factories bordering the canal, the seminary ordered new subdivision plans in 1857 and 1861. Here, along streets like Ropery, Manufacturers, and Grand Trunk, lots forty-five feet wide by one hundred feet deep were laid out. The seminary pushed the city to honour its agreement to pave Grand Trunk Street across the subdivision and the government to improve St Patrick Street along the canal. The seminary itself paid $1,425 to extend St Patrick and its sidewalks across the domain to Brewster Street. In 1860 it sold the city a market site for half price, in 1863 it ceded a school site, and a year later it allowed the first doctor in the subdivision, James B. Cowan, a six-month delay to make his down payment; in 1872 it sold a church site.[27]

Prices for Saint-Gabriel lots rose steadily. Between 1851 and 1853 John Redpath, John Young, and the Public Works Department paid between $0.02 and $0.04 a square foot for industrial lots along the canal. Housing lots sold from $0.07 to $0.09 a square foot in 1861 and between $0.09 and $0.14 in 1872. This progression in price can be traced on individual streets. Centre Street lots sold for $0.07 per square foot in 1861 and $0.10 in 1873: lots on Manufacturers Street rose from $0.06 or $0.08 in 1861 to $0.10 or $0.11 in 1872. Lots on newly opened streets like Brewster in the western part of the subdivision sold for $0.10 to $0.14 per square foot in 1872. Prices along St Patrick Street did not follow the general pattern dropping from $0.11 or $0.12 per square foot in 1862–3 to $0.07 or $0.08 in 1870–1 and then rising to $0.16 in 1878. The average price for a full lot with forty-five foot frontage rose from $232.00 in 1856 to $313.00 in 1861 and to $450.00 in 1873. Although most sales were for single lots, half-lot purchases, which gave the developer a higher return, were permitted. In 1861, for example, lots of twenty-two or twenty-three foot frontage sold for an average price of $237, whole lots for $313. Corner lots, with their attraction for shopkeepers, sold for premium prices. At Saint-Gabriel, the seminary – unlike its development on the Mountain domain – did not impose land-use covenants. In 1870, for example, steamboat engineer George Reid and machinist Bernard O'Brien put $80 down for a $840 double lot on Grand Trunk Street and built homes across the street from Alfred Savage's soap factory; Savage bought his two lots for $600 in 1866.[28]

Buyers of Saint-Gabriel house lots were good credit risks. Largely Irish and working for one of the surrounding industrial employers, they built single-family homes and duplexes and lived with their families, boarders, and tenants on the mortgaged property. Only three defaulters could be identified in seminary records. Labourer Patrick Clark bought a $295 lot on Roperty Street at the July 1857 auction. One of the rare purchasers permitted to make less than the $20 minimum down payment, Clark paid $12 down, returned in a week with another $4, and apparently made payments for several years. However, by 1867 he was living in Illinois and his property was repossessed for $216 outstanding principal and interest.[29]

Encircled by the canal, railway, lumber yards, and city waterworks,

Saint-Gabriel took on character after 1860 as a popular, mixed land-use and somewhat isolated suburb. The Montreal City Passenger Railway's tramway was extended along St Joseph Street (Notre-Dame) in 1872, but it was only in 1886 that the tramway was built south of the canal along Wellington to Centre Street. Although the western part of the subdivision remained undeveloped in 1880, the company's institutional structure was in place with a church, school, market, police station, fire-hall, and the Bull's Head Hotel. By 1879 the last vestige of the domain's earlier rural land use had disappeared with the demolition of the farm buildings to make way for a nail factory and expansion of the Redpath sugar refinery.[30]

THE MOUNTAIN DOMAIN

Subdivision of the Saint-Gabriel domain had been forced on the seminary and took shape in relation to industrial expansion along the Lachine Canal and the Grand Trunk shops in Pointe Saint-Charles. A mixed industrial/residential development, its manufacturing, milling, and warehouse sites sold because of proximity to water and rail facilities, and its small home sites sold because of their easy accessibility to industrial workplaces. Physically and symbolically, Saint-Gabriel was separated from the mountain, the river, and the city by the canal on one side, the railway on the other.

The seminary's subdivision of part of its Mountain domain took on a very different character as the response of a large land proprietor to bourgeois demand for suburban, single-family housing. On the slopes of Westmount the domain had been isolated from both urban and industrial activity. The Sulpicians had located their country estate and theological college here and worked to buttress the privacy of these institutional uses while shaping urban development in the area to their economic interest. Early in the century, seminary concessions of lots along the edge of the domain included covenants that limited land use to the construction of estates. The sixty-acre site along the east side of the domain for example, was ceded with the stipulation that no subdivision be undertaken, a condition that remained in effect from 1802 until 1835.[31]

Construction of road arteries was a major determinant in land subdivision. Enlargement of Dorchester Street along the front of the domain was carefully debated by the seminary's Consulting Council; the extension of Sherbrooke Street across the domain in 1847 was accompanied by construction of a high stone wall which to this day isolates the institution from secular traffic. Nor was the seminary opposed to the opening of the Boulevard, a road across the top of the domain which would open the mountain area to estate development. A condition of the right-of-way grant was that the Boulevard Company – in which the seminary invested – build an eight-foot fence along the entire northern length of the domain.[32] There were other early indications of seminary interest in marketing part of the domain. In 1846 the Consulting Council discussed possible construction of the governor's residence on the domain and in the same year it instructed its surveyor to draw up a subdivision plan for villa lots.[33]

David Hanna has effectively shown how the villa, terrace, and row-house subdivision of developers like John Redpath, Thomas Phillips, and Auld and McKenzie brought prestige housing to the western edge of the domain.[34] The area was further enhanced by continuing construction further up Mount Royal of the estates of the great capitalists: Hugh Allan, Judge John McCord, John Redpath, John J. Day, Samuel Monk, Henry Lyman and Alfred Savage. Development along Dorchester, Sainte-Catherine, and Sherbrooke was accompanied by road, water, and tramway services and the construction of suburban Episcopal, Presbyterian, Methodist, and Congregational churches.

Unlike the Saint-Gabriel domain which it was forced to sell, the seminary was able to await a favourable market at the Mountain. In the late 1850s Dorchester Street was opened into a major thorough-fare and urban expansion began skirting along the south side of the domain. In 1857 the Consulting Council decided to sell lots "in the part where there is less hope for a rise in value."[35] A new survey was ordered and special deeds printed to ensure a uniform, prestigious residential character. Access to the proposed subdivision was improved by the cession of land to the city for street enlargement at the corner of Guy and Dorchester and by the extension of Sainte-Catherine Street across the subdivision in 1862 (fig. 14).[36]

The tone of the subdivision was established in the first sales. In 1860 four large Guy Street lots were sold, all to merchants, as was an eleven-acre institutional site on the corner of Guy and Dorchester for construction of the Grey Nuns new mother house and orphanage.[37] In 1863–4 the seminary enhanced the prestige of the Sherbrooke Street entrance to the subdivision by selling estate lots to five prominent merchant and industrial families: merchant James Johnston, grocer Alexander McGibbon, miller A.W. Ogilvie, paper wholesaler and manufacturer Alexander Buntin, and refiner John Redpath's son Peter. Over the next twenty-five years, ninety-four individuals and two building societies bought lots; every purchaser but one had an English name.

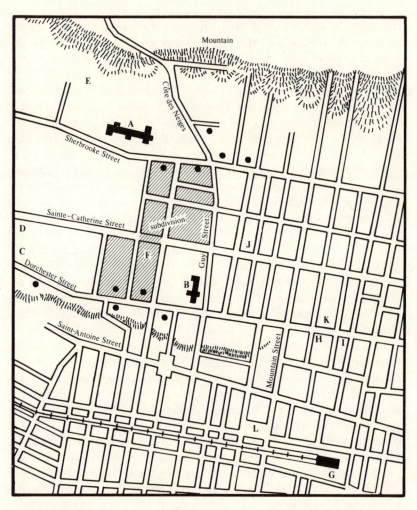

FIGURE 14
Subdivision of Mountain Domain, 1880

Legend
• estates
+↔ Grand Trunk Railway line
A Collège de Montréal and Grand
  Séminaire
B Grey Nuns convent and
  orphage
C Western Hospital
D public square
E domain farm

F 14 rental houses built by
  seminary
G Grand Trunk Railway station
H American Presbyterian Church
I Wesleyan Methodist Church
J Church of St James the Apostle
K Victoria Skating Rink
L Saint-Antoine market

Behind the Sherbrooke and Dorchester estates, smaller house lots were laid out between Guy and Atwater along streets named after disciples (St Matthew, St Luke, St Mark) and Sulpician superiors Baile and Quiblier. Lots varied in depth from 200 feet along Dorchester, Guy, and Sainte-Catherine to 60- and 75-foot lots on Quiblier and St Matthew. Frontages ranged upward from small 21-foot lots along Sainte-Catherine Street. Unlike Saint-Gabriel, the subdivision had lanes and was bounded by the open space of the Grey Nuns garden and the large estates along Dorchester, the seminary farm to the north, and a public square on Atwater.

The sales contract included seven clauses (reproduced in appendix 16) which ensured the homogeneous class and residential character of the subdivision. The seminary's covenant was very similar to those used by large developers in Boston. Purchasers had six months to fence their properties and to plant trees along their property fronts; a habitable house had to be completed within two years.[38] Deeds restricted land use to private residences, dictated fireproof roofs and the use of stone and brick building materials, and prohibited construction within twelve feet of the street. Factories, slaughterhouses, brick kilns, or other enterprises "detrimental to private residences" were forbidden. Quarrying for sand, clay, or stone – which the seminary itself practised on part of the domain – was prohibited. The covenant was perpetual and binding on subsequent owners.

The subdivision's reputation for exclusiveness, uniformity of land use, fire protection and pastoralism was further enhanced by improving tramway service. The Montreal City Passenger Railway opened its Sainte-Catherine line to Mountain Street in 1864. This was extended first to Guy and then in 1872 it crossed the subdivision to Greene Avenue permitting Mountain residents to travel along Sainte-Catherine and either Bleury or St Lawrence into the central business district.[39]

These amenities attracted purchasers from a cross-section of bourgeois occupations, or what Sam B. Warner Jr describes as upper middle class and central middle class occupations.[40] Thirty-four purchasers described themselves as merchants and eight others as wood merchants, grocers, or tailors (table 11). These general occupational terms – which pose added difficulties since they were reported in French by the notary preparing the deeds – covered a variety of exchange functions and sometimes included industrial production. John Foulds had his fancy goods shop on St Paul Street and bought a large 353 by 80 foot lot ($12,726) on St Matthew, commission merchant Nelson Davis had his office on Common Street and bought a 60 by 104 foot lot ($1,000) on St Mark. Like Davis and Foulds,

George Kemp worked in the old city. He had his gentleman's furnishings store on Notre-Dame Street and bought ($5,240) the relatively small but prestigious corner lot at Sherbrooke and Guy. John McGauvran described himself as a wood merchant but also owned an important saw and planing mill at the Saint-Gabriel locks. He was one of the rare heads of families who did not travel towards the city. From the domain he and most of the other industrial producers could travel down the Guy or Atwater hill to the canal.[41] The important contingent of clerks (thirteen), accountants (two), and bookkeeper probably took the tramway to downtown offices. Intellectuals and successful artisans were concentrated among the purchasers of lower-priced domain lots. Many of them benefited from transportation along Sainte-Catherine to the area of McGill University and central shops or offices; dentist James Alfred Bazin, for example, had his office on Beaver Hall terrace.[42]

Buyers in the subdivision needed a significant capital especially since purchase of the lot theoretically obliged house construction within two years. Although the seminary waived a down payment in eight instances over the period 1859–78, most buyers paid 20 to 30 per cent down, a percentage significantly lower than in Boston. First mortgages at the Mountain were for 70 to 80 per cent of property value and the situation is even more striking at Saint-Gabriel where the seminary normally took 10 per cent down payments and 90 per cent first mortgages. Warner gives 30 to 40 per cent of property value as the limit of first mortgages in Boston.[43]

With the exception of three buyers at the Mountain who paid off at the signing, purchasers took 6 per cent five-year, or occasionally four- or ten-year mortgages. The mortgage was repaid by a blended payment plan in which interest and principal were paid in equal annual instalments over the term of the loan. The term, blended-payment method, and interest rates of seminary mortgages differ significantly from Hamilton examples. Hamilton mortgages studied by Doucet and Weaver were for a shorter period (3.6 years on average) and did not offer a blended-payment method; holders of a mortgage from Hamilton realtors, Moore and Davis, paid the entire principal at the end of the mortgage term.[44] Doucet and Weaver also suggest that a much smaller percentage (43 per cent) of vacant Hamilton lots were mortgaged at the time of sale. Even more significant are differences in Montreal and Hamilton mortgage rates. At both Saint-Gabriel and the Mountain, interest rates remained at 6 per cent from 1853 to at least 1880 even though farm mortgages given by the seminary in the area of Saint-Jean, Quebec, rose to 8 per cent in 1874.[45] Rates in Hamilton were more unstable ranging from al-

TABLE 11

Home-Site Prices by Occupation: Mountain Subdivision, 1859–78

Occupation Reported on Deed	Number of Contracts	Average Price ($)
Merchant/hotelkeeper[1]	1	19,030
Publisher	1	5,832
Manufacturer	7	5,396
Merchant grocer	2	4,289
Merchant	34	4,060
Hotelkeeper	1	3,910
Insurance agent	1	3,048
Secretary of corn exchange	1	2,546
Bookkeeper	1	2,546
Merchant tailor	1	2,481
Architect	1	2,400
Dentist	1	2,280
Lumber merchant	5	2,273
Teacher	1	2,480
Professor of philosophy	1	2,254
Gentleman	4	1,717
Accountant[2]	3	1,046
Master shoemaker	1	1,004
Newspaper editor	1	971
Merchant clerk	3	851
Clerk	10	842
Machinist	1	680
Ex-colonel	1	629
Artist	1	600
Law student	1	600
Civil engineer	2	588
Plumber	1	576
Cambist	1	504

Note: In purchases by wife or widow, profession of husband is given on deed. The French terms used for these occupations are: merchant/hotelkeeper – marchand/hôtelier; manufacturer – fabricant, facteur; merchant grocer – marchand épicier; merchant – marchand, commerçant; merchant tailor – marchand tailleur; lumber merchant – commerçant de bois; master shoemaker – maître cordonnier; merchant clerk – commis marchand; clerk – commis; machinist – machiniste; cambist – agent de change. In addition, purchases by contractors (5) [$1,548; 3,840; 62,280; 1,500; 1,500], Montreal Building Society (3) [2,743; 5,681; 14,000], and Montreal Investment and Building Company (1) [1,600] not included since several were multi-lot purchases for subdivision or commercial housebuilding.

1 Maurice Cuvillier and Henry Hogan jointly bought "Aven Royale" in 1871.

2 Includes wife of George Marler, accountant for the seminary.

most 12 per cent in the early 1860s – a rate double that paid in Montreal – to an average of 7.5 per cent in the 1870s. As at Saint-Gabriel, the home-site buyer on the Mountain subdivision was a good credit risk. Aside from one buyer who was allowed to exchange his land for another lot, no defaults or retrocessions are evident from seminary accounts.

Sales at the Mountain were particularly strong from 1864 to 1871. After early sales along the Dorchester, Guy, and Sherbrooke perimeters, the seminary began selling Sainte-Catherine Street lots in 1868. In the same year it opened up St Matthew and St Mark streets and in 1871–2 St Luke, Fort, and Quiblier streets. Most early purchasers paid around $0.14 a square foot for Dorchester and Sherbrooke estate lots. Merchant tailor Stephen Mathews paid $0.15 a square foot (1865) for his 17,160 square-foot lot at the corner of Dorchester and Forts and Peter Redpath $0.14 a square foot (1863) for 56,000 square feet on Sherbrooke Street. The corner of Sherbrooke and Côte-des-Neiges was a choice site with lots selling for $0.19 a square foot in 1864 – substantially more than their Sherbrooke Street neighbours – and $0.31 in 1866.[46]

Prices on smaller lots inside the subdivision settled around $0.20 a square foot. In July 1864 dentist James Bazin paid $0.18 a square foot for a lot with a ninety-six foot frontage on St Matthew Street. Around the corner on Sainte-Catherine Street, bookkeeper David McFarlane paid $0.20 a square foot. Seven years later gentleman John Taylor paid $0.20 a square foot for his Sainte-Catherine Street lot and merchant John Binmore $0.19 for a lot on newly opened St Luke Street.[47]

After 1871 land prices on the domain rose sharply and sales dropped. Lots on Fort Street for example, sold for $0.13 and $0.20 a square foot in 1871, $0.28 in 1872, and $0.42 in 1874. It was in this period that building contractors began buying domain lots. Of twelve lots purchased between 1874 and 1880, five were bought by contractors or building societies. The Montreal Building Society paid $0.42 a square foot in 1874 and $0.54 in 1878 for adjoining lots on St Mark Street. Contractors Olivier DeGuise and Eugène Malo paid $0.50 a square foot for a large Sainte-Catherine Street lot in 1874. The seminary itself began constructing houses in 1875 and by the end of the decade was renting out fourteen single-family homes in the subdivision.[48]

Seminary activity as a land developer must be assessed as part of larger changes in the ground rules of class relations. In 1816 the seminary had gone to the courts to protect its seigneurial monopoly from an industrial miller at Lachine; its domains served as food, firewood, storage, and mission reserves. Later in the century, the two Montreal-area domains were being carved into industrial and residential subdivisions. The seminary had been forced to abandon much of its expropriation of surplus in feudal forms in return for new capitalist revenues. At Saint-Gabriel, hydraulic power, rail and canal transport, the changing disposition of capital, new worksites and work organization, and the evolving function of the state thrust the domain farm into the path of industrial expansion. On the Mountain, the very privacy and pastoral qualities that had led the Sulpicians to locate their country estate on their mission site attracted merchants, manufacturers, intellectuals, and members of expanding professions like managers, civil engineers, accountants, and dentists.

The seminary alienated domain land in freehold tenure, using the selling techniques of the land auction and salesmen; it lent money at legal interest and functioned as a modern mortgage institution. Its land sales were beamed at specific social classes which were increasingly segregated in terms of housing space. At Saint-Gabriel it did not impose land use, promoting rather the development of a mixed subdivision where housing for the popular classes was built alongside the factories, mills, and rail shops. This not only provided a handy industrial labour pool but proprietorship – with its accompanying mortgage debt and home owner ideology – was an important tool for *embourgeoisement* and class discipline. Put another way, the Saint-Gabriel home buyer was probably as faithful in his work performance as in his mortgage payments. Indeed, the major headaches in the seminary's Saint-Gabriel land business came from high-rolling industrial land developers who overestimated canal expansion and who were forced to default on their auction purchases.

On the Mountain, changing forms of business, family, and social organization led the seminary to structure a very different community. New forms of production and commercial activity, the tramway, waterworks, and a bourgeois ideology that sought suburban refuge brought a new single-family home clientele to the domain doorstep. Here the seminary did use covenants to reinforce the subdivisions' class and ethnic homogeneity; the greystone community was close to church, university, and countryside and isolated from industrial smoke and the popular classes.

CHAPTER SEVEN

Class Legitimation

Peace has been restored between the contending parties, by the intercession of a number of gentlemen deputed for that purpose, and the exertions of the very Reverend Sulpician Patrick Phelan, who, on Wednesday last addressed about 2,000 of the laborers after mass, and succeeded in inducing them to come to a reconciliation. A large number of guns were given up, and a subscription made by the laborers on behalf of those who had suffered during the riots ...   Montreal *Transcript*, 11 March 1843[1]

Living in such a place [Nazareth] and having so little means of acquiring wealth they necessarily were poor; not that degrading poverty which is fruit of laziness of dissipation, but that moderate ease which honest labour and a wise conduct will always afford.   Sulpician sermon, 1871[2]

Class struggle was an inherent part of the transition to the industrial stage of capitalism. Although feudal society was far from harmonious, nineteenth-century Montreal was marked by intense social division. Observers with as diverse political interpretations as H. Clare Pentland, Bryan Palmer, Margaret Heap, Peter DeLottinville, Gérard Filteau, George Rudé, Elinor Senior, Jack Little, and Thomas Chapais have presented a litany of labour struggle, peasant protest, cholera, religious, ethnic, and election riots, taxpayer revolts, church, school, convent, and mill desecrations, charivaris, and other individual or group political "crimes."[3]

On the work site, labour's resistance was shaped by changes in the form and place of work and by its declining ownership of the means of production. Labour militancy in Montreal has been well documented in the leather industry, construction, and transportation, sectors characterized by wage labour, capital accumulation, and particularly sharp changes in social relations. Along the St Lawrence canal system, for example, protest and strikes by Irish navvies at Lachine and other construction sites were episodic through the period 1822–77; the bloodiest confrontation occurred at Beauharnois (1843) where some twenty strikers were killed when troops intervened.

Popular resistance was never restricted simply to the work site as the rebellions of 1837–8 demonstrated. Preliminary studies of court records for the Montreal district show widespread political crime and suggest that the role of women in civil disturbances has been underestimated.[4] Boarding houses and taverns – of which Joe Beef's dockside tavern was the most famous – were important centres of resistance. Nor was disorder just an urban phenomenon. Nineteen of the some forty-five instances of popular resistance reported in the Montreal *Gazette*, 1821–64, occurred outside Montreal. George Rudé has shown that the south shore rebels of 1838 were locals and were "all men of settled residence and occupation and habitants ... About half of them were tenant farmers with a sprinkling of farm-workers ... others were innkeepers, blacksmiths, joiners, bakers, carriage-makers, with a smaller number of bailiffs, notaries, clerks, doctors, and merchants."[5] This rural independence from civil and religious authority had been a political reality faced by bishops and intendants in New France and its potential force was reconfirmed in the period 1848–50 with the burning of schoolhouses and threats against local priests, tax-collectors, and schoolmasters. School riots occurred on the seminary's seigneury at Sainte-Scholastique, while further up the Ottawa River on the Petite Nation seigneury the presbytery and nun's residence were attacked in protest against the replacement of the village teacher by nuns (1867).[6] In other communities, parishioners simply refused to support the church: "the hapless priest left Sherbrooke disgraced, broken in health, and £200 in debt to the British American Land Company for the fifty acres he had bought near his church."[7] We have already noted the general disregard on the Two Mountains seigneury for seigneurial privileges like wood-cutting rights and the fact that before 1840 there was massive resistance across the three seigneuries to *lods et ventes* collections. Indians at the Two Mountains mission, furious over their treatment by the Sulpicians, were apparently responsible for razing the mission church in 1877.

The Montreal bourgeoisie responded vigorously to the deepening inequality, poverty, and popular resistance that accompanied the industrial mode of production. And it was not just great capitalists like Redpath, Allan, or the Molsons who devoted energy outside their refineries, shipyards, manufactures, and breweries to check the temperance, religious, and benevolent activities of the popular classes.

These "philanthropic" efforts were aimed at throttling popular independence and in some cases (such as Hugh Allan's insurance schemes) served to collect capital. Peter DeLottinville has shown how Joe Beef's tavern and the popular culture it represented were undermined by the Young Men's Christian Association, the Law and Order League, the Montreal Sailors Institute, and the Knights of Labor.[8] Persistent bourgeois interest in the magistracy and militia testify to the usefulness of state force in controlling physical manifestations of popular resistance. And of course British troops were frequently used on the Montreal front. The move of the capital to Ottawa effectively isolated a vulnerable institution from popular pressure. To deflect Montreal's deepening social distress, hospitals, refuges, and soup kitchens were supported by bourgeois women. Agencies like the Grey Nuns were encouraged to expand their facility to deal with the growing number of unwanted Catholic births while doctors used maternity hospitals, new medical technology, and professionalization to distance midwives, the home, the family, and other popular support systems from birthing.[9]

New structures were also imposed on the countryside, where disciplinary forces such as judges, sheriffs, magistrates, and municipal councils were handicapped by the lack of bureaucratic structures. In 1840 Lower Canada had no general education system, no municipal code, and few district courthouses and jails. Until the 1850s circuit judges imposed the law in rural areas, and in the Eastern Townships it was unclear whether British or French civil law applied. The revised legal code, registry offices, libraries, and judicial and municipal institutions were introduced in tandem with the expansion of the freehold tenure property system and the development of road, canal, and rail grids. This forcing of structures on the countryside is also evident in the application of universal and centralized education systems.

How does the seminary fit into this class conflict? In pre-industrial Montreal the seminary enjoyed social and physical separateness. A Sulpician did serve as parish priest, another distributed alms to the urban flotsam, and others directed the Indian mission. As well, the seminary – through its patron and confessing function with the major Montreal female religious orders – had contact with the important social institutions. However, despite their original mandate, it was not training Canadian priests and its educational function was largely limited to its college for Catholic and male bourgeois. Its aloofness disappeared in the first decades of the nineteenth century. The seminary's increasing attentiveness to the industrial bourgeoisie, conditions attached to its corporate status and its right to collect capitalist revenues, and the increasing threat to its powers from episcopal clergy forced it to a new social activism.

The Sulpicians had only to look over their garden wall for dramatic evidence of distress in industrializing Montreal. The city was expanding rapidly, its population growing 56 per cent in the years 1851–61 and another 19 per cent in the following ten years; by 1871, 42 per cent of Montreal's work force was female and 25 per cent of boys aged eleven to fifteen were in the labour force. Poverty and vagrancy were the natural state for large numbers of Montrealers. In 1879 a single Irish hospice provided temporary lodging for 287 unemployed servants along with 10,497 evening meals and 14,355 "beds and breakfasts" for children and elderly vagrants.[10] Inadequate housing, sanitation, and water facilities encouraged fire, cholera, and typhoid. Two thousand east-end houses burned in the fire of 1852. In 1847 a nun who visited the immigrant sheds on the Saint-Gabriel domain was shocked to find 1,500 cholera victims, two to a bed, "suffering and abandoned." A year later 650 immigrants were lodged in the sheds; 332 died before being moved to alternate shelter. Even the impecunious dead caused problems. In the 1830s one-third of adults were buried without religious ceremony since they lacked the £1 to £2 cost of a coffin, transportation, and funeral mass.[11]

The seminary played an important ideological and institutional role in the legitimation of the social structures emerging in industrial Montreal. Its insistence on authority, isolation, and work discipline made it a useful vehicle by which the bourgeoisie could combat the vice, laziness, and rebelliousness perceived among the Catholic popular classes. The seminary had always had responsibility for Montreal's Irish, and in 1843 Sulpician Patrick Phelan – who had performed the same role in 1837 – was a central factor in defusing a Lachine Canal riot. Accompanied by St Patrick's Society members, Phelan marched to Lachine where he held a special mass attended by 2,000. At the mass, a collection for those injured in the riots was made, and Phelan enrolled ninety men in the Irish temperance society.[12]

The Sulpicians were far from amateurs in the techniques of institutionalization. In addition to their cumulative experience as aristocrats, priests, accountants, soldiers, seigneurs, schoolmasters, and wardens, they were heirs of a European religious-community tradition that – hundreds of years before nineteenth-century professionals began experimenting with prisons, asylums, and schools – had grappled with the relationship of isolation, work, prayer, discipline, and communal living. The Sulpician sense of totality, their instinct for a controlled and isolated environment, and their per-

ception of the integration of physical, spiritual, and psychological
needs gave form to the institutions they spawned, financed, and
directed. They knew how to separate and enclose, organize and
discipline, subdue and divide, order and chastise; the bell, the cell,
the wall, the gate, the desk, the refectory, and the confessional gave
an encompassing framework within which stomachs could be filled,
lessons learned, and resistance purged. The seminary's institutional
contribution took several forms. It acted as an intermediary expro-
priating capitalist and seigneurial revenues and financing land purchases for social institutions. It supervised other religious communities
directly and had special financial, advisory, and confessional relationships with lay groups performing diverse institutional functions.
As well, its pulpits, missions, schools, and newspaper were useful
missives for the diffusion of its social message.

IDEOLOGY

Two centuries of experience in directing two major pre-industrial
institutions – the parish and the seigneury – bequeathed the seminary a clear understanding of hierarchy and authority, useful qualities in nineteenth-century Montreal. In 1831 the superior reported
to Paris that

The Superior presides over everything which is done in the parish. He has
always had clear title to the parish charge. If there is an important marriage,
he blesses it, if there is a glittering procession or an important ceremony,
he announces and presides over it. The ex-officio parish priest does nothing
without ... a formal order from the Superior. The ex-officio parish priest
is only a simple priest that the Superior names each year.[13]

When a temperance society asked for the right to name its own
chaplain, the seminary refused with a notation in the minutes that
it was "contrary to the principle of authority and good administration."[14] It showed the same authoritarianism with candidates for the
priesthood:

in each of these establishments we begin by choosing from among those
destined for an ecclesiastical career those whom talent, character or piety
offer the greatest guarantee of becoming good teachers and we send the
rest directly to the Seminary. In that, we never consult their wishes, we order
them and they obey. For a long time – maybe from the very beginning –
this has been the discipline administered in Canada.[15]

This respect for authority took tangible political form. For the coronation of Queen Victoria in August 1837, the seminary rang the bells of Notre-Dame; the cathedral bells of the bishop remained silent. A year later with rebellion still in the air, the seminary invited the band of the 71st Regiment to provide music in the seminary garden for the Grand Rural Festival of the Montreal Horticultural Society. After the concert the band's commanding officer accompanied the superior for a visit to the Congregation of Notre Dame convent after which he was invited to dine with the priests at the seminary. In 1871 the seminary contributed $200 for construction of a statue of Queen Victoria.[16]

Work, sacrifice, and the pain of life as represented by circumcision, flagellation, or the nails of the cross were recurrent themes in Sulpician sermons. Manual labour was always described as a central feature of daily life, particularly for the institutionalized. The blind and poor residents of the Nazareth Asylum, for example, were encouraged to knit, sew, string pearls, and make baskets.[17] For their work model Sulpicians frequently used the example of the holy family. Superior Colin urged a mixed gathering of nuns, female students, and reformatory inmates to submit themselves to "humiliation" since Jesus sacrificed himself "for work, tough incessant work, even vile depending on the situation, work urgently ordered by the necessity to earn for himself his daily bread."[18] Every member of the family unit was urged to imitate the work, dress, and eating habits of Jesus, Mary, and Joseph:

St. Joseph, being a carpenter, spent his days in labouring for the support of Jesus and Mary. The Blessed Virgin attended the household duties of a mother, devoted her care and attention upon the infant savior and our Lord. He helped as far as his strength would allow, both the Blessed Virgin and St. Joseph. The village where they lived was separated from all centres of commerce and wealth, enclosed by ranges of little mountains and inhabited in great part by shepherds whose life was necessarily poor and simple; it was proverbial among the Jews that no good could come out of Nazareth. Living in such a place and having so little means of acquiring wealth they necessarily were poor; not that degrading poverty which is fruit of laziness or dissipation, but that moderate ease which honest labour and a wise conduct will always afford. Their food was most frugal ... their clothing was good and neat, but most plain and simple ... Mothers, why not imitate the Blessed Virgin? Why not think constantly ... Why not think of him and love him – it will not prevent you from working. You sweep the floor, you cook the dinner, you mend your children's clothes, you keep things in good order in the house. Why not do all this in a spirit of love of God. All those actions the Blessed Virgin performed. They were very ordinary actions but they were sanctified by the spirit of love and charity which animated the Blessed Virgin.[19]

Discipline and surveillance were other characteristics of a Sulpician regime. At their theological college it was the director himself who, lantern in hand, opened students' doors every day before 5:00 A.M. On Wednesdays each student met individually with the teaching staff for a broad-ranging fifteen-minute examination.[20] Seminary officials showed a particular obsession with the separation of the sexes, age groups, social classes, and even individual students. Detailed rule books were written and periodically revised for college and seminary students and even the college porter; instructions for the prudent operation of the infirmary at the Grand Séminaire covered twenty-one pages. Students were not allowed to enter the room of another student or the infirmary without permission from the superior. If admitted to the infirmary, the aspirant priest was to address only the male nurses – never the servants. Among themselves, students were to speak an absolute minimum and were to avoid touching or any other physical contact. They could be expelled for supporting "bad doctrine" or reading a forbidden book. The seminary porter delivered all student mail to the school director, issued tickets to students who left the grounds, and guarded the seminary entrance: "his vigilance on this point must be such that no one can enter or leave the house without having recourse to his service."[21]

Sulpician moral attitudes became more puritanical as the century progressed. In 1850 an important Sulpician from France reported that the college had too many doors, too much tobacco, and too many female servants. Rules for seminary outings were tightened in 1862 with students henceforth forbidden to attend the marriages of their brothers and sisters. Four years later the seminary's executive committee decided that Sulpicians – the Superior excepted – would no longer attend public concerts.[22]

Taken in their social context this censorship, control, and suspicion of popular culture, the family, and sex confirm Christopher Hill's emphasis on a changing work ethic preached by both Protestants and Catholics.[23] Perceiving the social implications of the industrial mode of production, seminary officials proposed far-reaching antidotes. Eustache Picard, an active Sulpician community worker, supported a lottery to subsidize a home for country girls which would protect their "innocence" and provide a work site where used clothing could be resewn into communion dresses for the poor. The refuge would also enable rural priests to exercise some control over female emigration to Montreal; girls would only be admitted to the refuge if they had a letter of recommendation from their parish priest.[24]

The seminary increasingly focused on the responsibility of each individual for his own economic condition, an accountability that extended to providing for one's own funeral. In 1851 the seminary sponsored a burial society which provided coffins, transportation, and a funeral mass for the popular classes. By 1863 the Union des Prières had 10,000 members, each contributing between thirty and sixty cents a year. With Sulpicians managing the society and keeping its books, the union soon accumulated an important capital which the seminary proposed to invest in low-cost housing, a refuge, or an asylum.[25]

Seminary paternalism is particularly clear in its relations with Indians and nuns. Although Indians at the Two Mountains mission contested Sulpician tutelage throughout the century, the seminary continued to treat them as children, granting them land "if they are well-behaved" and restricting their marriage and property rights.[26] Indians, the seminary explained in an 1876 pamphlet, "like racing, open fields and above all an easy existence." As a result, "for the purpose of accustoming the Indians to work, the seminary gave them certain work ... for which they were amply paid."[27]

The seminary always had special powers as confessors and financial supervisors of Montreal's senior female religious communities: the Grey Nuns, the Sisters of Hôtel-Dieu, and the Congregation of Notre Dame. Sulpician advisers approved all important business decisions by the three convents, managed their properties in France and their investments in Canada, subsidized their mission and hospital work, offered dowries for poor aspirants to the Congregation of Notre Dame, signed the notarized vows of novices in the Hôtel-Dieu convent, and maintained the carriages and horses of the teaching nuns.[28]

This influence assumed new significance with the rapid growth of female religious communities and their expanding role in Montreal's educational and social institutions. The proportion of nuns to single lay women jumped from 1.4 per cent in 1851 to 6.1 per cent in 1901; the most important teaching order in Montreal, the Congregation of Notre Dame, grew from 80 women in 1830 to 440 in 1870.[29] The seminary reinforced the legitimacy of this growing female profession, replacing lay teachers with nuns and praising the virtues of the convent. Sulpician Étienne-Michel Faillon was the best-known panegyrist, drawing up travel regulations for nuns and encouraging the cult of the Virgin. In his biographies of convent founders Marie d'Youville and Marguerite Bourgeoys and recluse Jeanne Le Ber, Faillon developed the nun as a model of female behaviour glorifying her submission, work habits, sacrifice, and asexuality. "Christian heroine" Le Ber, for example, was exemplary as a child, never speaking in the street nor entering strange houses. Retiring to the Congregation of Notre Dame convent she ate in her cell and was only visited by her father and Sulpician confessor.[30]

Propagation of Sulpician ideology was facilitated by the seminary's power over various lay organizations. It retained important constitutional privileges in many Roman Catholic social institutions in Montreal. St Brigitte's Refuge, a home for unemployed servants, the aged, and vagrants, for example, always had a Sulpician as director and its governing board could not have a quorum without the director's presence. The seminary had similar power at St Patrick's Orphan Asylum where the director, usually a Sulpician, was always named by the superior.[31] The Sulpicians subsidized, provided meeting sites, offered opening prayers, or sat on the boards of school commissions (Montreal Catholic School Commission), prayer groups (L'Adoration nocturne), women's charitable organizations (Ladies of Charity), national societies (Saint-Jean-Baptiste Society) and professional associations of lay teachers and doctors. They printed – at a cost of $6,034 – a history of Canada and published a weekly newspaper, *L'Écho du cabinet de lecture paroissial*. Taken cumulatively, a weekly all-night prayer vigil for women, the annual retreat for men, the provision of billiard rooms for youth in church halls, the organization of an annual orphans' picnic, the formation of the rules of a maternity hospital, the growing practice of home visits to the poor, and the introduction of a temperance band into a national festival represent a significant attack on popular culture. Seminary antennas were particularly sensitive to political elements that might encourage popular resistance. A stormy Institut canadien meeting in April 1858 apparently ended with Médéric Lanctot (leader of the Grande Association de protection des ouvriers du Canada in 1867) and Joseph Doutre smashing chairs and windows. The tumultuous meeting was held in a library sponsored by the seminary, and Sulpician officials quickly received written reports of damages, of the religiosity of the participants, and the future of the Institut canadien.[32]

FINANCING SOCIAL INSTITUTIONS

Historians generally locate the origins of specialized institutions in the mid-nineteenth century, particularly those that were organized to shape social behaviour. While some link this growth to humanitarian and reform impulses, Marxist historians explain institutionalization in terms of the social conflict accompanying the transition to industrial capitalism. It is the dynamic of this transition in Montreal that best explains Sulpician behaviour.[33]

The observer of early nineteenth-century Montreal is struck by the paucity and weakness of the institutional structure. Municipal government, for example, had hardly been constituted under the city's first charter (1833) when civil unrest led to its suspension until 1843. The local parish structure represented another weakness as, over several decades, the seminary fended off the bishop's attempts to divide the parish. Sulpician insistence on an undivided parish under its control left Montreal with increasingly inadequate parish facilities; the expanding Irish community, for example, had only one Irish priest and temporary church quarters until 1847. The seminary itself was grossly understaffed. Charged with the administration of three seigneuries, the parish of Montreal, an Indian mission, and a college, the chaplaincy of several convents, and the direction of expanding Catholic social services, the seminary in 1840 had only twenty priests, two of whom were over seventy years of age. Four of their number died in the cholera crisis in 1847–8, and a fifth fell to his death from a church under construction.[34] And although increasingly specialized in particular areas of education, Indian administration, accounting, or welfare work, individual Sulpicians always devoted much of their day to prayer, study, and other communal activities. Community service was generally limited to the hours 10:00 to 11:00 A.M and 3:30 to 6:00 P.M.

Support of the parish church of Montreal had been a seminary responsibility since the seventeenth century. Sulpicians had donated land for construction of Notre-Dame Church, blessed the cornerstone (1672), largely paid for its construction, and later added a chapel. In addition to naming the parish priest, the seminary supervised the accounts of the *fabrique*. All financial decisions were made by the church assembly, meetings of which were chaired by the superior. Until 1817 the chief warden kept *fabrique* accounts. The bankruptcy of this official and discovery that significant church funds had disappeared prompted a tighter accounting system and the naming of the seminary business manager as treasurer of the *fabrique*.[35]

The *fabrique*'s financial dependence on the seminary increased dramatically in the 1820s and the parish church remained in a debtor relationship to the seminary at least until the 1880s. Sharp growth of Montreal's Catholic population rendered Notre-Dame Church inadequate and forced church fathers to consider dismembering the parish, establishing "branch" churches, or building an enlarged central church. Given the seminary's power in parish affairs and its attachment to the principle of a single parish church, the decision to construct a new 4,968-seat Notre-Dame was not surprising. Despite efforts to cut costs by having habitants haul stone as part of their seigneurial obligations and an insistence that parishioners bear the major financial burden, construction costs of £55,700 placed the *fabrique* heavily in debt.[36] The seminary advanced £15,473 in interest-free loans to the *fabrique* between 1823 and 1840 and in 1835 borrowed an additional £9,140 in its own name from the Sisters of Hôtel-Dieu to pay off eight important *fabrique* creditors, including John Redpath and Peter McGill.[37] In 1842 the *fabrique*'s debt to the seminary was £36,953. Although some repayments were made, the *fabrique* increased its debt to the seminary with periodic loans, particularly for the interior decoration of Notre-Dame in the years 1870–77. In 1878 churchwardens appeared before the seminary's notaries to recognize and to consolidate their $160,749 interest-free debt and their loan of $36,560 at 5 per cent interest.[38]

Heavy immigration, clerical pressure for dismemberment of the parish, and demands for ethnic and suburban church facilities led to seminary sponsorship of St Patrick's. Land and construction of Montreal's first Irish church cost £29,211.[39] Industrialization along the Lachine Canal and growth of a largely Irish and popular suburb led to construction in 1854 of a second Irish church, St Anne's. The east-end site of the burnt cathedral was purchased by the seminary and a new Saint-Jacques Church was built (1854–6) and then rebuilt after a second fire. St Joseph's, a west-end church, was built (1860–3) with a seminary subsidy of £6,477 and in 1863 the seminary paid the Bishop £6,314 for the north-end Saint-Louis-de-France Church. Chapels in Saint-Henri and in the St Lawrence suburb (Notre-Dame-des-Anges) were enlarged and village churches constructed at Notre-Dame-de-Grâce and Côte-des-Neiges. In addition to church buildings, the seminary invested heavily in the purchase of church sites or land for other pious purposes. In the seven-year period 1859–66 the seminary bought twelve sites for school, church, or presbytery construction at a total cost of $52,116.[40]

The seminary strongly defended the property rights that accompanied its investment in churches. At Notre-Dame-de-Grâce it sent its notary to protest against a priest who usurped its powers, accusing him of changing church ornaments, disrupting its garden, inciting the parishioners to opposition, and collecting monies owed the seminary; the priest's continued occupation of the church was, in the seminary's view, "totally unjust, illegal, and contrary to their property rights."[41]

The seminary contribution to churches was not limited to major financial injections. Ongoing support was provided by paying building insurance and taxes, by buying church ornaments, or by subscribing to church improvement projects such as bells. The seminary's most important yearly support came in the form of firewood. This major contribution to schools and churches involved extensive cutting and hauling contracts with local suppliers, and the maintenance of extensive woodlots, particularly at the Sault-au-Récollet domain.[42]

Although the training of parish clergy was the primary social function of the Séminaire de Saint-Sulpice in France, the seminary of Montreal did not establish a Grand Séminaire during its first 177 years in Canada.[43] It was only in the 1830s that the need for parish clergy in the Montreal area forced the establishment of a theological college. With its financial security assured by the Ordinance of 1840, the seminary responded positively to Bishop Bourget's request and in November 1840 a concordat was signed. In addition to educating the prospective priest entirely by Sulpician rules and a perpetual right to name the director, the seminary insisted that students or their home dioceses assume the full cost of fees and lodging.[44]

With its Counter-Reformation roots and its founder's insistence that priesthood candidates experience "the mortification of all the roots of vice which are in us" and a "loathing for the vulgar things of this earth," the seminary was well equipped to train a moral, sober, and disciplined Quebec clergy.[45] In the Sulpician training, theological students were isolated from their families and peers, were subjected to an all-encompassing and authoritarian institutional regime, and received rigorous instruction particularly in morals, ritual, and theology. Instruction was given by Sulpician teachers rather than university theologians and Grand Séminaire rules – drawn up by Superior Quiblier in 1840 – emphasized prayer, conscience, weekly confession, and monthly meetings with the superior or director to examine the student's "interior."[46]

As site for the Grand Séminaire, the Mountain domain was chosen over urban locations at the Collège de Montréal, at the old cathedral site, or at the seminary itself. In 1854 the Sulpician general assembly approved architect Ostell's plans and, between 1855 and 1864, $213,341 was spent constructing the four-storey, 130-room building. The Grand Séminaire had an infirmary, library, parlour, park, and central staircase modelled on Sulpician seminaries in France. In the 1860s and 1870s an additional $91,579 was invested in construction of a new 80-room wing, private chapel, hot-water heating system, and crypt. Between 1840 and 1940, 7,529 priests were trained at the Grand Séminaire.[47]

The same direct institutional control was exercised at the Collège de Montréal. Founded by a Sulpician parish priest in 1767, the college moved into its new building in 1806 and took form as a major force in the selection of prospective priests and in the education of Montreal's male élite. By 1835 at least one hundred college graduates had become priests; by 1899 it had produced six archbishops, twenty-one bishops, seventeen founders of classical colleges, thirty-eight judges, thirty-five members of parliament, thirty members of the Quebec Legislative Assembly, and four Montreal mayors.[48]

Modelled on the French *petit séminaire*, the Collège de Montréal dispensed a classical curriculum in rhetoric, methods, philosophy, syntax, and literature. Traditional Sulpician virtues of authority, isolation, censorship, and discipline were applied with particular rigor to the college's teenage students. In 1861 the college had a staff of eight teaching priests and fifteen servants. Its student body of 129 residential students included 18 Americans and seventeen-year-old Louis Riel from the Red River settlement.[49]

In 1861 the college building on the western outskirts of Montreal was rented to the British government as a barracks for the 60th Rifles and, until opening of the new college nine years later, students were lodged in the Grand Séminaire.[50] The new college was built on the mountain adjacent to the Grand Séminaire at a cost of $237,018, and in the 1880s a separate college chapel was added. Particular attention was given to student amenities. The school's hot-water heating system cost $7,426, had 26,083 feet of pipe, and was guaranteed to maintain rooms at 65°F; in 1874, $6,000 was budgeted for construction of a games-court.[51] In addition to this capital investment and the furnishings, repairs, maintenance, insurance, and taxes for college buildings, the seminary provided the teaching staff – usually Sulpicians or theological students. Throughout the nineteenth century the seminary paid the college operating expenses not covered by student tuition including wine and rum for the faculty, books for the library, and apples for the students.[52] Firewood (£300), bread (£432), and washing were the major expenses paid by the seminary in 1840; in 1880 it delivered 180 tons of hard coal and 55 tons of soft coal to the college.[53] The seminary's average annual operating subsidy to the college was £727 in the 1840s and $3,473 in the 1860s (appendix 14). By the 1870s it was contributing substantial bursaries; in 1874, for example, it paid $1,260 to the college bursar for the fees of needy students.[54]

As with its college and Grand Séminaire, the seminary retained direct control over alms, a budget item that expanded rapidly with the deepening impoverishment of many in the popular classes. The seminary's average annual alms donation increased from £358 in the 1830s to £1,769 in the 1850s and $16,662 in the 1870s. In years of economic crisis (1836–7, 1849) or of surplus seminary income (1821, 1842), exceptional increases in alms were budgeted.[55]

Huguette Roy's study of social assistance emphasizes the Sulpician welfare was strongly influenced by French attitudes to pauperism. Insistent that alms not encourage laziness, the seminary almoner paid only part of the rent for the destitute, organized a discount system with bakers by which the poor paid half-price for bread, and offered land for construction of a House of Industry.[56] The seminary divided the city's destitute into two categories: "the shameful poor" (les pauvres honteux) and "the ordinary poor." The former were aided, presumably discreetly, from a special fund of £125 administered by the superior himself.[57] To help "the ordinary poor" and to avoid making cash handouts, the seminary established a "poor depot" where nuns distributed flour, potatoes, peas, and firewood. In the early 1840s two Sulpicians distributed sixty loaves of six-pound bread a month, a function later assumed by the Grey Nuns and Sisters of Providence.[58] The seminary paid £7 10s. a head for the upkeep of thirty to forty Irish orphans in the Grey Nuns orphanage and made periodic donations of £20 to £25 to the francophone orphanage. From 1816 to 1844 the seminary subsidized a ward for seven aged invalids in the Hôpital Général. In the early 1840s this subsidy was £169 a year, based on an annual consumption of twelve minots of wheat per invalid.[59]

In addition to alms, the seminary had a "subscription" budget for special donations to public-works projects, catastrophe victims, missions, and retreats. A highly visible, political, and "one-time" form of support, this budget grew from an annual average of £454 in the 1840s to $6,663 in the 1860s (appendix 14). Seminary policy, as defined by the superior, was to make the largest individual contribution; the seminary donated church bells, gifts of books and pictures for children at communion, £25 for a maternity hospice, £7 10s. to support the German Catholic community in Montreal, £250 for flood victims in southern France, a £75 subscription for a Montreal Catholic newspaper, True Witness, and £250 for the papal zouaves.[60] Fire victims were the most recurrent benefactors with seminary contributions to fire-disaster funds in Montreal, the Saguenay, Chicago, Boucherville, London (Ontario), and £15 to a retired seminary servant who lost his house in a fire. It was from the subscription fund that funds were drawn for the seminary's political gestures: equipping government volunteers in the rebellions of 1837–8 (£150), Grand Trunk Railway celebrations (£100), festivities during the visit of the Prince of Wales (£100), the statue to Queen Victoria (£50), a donation to the newly founded Institut canadien-français (£75).[61]

Until the formation of the Montreal Catholic School Commission, the education of Montreal's Catholic population was largely a financial responsibility of the seminary. To manage this growing jurisdiction the seminary normally subsidized other religious communities which in turn directed the schools. The Congregation of Notre Dame, an order specializing in female education, had been in Montreal since 1659. Living on revenues from the rent of commercial properties, the produce of its two farms, student tuition, and the sale of religious bric-à-brac, the congregation received only small subsidies from the seminary in the 1820s and 1830s to cover tuition for a few indigent students.[62] The 1840s was a decade of rapid institutional expansion and by 1846 the one hundred sisters had 1,359 girls enrolled in three schools. Seminary financial support escalated rapidly. In the period 1848–76 the seminary built four schools for the congregation, reconstructed another, and renovated two others at a total cost of $40,638 (appendix 17); by 1891 the sisters had ten schools in Montreal.[63] The seminary average annual operating subsidy for repairs, caretakers, insurance, firewood, and carriages increased from £85 in the 1830s, to £545 in the 1840s, and to $7,930 in 1871–6.

Although local convents filled many of the female social-service needs, the seminary had to turn to France – an expensive alternative – to find male clerics to staff the male schools projected for Montreal's popular classes. The Christian Brothers, an important French order which specialized in popular education, had historic links with the Sulpicians. Their founder, Jean-Baptiste de La Salle, lived at the Séminaire de Saint-Sulpice while studying at the Sorbonne and modelled his order on the Sulpician example. His schools were quickly known for their "discipline and good behaviour," and in 1688 La Salle was invited to open a school in the seminary's parish of Saint-Germain.[64] Negotiations for the Brothers' immigration to Canada began in 1829 and eight years later they accepted Sulpician terms of sponsorship. The first Brothers arrived in the midst of the 1837–8 rebellions and were lodged in the seminary until completion of their St Lawrence school and residence. These facilities with their furnishings and the Brothers' transportation from France cost the seminary £15,045.[65] By 1846 St Brigitte's, an Irish school, had been built, and a total of 1,900 boys were enrolled in the two schools.

Four suburban schools – Sainte-Marie, Saint-Jacques, St Anne, and St Joseph – were built by the seminary before 1876 along with an enlarged noviciate, a second residence, and a school of agriculture at Oka. The seminary's total capital investment in the Christian Brothers and their schools in Montreal between 1837 and 1876 was some $180,000. The operating subsidy for the Christian Brothers' schools was also consistently higher than that for the Congregation of Notre Dame's schools partly because the Brothers received a small salary. The average annual operating subsidy was £1,333 in the 1850s and $15,847 in the early 1870s.[66]

The seminary's social investment cannot be explained in terms of the institution's own momentum but rather as one facet of the transition in Montreal to industrial capitalism. This becomes clearer if we look at the changing form of seminary aid over time. In pre-industrial Montreal the seminary's major social activities were its parish and mission. In 1806, after some false starts and in the midst of its own corporate crisis, the seminary built the Collège de Montréal. Much more than a means of incubating candidates for the-priesthood, this involvement with bourgeois education gave the seminary important ideological and institutional power with the very group of intellectuals capable of leading the popular classes. The burning in effigy of the college director, the raising of the tricolour on the school flagpole, and Sulpician expressions of their fears of revolution emphasize the seminary's front line position against radicalism.

Construction of the new parish church in the 1820s heralded a new scale of seminary-directed social institutions. Notre-Dame and the Lachine Canal were the first of Montreal's "mega" construction projects and were important means by which contractors like Redpath, Phillips, and Bagg accumulated capital and moved away from artisanal modes. Construction of churches, schools, the Grand Séminaire, and the new Collège de Montréal brought the seminary into increasingly complex credit, real-estate, social, ideological, and political relationships with industrial producers; as examples, we need only recall the multiple relationships with the seminary of John Redpath or John Ostell.

By the late 1830s education of the male bourgeoisie and its parish and mission duties were being lapped by dramatically expanding ideological and social responsibilities with the urban popular classes. Over the next decades the seminary established its presence everywhere in Catholic Montreal introducing the Christian Brothers, sponsoring girls schools, orphanages, reading-rooms, hospices,

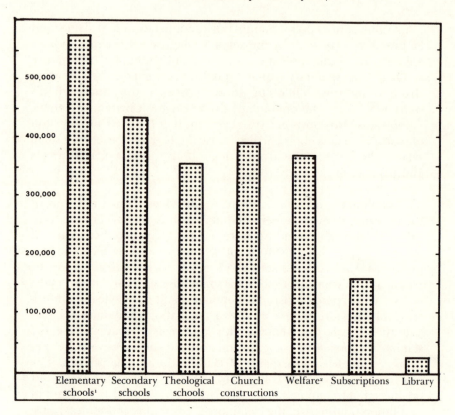

FIGURE 15
Social Investment by the Seminary in Montreal, Operating and Capital
Costs, 1841–76 (dollars)

Source: Appendix 12.
Note: Figures do not include Indian mission or schools outside Montreal. The actual totals are:
elementary schools $575,684; secondary school $438,034; theological school $357,087;
church construction $391,595; welfare $371,425; subscriptions $162,351; and
library $29,138.
1 Determined by adding grants to Congregation of Notre Dame and Christian Brothers
schools.
2 Determined by adding alms and subsidies to Grey Nuns.

workshops, and burial societies, and co-opting national, temperance,
intellectual, and sports activities. This Sulpician preoccupation with
authority, the family, social order, public morality, labour discipline,
and poor relief had roots in seminary traditions that reached back
to France and the Counter-Reformation. But when this institutional
response is related to the larger struggle of labour and capital in
nineteenth-century Montreal we see that seminary concerns meshed

nicely with the needs of industrial producers. Taken in this perspective, Sulpician defusing of the Irish in the Lachine strikes, their direction of social capital into St Patrick's Church and dozens of institutions that could shape social relations, their control of the training of priests in the Montreal region, and their ideological hammering from pulpits, confessionals, schools, newspaper, and libraries is more than coincidental with their corporate revitalization and their accession to new revenues after 1840.

Conclusion

So he [the Angel] took me thro' a stable and thro' a church and down into the church vault at the end of which was a mill ...   William Blake, 1793[1]

Nineteenth-century Quebec is crucial turf for the historian of both institutions and business. For the former it represents a period of institutionalization when schools, law, government, social services, and the professions developed structures in an industrializing society that would last into our lifetimes. For the business historian it is an immensely significant time when Lower-Canadian owners and their managers had to contend with changing forms of capital and property, with new markets and products, with the formation of the modern business institution and with a labour force that had to be utilized and disciplined in revolutionary ways – and all this in the cadre of a resistant, seigneurial, and Catholic society.

Institutional persistence is a striking feature of the seminary of Montreal. In the passage across two modes of production from New France into industrial Montreal the centrality of Sulpician religious belief must be re-emphasized. Products of the Counter-Reformation, the Sulpicians' faith in God, the promise of Heaven, and the reality of Original Sin ensured strength and coherence to the community. This religious bedrock was buttressed by a sound constitution, a skilful recruitment policy, and an administrative structure that diluted the essential social exclusiveness and authoritarianism of the institution with the equality implied by membership in a closed organization. The dominance of the symbol of the Virgin and the reality of Man as fallen in their world-view was combined with their power over the sacraments to give the Sulpicians the superiority, confidence, toughness, and discipline to wage perennial war against the perceived laziness, distress, sin, and ignorance of native peoples, women, youth, and other social constituencies.

As late as the rebellions of 1837–8, the seminary supported itself and its mission and parish activities from income drawn from three seigneuries acquired in Canada before 1717. Seigneurialism implied a series of strict property relations that seigneurs were able to exploit in a variety of rural, urban, and industrial circumstances. Although a quarry, sawmills, carding mills, a fur-trade post, and brick kiln contributed to its revenues, the seminary's main income before 1840 came from seigneurial levies on production taken to its mills, from annual rents on all ceded lands, from mutation levies applied when properties were transferred, and from the harvest on its domains.

Although the historian of an institution is not well placed to see all dimensions of the social struggle that marked Lower Canada in the first half of the nineteenth century, Sulpician fears of physical retribution, particularly from the popular classes, can be perceived across the period. As early as 1819, the superior expressed fear that the peasantry would rebel if the seminary tightened its seigneurial collections, and in 1827 the business manager worried about popular repercussions if the seminary made a private settlement with the Colonial Office. The Sulpicians were horrified by the rebellion of their students in 1830 which raised for them the spectre of the revolutions in France. Months before the outbreak of the rebellion in October 1837 there were riots and shooting on the Two Mountains seigneury; in July the priest in Saint-Benoît had his barn burned because, in the words of the Montreal *Gazette*, he was "pious to God and loyal to his king." The local constable made arrests but refused to keep prisoners in the region since he "was certain a rescue would have been successful."[2] In the violent year of 1849 the Sulpicians described themselves as on a smoking volcano and they were forced to guard their properties from arsonists throughout the summer. In the 1850s riots and arson were not uncommon as rural protest mounted against municipal taxation and schooling. The priest at Sainte-Scholastique was physically threatened while in Saint-Liquori the schoolhouse was attacked and defaced in an attempt to frighten away the teacher.[3] Deteriorating relations between the Sulpicians and mission Indians concerning property rights and freedom of religion culminated in the burning of the mission church at Oka in 1877.

Part of this broad popular hostility was due to the seminary's front line role in maintaining social order. They helped raise troops for the British in 1812 and 1837 and used their full weight as parish priests to defuse Irish participation in the 1837 rebellions and to disarm strikers on the Lachine Canal in 1843. After the 1830s, a period of immature institutional and state structures, the Sulpicians were a consistent and reliable conservative force in Catholic Montreal, legitimizing changing class relations in their schools, pulpits, newspaper, alms-giving, and self-help associations.

By 1816 the seminary's property rights, and ultimately the form of its social relations and its power in Montreal, were being challenged. Without a fuller prosopography of the Montreal bourgeoisie, one cannot identify all the characteristics of the group that hounded the seminary in the courts, newspapers, assembly, government councils, and finally to Westminster. However, attacks on the seminary's feudal property privileges came particularly from the sector of largely Protestant industrial producers and large capitalist landowners. The characteristics of the thirty-eight individuals who can be located definitely as opposing the seminary raise the *voies de passage* debate. Some, like David Torrance or George Moffatt seem to have directed their capital from the commercial circuit into industrial pursuits and land accumulation. Others like mason John Redpath, utilizing megaprojects like construction of the seminary's churches, took the "really revolutionary path" from the artisanal to industrial mode.[4] From the perspective of the seminary, it would appear to be this emerging and still amorphous industrial bourgeoisie that was particularly resentful of seigneurial restraints on the free exchange of property, of seigneurial levies and particularly mutation fees, of the banal privilege on milling, of the presence of the seminary's domain on potential water-power sites and industrial lands, and of the restrictions of auxiliary structures such as the *Coutume de Paris* and the secret and general hypothec.

The miller Fleming, who led early opposition, did not attack the institution of seigneurialism but rather the seminary's corporate existence. This jeopardized the foundation of the seminary's business operation in Canada: its right to hold property and to call on the coercive power of the state, a vital force if the seigneur was to enforce his privileges. Faced with growing rural and urban opposition to its seigneurial levies – resistance expressed most clearly in the refusal to pay *lods et ventes* – and an increasing imbroglio in its judicial action against Fleming, the seminary admitted the odiousness of feudal levies as early as 1819 and concentrated on finding a political solution that would assure it a modicum of property rights and revenues. After two decades of lawyers, fruitless negotiations with the Colonial Office and episcopal officials, and serious division within its own walls as to the magnitude of the concessions to be made, the seminary was rescued by the failure of the rebellions of 1837–8. Behind Lord Durham's publicized disdain for feudal and Catholic structures, his officials recognized the seminary's practical aid during the rebellions, its contribution to the maintenance of social order, particularly among the Montreal Irish, and its ideological and institutional potential in the Catholic sector of industrializing Montreal. Seigneurialism would be abandoned but only in piecemeal fashion, with full compensation for lost seigneurial revenues and state backing for the seminary's reconstituted corporate rights.

The Ordinance of 1840 did not destroy seigneurialism; that institution would persist, albeit fragmented, over the next century.[5] But, along with measures like the revised civil code and the registry law, the ordinance recognized and extended the realm of capitalist property relations in the Montreal region. This recognition was symbolized by the obligation of the seminary to accept all legitimate demands to commute property into freehold tenure. The evolution of this process towards what has been called "an exclusive, alienable, 'absolute,' individual or corporate right in things" can be perceived in the changing business behaviour of the seminary.[6] Assisted by the law, improving roads and mails, new professionals, and updated office and accounting systems, the seminary was able to monitor its seigneurial debtors and to force them before its notaries.[7] Between 1842 and 1847, 1636 debtors on the seigneuries of Montreal and Saint-Sulpice signed debt-recognition contracts. Of course, debt and debt-contracts were not a new phenomenon for the Lower-Canadian *censitaire*. But Sulpician attitudes to these contracts and their collection emphasize that the ground rules surrounding them had changed significantly. After 1840 debt-recognition contracts signed with the seminary locked the debtor into a cycle of legal interest and gave the seminary a much stronger, preferred, and specific mortgage as security for principal and interest.[8] Even more symptomatic of the seminary's changing property relations was its alienation of seigneurial debts. The sale of hundreds of overdue accounts extricated the religious community from direct participation in subsequent land dispossession procedures.

This conception of land as a disposable commodity was evident in the seminary's expanding participation in the urban rental market. From six downtown rental properties in the early decades of the century, the seminary increased its commercial rental properties to twenty-nine in the late 1870s at the same time as it was building and renting a large warehouse and nineteen houses. With a view to maximizing office rents from its insurance, banking, and professional tenants, the seminary invested in improved security, lighting, heating, and plumbing systems. A telegraph antenna in their church belfry, installation of special office windows, and new vaults for a bank tenant are witness to the seminary's development as an urban *rentier*.

The seminary's real-estate business – which was in good part based on land sales it was forced by the ordinance to conduct – provides another example of the new freedom in its property relations. In mid-century, its Saint-Gabriel domain and a large part of its Mountain domain were subdivided and sold for urban land uses. Expensive zoned land was provided for one market, cheaper multi-purpose lots for the other. On the Saint-Gabriel flat along the Lachine Canal, a creek was filled in and farm buildings torn down to develop the housing and industrial potential of an area surrounded by railway, canal, waterworks, and port. The site served diverse land uses: immigrant sheds, manufactures, turning basins, railway yards, and housing for the popular classes. On the Mountain domain the seminary responded to the housing aspirations of elements in the bourgeoisie who sought single-family housing isolated from insalubrity and social unrest. The building, fencing, and tree-planting requirements incorporated into the deeds on these lots ensured that the community would be green, safe, and homogeneous.

The unleashing of land from seigneurial restrictions triggered new sales, professional, and contractual forms. The private sale and the salesman superseded the public auction and the priest / business manager. Since these land sales, unlike seigneurial concessions, involved a significant sale price and often an accompanying loan, interest and the term and surety of mortgages had new significance. At the bottom line, buyer and seller had a purely financial relationship. For its investment in farm mortgages in the 1870s, the seminary chose a region outside its seigneuries and operated through professional intermediaries. Other signs of the seminary's orientation are evident from its account books and minutes. From representing well over 90 per cent of its income in 1834, seigneurial revenues fell to only 1 per cent of total seminary income in 1890. Seminary minutes after 1840 contained increasing references to urban considerations like road extensions across the Saint-Gabriel suburb, tramway routes, the location of city markets, and investment in ancillary development projects like the Boulevard Company. The investment of the seminary surplus in bonds, stocks, and municipal issues, its assumption of the functions of a deposit bank, its entry into the mortgage market, the accelerating role of interest in its business operations, and its support for the most important transportation industries are clear indicators of the domination of capitalist forms of incomes.

This evolution in the form of its business prompted sharp change in the seminary business office and over several decades its management became more secular, specialized, professional, and centralized. Early in the nineteenth century the seminary business operation was a one-man office run from the procurator's bed-sitting-room and adjoining office. The procurator – a Sulpician priest with an in-house training in accounting, the law, and surveying – handled all seminary business; in particular situations he retained an individual lawyer, notary, or surveyor. After 1840 seminary business operations escalated. Its notarial business tripled between 1839 and 1840 and doubled again in the following year. Swamped with this increasing business, the procurator was forced to delegate responsibilities to full-time office employees and professionals: notaries, architects, accountants, lawyers, surveyors, and clerks. While inspecting the books at the Saint-Sulpice seigneury, the procurator had to leave his surveyor in charge of the important Lachine Canal negotiations with the government. Official agents were named to represent the seminary in bankruptcy court, and to handle banking operations in Paris, Quebec City, and Toronto. After the death of powerful procurator Joseph Comte in 1863, notary Édouard Lafleur handled most collections and accountant George Marler kept the books. By 1875 the business office had five full-time employees – two notaries, two clerks, and an accountant – in addition to the procurator. The seminary's board of directors or Consulting Council revised its procedures after 1840 adopting more formal minutes and centralizing its accounting and signing procedures.

The seminary's emerging managerial structure, its increasing revenues, its boldness as a model corporate citizen, and its renewed access to state coercion to enforce its property rights must not obscure the institution's marginalization from real power. From a feudal mode of production at the beginning of the nineteenth century in which the Sulpicians wielded direct power as seigneurs, we move in the 1870s to a position in which the seminary has ceded its centrality in property relations. Confederation, the National Policy, and the new freedom of land and labour in Quebec were signs of a maturing capitalism in which the seminary would be but a minor force.

Appendixes

APPENDIX 1
Individuals Attacking the Seminary's Seigneurial Privileges, 1816–40

Individual	Occupation	Year of Protest	Type of Protest	Real Property		Year of Commutation
William Fleming	miller	1816–26	lawsuit			
Thomas Porteous	grain merchant, mill operator, waterworks-entrepreneur	1819	built non-banal mill			
Joseph Leduc	bourgeois/commerçant	1825	petitioner for steam-operated mill	£104	city	1843
Walter Benny	baker	1825	petition for steam-operated mill	£5,650	Sainte-Anne	1842
Samuel Gale	judge, rail petitioner (1833), lawyer for Selkirk and Handyside distillers (1824)	1825	petitioner against *lods et ventes*	£1,500	Sainte-Marie	1841
				£4,000	city	1845
				£12,000	city	1845
				£400	Sainte-Marie	1850
				£1,265	Sainte-Marie	1853
				£200	Sainte-Marie	1860
Thomas Cringan	import-export merchant (potash)	1836	testimony	£8,000	city	1841
Benjamin Holmes	cashier of Bank of Montreal, Champlain and St. Lawrence Railway interests (1832)	1836	testimony	£40	Sainte-Marie	1848
				£500	Côte-des-Neiges¹	1841
John Fisher	textile importer	1839	petitioner against Ordinance of 1840	£1,900	Saint-Antoine	1841
				£200	Sainte-Marie	1842
				£3,000	city	1842

APPENDIX 1 — *Continued*

Individual	Occupation	Year of Protest	Type of Protest	Real Property		Year of Commutation
John Fisher — *Continued*				£1,100	Saint-Antoine	1842
				£800	Saint-Antoine	1842
Thomas Phillips	mason/contractor, partner of John Redpath, brewer, railway petitioner 1833	1839	petitioner	£4,400	Saint-Antoine	1841
				£2,500	Saint-Laurent	1842
				£600	Saint-Laurent	1843
				£4,850	Saint-Laurent	1861
Henry Griffin	notary, railway petitioner (1833)	1839	petitioner			
Benaiah Gibb	tailor	1839	petitioner	£2,300	city	1841
				£3,500	Saint-Pierre river[1]	1841
				£2,300	city	1841
				£390	Saint-Laurent	1847
				£120	Saint-Laurent	1860
James Duncan Gibb	tailor/esquire	1839	petitioner	£2,000	city[2]	1841
				£25	Sainte-Anne	1841
				£600	city	1841
				£675	Saint-Antoine	1841
				£2,600	city	1841
				£300	Saint-Laurent	1841
				£1,350	Saint-Laurent	1856
James H. Lambe	lawyer	1839	petitioner	£200	Saint-Antoine	1844
Archibald Hume	candle maker	1839	petitioner	£555	Sainte-Marie	1841
				£9,000	city	1865
William Watson	flour inspector; his capital helped found Ogilvie milling	1839	petitioner	£1,750	Saint-Pierre river[1]	1845
Jesse Thayer David Handyside	distiller	1839	petitioner	£6,020	Sainte-Marie	1847

Name	Occupation	Year	Role	Amount	Location	Year
Robert Handyside	distiller & brewer	1839				
James Ferrier	importer/esquire; tramways (1840), Montreal & Lachine Railway (1846)	1839	petitioner petitioner	£1,228	Saint-Laurent	1840
				£8,500	city	1841
				£2,000	city	1842
				£1,100	city	1844
				£750	Sainte-Marie[2]	1850
				£100	Saint-Antoine	1861
John Redpath	mason/contractor, Lachine Canal interests, sugar	1839	petitioner	£4,000	Saint-Antoine	1840
				£480	Saint-Antoine	1841
				£5,000	Saint-Antoine	1844
				£750	Pointe-aux-Trembles[1]	1845
				£1,800	city	1853
David Torrance	general merchant especially food wholesaling, steamship operator, railway and water company interests	1839	petitioner	£1,500	city	1841
				£860	city	1842
				£1,770	Sainte-Anne	1843
Andrew White	carpenter/joiner contractor for Anglican cathedral	1839	petitioner			
Robert Howard		1839	petitioner			
James Holmes	merchant/esquire	1839	petitioner	£1,200	city	1841
				£500	Côte-de-la-Visitation[1]	1847
				£100	Sainte-Marie	1847
				£77	Sainte-Marie	1850
Stanley Bagg	commodity trader, Lachine Canal contractor, steamboat & rail interests	1839	petitioner	£2,000	city	1840
				£137	Saint-Laurent parish[1]	1841
				£600	Saint-Laurent	1842
				£4,500	Sainte-Anne	1844
				£2,750	Saint-Laurent	1844

APPENDIX 1 — Continued

Individual	Occupation	Year of Protest	Type of Protest	Real Property		Year of Commutation
William Lunn	merchant, director of Bank of Montreal; insurance, gas, & Savings Bank interests	1839	petitioner	£300	Sainte-Anne	1843
				£19,000	city²	1845
				£600	parish of Saint-Laurent¹	1846
John Mathewson	soap and candle factory, gas & insurance, wife ran largest millinery shop in Montreal	1839		£1,250	Saint-Antoine	1841
				£1,500	city	1841
				£770	Saint-Laurent	1843
				£2,750	Sainte-Anne	1844
				£500	Saint-Antoine	1844
				£145	Saint-Antoine	1850
William Badgley	lawyer	1839	petitioner			
George Moffat	import-export merchant, landowner along Lachine Canal, Phoenix Fire Assurance, Champlain and St. Lawrence Railway interests, director of Bank of Montreal, commissioner & president of Board of Trade	1840	votes against Ordinance on Special Council	£1,200	city	1843
				£1,900	Pointe-Claire¹	1845
				£3,500	city²	1846
				£1,050	city	1854
				£200	St Louis	1854
John Molson Jr	brewer, steamship owner, warehouser, St Mary's Foundry, land speculator	1840	votes against Ordinance on Special Council	£19,400	city, Sainte-Marie, Saint-Laurent, Sainte-Anne, Côte-de-la-Visitation	1841

Name	Occupation		Committee	Amount	Location	Year
John Adams	merchant	1840	committee of proprietors, 1840	£800	Saint-Laurent	1840
Perkins				£2,000	Sainte-Anne	1842
				£220	foot of mountain[1]	1842
Richard Robinson	master carpenter & contractor	1840	committee	£175		1841
Joseph Knapp	merchant/gentleman	1840	committee	£610	Saint-Laurent[2]	1842
				£250	Côte-de-la-Visitation[1]	1845
				£1,800	city	1853
				£450	city	1853
				£720	Sainte-Anne	1854
Orlin Bostwick	merchant; active in mill sites & as surety in Lachine Canal contracts					
John E. Mills	banker/exchange broker in grain export to United States			£2,500	Sainte-Anne	1845
				£750	Saint-Antoine	1847
Charles Castle	cashier, City Bank	1840	committee	£1,460	Sainte-Anne, Saint-Laurent, Sainte-Marie	1842
				£600	Saint-Antoine	1844
C. Fitts		1840	committee			
Joseph R. Brondson	master carpenter	1840	committee	£1,200	Saint-Laurent	1844

1 Outside city and suburbs of Montreal
2 Commutation with partners or family members

APPENDIX 2
Debt-Recognition Contract (*Reconnaissance de dette*), 1842

Pardevant les notaires publics pour cette partie du Canada ci-devant appeleé la province du Bas-Canada, résidant dans le district de Montréal, soussignés, a comparu *Jean Baptiste Poirier, cultivateur, demeurant à la Côte St. Luc, paroisse de Montréal*

Le Quel a par ces présentes, reconnu et confessé devoir bien légitimement à MM. les Ecclésiastiques du Séminaire de St. Sulplice de Montréal, demeurant en la cité de Montréal, seigneurs propriétaires en possession des fiefs et seigneuries de l'Ile de Montréal, de St. Sulpice et du Lac-des-deux-Montagnes,

Ce Qui a été accepté, pour et au nom des dits sieurs seigneurs, par *Messire Joseph Comte ptre*, leur procureur demeurant en la paroisse de *Montréal*, à ce présent,

La somme de *sept cent soixante livres treize sols ancien cours, selon compte reglé et arrêté conforme*, pour arrérages de droits seigneuriaux dus et échus sur *une terre et emplacement* ci-après désignés, que le dit *J. Bte. Poirier* a déclaré tenir et posséder dans la censive de la dite seigneurie de *Montréal* à titre de cens et rentes, portant profit de lods-et-ventes, saisines, amendes et autres droits seigneuriaux; les dits cens et rentes payables, au lieu de la recette de la dite seigneurie, le onze de novembre de chaque année, à raison *d'une demi sol tournois et d'une pinte* de bled froment, bon, sec, net, loyal et marchand, pour chaque arpent de terre en superficie, *situés en la dite Côte St. Luc de la contenance d'un arpent et demi de front sur vingt arpents de profondeur, tenant devant au ruisseau ou Petite Rivière St. Luc, derrière aux Terres de la Côte de Liesse, et des deux Côtés à Antoine Goujon; avec maison, grange et dépendances dessus construites,*

Savoir: Deux cent six livres douze sols pour balance des arrérages de rentes du dit Antoine Goujon au onze novembre milhuit cent vingt neuf selon Reconnaissance du dit J. Bte Poirier en date du 3 Janvier (Lorimier notaire) cy –   206.12

Plus, quatre cent quatre vingt quatre livres cinq sols pour lods et ventes du dit J. Bte Poirier sur l'acquisition qu'il a faite de la dite terre et emplacement, le 4 octobre 1830, et le 30 avril 1832 (Lorimier notaire) cy –   484.5

Enfin Soixante et dix livres, pour douze années d'arrérages de rentes sur la dite tearre, échu au onze novembre dernier cy   70.0

total   769.13[sic]

Laquelle dite somme de *sept cent soixante livres treize sols* le dit Tenancier s'est obligé de payer et remettre aux dit sieurs seigneurs, ou à toute personne autorisée à la perception de leurs droits, au lieu ordinaire de leur recette, en la dite seigneurie, ou au porteur des présentes, ou ordre, *comme suit: deux cent six livres douze sols, d'ici au premier avril prochain et la balance au premier mars de l'année suivante mil huit cent quarante quatre.*

Le tout sans intérèt pendant les délais ci dessus, mais avec intérèt légal de six par cent, par an, à compter des échéances.

En Garantie du paiement de la présente reconnaissance, tant en principal qu'intérêt, l'héritage ci-dessus désigné demeurera spécialement affecté et hypothéqué aux dits sieurs seigneurs, qui se réservent expressément et dans leur intégralité, tous les droit de préférence et privilèges qui leur sont acquis sur le dit héritage, sans aucune novation ni dérogation.

Enfin le dit Tenancier a consenti que toute inscription de privilèges et hypothèques soit prise, à ses frais, contre lui, au profit des dit sieurs seigneurs; à l'effet de quoi tout pouvoir est donné aur porteur d'une expédition ou de tout extrait, bordereau ou sommaire.

Et pour l'exécution des présentes le dit Tenancier a fait élection de domicile sur l'héritage ci-dessus désigné.

Dont Act: fait et passé *à Montréal, en la procure du Séminaire* l'an mil-huit-cent-quarante-*deux, le premier octobre, et le dit J Bte Poirier fait sa marque ayant déclaré ne savoir signer ...*

Joseph Comte ptre   J. Bte X Poirier

marque

P. Lacombe N.P.   H. Valotte N.P.

Source: ANQM, Valotte, 181, 1 October 1842, Jean-Baptiste Poirier to seminary
Note: Sections in italics handwritten; rest of act printed

APPENDIX 3
Notarial Acts Completed by Seminary Notaries and Deposited in ANQM, 1835–80

Year	Notary	Debt-Recognition Contracts	Commutations	Sale	Other	Total
1835	Lacombe	3	–	–	18	21
1836	Lacombe	5	–	–	14	19
1837	Lacombe	8	–	–	27	35
1838	Lacombe	13	–	–	25	38
1839	Lacombe	5	–	–	26	31
1840	Lacombe	9	51	–	29	89
1841	Lacombe	6	142	–	16	164
1842	Lacombe, Valotte, Jobin	1,382	194	–	26	1602
1843	Lacombe, Valotte, Jobin	107	135	–	32	274
1844	Lacombe, Valotte	14	166	–	32	212
1845	Lacombe, Valotte	84	209	40	65	398
1846	Lacombe, Valotte	36	120	3	41	200
1847	Lacombe, Valotte	13	78	1	35	127
1848	Lacombe	5	60	–	18	83
1849	Lacombe	3	42	–	51	96
1850	Lacombe	10	51	2	44	107
1851	Lacombe, Lafleur	44	60	4	30	138
1852	Lacombe, Lafleur	117	71	1	30	219
1853	Lacombe, Lafleur	18	125	33	50	226
1854	Lacombe, Lafleur	2	107	33	41	183
1855	Lacombe, Lafleur	4	67	1	23	95
1856	Lacombe, Lafleur	1	68	39	27	135
1857	Lacombe, Lafleur	2	72	65	45	184
1858	Lacombe, Lafleur	1	73	21	28	123
1859	Lacombe, Lafleur	11	110	3	48	172
1860	Lacombe, Lafleur	40	113	16	48	217
1861	Lacombe, Lafleur	38	93	34	39	204
1862	Lacombe, Lafleur	17	74	28	30	149
1863	Lacombe, Lafleur, Moreau	20	92	38	44	194
1864	Lafleur, Moreau	13	107	30	58	208
1865	Lafleur, Moreau	9	73	7	37	126
1866	Lafleur, Moreau	6	80	14	62	162
1867	Lafleur, Moreau	6	52	19	45	122
1868	Lafleur	1	–	27	24	52
1869	Lafleur	0	–	25	28	53
1870	Lafleur	2	26	23	30	81
1871	Lafleur	3	–	56	40	99
1872	Lafleur, Bonin	218	24	35	40	317
1873	Lafleur, Bonin	20	110	57	59	246
1874	Lafleur, Bonin	10	106	9	100	225
1875	Lafleur, Bonin	3	51	1	47	102

APPENDIX 3 — *Continued*

Year	Notary	Debt-Recognition Contracts	Commutations	Sale	Other	Total
1876	Lafleur, Bonin	3	22	2	59	86
1877	Lafleur, Bonin	5	27	1	78	111
1878	Lafleur, Bonin	27	31	3	63	124
1879	Lafleur, Bonin	29	31	2	58	120
1880	Lafleur, Bonin	9	52	5	75	141

Source: Compiled from the records of notaries Bonin, Jobin, Lacombe, Lafleur, Moreau, and Valotte; it does not include Two Mountains' acts completed by Jean-Jacques Girouard or F. Hyacinthe Lemaire.

APPENDIX 4
Excerpt of Transfer of Seigneurial Debts due to Seminary, 1862

Lacombe N.P. #4112, 11 septembre, 1862
Transport par le Séminaire de St. Sulpice de Montréal à l'Honorable J.A. Berthelot sur Louis Franche dit Laframboise

Pardevant les notaires publics ... ont comparu Messieurs les Ecclésiastiques du Séminaire ... agissant par Messire Dominique Granet, leur Supérieur, assisté de Messire Joseph Comte, l'un d'eux, leur procureur ...

Lesquels ont, par ces présentes, cédé et transporté, sans aucune garantie,

A l'Honorable Joseph-Amable Berthelot, demeurant en la dite cité de Montréal, l'un des Juges de la Cour Supérieure ... présent et acceptant,

La somme de trente neuf livres dix chelins et onze deniers, cours actuels due aux dits Sieurs Ecclésiastiques, Savoir

1. Celle de trente et un livres dix huit chelins onze deniers et demi dit cours, pour arrérages de cens et rentes et autres droits seigneuriaux, échus au onze novembre ... 1860 ... sur deux terres contiguës, situées ... dans la censive de la Seigneurie du Lac des Deux Montagnes, l'une, de deux arpents de front sur vingt un arpents de profondeur ... au cadastre seigneurial, sous le Numéro 849 ... avec maison, grange et autres bâtiments, circonstances et dépendances. Et l'autre, de trois arpents de front sur vingt et un arpents de profondeur ... au cadastre seigneurial, sous le numéro 850 ... avec maison, grange en bois depuis construits; la dite somme actuellement exigible, avec l'intérêt de six pour cent par année, à compter du premier janvier mil huit cent soixante jusqu'à parfait paiement.

2. Celle de seize chelins sept deniers et demi, dit cours, pour une année de cens et rentes seigneuriales échues au onze de Novembre dernier, sur les deux terres ci-dessus décrites et exigible à première demande.

3. Enfin, celle de six louis quinze chelins et quatre deniers dit cours, pour frais encourus, jusq'à ce jour, dans une poursuite, No. 236 que les dits Sieurs Ecclésiastiques ont faite, devant la Cour de Circuit, pour le Circuit de Terrebonne, pour le recouvrement de 31£ 18s 11d ... et pour laquelle somme les dits Ecclésiastiques auraient obtenu jugement le 17 jour d'octobre 1861, contre Louis Franche dit Laframboise, alors propriétaire des susdites deux terres, avec, intérêt de six pour cent par année, à compter du dit jour premier janvier 1860, jusqu'à parfait paiement de la dite somme ...

Pour toucher et percevoir par le cessionnaire, sur ses simples quittances, de qui'il appartiene la dite somme ... ou pour en faire et disposer autrement et comme bon lui semblera; à l'effet de quoi les dits Sieurs Ecclésiastiques mettent et subrogent le dit cessionnaire, dans tous leurs droits et actions, privilèges et hypothèques, jusqu'à ... concurrence, mais dans aucune garantie, ni préférence.

Ce transport est fait pour valeur et bon paiement que les dits Sieurs Ecclésiastiques ont reconnu avoir reçu du cessionaire dont quittance ...

Dont acte fait et passé .... en la Procure du dit Séminaire ... Les parties ont signé avec les dit notaires, après lecture faite ...

Joseph Comte, ptre

J.A. Berthelot

D. Granet Sup.

P. Lacombe N.P.

E. Lafleur N.P.

APPENDIX 5
Summary of the Ordinance of 8 June 1840

Incorporation
Seminary incorporated, given renewed title to its seigneuries, and the right to recruit members.

Function
Seminary responsible for parish of Montreal and Indian mission at Two Mountains; seminary to sponsor Collège de Montréal, schools in the parish of Montreal, orphanages, and invalid institutions, and other religious, charitable and educational institutions as approved by the government.

Collection of Seigneurial Debts
All seigneurial arrears now payable and collectible with force of law.

On property within the City of Montreal which (including buildings) had value of more than £500, seminary not to claim more than 5 per cent of property's value for each time *lods et ventes* not paid before 1840.

For seigneurial debt of more than £41, seminary cannot demand payment except over seven years and in seven equal annual payments.

The amount collected for *lods et ventes* debts not to exceed £44,000 on seigneury of Montreal and £12,000 on the seigneuries of Two Mountains and Saint-Sulpice. Any excess sum to be paid to government.

Mortgages or other forms of security taken by seminary to ensure payment of seigneurial debts to have priority over other liens on the property including commutations.

Commutation to freehold tenure
Conversion (i.e. commutation) from seigneurial to freehold tenure possible on seminary's seigneuries on demand of *censitaire*. Seminary cannot refuse commutation.

No reimbursement provided for loss of milling right. Provision, however, for commutation of annual charge (*cens et rentes*) and transfer levy (*lods et ventes*) into a fixed capital. If not paid off immediately and if more than £100, this capital could be formed into a quitrent (*rente constituée*) with the commuted property acting as security.

The fixed capital to be settled by voluntary agreement or by arbitration. The amount to vary from 5 percent to 12 percent of value of property (including buildings), the actual percentage to depend on whether property evaluated at more than £500, on the location (urban-rural), and the time elapsed between 1840 and the commutation.

Sale of the Saint-Gabriel Farm

Farm to be sold in freehold tenure by public sale and within twenty years. Parts of farm not sold to revert to crown.

Disposal of Capital

£30,000 could be invested in income-producing real estate in Canada.

Seminary not restricted in its investments in non-income producing real estate such as religious or charitable institutions.

Balance of capital to be invested in public securities of Great Britain or colonies.

Supervision

Seminary to provide full financial statement as required by government.

Crown inherits French king's power of visitation for temporal matters.

Source: "An Ordinance to incorporate the Ecclesiastics of the Seminary of Saint Sulpice ... ," No. 164, 8 June 1840, printed in *Copy of Ordinances passed by the Governor and Special Council of Lower Canada*, 3–4, Vict. 1841.

APPENDIX 6
Commutations of Seminary of Montreal, 1840–80

Year	No. of Commutations	Evaluation			Location						Demander[2]			Amount of Commutation			Capital Paid off Day of Commutation[3]
		Mutual Agreement	Arbitration	Recently[1] acquired	City	Suburbs	Island of Montreal outside suburbs	Saint-Sulpice	Two Mountains	Institution	French	English	Other	–$399	$400–1,999	$2,000+	
1840	51	44	7	7	15	32	1	3	0	0	17	33	0	2	19	30	–
1841	142	140	2	68	38	133	12	1	1	2	39	110	0	19	42	73	127
1842	194	194	0	143	44	216	20	0	2	1	70	124	0	26	77	95	163
1843	135	133	2	103	16	120	30	0	0	1	76	76	0	28	56	53	115
1844	166	164	2	46	29	157	19	0	0	3	63	97	0	24	47	100	137
1845	209	206	3	86	42	175	39	3	0	4	69	136	0	35	66	104	171
1846	120	119	1	42	23	94	14	3	1	1	57	68	1	21	53	50	91
1847	78	78	0	34	10	63	10	2	1	2	23	44	0	12	23	34	62
1848	60	59	1	32	7	49	6	1	2	1	23	38	0	9	31	20	56
1849	42	42	0	20	1	36	14	0	0	1	17	24	1	9	23	8	37
1850	51	50	1	17	6	59	15	0	0	2	30	23	0	13	25	12	48
1851	60	60	0	18	3	51	6	1	0	2	20	36	0	13	30	11	55
1852	71	71	0	17	15	45	9	0	2	6	23	37	1	7	29	31	64
1853	125	125	0	19	27	86	11	2	2	2	52	65	1	20	55	45	114
1854	107	107	0	28	22	94	13	2	2	3	47	53	2	14	46	44	94
1855	67	67	0	17	7	51	9	1	0	2	25	41	1	14	27	28	59
1856	68	68	0	10	6	58	8	1	0	0	29	36	0	7	33	24	57
1857	72	72	0	25	7	65	4	0	0	1	28	41	1	7	32	30	64
1858	73	73	0	39	9	63	13	1	0	1	36	36	0	15	29	30	67

Seigneurial Amendment of 1859

Year															
1859	110	110	0	68	9	19	8	7	48	55	1	16	42	48	78
1860	113	113	0	81	11	114	8	4	65	40	0	8	56	51	55
1861	93	93	0	66	10	114	4	4	54	29	0	14	64	24	38
1862	74	74	0	50	9	73	11	2	30	39	0	9	34	31	42
1863	92	92	0	49	7	70	13	5	40	42	1	11	45	34	56
1864	107	107	0	40	11	98	9	7	54	37	0	13	48	42	60
1865	73	73	0	25	20	58	11	4	32	32	0	3	31	39	34
1866	80	80	0	34	13	51	24	6	41	32	0	7	31	42	42
1867	52	52	0	24	12	42	11	4	30	19	0	8	18	23	44
1868	—	—	—	—	—	—	—	—	—	—	—	—	—	—	—
1869	—	—	—	—	—	—	—	—	—	—	—	—	—	—	—
1870	26	26	0	10	0	27	17	0	12	12	0	2	9	14	16
1871	—	—	—	—	—	—	—	—	—	—	—	—	—	—	—
1872	24	24	0	4	0	21	9	3	14	7	0	2	5	11	11
1873	110	110	0	24	7	79	40	7	59	40	1	9	32	59	57
1874	106	106	0	22	4	66	51	3	63	39	0	8	36	56	52
1875	51	51	0	16	9	37	13	5	27	19	0	4	17	27	28
1876	22	22	0	6	0	20	2	2	13	7	0	2	9	7	15
1877	27	27	0	6	3	22	0	1	17	9	0	2	11	12	18
1878	31	31	0	7	1	26	5	3	14	15	0	3	9	17	21
1879	31	31	0	2	4	23	4	3	19	9	0	1	6	22	20
1880	52	52	0	1	4	30	7	2	36	3	0	3	24	26	28

Source: Commutation acts deposited in the ANQM by Patrice Lacombe, Edward Lafleur, Édouard Moreau, and Joseph Bonin.

Note: Not all totals in the Evaluation, Location, Demander, and Form of payment categories correspond to the number of commutations because certain commutations were multiple-property transactions, individual property owners sometimes included several parties, and so on.

1 Recently acquired refers to an acquisition in the year of commutation. Many other properties were sold shortly after commutation.

2 Since all commutations were written in French, individual names were used as a rough indication of ethnicity. Although error undoubtedly arises from using names, the approximation may be useful. Most in the "other" category had German or Italian names.

3 Most of those who commuted but did not pay off their debt at the signing took a debt in the form of an *obligation* or *rente constituée*.

APPENDIX 7
Commutation: Example under Ordinance of 1840

Devant les Notaires Publics ... soussignés:

FUT PRÉSENT, MESSIRE *Joseph Vincent Quiblier* Prêtre, résidant en la dite Cité, Supérieur de Messieurs les Ecclésiastiques du Séminaire de Montréal, Seigneurs des Fiefs et Seigneuries de l'Ile de Montréal, de St. Sulpice et du Lac des Deux Montagnes, assisté à l'effet des présentes de MESSIRE *Joseph Comte,* Prêtre du même lieu et Procureur du dit Séminaire:

Lequel, sur la Réquisition à lui faite par *Stanley Bagg, Ecuier, Marchand résidant en la dite Cité, à ci présent,*

de *lui* accorder Commutation, Rachât et Affranchissement conformément à l'Ordonnance ci-après mentionnée, de tous Droits de Lods et Ventes, Cens et Rentes, et autres Droits Seigneuriaux, auxquels *peut* être sujet *un* ter*re*in dont *il est* Propriétaire et détemp*teur*; situé *en la dite Seigneurie de l'Ile de Montréal, au faubourg St. Joseph ... Borné en front par la Rue McGill ...*

Acquis par le dit Stanley Bagg de James Kipp le 11 juin 1816 (Desautels) pour Lods de laquelle acquisition, ainsi que pour ceux du dit James Kipp son auteur sur son acquisition du 14 avril 1815 (même notaire) il reconnait devoir aux dits Seigneurs, la somme de Cinquante Livres courant − £50 ...

A par les présentes, tant pour lui-même ès dits nom et qualité, que pour et au nom des dits Sieurs Ecclésiastiques, acquitté, affranchi et déchargé, de ce jour à toujours, *le* dit ter*ra*in de tous Droits de Lods et Ventes, Cens et Rentes, Droits de Banalité de Moulin, de Retrait, et de tous autres Droits Seigneuriaux quelconques, auxquels *le* dit ter*ra*in *peut* être sujet ou obligé; en sorte qu'au moyen des présentes, *le* dit ter*re*in *sera* de ce jour à toujours converti EN FRANC ALEU ROTURIER conformément à l'Ordonnance du Conseil Spécial de la dite Province, passée dans la 3ᴱ année du régne de Sa Majesté la Reine Victoria, chapitre XXX. qui a pour objet, entre autres dispositions y conténues, de "pourvoir à l'extinction graduelle des Redevances et Droits Seigneuriaux dans les limites Seigneuriales des Fiefs et Seigneuries" ci-dessus mentionnées, et ne pourra plus être tenu et possédé à aucun autre titre par *le* dit *Stanley Bagg, ses* hoirs et ayant cause, à l'avenir.

CETTE COMMUTATION, QUITTANCE et DÉCHARGE, ainsi consenties et accordées pour et moye*nnant* la somme de *cente cinquante livres et deux deniers,* du cours actuel de la dite Province, savoir, la somme de *deux deniers,* dit cours, principal de la somme de *trois deniers tournois ancien* cours, montant annuel des Cens et Rentes, dont *le* dit ter*re*in *est* chargé suivant le Tître de Consession, et celle de *cent cinquante Livres dit cours actuel,* afférante en vertu de la dite Ordonnance, aux dits Sieurs Ecclésiastiques, dans la somme de *Trois Mille Livres,* même cours, à laquelle *le* dit ter*re*in *a* été estimé *à l'amiable entre les parties; Pour laquelle somme de Cent Cinquante Livres et deux deniers dit cours actuel, le dit Stanley Bagg a, par les présentes crée et constituée en faveur des dits*

Sieurs Ecclésiastiques, ce acceptant par le dit Messire Quiblier, assisté comme cidessus, une Rente annuelle et perpétuelle mais à toujours rachetable de Neuf Livres du dit cours actuel, payable au premier Mai chaque année à compter du premier mai prochain, à Montréal en la Procure du Séminaire; La dite rente rachetable en tout temps, à la volonté du dit Stanley Bagg ou de ses hoirs et ayans cause, en-par lui ou par eux remboursant en un seul payement la dite somme principale de Cent Cinquante Livres, outre les arréges alors dus et échus, frais, mises et loyaux coûts;

Pour sûreté de lesquelles sommes tout en principal qu'intérêt, le dit Messire Quiblier, assisté comme cidessus, en vertu de l'article VIII de la dite Ordonnance, se réserve expressément et sans aucune novation, les mêmes recours legaux, privilèges et priorité d'hypothèque que les dits Sieurs Ecclésiastiques auraient eus pour les Droits de Lods et Ventes et Cens et Rentes éteints par la présente commutation ...

Et quant à la somme de cinquante Livres pour Lods et Ventes mentionnés en l'autre part, le dit Stanley Bagg promet et s'oblige la payer moitié au premier Mai mil huit cent quarante cinq, et l'autre moitié au premier Mai mil huit cent quarante six.

ET POUR L'EXÉCUTION ...

Joseph Comte ptre
Joseph Quiblier supérieur
Stanley Bagg
Henri Valotte N.P.
Patrice Lacombe N.P.

Source: ANQM, Lacombe, 1531, commutation, seminary to Stanley Bagg, 9 March 1844.

Note: Sections in italic are handwritten; the rest is a printed form.

APPENDIX 8
Commutators of Property Evaluated at over £5,000, 1840–59

Commutator	Year	Profession	Major Interests	Location	Property Evaluation (£)
John Donegani	1842	esquire	land speculator	city	3,000
	1842			city, Saint-Antoine, Sainte-Marie, Saint-Laurent	11,000
	1843			Saint-Laurent	600
	1845			city	2,620
	1845			city	1,900
	1846			Saint-Laurent	5,200
	1846			Sainte-Marie	1,600
	1848			Sainte-Anne	650
					26,570
City of Montreal	1844		institution	city	14,000
	1853			city	1,750
	1857			city	725
	1858			city	1,585
	1859			city	4,150
	1859			city	600
	1859			city	500
	1859			city	605
					23,915

Name	occupation	business	year	location	amount
William Molson	merchant	brewing, shipping	1841	Sainte-Marie	6,800[a]
			1843	Sainte-Marie	951
			1844	Longue-Pointe	7,875[a]
			1845	Sainte-Marie	7,500
			1845	Sainte-Marie	100
			1851	Sainte-Marie	195[3]
			1854	Sainte-Marie	475
					23,896
William Lunn	esquire	banking insurance, gas	1843	Sainte-Antoine	300
			1845	Saint-Antoine	19,000[4]
			1846	Saint-Antoine	600[4]
					19,900
John Molson	esquire	brewing, shipping	1841	city, Sainte-Marie, Saint-Laurent	19,400
Bishop of Montreal		institution	1850	Saint-Laurent	500
			1855	Saint-Laurent	600
			1859	Saint-Antoine	1,000
			1861	city, Saint-Antoine, Saint-Laurent	15,900
					18,000
John Torrance	esquire, merchant	merchant, shipping	1841	city	1,500[5]
			1842	city	3,300
			1845	Saint-Antoine	1,600
			1846	city	1,160
			1849	Saint-Antoine	90

APPENDIX 8 — *Continued*

Commutator	Year	Profession	Major Interests	Location	Property Evaluation (£)
John Torrance *Continued*	1852			Saint-Antoine	456
	1854			Sainte-Anne	800
	1854			Sainte-Anne	5,350
	1855			city	900
	1856			Saint-Laurent	280
	1859			Saint-Antoine	1,700
					17,136
Joseph Masson	1841	esquire	import-export, bank director	city	3,700
	1842			city	850
	1842			city	6,900
	1844			city	3,890
	1856			city	1,200[6]
					16,540
Samuel Gale	1841	judge	land developer, railway director	Sainte-Marie	1,500
	1845			city	12,000
	1850			Sainte-Marie current	400
	1852			Sainte-Marie current	1,265
					15,165

Name	Year	Title	Occupation	Location	Amount
James Ferrier	1840	esquire, banker	merchant	Saint-Laurent	1,228
	1841		banker, merchant, mayor	city, Sainte-Marie	8,500
	1842			city	2,000
	1844			city	1,100
	1850			Sainte-Marie	725[7]
					13,553
John Redpath	1840		stone mason, contractor, sugar refiner	Saint-Antoine	4,000
	1841			Saint-Antoine	480
	1844			Saint-Antoine	5,000
	1845			Pointe-aux-Trembles	750
	1853			city	1,800
					12,030
John Mills	1845	esquire, banker	banker, merchant	Sainte-Anne	2,500
	1847			Saint-Antoine	750
	1855			Saint-Antoine	8,000[8]
					11,250
Peter McGill	1840	esquire	merchant, banker, shipping, railways	city	1,530
	1844			city	5,000
	1847			city	4,700
	1853			Sainte-Anne	200
					11,430

APPENDIX 8 — *Continued*

Commutator	Year	Profession	Major Interests	Location	Property Evaluation (£)
Hugh Allan	1841	esquire, merchant	merchant, shipping	city	3,966
	1844			Saint-Laurent	1,302
	1845			Saint-Laurent	750
	1857			Pointe-à-Callières	5,000[9]
					11,018
Congregation of Notre Dame	1854		institution	Côte Saint-Antoine	9,000
	1860			Pointe Saint-Charles	1,300
					10,300
John Frothingham	1842	esquire, merchant	hardware merchant, iron manufacturer	city	2,500
	1842			Saint-Laurent & foot of mountain	4,400
	1845			Saint-Laurent	600
	1854			Saint-Laurent	2,000
					9,500
Banque du Peuple	1852		institution	city	3,000
	1852			Sainte-Anne	3,925
	1852			Saint-Laurent	1,000
	1853			Sainte-Anne	200

Name	Year				Amount
	1854			Saint-Antoine, Sainte-Marie	830
	1855			Saint-Antoine	400
					9,355
William Dow	1841	merchant, brewer	brewing	Sainte-Anne	8,628
	1845			Sainte-Anne	50
	1849			Sainte-Marie	200
					8,878
Thomas Cringan	1841	merchant	railways	city & Pointe-à-Callières	8,000[iii]
	1848			Sainte-Marie	40
					8,040
George Moffatt	1843	esquire	merchant, railways	city	1,200
	1845			Pointe-Claire	1,900
	1846			city	3,500
	1854			city, Saint-Louis	1,250
					7,850
Hubert Paré	1840	merchant	grain merchant	city	4,000
	1841			city	755
	1844			Saint-Laurent	1,800
	1845			Sainte-Marie	200
	1846			Sainte-Marie	830
					7,585

APPENDIX 8 — *Continued*

Commutator	Year	Profession	Major Interests	Location	Property Evaluation (£)
Jacob Joseph	1845	esquire, merchant	commission merchant	Saint-Antoine	49
	1853			city	1,200
	1853			Saint-Laurent	720
	1856			Saint-Antoine	5,600
					7,569
Thomas Phillips	1841	esquire	contractor	Saint-Antoine	4,400
	1842			Saint-Laurent	2,500
	1843			parish of Saint-Laurent	600
					7,500
Olivier Berthelet	1840	esquire	rentier	Saint-Antoine	900
	1841			Saint-Laurent	24
	1841			Saint-Laurent	50
	1842			Saint-Laurent	800
	1842			Saint-Laurent	119
	1843			Saint-Laurent	23
	1843			Sainte-Marie	80
	1844			Sainte-Anne	471
	1850			Saint-Laurent	200
	1850			Saint-Laurent	3,805
	1854			Sainte-Anne	350

Name	Year	Occupation	Location	Value
	1858		Saint-Laurent	375
	1859		Saint-Laurent	39
				7,236
Stanley Bagg	1841	esquire, commer- cant, merchant / contractor	city	2,000[a]
	1842		parish of Saint-Laurent	300
	1844		Sainte-Anne	1,500
	1844		Saint-Antoine	3,000
				6,800
William Watson	1843	esquire, flour inspector / miller	Saint-Laurent	240
	1845		Saint-Laurent	150
	1845		Saint-Pierre creek	1,750
	1849		Saint-Antoine	25
	1851		Saint-Laurent	920
	1859		Sainte-Anne	3,700
				6,785
Toussaint Pelletier	1858		city	6,750[b]
George Auldjo	1853	general merchant	city	6,750[b]
Alexandre Delisle	1842	esquire / lawyer, banker	Saint-Laurent	910
	1843		city	1,205
	1844		Saint-Antoine	2,840
	1845		city	650
	1856		Saint-Antoine	150
	1858		Côte Saint-Luc	950
				6,705

APPENDIX 8 — *Continued*

Commutator	Year	Profession	Major Interests	Location	Property Evaluation (£)
Jacob DeWitt	1843	esquire, banker	banker	Sainte-Anne	1,550
	1843			city	1,200
	1846			Sainte-Antoine	500
	1852			city	3,000
					6,250
Bank of Montreal	1842		institution	city	4,000
	1848			city	2,000
					6,000
David L. Macpherson	1845	esquire, merchant	forwarder	Sainte-Marie	2,000[12]
	1845			Côte Saint-Antoine	4,000
					6,000
Sisters of Hotel Dieu	1859			Saint-Laurent	6,000
Samuel Gerrard	1841	esquire	merchant	Saint-Antoine	2,000
	1841			Sainte-Marie	100
	1842			city	2,370
	1843			city	1,000
	1845			Saint-Laurent	480
					5,950

Benaiah Gibb	1841	esquire	merchant tailor	Saint-Antoine	3,500
	1841			city	2,300[13]
	1847			Saint-Laurent	390
					5,890
Thomas Stayner	1845	esquire	railway interests	Saint-Louis	1,800
	1846			Sainte-Marie current	4,000
					5,800
McGill University	1845		institution	Saint-Antoine	5,250
David Ross	1855			city	5,000[6]
	1855			Saint-Laurent	200[6]
					5,200
Harrison Stephens	1845	esquire, merchant		city	5,000

1 With Benjamin Lemoine
2 With Thomas Molson
3 With Thomas and John Molson
4 Commuted by his wife Margaret Fisher, widow of William Hutchison
5 With David Torrance
6 Commuted by heirs
7 With Alexander Bryson
8 Commuted by widow Hannah Lyman
9 With William Edmonstone
10 With William Edmond, William and Hart Logan, and Kentwell Hall
11 With Abner Bagg
12 Commuted by wife Elizabeth Sarah Molson
13 Commuted by heir James D. Gibb

APPENDIX 9

Laws Affecting Seigneurial Tenure and Disposal of Revenues, 1840–73

	Ordinance of 1840 3–4 Vict. c. 30	Amendment to St. Lawrence and Atlantic Railroad Act (1849) 12 Vict. c. 176	Seigneurial Act of 1854 18 Vict. c. 3	Seigneurial Amendment of 1859 22 Vict. 48	Seigneurial Act of 1860 23 Vict. c. 60	Act to Amend Revised Stat. of Canada, 1873 36 Vict. c. 70
Status of seminary	– seminary given absolute ownership in freehold tenure of its buildings and unconceded lands; can sell or dispose of them as it wishes		seminary exempted from all clauses	– seminary given absolute ownership of buildings and unconceded lands; can sell or dispose of them as it wishes	seigneurial tenure abolished on fiefs	
Right to collect seigneurial arrears	– full power to collect seigneurial arrears and to charge interest; mortgages on these arrears have priority – *lods et ventes* arrears of under £41 payable on demand – *lods et ventes* arrears of over £41 payable in instalments before 1847			– seigneurial arrears to be collected and interest exigible – *lods et ventes* arrears of under $100 payable on demand¹ – *lods et ventes* arrears of over $100 due in four annual payments before 1862		

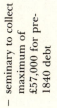

– seminary to collect maximum of £57,000 for pre-1840 debt

Commutation
– *censitaire* may ask for commutation; seigneur cannot refuse
– *cens et rentes* converted into a capital on which legal interest returns equivalent amount
– capitalization of *lods et ventes* on property worth more than £500 on seigneury of Montreal:
  5% of value of property if commuted within 7 years
  5.6% of value of property if commuted 7 to 14 years
  6.25% of value of property if commuted after 14 years

– capitalization of *cens et rentes* to be calculated as under Seigneurial Act of 1854
– commutation of *lods et ventes* within city and parish of Montreal continues under terms of 1840
– *censitaire* may commute voluntarily but commutation is obligatory when there is a sale and within 10 years of a succession
– corporate bodies to commute within 20 years
– capitalization of *lods et ventes* outside city and parish of Montreal at 8.3% of assessed value; amount to be paid

APPENDIX 9 — *Continued*

Ordinance of 1840 *3–4 Vict. c. 30*	*Amendment to St. Lawrence and Atlantic Railroad Act (1849)* *12 Vict. c. 176*	*Seigneurial Act of 1854* *18 Vict. c. 3*	*Seigneurial Amendment of 1859* *22 Vict. 48*	*Seigneurial Act of 1860* *23 Vict. c. 60*	*Act to Amend Revised Stat. of Canada, 1873* *36 Vict. c. 70*
– capitalization of *lods et ventes* on property worth more than £100 to £500 on seigneury of Montreal: 6.25% of value of property if commuted within 7 years 7.1% of value of property if commuted 7 to 14 years 8.33% of value of property if commuted after 14 years – capitalization of any property outside city of Montreal and on property within city evaluated at less than £100:			by crown with interest from £35,000 in Consolidated Revenue Fund¹; seminary has option of taking a 75% lump-sum payment – this settlement from crown in lieu of any commutation for crown properties on seminary seigneuries		

Assessment of land of which commutation based	8.33% of value of property if commuted within 7 years 10% of value of property if commuted 7 to 14 years 12.5% of value of property if commuted after 14 years – for capitalization of over £100, *censitaire* may ask Seminary to take quit rent (*rente constituée*)	– if no amicable agreement, assessment by arbitrators		
Investment rights	– unlimited right to invest in non-profit religious or charitable organizations. – £30,000 could be invested in revenue-producing real estate. – surplus capital to be invested in public	– Seminary (and other civil and ecclesiastical bodies) right to lend with interest to St. Lawrence & Atlantic Railway	– seminary has right to invest in mortgages and securities of its choice but not more than £30,000 in revenue-producing real estate	– Seminary and other religious bodies can lend at up to 8% interest

APPENDIX 9 — *Continued*

	Ordinance of 1840 *3-4 Vict. c. 30*	*Amendment to St. Lawrence and Atlantic Railroad Act (1849)* *12 Vict. c. 176*	*Seigneurial Act of 1854* *18 Vict. c. 3*	*Seigneurial Amendment of 1859* *22 Vict. 48*	*Seigneurial Act of 1860* *23 Vict. c. 60*	*Act to Amend Revised Stat. of Canada, 1873* *36 Vict. c. 70*
	securities of Great Britain or colonies.					
Sale of Saint-Gabriel farm	– sell in public sale within 20 years and in freehold tenure			– 20-year extension for sale of Saint-Gabriel farm – can sell privately or in public sale		

1 The act uses pounds and dollars in different sections.

APPENDIX 10

Seminary Income, 1795–1839 (*livres tournois*)

Year	Cens et rentes (paid in cash) & lods.	Cens et rentes et dîmes (paid in kind)	Domains	Flour Mills	Saw-mills	Other Seigneurial Dues (fishing, dimes in cash, wood)	Urban Property Rents	Other	Total
1795	34,115	–	1,453	44,220	736	–	600	1,200	82,324
1805	56,152	18,565	18,565	24,378	–	295	–	24,717[1]	142,705[2]
1815	85,217	29,881	24,154	51,551	2,065	647	3,909	3,009	200,433
1825	111,710	48,500	18,833	19,723	1,215	1,064	3,650	10,421[3]	215,116
1830	90,739	8,321	7,489	19,920	636	817	3,291	8,754	139,967
1831	140,796	11,581	8,416	23,048	1,716	1,170	1,538	5,118	186,685
1832	157,705	14,819	9,293	27,617	881	1,093	3,214	4,166	218,788
1833	146,844	9,540	9,343	20,888	2,172	1,625	4,674	8,507	203,593
1834	135,846	18,365[4]	4,175	–	–	1,292	5,600	9,076	174,354
1835	119,411	6,434	4,766	9,241	–	391	4,949	4,290	149,482
1836	120,654	9,090	6,352	9,414	–	1,453	3,464	5,460	155,887
1837	141,852	13,961	6,686	13,366	–	1,591	2,820	4,210	184,486
1838	79,438	7,727	10,474	16,205	–	577	5,166	8,692	128,279
1839	114,832	11,349	4,800	19,225	–	603	6,552	3,540	160,901

Source: ASSM, arm. 2, vol. 24: arm. 2, vol. 225.

Note: Includes income of both procurator and bursar.

1 Land sale

2 Does not include 87,639 *livres tournois* borrowed in 1805 to build the Collège de Montréal

3 Includes a 7,200 *livres tournois* reimbursement from Séminaire de Québec

4 Rentes and flour mills lumped into one figure for 1834

APPENDIX 11
Seminary Income, 1841–1915 (dollars)

Year	Mills	Lods et ventes, cens et rentes	Domains	Total Seigneurial Income	Mill Sales	Land Sales	Rents	Transfers, Debts, Reimbursements	Interest on rentes constituées and obligations	Borrowed Capital	Commutations	Collection of pre-1840 Seigneurial Debts	Government Indemnity for lods et ventes	Other	Total
1841	3,249	5,592	636	9,477	4,532	2,236	—	4,480	3,184	16,580	47,632	30,476	—	—	120,522
1842	2,232	12,032	5,143	19,407	584	2,484	1,925	21,096	8,528	—	46,924	34,536	—	—	136,643
1843	888	12,704	2,897	16,489	208	1,140	3,094	6,156	6,968	—	41,024	27,672	—	—	103,045
1844	1,892	17,164	3,655	22,711	2,916	2,316	3,388	2,580	7,112	—	35,144	25,132	—	—	101,299
1845	1,796	16,356	3,487	21,639	1,200	1,072	5,042	2,112	12,772	—	82,584	17,904	—	1,796	146,921
1846	1,280	20,792	2,679	24,751	—	648	5,975	750	16,040	—	40,580	14,900	—	4,272	107,916
1847	2,464	18,460	3,206	24,130	—	744	5,911	608	19,792	—	21,756	14,604	—	200	87,745
1848	2,516	14,924	4,489	21,929	14,556	—	3,116	616	19,484	—	15,788	8,324	—	—	69,257
1849	2,520	12,880	2,578	17,978	—	1,884	4,460	1,236	20,784	—	7,540	7,588	—	—	74,142
1850	3,068	14,232	3,116	20,416	—	200	2,432	1,272	20,468	5,732	8,036	7,308	—	—	67,548
1851	2,584	14,220	457	17,273	1,200	—	2,768	248	20,844	21,000	26,796	6,044	—	—	95,173
1852	2,088	13,080	811	15,979	—	27,020	2,748	4,432	17,540	11,400	31,148	8,636	—	15,984[1]	136,087
1853	1,892	18,792	910	21,594	—	90,204	3,172	10,392	19,596	2,720	84,684	9,056	—	3,364[1]	244,782
1854	2,072	16,348	1,416	19,836	388	10,564	4,865	176	22,392	—	36,352	8,972	—	924[2]	104,469
1855	1,892	19,488	1,508	22,888	—	4,668	4,995	112	21,884	14,200	17,100	3,364	—	1,176[1]	90,385
1856	324	20,720	1,436	22,480	868	12,188	4,808	8	25,736	26,688	21,232	5,512	—	3,600[3]	123,120
1857	328	21,236	724	22,288	5,840	21,392	5,384	996	24,428	28,760	21,256	4,224	—	4,500	139,068
1858	420	21,816	16,220	38,456	1,124	12,012	5,064	440	20,480	95,048	19,224	3,608	—	—	195,456
1859	468	24,148	13,192	37,808	3,552	17,324	4,720	160	20,876	5,564	21,904	3,832	—	24,000[1]	139,740

Year															
1860	468	41,352	12,232	54,052	1,084	43,112	6,412	540	18,864	24,596	30,512	8,488	9,708	800	198,168
1861	236	22,156	15,376	37,768	1,388	20,056	6,980	100	21,800	1,512	30,844	4,940	33,848	–	159,236
1862	650	19,841	10,608	31,099	336	19,797	12,178	326	36,913	22,650	23,856	3,476	20,202	–	170,833
1863	476	19,108	11,423	31,007	1,696	17,047	14,090	837	33,541	1,360	23,330	3,834	20,202	12,390[2]	159,334
1864	400	19,106	11,222	30,728	1,378	48,925	15,034	–	34,218	1,327	32,338	3,489	20,202	1,947	189,586
1865	400	19,128	1,171	20,699	950	82,207	14,026	–	37,295	3,900	30,099	5,580	20,202	11,739	226,697
1866	300	32,118	439	32,857	390	20,605	14,887	–	50,465	9,815	32,239	4,928	20,202	–	186,388
1867	–	16,515	726	17,241	1,173	34,901	15,444	6,962	40,492	12,364	35,152	3,658	20,202	–	187,589
1868	–	17,485	614	18,100	1,290	53,372	16,507	–	39,103	32,497	25,857	2,710	20,202	–	209,637
1869	–	11,857	506	12,363	330	49,173	17,698	–	36,857	55,376	41,581	1,557	20,202	–	235,137
1870	–	4,890	119	5,009	956	37,044	14,764	–	37,932	147,018	31,401	10,004	20,202	–	304,330
1871	–	3,701	3,874	7,575	240	121,945	14,499	3,269	43,239	59,067	54,499	10,265	20,202	–	334,800
1872	–	4,907	43	4,950	300	44,093	15,493	11,077	42,523	39,336	53,946	12,906	20,202	–	244,826
1873	–	7,135	956	8,091	–	49,698	17,809	–	53,231	93,972	52,768	9,672	20,202	–	305,443
1874	–	3,445	110	3,555	300	58,245	17,856	650	44,346	92,929	95,730	10,498	20,202	475	344,786
1875	–	4,778	150	4,928	700	63,124	20,697	9,632	61,121	54,718	51,975	10,720	336,719	–	614,334
1876	–	2,554	–	2,554	600	86,522	23,667	7,296	59,356	6,043	22,114	8,218	–	–	216,370
1890	–	2,165	206	2,371	–	63,928	25,369	35,936[4]	58,493	–	29,798	6,578	–	–	222,473
1900	–	1,249	2,216	3,465	–	44,646	22,508	70,715[5]	64,364	–	12,230	7,730	–	–	225,658
1915	–	–	–	–	–	115,387	50,976	28,306	61,529	–	4,529	3,043	–	–	263,770

Source: ASSM, arm. 2, vol. 157; arm. 3, vol. 402.

1 Insurance settlements

2 Indemnity for quints or fiefs

3 Gift for schools

4 Includes $8,000 reimbursement by Notre-Dame *fabrique,* bond income, and various debts

5 Includes bond and bank income

APPENDIX 12

Bonds, Debentures, and Shares Held by the Seminary, 1882–1909

Investment	Type of Enterprise		Form	Amount ($)
Acton Vale, Quebec	municipality		bonds	10,000
Banque d'Hochelag	financial	685	shares	
Bell Telephone Co. of Canada	industry		debentures	4,000
Birtle, Manitoba	municipality		debentures	9,800
Canadian Electric Light Co.	industry	112	shares	
Canadian Colored Cotton Co.	industry		bonds	12,200
Cartierville, Quebec	municipality		debentures	11,000
Chambly, Quebec	municipality	21	bonds	
Champlain and St. Lawrence Jct. Ry.	transportation		debentures	94,000
Chemins à Barrières	transportation	6	shares	
Chicoutimi Pulp Co.	industry	94	debentures	
Coteau Saint-Louis, Quebec	municipality	20	bonds	8,000
Detroit United Railway	transportation	341	shares	
Dominion Coal (Boston)	industry	93	debentures	
Dominion Cotton Mills Co.	industry		bonds	85,000
Dominion Iron and Steel Co.	industry	4,855	shares	
		43	bonds	
Dominion Textile Co.	industry	443	shares	
Garthby	municipality	6	bonds	
Grantham	municipality	1	bond	
Grand Forks, British Columbia	municipality	46	bonds	
Government of Quebec	government	45	bonds	22,500
Halifax and Eastern Railway	transportation	87	bonds	
Hamilton Power Co.	industry	73	debentures	73,000
Heinks Township	municipality	25	debentures	11,875
Hull, Quebec	municipality	492	bonds	
Iberville, Quebec	municipality	49	bonds	49,000
International Coal Mining Co.	industry	55	debentures	27,500
Joliette, Quebec	municipality	15	debentures	15,000
Laprairie, Quebec	municipality	85	debentures	33,850
Longueuil, Quebec	municipality	36	bonds	18,000
Louisville, Quebec	municipality	9	debentures	4,500
Lake of the Woods Milling Co.	industry	43	debentures	43,000
Marie-Ville, Quebec	municipality	18	debentures	9,000
Merriton, Ontario	municipality	5	debentures	15,887

APPENDIX 12 — *Continued*

Investment	Type of Enterprise	Form		Amount ($)
City of Montreal	municipality	75	debentures	
Montreal Harbour Board	public body	73	debentures	
Montreal Catholic School Commission	public body	98	debentures	
Montreal Light, Heat and Power Co.	industry	42	bonds	42,000
		1,948	shares	
Mount Royal Assurance Co.	financial	685	shares	
New Glasgow, Quebec	municipality	20	debentures	$2,000
Ogilvy Flour Mills	industry	8	debentures	8,000
Port Arthur, Ontario	municipality	105	debentures	90,000
Port Hood Coal Co.	industry	10	debentures	10,000
Payne Mining Co.	industry	3	debentures	
Quebec, Montmorency and Charlevoix Railway Co.	transportation	183	debentures	
Roberval, Quebec	municipality	46	bonds	36,202
Richelieu and Ontario Navigation Co.	transportation	380	debentures	169,000
Roxton Falls,	municipality	36	debentures	17,500
Royal Electric Light Co.	industry	15	debentures	15,000
Sault Ste Marie, Ontario	municipality	89	debentures	89,000
Sutton Township, Quebec	municipality	1	bond	
Saint Cesaire, Quebec	municipality	44	debentures	4,400
St Boniface, Manitoba	municipality	10	debentures	10,000
Stanbridge, Quebec	municipality	21	bonds	
Sorel, Quebec	municipality	142	debentures	142,000
Sainte Sophie, Quebec	municipality	37	debentures	3,700
Saint Die parish, Quebec	municipality	30	debentures	3,000
Salaberry of Valleyfield	municipality	61	debentures	30,500
Sandon,	municipality	15	debentures	15,000
Shawinigan Falls, Quebec	municipality	10	debentures	10,000
Tadoussac, Quebec	municipality	13	debentures	13,000
Toronto Street Railway	transportation	525	shares	
Trois-Rivières, Quebec	municipality	387	bonds	
Valleyfield, Quebec	municipality	44	debentures	22,000
Valleyfield Aqueduc Co.	transportation	3	debentures	27,000
Verdun, Quebec	municipality	40	debentures	
Wickham,	municipality	8	bonds	
Winnipeg, Manitoba	municipality	40	debentures	20,000
Winnipeg Electric Street Railway Co.	transportation	50	debentures	25,000

Source: ASSM, arm. 2, vol. 267.

APPENDIX 13

Procurator's Ordinary and Capital Expenditures, 1805–39 (*livres tournois*)

ORDINARY EXPENDITURES

Year	Bursar	Travel & Purchases in France	Collège de Montréal	Grey Nuns	Congregation of Notre Dame	Christian Brothers	Alms	Sub-scriptions	Indian Mission	Lawyers	Survey-ors	Notaries	Office Expenses	Other[1]
1805	51,740	228	648	–	–	–	652	420	5,496	990	–	514	–	120
1815	38,082	8,886	17,856	–	–	–	4,800	2,436	1,590	120	–	720	–	96
1820	47,586	636	4,855	2,400	2,100	–	9,600	2,595	–	3,596	2,565	760	–	–
1825	55,017	3,180	13,668*	6,831	600	–	9,600	7,002*	1,740	4,417	1,620	1,768	648	16,560
1830	46,920	–	10,110*	8,185	1,200	–	7,200	1,152	1,080	3,070	–	3,009	–	432
1831	47,679	1,494	9,084*	6,551	600	–	8,130	6,180	–	2,434	131	1,655	942	1,854
1832	51,172	2,844	18,354*	7,147	1,500	–	8,208	3,678	–	2,908	379	1,317	1,254	25,758
1833	51,995	720	13,920	8,826	1,800	–	9,600	3,006	1,848	3,072	1,589	10,914	1,914	21,246
1834	49,602	216	22,140*	9,416	720	–	9,000	8,826	–	2,746	–	3,943	3,858	11,256
1835	43,330	–	14,364*	8,366	2,400	–	9,600	5,436	–	4,712	2,467	3,203	–	13,164
1836	58,741	–	19,776*	10,021	2,400	–	11,076	7,686	–	2,336	466	3,900	996	2,502
1837	78,041	1,110	26,436*	9,316	2,400	–	11,160	11,382	–	2,958	624	5,588	–	38,004
1838	48,876	2,328	10,758*	8,253	2,400	15,264	9,600	9,966*	–	5,022	180	4,398	–	10,686
1839	41,206	240	15,582*	8,454	4,272	30,618	9,600	4,536	–	5,740	844	4,536	–	4,374

CAPITAL EXPENDITURES

Year	Capital Expenses at Seminary	Church Construction	Collège de Montréal Construction	Repairs & Construction of Mills, Domains, Rental Properties	Other²
1805	–	–	162,078	9,300	–
1815	–	–	–	49,932	2,772
1820	–	–	–	20,210	13,567³
1825	24,102	18,000	–	6,726	–
1830	–	8,640	2,214	36,420*	–
1831	3,252	17,142	–	10,272	–
1832	7,734*	6,120	–	39,204	–
1833	6,324	10,374	–	54,252	–
1834	1,782	13,158	–	25,458	4,344
1835	–	–	–	1,956	–
1836	–	–	–	32,034	600
1837	1,836	143,274	12,780	51,738	–
1838	966	–	–	9,402	–
1839	–	16,002	–	6,210	–

Source: ASSM, arm. 2, vol. 24; arm. 2, vol. 225.
* denotes inclusion of expenditures of bursar
1 Includes items like insurance, bailiff, firewood, taxes
2 Mainly school repairs and construction
3 Sulpician sent to London on political mission

APPENDIX 14

Procurator's Ordinary and Capital Expenditures, 1840–1915 (dollars)

ORDINARY EXPENDITURES

Year	Bursar	Travel & Purchases in France	Collège de Montréal	Grand Séminaire	Grey Nuns	Congregation of Notre Dame	Christian Brothers	Other Schools	Alms	Subscriptions	Indian Mission	Lawyers	Surveyors	Office Employees	Others[1]
1840–1	14,560	2,068	4,484	—	2,640	3,404	37,712[3]	—	2,168	2,212	—	540	192	1,828[4]	2,664
1842	10,608	528	2,724	—	1,452	3,648	5,752	—	10,540	—	—	824	80	1,684[5]	4,344
1843	7,672	2,728	2,192	—	1,760	756	3,616	—	1,664	2,296	—	636	108	4,100	312
1844	5,784	—	1,964	—	1,596	872	3,216	872	2,548	1,508	—	640	—	4,224	716
1845	7,164	3,584	2,032	—	1,216	5,156	10,956[3]	15,784[3]	2,548	3,476	—	1,088	340	2,880	1,252
1846	7,172	2,436	3,176	—	1,452	1,792	14,140[3]	5,376	2,188	2,408	—	664	188	3,724	1,324
1847	6,972	396	1,658	—	1,176	1,352	4,504	2,784	2,920	2,132	—	412	1,000	2,876	934
1848	10,436	3,688	4,248	—	1,196	1,208	4,032	2,584	3,380	2,540	—	1,292	120	2,640	776
1849	11,040	4,148	3,696	—	2,084	1,416	6,138	1,944	6,018	1,580	—	78	—	2,268	1,064
1850	15,900	1,492	3,784	—	1,712	1,444	4,988	1,164	3,652	2,568	—	488	—	2,388	1,440
1851	13,096	3,020	2,908	—	1,440	1,452	4,972	1,696	4,440	1,508	—	232	196	2,532	940
1852	15,104	912	3,288	—	1,396	1,280	4,892	1,480	4,064	3,352	—	132	—	3,188	10,732
1853	14,896	1,744	4,756	—	1,500	1,204	4,608	4,260	4,376	2,828	—	572	180	3,276	432
1854	19,132	2,900	4,760	—	1,508	2,740	5,284	1,484	6,452	2,304	1,000	572	—	3,084	600
1855	21,724	968	4,540	—	1,564	15,088[3]	13,088[3]	1,660	5,960	2,672	780	172	—	3,112	648
1856	22,464	532	5,004	—	1,444	8,608	11,728[3]	812	4,948	1,996	1,104	196	184	3,000	804
1857	26,400	488	4,252	—	1,600	3,188	6,044	1,636	4,796	3,144	208	408	—	2,900	836
1858	21,792	2,828	3,976	—	1,500	2,596	5,500	2,036	5,364	2,248	1,896	264	—	3,364	784
1859	19,940	4,384	3,256	—	1,512	2,592	6,364	1,840	6,716	1,680	4,988	—	92	3,576	1,132
1860	22,216	4,148	5,544	—	1,680	3,520	6,628	1,656	5,532	4,192	4,140	316	284	3,768	1,236
1861	25,440	1,048	2,996	—	1,828	5,864	6,044	1,656	7,112	4,180	8,124	156	—	5,128	8,696

Year	Capital Expenses for Sulpician Community	Church Construction	New Collège de Montréal	Grand Séminaire	Cabinet de Lecture	Mills, Domains, & Rental Properties (till 1853)	Rental Properties (after 1853)	Land Purchases	Loans, Bonds	Reimbursement of Capital	Interest Payments	Other
1862	23,844	1,086	3,102	1,404	3,197	6,887	5,802	9,203	6,516	253	77	8,214
1863	28,853	1,580	3,107	1,393	3,344	9,926	6,576	11,382	6,021	106	925	3,090
1864	36,444	4,404[8]	2,978	1,502	8,587	7,864	10,933[3]	10,887	4,454	156	315	1,108
1865	33,735	1,861	3,478	1,566	9,864	11,341	32,685[3]	12,716	5,148	222	—	581
1866	33,880	1,919	3,249	1,630	3,567	11,370	10,093[3]	14,524	4,396	456	—	2,090
1867	34,709	4,737	2,480	1,678	6,143	10,613	1,151	12,439	5,406	333	—	6,734
1868	39,160	2,493	4,451	1,883	6,710	12,261	1,273	13,327	6,510	131	—	1,088
1869	36,327	2,940	3,531	1,467	17,779[3]	12,189	1,791	16,447	13,156	111	—	4,096
1870	38,757	2,032	3,095	1,524	16,312[3]	15,287	970	16,538	2,159	—	—	—
1871	41,023	2,761	4,195	1,684	9,426	15,895	709	16,747	3,168	1,266	—	1,354
1872	39,705	3,224	9,953	1,517	8,112	22,515[3]	717	15,437	2,614	1,012	—	361
1873	44,060	2,752	5,467	1,399	7,660	29,011[3]	3,719	15,137	6,306	345	—	585
1874	47,393	11,283	8,793	1,559	7,835	15,106	673	19,478	5,339	168	—	1,194
1875	43,570	3,134	13,500	1,417	7,664	16,114	681	16,300	10,259	2,434	—	1,394
1876	41,505	4,795	21,745	1,598	6,883	16,836	530	17,000	8,839	—	—	8,435
1890	33,681	—	14,554	429	5,070	5,897	—	10,900	7,605	222	—	1,679
1900	29,271	2,401	10,815	429	3,537	12,237	—	9,655	6,362	—	—	6,366
1915	27,792	4,869	18,773	—	4,830	14,260	28,652[3]	4,000	20,559	—	—	—

CAPITAL EXPENDITURES

Year	Capital Expenses for Sulpician Community	Church Construction	New Collège de Montréal	Grand Séminaire	Cabinet de Lecture	Mills, Domains, & Rental Properties (till 1853)	Rental Properties (after 1853)	Land Purchases	Loans, Bonds	Reimbursement of Capital	Interest Payments	Other
1840–1	160	8,812	—	—	—	3,416	—	—	—	2,000	60	5,708
1842	—	—	—	—	—	17,016	—	—	4,452	9,004	—	4,052
1843	—	4,216	—	—	—	4,856	—	—	4,508	9,372	—	—

CAPITAL EXPENDITURES — Continued

Year	Capital Expenses for Sulpician Community	Church[2] Construction	New Collège de Montréal	Grand Séminaire	Cabinet de Lecture	Mills, Domains, & Rental Properties (till 1853)	Rental Properties (after 1853)	Land Purchases	Loans, Bonds	Reimbursement of Capital	Interest Payments	Other
1844	192	2,032	—	—	—	7,220	—	—	3,464	—	—	—
1845	6,768	—	—	—	—	7,512	—	—	7,476	—	—	—
1846	4,244	6,000	—	—	—	6,204	—	—	400	—	864	—
1847	3,684	2,000	—	—	—	10,212	—	—	—	—	1,220	1,200
1848	18,498	—	—	—	—	2,500	—	—	—	—	1,220	—
1849	—	84	—	—	—	648	—	—	—	—	1,220	14,556[6]
1850	—	—	—	—	—	1,948	—	—	—	—	1,220	—
1851	—	—	—	—	—	—	—	—	—	—	1,156	—
1852	—	—	—	—	—	992	—	—	—	—	1,060	—
1853	—	23,072	—	—	—	—	15,376	—	400	2,876	—	—
1854	—	18,740	—	—	—	—	3,036	—	—	19,732	1,964	17,000[7]
1855	—	22,716	—	38,740	—	—	44	—	—	—	184	—
1856	—	24,976	—	39,000	—	—	220	—	2,108	4,264	692	2,180[7]
1857	—	30,400	—	49,690	—	—	1,656	—	—	4,552	2,308	—
1858	—	2,304	—	41,712	—	—	2,524	—	1,000	15,408	3,616	—
1859	—	1,304	—	6,696	—	—	8,324	—	600	12,452	7,164	—
1860	—	73,720	—	2,356	—	—	3,072	—	960	25,760	7,700	—
1861	—	25,456	—	11,069	6,420	—	2,864	10,000	2,524	7,556	9,964	—
1862	—	9,394	—	1,208	94	—	5,269	8,257	10,800	20,432	7,635	—
1863	—	14,228	—	5,525	—	2,825	1,646	—	—	12,528	7,708	—
1864	—	21,481	—	17,345	5,076	—	—	3,348	—	1,700	4,531	—
1865	—	6,895	—	—	—	223	—	13,872	2,000	1,857	6,927	4,393[9]
1866	—	78	—	—	—	—	—	—	—	14,855	6,310	2,592[10]

Year												
1867	–	6,116	–	–	–	–	3,852	1,277	21,733	16,579	7,274	2,000[11]
1868	–	13,911	36,071	1,516	–	382	1,217	–	5,340	10,557	6,498	16,000[12]
1869	–	16,866	85,465	–	–	5,996	–	–	–	16,096	7,742	–
1870	–	19,232	75,275	3,110	6,379	–	10,985	10,604	–	63,173	8,086	–
1871	11,829	–	40,314	–	3,862	–	8,370	8,040	500	61,250	16,540	–
1872	–	18,657	6,245	–	985	–	–	3,140	32,606	37,618	15,526	–
1873	3,127	15,666	1,000	6,449	833	–	–	6,884	2,000	58,910	17,130	–
1874	–	13,577	11,486	–	4,152	1,999	13,000	23,819	8,183	53,410[13]	[14]	–
1875	–	8,894	5,137	26,505	1,337	767	49,236	12,473	105,487	80,459[13]	[14]	–
1876	–	–	8,859	34,511	–	347	52,309	–	250	–	–	–
1890	–	–	–	–	631	–	–	–	79,978	–	–	113,263[15]
1900	–	–	–	–	1,115	–	–	–	106,628	–	–	3,976
1915	–	1,805	–	1,300	12,538	–	–	5,391	25,062	–	–	78,936[16]

Source: ASSM, arm. 2, vol. 24; arm. 2, vol. 225; arm. 2, vol. 264; arm. 2, vol. 157; arm. 3, vol. 402.

1 Includes payment to city for street improvements and expenditures for firewood, insurance, other expenses
2 Certain maintenance costs included
3 Includes capital expenditure for school and residence construction
4 Notary only
5 $824 for outside notary or office employees
6 Taking over mill
7 Transfer of John Donegani's debt
8 Represents 1864–5
9 $3443 for publishing *Histoire du Canada*; $950 for St Patrick's
10 Publishing costs for *Histoire du Canada*
11 Loan to Hôtel-Dieu
12 Transfer to Grey Nuns
13 Includes interest
14 Lumped with capital reimbursement in seminary books
15 Includes $27,937 for construction of Collège canadien in Rome
16 Includes $17,056 for construction of library on Saint-Denis street and $60,585 for Philosophy College on Côte-des-Neiges

APPENDIX 15

Auction Sales on the Saint-Gabriel Domain, 1853–9

Date	Number of Purchasers	Number of Lots Sold	Total Sales $	Terms	Service Charges	Other
12 April 1853	8	62	16,528	25% down; rest in equal instalments over 10 years	£1 10s. per title	– purchaser to erect fences – purchasers of basin lots accept mill and factory discharge from Young-Gould property
19 Oct. 1853	16	106	47,992	25% down; rest in equal instalments over 10 years	20s. per title for small lots, ½% of sale for larger lots	
12 June 1854	11	21		25% down; rest in equal instalments over 10 years	1% of sale price	
22 Aug. 1854	2	2		25% down; rest in equal instalments over 10 years	1% of sale price	
6 Sept. 1854	3	7	22,380	25% down; rest in equal instalments over 10 years	1% of sale price	
27 September 1854	4	8		25% down; rest in equal instalments over 10 years	1% of sale price	
18 October 1854	2	5		25% down; rest in equal instalments over ten years	1% of sale price	

Date				Conditions	Price
8 July 1856	0	0	0	25% down; rest in equal instalments over ten years. Interest from October 1857	£1 15s. per title
5 August 1856	7	7	2,040	25% down; rest in equal instalments over ten years. Interest from October 1857	£1 15s. per title
2 September 1856	16	47 & two blocks	21,580	$20 down for sale under $400; 5% down if more than $400. Balance in five equal payments over five years	£1 15s. per title
7 October 1856	5	10	2,564	$20 down for sale under $400; 5% down if more than $400. Balance in five equal payments over five years	£1 15s. per title
14 November 1856	5	19	10,240	same conditions as above if on south side of canal; 25% down if on north side	$8 per title
29 July 1857	22	32	9,040	10% down; interest from 1 October; balance in five equal payments over five years	$8 per title
26 August 1857	33	50	16,128	10% down; interest from 1 October; balance in five equal payments over five years	$8 per title

APPENDIX 15 — *Continued*

Date	Number of Purchasers	Number of Lots Sold	Total Sales $	Terms	Service Charges	Other
23 September 1857	7	11	3,152	10% down; interest from 1 October; balance in five equal payments over five years	$8 per title	
28 October 1857	4	5	1,524	10% down; interest from 1 October; balance in five equal payments over five years	$8 per title	
25 November 1857	?	?	?	10% down; interest from 1 October; balance in five equal payments over five years	$8 per title	
21 July 1858	10	16	3,952	10% down; interest from 1 October; balance in five equal payments over five years	$8 per title	
30 September 1858	2	2	480	10% down; interest from 1 October; balance in five equal payments over five years	$8 per title	
27 October 1859	4	7	1,700	10% down; interest from 1 October; balance in five equal payments over five years	$8 per title	

1 July 1861	24	27	7,528	10% down; interest from 1 October; deed to be signed within 24 hours of auction	$8 per title
2 July 1862	14	20	3,660	10% down; interest from 1 October; deed to be signed within 24 hours of auction	$8 per title
2 July 1863	3	5	804	10% down; interest from 1 October; deed to be signed within 24 hours of auction	$8 per title
29 August 1866	1	2	600	10% down; interest from 1 October; deed to be signed within 24 hours of auction	$8 per title

Source: ANQM, Lafleur, and ASSM, unindexed, arm. 5, tir. 47, St. Gabriel, livre d'encan, no. 1, no. 2.

APPENDIX 16
Conditions of Sale of Building Lots on Mountain Domain, 1860–80

Cette vente est ainsi faite aux charges, clauses et conditions suivantes que le dit acquéreur ses successeurs et ayant-cause, seront tenus d'exécuter comme conditions expresses de présentes, savoir:

1. De clore mitoyennement et à frais communs avec leurs voisins selon la loi, et à leurs frais seuls sur les rues et dans les lignes des vendeurs tant qu'il seront propriétaire de lots voisins, sous six mois de cette date, et de planter dans le même délai, des arbres sur le front du dit terrain.

2. De bâtir sur le dit terrain une maison logeable sous deux ans de cette date, et à pas moins de douze pieds de l'enlignement de la rue.

3. De ne pouvoir jamais y constuire d'autres bâtisses que des résidences privées, en pierre our en briques, couvertes en fer blanc ou autres matériaux à l'épreuve du feu, ni y ériger par conséquent aucune espèce de manufacture, d'usine, de boucherie où autres établissements nuisibles à des résidences privées.

4. De ne pouvoir détériorer le dit terrain, soit en l'exploitant comme Briqueterie ou en le creusant, pour en sortir du sable, de la glaise ou de la pierre, ou d'aucune autre manière.

5. Dans le cas de vente ou autre transport du dit terrain, de fair agréer et accepter par le Séminaire, dans le même acte, le nouvel acquéreur ou propriétaire, leguel sera tenu de fournir à ses frais au Séminaire une Copie Authentique et enrégistrée de son titre, dans les quinze jours qui suivront la passation d'icelui.

6. Dans le cas de vente ou autre cession d'une partie seulement du dit terrain, de fournir aussi au Séminaire une copie du titre de vente ou autre cession dans le même délai, et tout ce qui lui sera dû sur la partie ainsi vendue ou cédée, sera exigible et devra être alors payé et acquitté, nonobstant tous termes ou délais antérieurement accordés.

7. Dans le cas de contravention à, ou de non exécution d'aucune des charges, clauses ou conditions ci-dessus, tant pour le dit acquéreur que par ses représentants ou successeurs à l'avenir, tout ce qui sera alors dû aux dits Sieurs Ecclésiastiques sur le dit terrain, en capital et intérêts, deviendra alors aussi échu sera payable en entier, sans qu'il soit besoin d'aucun avis ou signification.

Source: Printed sale deed, ANQM, Lafleur, 1173, vente, seminary to Charles Binmore, 6 September 1860.

APPENDIX 17
Major Capital Expenses of Seminary for Social Purposes, 1848–78

Institution	Project	Year	Function	Cost ($)	Other
Congregation of Notre Dame School (Saint-Antoine suburb)	– reconstruction after fire	1848–9	school for girls	1,192	$1,192 from insurance on old building
Grand Séminaire	– construction	1855–64	theological school	213,341	
	– add wing	1875–8		91,579	
Saint-Jacques Church	– reconstruction after fire	1854–6	church	121,004	$24,000 from insurance
	– reconstruction after second fire	1859–60		24,000	represents insurance payment
	– belfry	1863		2,462	
	– enlarge presbytery	1873–4		14,312	
St Anne's Church	– construction	1851–9	church for Irish	44,600	
	– fence	1863–4		504	
	– vestry	1874		1,148	
Notre-Dame de Grâce Church	– construction	1850–9	church	51,160	
Christian Brothers School (Sainte-Marie suburb)	– construction	1854–5	school for boys	7,968	
Congregation of Notre Dame School (Sainte-Anne suburb)	– construction	1856–7	school for girls	5,480	
	– caretaker's house at school	1863–4		1,164	
Saint-Henri des Tanneries Chapel	– enlarge	1860	chapel	2,392	
Congregation of Notre Dame School (Saint-Laurent suburb)	– construction	1860–1	school for girls	2,632	
	– enlarge	1864–5		5,393	
St Joseph's Church	– construction	1860–3	church	25,911	

APPENDIX 17 — *Continued*

Institution	Project	Year	Function	Cost ($)	Other
Congregation of Notre Dame School (Visitation St)	– construction	1861	school for girls	4,250	
Christian Brothers School (Saint-Jacques)	– construction	1865–6	school for boys	25,965	
Côte-des-Neiges School and Chapel	– construction	1863	school & chapel	2,710	
Saint-Louis-de-France Church (Coteau-Saint-Louis)	– construction	1862–5	church	6,548	
Christian Brothers School (Sainte-Anne suburb)	– construction	1864–6	school for boys	19,013	
	– residence for teaching bros. at school	1876		1,000	
St Patrick's Orphan Asylum	– renovate	1865	orphanage	950	
Notre-Dame-des-Anges Chapel	– enlarge	1866–7	chapel	7,291	
Collège de Montréal	– construction on mountain	1867–73	college for boys	237,018	
Collège de Montréal and Grand Séminaire	– construction of wall along Sherbrooke St	1870–	college & seminary	11,198	
Congregation of Notre Dame School (St Patrick's)	– construction	1869–72	school for girls	22,272	
Congregation of Notre Dame School (St Joseph St)	– enlarge	1869–70	school for girls	1,562	
Cabinet de Lecture	– construction	1870–5	reading-room & meeting hall	17,549	
Residence for Christian Brothers (St Joseph's Church)	– construction	1870–1	residence	7,253	

add bedrooms & bathrooms

Christian Brothers Noviciate (Côté St)	– enlarge	1872–5	novitiate for teaching brothers	24,281
Congregation of Notre Dame School (Bonsecours)	– renovate	1872	school for girls	2,530
Christian Brothers School (St Joseph's suburb)	– construction	1874–6	school for boys	29,271

Source: ASSM, arm. 2, vol. 219, Dépenses pour construction du Séminaire, églises en ville, 1848–59; arm. 2, vol. 237, Dépenses pour construction.

Note: Does not include land purchases or expenses under $300

In 1859–60 the Seminary paid $13,800 for lumber, presumably for construction of churches and schools.

Notes

The following abbreviations or shortened references are used in the notes.

ANQM   Archives nationales du Québec, Montréal
ASSM   Archives du Séminaire de Saint-Sulpice de Montréal
ASSP   Archives du Séminaire de Saint-Sulpice de Paris
BNQM   Bibliothèque nationale du Québec, Montréal
DCB   *Dictionary of Canadian Biography* / *Dictionnaire biographique du Canada*
Fifth Report   Great Britain, *Report of the Committee on Grievances in Lower Canada*, 1838
Minutes   ASSM, Procès-Verbaux, Assemblées des Quatre Consultateurs
Notice   ASSM, tir. 70, Joseph-Vincent Quiblier, "Notice sur le Séminaire de Montréal"
Ordinance of 1840   Lower Canada, *Copy of Ordinances*
PAC   Public Archives of Canada
RHAF   *Revue d'histoire de l'Amérique française*

INTRODUCTION

1 Chandler, *The Visible Hand.*
2 McCalla, "The 'Loyalist' Economy of Upper Canada," 299.
3 Dobb, *Studies in the Development of Capitalism*, 35–6; K. Takahashi, "A Contribution to the Discussion," in Hilton, ed., *Transition*, 71–2; Bois, *Crise du féodalisme*, 195; Dechêne, *Habitants et marchands*, 256–7; for evidence of the rigour of seigneurialism after the conquest, see Beutler, "Les moulins à farine," 198; Harris, "Of Poverty and Helplessness," 336–46, and Ouellet, "Libéré ou exploité," 341–7.
4 For the transition, see Albert Soboul, *Contributions à l'histoire paysanne; Problèmes paysans de la révolution*, or "Du féodalisme au capitalisme"; also

of great importance are Hilton, ed., *Transition*, and Marx, *Grundrisse*, 471–533 and *Capital* 3: 323–37, 802–13; for changes in land tenure in other countries, see Pollard, *Peaceful Conquest*, 47, 55.

5 Donald Creighton, *Empire of the St. Lawrence*, 53, 96; for Japan, see Takahashi, "Place," 247; for England, see Marx, *Capital* 3: 327, or Hill, *English Revolution*, 4.

6 Ouellet, "Propriété seigneuriale," 194, 203.

7 Beauharnois is described in Colthart, "Edward Ellice," Lavaltrie in Robert, "Un seigneur entrepreneur," and Terrebonne in Ouellet, "Simon McTavish"; ANQM, Valotte, 397, "Vente et transport," Seminary to Jean-Baptiste Demers, 20 March 1845. For masons, see Lauzon, "Pierre sur pierre," 6–7. Carpenters, joiners, and masons are treated in Stewart, "Structural Change and the Construction Trades."

8 Braverman quoted in Katz, "Origins of the Institutional State," 17; Soboul, "Du féodalisme au capitalisme," 66.

9 ASSM, tir. 63, no. 206, Déclaration du Séminaire produite devant la cour du Banc du Roi, 28 June 1816; tir. 5, no. 42, Remarks on the proposed ordinance to erect and endow an ecclesiastical corporation in the Province of Lower Canada, 1840, 1; tir. 4, no. 8, Samuel Gale to A.W. Cochran, 15 April 1826.

10 ASSM, tir 3, no. 36b, Procès-verbaux d'une conversation entre Col. Ready and H.A. Roux, 28 August 1819.

11 Conditions under which interest could be collected are examined in Zoltvany, "Esquisse," 369.

12 Ouellet, *Papineau*, 83.

13 Lemieux, *L'établissement*; Pouliot, *Monseigneur Bourget*; Rumilly, *Histoire de Montréal*; Chabot, *Le curé de campagne;* Eid, *Le clergé*; Chaussé, *Jean-Jacques Lartigue*; Lajeunesse, *Les Sulpiciens*; Rousseau, *La prédication à Montréal*; Lambert, "Monseigneur, the Catholic Bishop."

14 For conversions in seminary accounts, see ASSM, arm. 3, vol. 403; see also *A Remedy for the Evils of Banking*, 8, and McCalla, *Upper Canada Trade*, 176.

15 For these documents see ASSM, unindexed and unshelved boxes in arm. 5 entitled "Vente de la ferme St. Gabriel et emploi des deniers en provenant," and "Gestion: Not. Le Maire (1849–79); Not. Parent (1826–47); Arp. Ostell (1840–48); Arp. Perrault (1862–79); and arm. 5, tir. 47, "St. Gabriel, livre d'encan," no. 1, no. 2.

16 Sweeny, "Internal Dynamics and the International Cycle: Questions of the Transition in Montreal, 1821–28"; the papers collected as *Protesting History* are entitled "Problématique de la transition," "Colony and Crisis: Montreal and the First Capitalist Crisis," "Financing the Transition in a Colonial City: Montreal 1820–28," and "Beyond the Staples: Firms and Functions of Lower Canadian International Trade."

CHAPTER ONE

1 The term "holy housekeeping" is Werner Sombart's and is quoted in
  K. Samuelson, *Religion and Economic Action: A Critique of Max Weber*
  (New York: Harper and Row, 1964), 69; H. d'Antin de Vaillac, "Les
  constitutions de Saint-Sulpice," 81.

2 ASSM, arm. 3, vol. 115, "Compte de sommes remises à Joseph Comte
  et autres," Comte to F. Lemaire, 20 September 1861.

3 For a description of the Counter-Reformation and a full bibliography
  see Jean Delumeau, *Le Catholicisme*; French seminaries are described
  in Bernard Plongeron, *La vie quotidienne*, 53–61; the origins of the
  Séminaire de Saint-Sulpice have been fully described by three Sulpician
  historians: Pierre Boisard, *La compagnie de Saint-Sulpice*; Étienne-Michel
  Faillon, *Vie de M. Olier*; and d'Antin de Vaillac, "Les constitutions de
  Saint-Sulpice"; for the seminary's role in the Counter-Reformation outside Paris see Philip T. Hoffman, "Le rôle social des curés," 7.

4 As late as the nineteenth century the constitution was open only to
  members, although a copy in Latin was provided to British authorities
  in 1840. Important parts of the constitution are reproduced in d'Antin
  de Vaillac, "Les constitutions de Saint-Sulpice," 121, 300.

5 Delumeau, *Le Catholicisme*, 85; Plongeron, *La vie quotidienne*, 59.

6 Faillon, *Vie de M. Olier* 1: 406.

7 Tackett, *Priest and Parish*, 82, 153.

8 Faillon, *Vie de M. Olier* 3: 183; for the history of Issy, see Boisard, *Issy*.

9 Olier's parish work is treated fully in Faillon, *Vie de M. Olier* 2.

10 Ibid.

11 d'Antin de Vaillac, "Les constitutions de Saint-Sulpice," 111.

12 Ibid., 207; Gauthier, *Une âme sacerdotale*, 35.

13 Boisard, *La compagnie de Saint-Sulpice*, 81; the concession acts, 17 December 1640, 21 April 1659, and the act of donation, 9 March 1663,
  are in Roy, *Inventaire des concessions* 1: 180–2. In 1679 the seminary was
  granted five small islands in the Rivière des Prairies and in 1735 the
  crown enlarged the seigneury at the Lake of Two Mountains. Roy,
  Inventaire des concessions 1: 185; Canada, Province of, *Journals of Legislative Assembly*, app. F, 1843, testimony of Joseph Comte.

14 ASSM, tir. 5, no. 23, Recueil des principaux documents relatifs à l'enquête Durham.

15 The original seminary on Saint-Paul was sold and was known as the
  Commercial Hotel until it burned in 1850. Maurault, *La paroisse*, 251;
  detailed descriptions of the seminary's construction are included in
  Maurault and especially Lahaise, *Les édifices conventuels*, 223–8.

16 Lahaise, *Les édifices conventuels*, 259; Minutes, 14 December 1859; 9
  December 1870; ASSM, arm. 2, vol. 294, data for winter of 1884–5.

17 Lahaise, *Les édifices conventuels,* 241, 268.

18 In two separate reports Superior Quiblier stated that the Mountain domain was 300 acres. ASSP, no. 98, Quiblier to superior general, 14 July 1831; "Notice," 13.

19 Photos, maps, and a description of the estate are in Lahaise, *Les édifices conventuels,* 275–95; in the mid-nineteenth century the site was used for construction of the new Collège de Montréal and the Grand Séminaire. Alain Duhamel, *Le Devoir,* 3 November 1980, notes that the only other *plan d'eau* in Montreal was on the Congregation of Notre Dame grounds at Villa Maria.

20 Lahaise, *Les édifices conventuels,* 292; quote in Edward Watkin, *Canada and the United States,* 358.

21 Rules of the seminary of Montreal, 10 November 1764, quoted in Bruno Harel, "Saint-Sulpice et la conquête," 271.

22 ASSM, tir. 3, no. 1, Superior Roux to Lieutenant-Governor Milnes, 19 February 1800; comparison can be made with the administrative structure of the mother house described in d'Antin de Vaillac, "Les constitutions de Saint-Sulpice," 68–83.

23 ASSM, arm. 2, vol. 134. In 1858 the seminary subscribed to *La Minerve, Le Courrier du Canada* (two copies, one of which was for the superior), *Le Journal de l'instruction publique, L'Écho, L'Union, L'Ordre, Le Pilote,* Montreal *Gazette, Transcript, L'Argus, Catholic Citizen, Canadian Freeman, Freeman's Journal, True Witness* (four copies: two for the seminary, one for the Lake of Two Mountains mission, one for the Oeuvre des bons livres), *Bronson's Review.*

24 ASSM, arm. 2, vol. 133; ASSP, dossier 59, Joseph Comte to Joseph Carrière, n.d. 1843; Minutes, 26 July 1855.

25 Maurault, *La paroisse,* 256; ASSM, arm. 2, vol. 210, accounts with James Flynn, Mlle Girouard.

26 Lahaise, *Les édifices conventuels,* 230.

27 For employee rules, see BNQM, bobine 28, no. 48, "Coutumier pour les serviteurs," n.d.; for employee records, see ASSM, arm. 2, vol. 154; and arm. 2, vol. 134.

28 ASSM, arm. 2, vol. 154, 36; BNQM, bobine 28, no. 48, "Coutumier pour les serviteurs."

29 ANQM, Lacombe, 2515, lease, seminary to Isaac Aaron, 30 April 1850; lease, seminary to James Thompson, 3 March 1849.

30 ASSM, arm. 2, vol. 154; for porter rules, see BNQM, bobine 30, "Coutumier à l'usage du portier."

31 Minutes, 20 April 1855.

32 Louis Rousseau, *La prédication à Montréal,* 62.

33 ASSM, arm. 2, vol. 154.

34 Maurault, *Grand Séminaire de Montréal*, 128.
35 ASSM, Billaudèle correspondence, Billaudèle to brother, Rome, 24 January 1840; Gauthier, *Une âme sacerdotale*, 128.
36 Minutes, 9 September 1841, 26 December 1849.
37 ASSM, Comte correspondence, Joseph Comte to Claude-Joseph Bardey, 16 July 1850.
38 Minutes, 1 December 1851.
39 Beaubien, *Le Sault-au-Récollet*, 140. The remnants of the fort built by François Vachon de Belmont are visible in the two stone towers in front of the Grand Séminaire on Sherbrooke Street.
40 Beaubien, *Le Sault-au-Récollet*, 154; Marcel Trudel, *L'église canadienne*, 48.
41 Maurault, *La paroisse*, 149, 159, 163, 195.
42 ASSM, arm. 2, vol. 282.
43 Minutes, 16 September 1841.
44 Ibid., 30 March 1857, 21 May 1858, 10 February 1863, 13 May 1870.
45 See, for example, the dispute over the right of Indians to sell wood gathered on mission property, Minutes, 15 October 1858.
46 Minutes, 8 November 1843, 7 November 1853. The Council met an average of twenty times a year in the 1840s, fourteen times a year in the 1850s, nine times in the 1860s and an average of twenty-six times a year in 1870, 1874, and 1875.
47 Ibid., 4 August 1874.
48 Ibid., 4 February 1850, 22 December 1856, 10 December 1863.
49 Ibid., 15 July 1846, 29 November 1884, 27 April 1856, 30 July 1857, 15 March 1847.
50 Ibid., 9 December 1875, 26 March 1863, 25 May 1874.
51 D'Antin de Vaillac, "Les constitutions de Saint-Sulpice," 511–12.
52 For the signature of the superior, see ASSM, arm. 2, vol. 225.
53 ASSM, arm. 2, vol. 128.
54 ASSM, arm. 2, vol. 10, entries for June 1854; 9, 18 March, 15 June 1861.
55 ASSP, doss. 59, Joseph Comte to Joseph Carrière, 26 November 1846.
56 ASSP, doss. 52, J.A. Baile to Louis de Courson, 24 September 1845.
57 ASSM, Comte correspondence, Comte to Claude-Joseph Bardey, 23 May 1850.
58 Minutes, 30 June 1845.
59 ANQM, Lacombe, 3347, vente, Hôpital général to William Edmonston and Hugh Allan, 19 December 1856.
60 ANQM, Lacombe, 3500, quittance, Joseph Comte to Paul Leblanc; see also the procurator's threat to resign as *fabrique* treasurer, Minutes, 1 May 1844.

61 Minutes, 11 February 1876; Thérèse Berthelet's legacy to support Christian Brothers schools was administered by the seminary. ANQM, Lacombe, 2134, testament, 10 January 1847.

62 Minutes, 12 December 1845; ASSP, doss. 59, Joseph Comte to Louis de Courson, 25 May 1847.

63 Minutes, 15 April 1841; ASSP, J.A. Baile to Louis de Courson, 24 January 1849.

64 ASSM, Répertoire général des Archives du Séminaire de Montréal, "Liste des procureurs."

65 D'Antin de Vaillac, "Les constitutions de Saint-Sulpice," 511–12.

66 ASSM, arm. 6, carton 132, no. 3 (typed and hanging on cabinet door in vault), "Instruction sur la procure de Séminaire de Montréal, François Citoys de Chaumaux, 1721.

67 ASSM, arm. 2, vol. 65; arm. 2, vol. 134; arm. 2, vol. 10; arm. 2, no. 192.

68 ASSM, arm. 2, vol. 56; arm. 2, vol. 30.

69 ASSM, tir. 91, "Notes sur les droits seigneuriaux."

70 The inventory of Comte's father was pointed out to me by Alan Stewart and can be found in ANQM, Cadieux, 255, inventaire, 20 May 1817; for discussion of the transition in the trades see Gilles Lauzon, "Pierre sur pierre."

71 Comte's obituary is in the Montreal *Gazette*, 18 April 1864.

72 ASSM, Comte file, Comte to George-Étienne Cartier, 9, 13 November 1854, see also the author's *George-Etienne Cartier*, 105; Minutes, 26 March 1859.

73 ASSM, Comte correspondence, 1830–9, Comte to —, 10 May 1832; John Taylor to Comte, 17 May 1830.

74 Ibid., Comte to Claude-Joseph Bardey, 4, 6 August, 1850.

75 For the Chandler model of managers, see his *The Visible Hand;* ASSP, doss. 52, J.A. Baile to Louis de Courson, 9 September 1848; Rousseau, *La prédication à Montréal*, 63, notes that Comte was reprimanded – but not expelled – for sexual misdemeanours that stretched over seven years.

76 *L'Écho du cabinet de lecture paroissial*, 6 (1864): 133.

77 For a description of the role of the notary in the Lyons area, see M. Toublanc, "Le notaire rural, intermédiaire entre les paysans et les propriétaires seigneuriaux et urbains: un type social des campagnes lyonnaises," in Vogler, *Les actes notariés*, 85–104. This volume contains several articles explaining the notarial function in different European centres.

78 Louise Dechêne, *Habitants et marchands*, 245.

79 Doucet, whose office was opposite the seminary, handled many of the seminary's land concessions in the 1820s, registered pew rentals for the *fabrique*, and displayed the architect's plans for the new Notre-Dame

Church in his office. Notaries used by the seminary before 1800 include A. Adhémar (1697–8), P. Raimbault (1711–25), J. David (1720–4), N. Senet (1721–7), C.J. Poslier (1735–44), F. Comparet (1750), Danré de Blanzy (1753), P. Panet (1761–7), J. Papineau (1788), J.B. Desève (1792), L. Chaboillez (1793–8). Objois, "Les meuniers," 238–9.

80 For biographies of Lacombe, see *Le Bulletin des recherches historiques* 32 (1926): 116–18; 45–6 (1939–40): 180; and Lemire, "Patrice Lacombe," *DCB* 9: 439–40. In 1846 Lacombe published a novel, *La terre paternelle*; it describes the disintegration of the Chauvins, a habitant family which lost its land and was forced to emigrate to Montreal.

81 Statistics on the growth of the Quebec notariat are in Ouellet, *Le Bas Canada*, 270. Workload figures were compiled from the Lacombe, Lafleur, Valotte, and Moreau dossiers in the ANQM.

82 ANQM, Lacombe, 2274, procuration, 31 March 1848; at least from the perspective of his doodles, Valotte may not have been a sober enough notary for the seminary. Blank spaces on his contracts were often filled with impressive drawings, the debt-recognition act of 25 August 1842 containing a particularly large woman's head. The seminary also had trouble collecting money that it had loaned to Valotte. ANQM, Valotte, 127, reconnaissance, 24 August 1842; Lacombe, 2570, Sommation par ... Joseph Comte à Dame Henri Valotte, 16 October 1850.

83 *Le Bulletin des recherches historiques* 39 (1933).

84 These averages can be misleading because of yearly fluctuations in seminary business. Lafleur, for example, recorded only 36 acts in the slow year of 1855 but wrote 331 acts in 1872.

85 Moreau averaged 160 acts a year for the seminary between 1864 and 1866. For information on the seminary's notaries, see ASSM, arm. 2 vol. 296, and their individual registers in the ANQM.

86 For the transfer of debts see chapter three; an example of the rural notary's role as informant can be seen in André Jobin's letter to Joseph Comte, 10 May 1850, in which Jobin reports on the financial and personal circumstances of eighteen of the seminary's debtors in the Sainte-Geneviève area. ASSM, arm. 2, vol. 65.

87 Chassé, "Le notaire Girouard," 242–309; ANQM, Lacombe, 1048, procuration, seminary to J.J. Girouard, 8 March 1842; 2045, procuration, seminary to J.J. Girouard, 6 June 1845.

88 ASSM, unindexed and unshelved box entitled "Gestion: Not. Lemaire, 1849–79 ... Ostell, 1840–48"; ASSM, arm. 3, vol. 115.

89 *Le Bulletin des recherches historiques* 39 (1933): 512; ASSM, arm. 2, vol. 264.

90 Expenses of £8 2s. for notarial services at Achigan in 1847 are listed in ASSM, arm. 2, vol. 153; Faure is mentioned in arm. 2, vol. 264; Bonin's

records are in the ANQM and should not be confused with those of Jean-Baptiste Bonin who began work in the seminary office in 1876. Notarial records for the Saint-Sulpice seigneury were not consulted.

91 ASSM, arm. 2, vol. 264.

92 Ibid., vol. 223.

93 See, for example, Glackmeyer's role in ASSM, arm. 2, no. 209.

94 ASSM, unindexed and unshelved box entitled "Gestion: Not. Lemaire, 1849–79 ... Ostell, 1840–48"; for full treatment of the development of modern business management, see Chandler, *The Visible Hand*, 1–49.

95 For Valotte's debt, see ANQM, Lacombe, 2570, Sommation par M. Comte à Dame Henri Valotte, 16 October 1850; the sale to Marler's son is noted in the Minutes, 12 November 1874, 4 October 1875.

96 Antonio Dansereau, "Jacques-Victor Arraud," *DCB* 10: 16–17; in 1864 Marler's salary was increased in $120 a month and it remained at this level until his death in 1884. The difference between the accountant's and notaries' salaries was reduced by the fact that the latter had supplemental fees in addition to their retainers. ASSM, arm. 2 vol. 264; arm. 2, vol. 296.

97 For a description, including photos and floor plan, of the seigneurial office at Terrebonne, see Daoust and Viau, eds., *L'île des moulins*, 49–56. This building has been restored and can be visited; the seminary's business office was replaced by new facilities on the same site in the wing built in the period 1848–51. Around 1900 the office was moved to its present second-floor location. It is the contemporary staff who reported the peep-hole.

98 ASSM, arm. 2, vol. 160, 2 November 1843; for a description of the office and its darkness, see Gauthier, *Une âme sacerdotale*, 110. Little is known of office hours and conditions of work in Canadian offices. Notaries in Lyons, France, started later in winter because of darkness and invariably received more rural clients on rainy days: "Le notaire reçoit sa clientèle en liaison étroite avec le cycle naturel des cultures et l'état du temps." M. Toublanc, "Le notaire rural," in Vogler, *Les actes notariés*, 89; for the procurator's hours, see ASSM, arm. 2, vol. 223.

99 ANQM, Lacombe, 2222, accord, seminary and Jean-Baptiste Chevalier and his children, 14 October 1847; a few leases that were in the bursar's jurisdiction were signed by that official rather than the procurator.

100 ASSP, doss. 68, Antoine Mercier to superior general, 7 February 1865; ASSM, Comte correspondence, Comte to Antoine Mercier, various dates; Mercier to Comte, 9 August 1862.

101 ASSM, arm. 2, vol. 153, March, April 1850, 7 June 1853.

102 ASSM, arm. 2 vol. 223.

103 ANQM, Bonin, 1682, marché, seminary and Edmond Piché, 21 February 1877; Lafleur, 624, vente, Seminary to Jean-Baptiste Hénault, 30 October 1856.

104 ANQM, Lacombe, 2244, déclaration et arrangement, seminary and Jacques Piquet, 24 January 1848.
105 ANQM, Biens du Séminaire, no. 193, Superior M.D. Granet to Comte, 3 March 1859.
106 ASSM, arm. 2, vol. 180.
107 Ibid., arm. 2, vol. 20.
108 Ibid., arm. 2, vol. 67.

CHAPTER TWO

1 Vilar, *Une histoire en construction*, 269.
2 Marx and Engels, *The Communist Manifesto* (Middlesex: Penguin, 1967), 82.
3 Trudel, *L'église canadienne*, 124; Munro, *Seigneurial System*, 181; Harel, "Saint-Sulpice et la conquête," 264; Frégault, *Le XVIIIe siècle*, 130, notes that the seminary was granted 6,000 French pounds in 1744.
4 For discussion of the role of the conquest on clericalization in Quebec, see Fernand Ouellet's review of Serge Gagnon's *Le Québec et ses historiens* in *Social History* 13, no. 25 (May 1980): 269–74.
5 Boisard, *La compagnie de Saint-Sulpice*, 124; Harel, "Saint-Sulpice et la conquête," 270; BNQM, bob. 34, Mémoire, Étienne Montgolfier to James Murray, 16 June 1766.
6 BNQM, bob. 34, Biens du Séminaire, Instructions officielles du gouvernement anglais, 23 August 1786. These privileges were denied to the Jesuits and Récollets.
7 The results of these court cases seem to have been inconclusive, but it was not possible to locate court dossiers in the Judicial Archives of Montreal. See also BNQM, bob. 34, Biens du Séminaire, no. 9, 5 November 1798.
8 Lemieux, *L'établissement*, 17; BNQM, bob. 34, no. 14, J.H.A. Roux to W. Horton, 22 July 1826, Lord Bathurst to Roux, 24 October 1826; Baillargeon, *La survivance*, 231.
9 "Notice," 5.
10 Creighton, *Empire of the St. Lawrence*, 53, 96.
11 In 1816 Sulpician J.H.A. Roux lent £400 to William McGillivray, a partner in the North West Company, taking a mortgage on his country residence on Côte-Saint-Antoine. AJQM, Court of Kings Bench, 1828, no. 787, François Desrivières and Peter McGill vs. John McLeod. In mid-century, this situation reversed as the seminary began borrowing from important merchant fortunes like that of Joseph Masson (chapter four).
12 ASSM, tir. 63, no. 206, Déclaration du Séminaire ... devant la cour du Banc du Roi, 28 June 1816.

13 ASSM, tir. 63, no. 312, Extraits des témoignages de Jean-Baptiste Parent et Joseph Mattel à la cour du Banc du Roi, Roux vs. Fleming, 1818.

14 ASSM, tir. 64, no. 229.5, Lettre donnant un résumé de l'affaire Fleming et exposant l'opinion de O'Sullivan, avocat du Séminaire de Montréal, Paris, 19 September 1824; aside from these fears on the part of the seminary, later pamphlets published by Montreal property owners suggest that Fleming's backers saw the suit as a test case which, if lost, would be appealed in British courts. ASSM, tir. 5, no. 42, Remarks on the Proposed Ordinance to erect and endow an Ecclesiastical Corporation ... 1840, 1.

15 ASSM, tir. 63, no. 207, Exceptions et défenses de William Fleming présentées ... par son avocat James Stuart, 1 December 1816; tir. 64, no. 230.4, Trois mémoires ... cités ... pour prouver le droit de plaider du Séminaire de Montréal, unsigned, 1824; tir. 64, no. 228.12, Défense du Séminaire ... la cour d'appel, 15 November 1823.

16 For early complaints against the seminary banal monopoly, see Louise Dechêne, "L'évolution du régime seigneurial," 161; ASSM, Comte file, Joseph Leduc to Comte, 19 February 1825; Comte file, Petition of Joseph Leduc and Walter Benny ... to erect steam flour mill in Récollets suburb, 31 January 1825.

17 Beutler, "Les moulins à farine," 191, 201; see the letter from distiller Andrew Lang asking for the right to grind *censitaires*' grain in his grist mill on the Saint-Esprit River at the Saint-Sulpice seigneury. ASSM, Comte correspondence, Andrew Lang to Comte, 4 July 1827.

18 For a chart of seminary mills, see Beutler, "Les moulins à farine," 186; see also Beutler, "Le rôle du blé," and Objois, "Les meuniers"; for examples of sales and leases of mills, see ANQM, Lacombe, 479, concession, seminary to Anne Smith, 4 October 1837; 481, concession, seminary to Alexander McKenzie, 12 October 1837; 458, vente, seminary to Charles Perry, 19 July 1837.

19 ASSM, tir. 63, no. 214, Jugement du Conseil Législatif ne reconnaissant pas au Séminaire de Montréal ses droits à une existence légale, 16 April 1819.

20 *Fifth Report*, 169.

21 In "the public interest" the seminary later reduced its claim on this land to £2,246. ASSM, tir. 37, Joseph Comte to — Atterton, 12 August 1843.

22 BNQM, bob. 34, no. 14, Samuel Gale to A.W. Cochrane, 13 April 1826; Commissioners A. Buchanan, J.A. Taschereau, and James Smith, 4 October 1843, in Canada, Province of, *Pièces ... à la tenure seigneuriale*, 49.

23 Commutation file on deposit at Montreal Business History Project, McGill University.

24 ASSM, tir. 4, no. 8, Petition and accompanying letter of Samuel Gale to A.W. Cochran, 15 April 1826.

25 Of the five remaining property holders, one apparently left Montreal. Richard Robinson, a master carpenter and contractor in the 1820s and 1830s, described himself as a "gentleman from St. Jérôme" in 1844, Commutation file, no. 1870.

26 ASSM, tir. 91, no. 40, vol. 3, Notes sur les moulins et les meuniers ... (*c.* 1800–11); also in Objois, "Les meuniers," 197.

27 ASSM, tir. 5, no. 23, Recueil des principaux documents relatifs ... à l'enquête Durham, Joseph Quiblier to Charles Buller, 15 September 1838.

28 Lambert, "Monseigneur, the Catholic Bishop," 938.

29 Canada, Province of, *Journals of Legislative Assembly*, 1843, app. F, testimony of J.R. Raymond.

30 Ibid., testimony of Joseph Comte.

31 For violent opposition to seigneurialism on other seigneuries, see George Rudé, *Protest and Punishment*, 50, and Murray Greenwood, "L'insurrection appréhendée," 63. F.B. Ricard, parish priest in Saint-Marc told the Seigneurial Commission in 1842 that seigneurial rights were "so onerous, so detested, and the people wish so ardently for their extinction, that in '37 and '38 they were excited and led to rush to destruction, by being told 'you shall pay no more rents you shall pay no more lods ... [Do away with seigneurial rights] and you will lessen by one half the general discontent.' However, notwithstanding their hatred for Seigneurial rights, notwithstanding their desire to be freed from them, the Censitaires will not contend with the Seigniors, because they have not the means, the people ... are poor," Canada, Province of, *Report of the Seigneurial Commission*, app. F. For petitions of *censitaires*, see Bernier and Salée, "Appropriation foncière et bourgeoisie marchande," 176. Examples of resistance on the seminary's seigneuries can be found in Dessureault, "La colonisation," and Tremblay, "La politique des Sulpiciens."

32 ASSM, tir. 91, no. 40, vol. 3, Notes sur les moulins ... par M. Molin, économe du Séminaire, n.d. (*c.* 1800–11), cited in Objois, "Les meuniers," 202.

33 Figure calculated by counting debt-recognition contracts; see chapter three.

34 Gagnon and Gagnon, "Le milieu d'origine," 379, 374; Richard Chabot, *Le curé de campagne*, 96; Ouellet, *Le Bas Canada*, 113; Wallot, *Un Québec qui bougeait*, 200; Lemieux, *L'établissement*, 66; Savard, "La vie du clergé," 261.

35 Chabot, *Le curé de campagne*, 96.

36 ASSP, Superior Quiblier to Superior General Louis de Courson, 28 April 1831.

37 Ibid., doss. 52, J.A. Baile to Superior General Louis de Courson, 26 November 1836.

38 Ibid., Baile to Courson, 20 June 1834; descriptions of the revolt can be

found in ASSM, tir. 47, no. 83, clipping from *L'Observateur*, 13 November 1830; Maurault, *Le Collège de Montréal*, 125, ASSP, doss. 98, Quiblier to superior general, 29 October 1830, 10 November 1830.

39 Chaussé, *Jean-Jacques Lartigue*, 188, 218.

40 Ouellet, *Discours de Papineau*, 69; Lower Canada, *Journals of the House of Assembly*, 1835–6, app. EE, Morin testimony.

41 ASSM, tir. 5, no. 11, 23 January 1834, E. Bédard to Superior Quiblier; no. 12, J.J. Girouard to Quiblier, 23 January 1834.

42 ASSM, tir. 5, Report ... to the property of the Seminary, 1834.

43 Ouellet, *Discours de Papineau*, 83.

44 Lambert, "Monseigneur, the Catholic Bishop," 288; Doughty and McArthur, *Documents*, 400, James Craig to Robert Banks Jenkinson, Liverpool, 1 May 1810.

45 ASSM, tir. 5, no. 23, Recueil des principaux documents relatifs ... à l'enquête Durham, 12–14.

46 ASSM, tir. 3, no. 36b, Procès-verbaux d'une conversation H.A. Roux et Col. Ready, 28 August 1819.

47 ASSM, tir. 4, no. 25, Joseph Comte to C.M. LeSaulnier, 2 February 1827.

48 Lambert, "Monseigneur, the Catholic Bishop," 937; for class association see, for example, Creighton, *Empire of the St. Lawrence*, 37–40.

49 ASSM, tir. 4, no. 22, Recueil des principaux documents ... 1826–30, 75; tir. 4, no. 51, Histoire des négociations ... avec le gouvernement ... en 1827, Pierre Rousseau, c. 1890.

50 ASSM, Comte file, misc., T. Coffin to Joseph Comte, 13 September 1826; ASSP, doss. 98, Joseph Quiblier to Joseph Carrière, 19 June 1831; doss. 52, J.A. Baile to Superior General Louis de Courson, 28 February 1839.

51 Chaussé, *Jean-Jacques Lartigue*, 76–81; for Porteous' activity, see nominative file, Montreal Business History Project.

52 ASSM, tir. 4, no. 55, Mgr Panet to C.M. LeSaulnier, 18 January 1828; full descriptions of the struggle between seminary and episcopacy are in James Lambert, "Monseigneur, the Catholic Bishop"; Chaussé, *Jean-Jacques Lartigue*; Lemieux, *L'établissement*.

53 ASSM, tir. 3, no. 40, Journal de M. Thavenet, 1819–20; the probable offer is mentioned in marginal comments of Joseph Comte on letter of Mgr Panet to C.M. LeSaulnier, 22 December 1827, ASSM, tir. 4, no. 44.

54 Lambert, "Monseigneur, the Catholic Bishop," 1084.

55 ASSM, tir. 4, no. 20, Lord Bathurst to Superior Roux, 24 October 1826.

56 Ibid., Joseph Comte to Governor Dalhousie, 5 February 1827.

57 Ibid., no. 25, "Memorandum," Joseph Comte, 20 February 1827.

58 ASSM, tir. 4, no. 38, Précis of six interviews, Roux and Wilmot Horton, 12 September – 2 October 1827; no. 43, Instructions from Secretary Huskisson to Lord Dalhousie, 8 December 1827.

59 Ibid., no. 50, Projet d'accommodement ... avec le gouvernement, handwriting of Joseph Comte, 1827.

60 Ibid., tir. 64, no. 230.11, Mémoire sur l'existence légale du Séminaire, Joseph Quiblier handwriting, n.d. (*c.* 1830s); tir. 4, no. 21, Catholic bishops to Governor James Kempt, 27 December 1828.

61 Ibid., tir. 5, no. 1, Lord Goderich to Lord Aylmer, 13 September 1831.

62 Ibid., no. 5, Mgr Panet's "Notes" on Lord Goderich's despatch of 25 May 1832; no. 6, La Propagande (Rome) to Superior Quiblier, 2 June 1832.

63 Ibid., Joseph Quiblier testimony to Special Committee of Assembly, 5 February 1834.

64 Lower Canada, *Journals of House of Assembly*, 1836, app. EE.

65 Ormsby, *Crisis in the Canadas*, 20.

66 Lemieux, *L'établissement*, 438; Notice, 103–7; Chaussé, *Jean-Jacques Lartigue*, 225.

67 Lucas, ed., *Report of the Earl of Durham* 2:140.

68 Chaussé, *Jean-Jacques Lartigue*, 186.

69 See Canada, *Statutes*, 4 Vict., c. 30, 9 February 1841, Ordinance for the Registering of Titles; also Careless, *Union of the Canadas*, 16–17, 53; Faucher, *Histoire économique*, chap. 2.

70 ASSM, tir. 3, clipping from Quebec *Morning Chronicle*, 10 May 1839; for biographies of Thom, see Bindon, "Adam Thom," *DCB* XI: 874–7, and Bindon, "Hudson's Bay Company Law: Adam Thom and the Institution of Order in Rupert's Land, 1839–54," in David Flaherty, ed., *Essays in the History of Canadian Law* (Toronto: University of Toronto, 1981), 1: 43–87.

71 ASSM, tir. 5, no. 23, Recueil des principaux documents relatifs ... à l'enquête Durham; Lemieux, *L'établissement*, 438; Notice, 103–7.

72 ASSM, tir. 3, Quebec *Morning Chronicle*, 10 May 1839.

73 ASSM, tir. 5, no. 33, Requête de quelques censitaires relative à l'affranchissement des charges féodales dans les seigneuries du Séminaire de Montréal, 28 March 1839.

74 Montreal *Gazette*, 2, 9 June, 1840; ASSM, tir. 5, no. 42, Remarks on the proposed Ordinance to erect and endow an Ecclesiastical Corporation in ... Lower Canada, 1840.

75 ASSM, tir. 5, no. 53, Refutation of the Opinion of the Crown Lawyers on the Question of the Rights and Titles of the Seminary, Montreal, 1840.

76 Lower Canada, *Journals of the Special Council*, 1840, 113; Montreal *Gazette*, 7 May, 2, 8, 16 June, 1840; *Hansard*, 4 March 1841, 1336; Notice, 114.

77 Ordinance of 1840.

CHAPTER THREE

1 Wrong, *A Canadian Manor*, 45.

2 Dechêne, *Habitants et marchands*, 256–7.

3 Minutes, 15 July 1846.

4 The tithe of 1/26 of the grain harvested was payable to the seminary only at the Two Mountains mission and in rural parts of the parish of Montreal. As the parish was urbanized and farmers switched to peas and other market vegetables, tithe income remained small. The tithe collected in 1820 amounted to 469 *livres tournois* in cash and 199 minots of grain. In 1846 annual tithe revenues were calculated by the superior at about £120, a sum less than the approximately £340 collected annually for burials, marriages, and offerings. See ASSM, arm. 2, vol. 195; arm. 2, vol. 225; Notice, 18.

5 Christian Dessureault, "La colonisation," 37; ASSM, tir. 5, no. 18, État des arrérages du Séminaire, Joseph Quiblier, 23 July 1836; ASSM, arm. 2, no. 19, Baux à ferme et à loyer et conventions, 1808–15; Notice, 15–5; in 1845 the seminary added to its reserve by purchasing the Gregory estate, a farm adjacent to the Saint-Gabriel domain.

6 Minutes, 1 February 1853; ANQM, Lafleur, 1274, Bail, seminary to Grey Nuns, 13 April 1861.

7 For the capital investment in mills, see ASSM, arm. 2, vol. 225; figures on the number of mills are taken from Beutler, "Le rôle du blé"; seventeenth century *banalités* are discussed in Dechêne, *Habitants et marchands*, 253–4; milling contracts and income can be traced in ASSM, arm. 2, vol. 195; for the seminary's insistance that it did not exercise banal rights within city limits, see ASSM, tir. 5, no. 51, Extrait des quelques articles ... 1840.

8 In an 1856 sale of two mill sites at Saint-Sulpice, the seminary ceded its seigneurial milling privileges and gave the new owner the right to demand from the *censitaires* "la mouture ordinaire." ANQM, Lacombe, 687, concession, seminary to François Tellier, 16 March 1840; Lafleur, 624, vente, seminary to Jean-Baptiste Henault, 30 October 1856.

9 Seigneurial fishing privileges are outlined in ANQM, Lacombe, 458, vente, 19 July 1837, seminary to Charles Perry, and in various leases noted in ASSM, arm. 2, vol. 19, Baux à ferme et à loyer et conventions, 1808–15. In contrast to its interest in seigneurial fishing rights, the seminary does not seem to have exercised a seigneurial hunting privilege. This confirms Dechêne's findings for the seventeenth century, *Habitants et marchands*, 254.

10 Minutes, 15 March, 6 October 1843; ASSM, arm. 2, vol. 77; Claude Perrault, *Montréal en 1825* (Montréal: Groupe d'études, 1977) 349; ASSM, tir. 45, lease, seminary to Joseph Weydenbaker and Charles Perry, 4 September 1832.

11 ASSM, tir. 5, no. 18, État des arrérages dûs au Séminaire, Joseph Quiblier, 23 July 1836; ANQM, Lacombe, 985, bail, seminary to Joseph Frechette, 2 October 1841; Lacombe, 498, lease, seminary to Hudson's Bay

Company, 22 October 1837. The company had leased the store site since 1808 and paid a rent of £20 a year (1837); ASSM, arm. 2, vol. 157.

12 ASSM, tir. 91, no. 40, vol. 3, Notes sur les moulins et les meuniers faites par M. Molin, économe du Séminaire, n.d. (1800–11?), quoted in Objois, "Les meuniers," 201.

13 ASSM, arm. 2, vol. 78, accounts of François Lanthier.

14 ASSM, arm. 2, vol. 19, Baux à ferme et à loyer et conventions, 1808–15; ASSM, arm. 2, vol. 75; in 1852 they made ten trips for firewood to Achigan on the Saint-Sulpice seigneury and to Belle Rivière on the Two Mountains seigneury; Notice, p. 13; ASSM, arm. 2, vol. 77; for the condition of the farm, see ASSM, carton 133, dossier 4, no. 65b, bail, seminary to Paul Deschamps, 31 March 1886.

15 See in particular ASSM, arm. 2, vol. 19, Baux à ferme et à loyer et conventions, 1808–15, and ASSM, arm. 2, vol. 195.

16 ANQM, Lacombe, 2303, bail, seminary to Joseph Metayer, 12 April 1850; Lacombe, 2648, bail, seminary to Gervais Descary, 17 April 1851.

17 See, for example, the Council decision to sell the island in Rivière des Prairies and the debate over a tenant, Minutes, 10 December 1841, 26 March 1863.

18 Dessureault, "La colonisation," 86, describes the changing use of the domain at Two Mountains in the mid-nineteenth century.

19 ANQM, Valotte, 339, bail, seminary to Jean Dupont, 6 May 1844; Valotte, 343, bail, seminary to Benjamin Corrigan, 17 May 1844; Lafleur, 848, lease, seminary to Michael Hennessy, 19 March 1858.

20 ANQM, Lacombe, 428, accord, seminary and Paschal Persillier, 14 March 1837; Lacombe, 2246, accord et bail, seminary and F. Babineau and François Grenier, 25 January 1848.

21 Dessureault, "La colonisation," 77–8; ANQM, Jobin, 5280, bail, seminary to Denis Walsh, 28 January 1837.

22 ANQM, Lacombe, 1010, bail, seminary to Paschal St. Gebert, 19 November 1841; Jobin, 5371, bail, seminary to Abraham Forest, 21 January 1839; Valotte, 336, lease, seminary to Lancelot Franklin, 28 March 1844; Valotte, 648, obligation, Joseph Guilbault to seminary, 30 November 1846.

23 See appendixes 10 and 11.

24 ASSM, arm. 2, vol. 24; arm. 2, vol. 77. Despite its title vol. 77 contains receipts for all farms on the island. For Two Mountains, see arm. 2, vol. 157.

25 ANQM, Lafleur, 1848, bail, seminary to Jean-Baptiste Pilon, 14 September 1864; this careful protection of manure in seminary leases emphasizes McInnis's point that the disposal of farm manure by dumping it into rivers was a "colourful story" told to ridicule the Lower-Canadian peasant, "A Reconsideration of the State of Agriculture," 21.

26 ASSM, arm. 3, vol. 69, entries for 9 July, 16 August 1867, 19 June 1868; see also arm. 3, vol. 42: Minutes, 4 February 1848.

27 Louis Michel suggests that sharecroppers – at least on the estates of F.A. Bailly, 1733–71 – came from the poorest peasant elements, those who were forced to work the lands of others. The social origins of the seminary's tenant farmers cannot be determined. Louis Michel, "Un marchand rural en Nouvelle France."

28 ASSM, carton 133, dossier 4, no. 65b, bail à ferme, seminary to Paul Deschamps, 31 March 1886.

29 The seminary's levy on the work accumulation in ceded lands was expropriated by the seminary at the time of *lods et ventes* or of commutation, both of which were based on the market value of the property including improvements; see chapter four.

30 Tremblay, "La politique missionnaire," 87, 108, 134; see also Marx, *Capital* 1: 168–85.

31 ANQM, Lacombe, 2648, bail, seminary to Gervais Descary, 17 April 1851; Jobin, 5372, bail, seminary to Michel Cadire, 21 January 1839; Valotte, 356, bail, seminary to Benjamin Talon, 26 August 1844; ASSM, carton 133, dossier 4, no. 65b, bail, seminary to Paul Deschamps, 31 March 1886. Deschamps's lease stated that the tenant could not undertake any improvements without informing the landlord since he would be obliged to cede them.

32 ANQM, Lafleur, 1848, bail, seminary to Jean-Baptiste Pilon, 14 September 1864.

33 ASSM, arm. 2, vol. 19, baux à ferme et à loyer et conventions, 1808–15; arm. 3, no. 42; arm. 2, vol. 195; ANQM, Valotte, 695, protest, seminary to Edward Dunwoody, 6 August 1847.

34 ASSM, tir. 5, no. 23, Recueil des principaux documents relatifs ... à l'enquête Durham, 4–6.

35 Notice, 9; Bouchette, *Description topographique*, 236, 134, 156; Dechêne, *Habitants et marchands*, 233–46, 264–70.

36 ANQM, Valotte, 665, concession, seminary to J.J. Girouard, 5 March 1847; Valotte, 666, concession, seminary to Joseph Guilbault, 8 March 1847; Lacombe, 272, concession, seminary to Jean-Baptiste Blais, 3 July 1835; Lacombe, 3219, concession, seminary to Charles Personne, 28 August 1855.

37 See, for example, the George Wrong quote at the beginning of the chapter. The similarities between the seminary's concession contract in the 1830s and the conditions noted in Dechêne, *Habitants et marchands*, 250–8, are clear. The seigneur's duties were outlined in his original cession.

38 ASSM, tir. 5, no. 51, Extrait des quelques articles ... 1840; it is not clear how often the seminary exercised this right in the seventeenth and

eighteenth centuries. Dechêne, "L'évolution du régime seigneurial," 168–9.

39 ANQM, Lacombe, 265, concession, seminary to Luc Poirier, 16 June 1835.

40 John McCallum, *Unequal Beginnings*, 29.

41 Ouellet, *Le Bas Canada*, 282–3; ASSM, arm. 2, vol. 225.

42 McInnis, "A Reconsideration of the State of Agriculture," 9–49; Ouellet, *Le Bas Canada*, 177–96; McCallum, *Unequal Beginnings*, 25–44.

43 ASSM, tir. 6, no. 23, Recueil des principaux documents relatifs ... à l'enquête Durham, Quiblier to Charles Buller, 15 September 1838.

44 Quiblier, Notice, 18, notes that the tithe was payable only on grains; Ouellet, *Le Bas Canada*, 181, states that it was applicable to grains and peas.

45 Joseph Comte testimony, *Fifth Report*, 10; for seigneurs raising seigneurial dues, see Lower Canada, *Journals of the House of Assembly*, 1833, app. NN; Ouellet, "Libéré ou exploité," 344; Bernier and Salée, "Appropriation foncière," 177.

46 *Fifth Report*, 10; *lods* were due within twenty days of a sale.

47 Dechêne, *Habitants et marchands*, 258.

48 ASSM, tir. 5, no. 23, Recueil des principaux documents relatifs ... à l'enquête Durham, Quiblier to Charles Buller, 27 October 1838.

49 *Fifth Report*, 178, testimony of Turton Penn, John Molson.

50 ANQM, Lacombe, 1976, reconnaissance, Jacob DeWitt to seminary, 31 January 1846; Lacombe, 809, reconnaissance, John Redpath to seminary, 22 December 1840; Valotte, 144, reconnaissance, widow Jean-Baptiste Thibault to seminary, 5 September 1842; Valotte, 136, reconnaissance, Jean-Baptiste St. Germain to seminary, 30 August 1842.

51 These figures were calculated by counting the debt-recognition acts for Saint-Sulpice and rural parts of the island of Montreal notarized by André Jobin and Henri Valotte. Debt recognitions for Two Mountains were not examined but seminary accounts make clear that they can be found in the records of notary Jean-Jacques Girouard. ASSM, arm. 3, vol. 110.

52 ASSM, tir. 5, no. 23, Recueil des principaux documents relatifs ... à l'enquête Durham, Quiblier to Charles Buller, 15 September 1838; Notice, 11; figures given by seminary officials to the government in 1852 put the pre-1840 arrears at £48,414 on the island of Montreal and £13,363 on the seigneuries of Saint-Sulpice and Two Mountains. Canada, Province of, *Journals of the Legislative Assembly*, 1852–3, app. YYYY, no. 5. A good example of arrears can be seen in Jacob DeWitt's debt recognition, ANQM, Lacombe, 1976, 31 January 1846; Lacombe, 255, reconnaissance, Sophia Loo (widow) to seminary, 5 May 1835.

53 ANQM, Lacombe, 298, reconnaissance, Ernest Idler to seminary, 1 October 1835; Lacombe, 438, reconnaissance, Alexandre Brunet to semi-

nary, 11 April 1837; Lacombe, 202, reconnaissance, James Carswell to seminary, 19 September 1834.

54 Ordinance of 1840.

55 This differentiation was repeated in the Seigneurial Act of 1859 which made seigneurial debts of less than £25 payable immediately. Arrears of more than £25 were payable in four instalments over four years. "Extrait de l'acte d'amendement seigneurial de 1859," *La Minerve*, 9 May 1859.

56 ANQM, Valotte, 103, reconnaissance, Joseph Leduc to seminary, 8 August 1842; Valotte, 134, reconnaissance, Narcisse Vinet to seminary, 27 August 1842; Valotte, 184, reconnaissance, Pierre Cousineau to seminary, 3 October 1842.

57 ANQM, Lacombe, 213, reconnaissance, Olivier Barbary to seminary, 16 November 1834.

58 ANQM, Valotte, 191, reconnaissance, Dame Sophie Lindsay to seminary, 27 October 1842.

59 ANQM, Valotte, 181, reconnaissance, Jean-Baptiste Poirier to seminary, 1 October 1842.

60 *La Minerve*, 9 May 1859.

61 ASSM, arm. 3, vol. 115.

62 ANQM, Valotte, 169, 170, 171, reconnaissances, Jesse Thayer, Samuel Hart, and Robert Robinson to seminary, 24, 26 September 1842.

63 ASSM, arm. 3, vol. 110; arm. 2, vol. 64, 297.

64 See appendix 11.

65 ANQM, Lacombe, 2753, reconnaissance, Jean-Baptiste Le Roux to seminary, 24 March 1852; Lacombe, 2340, quittance, seminary to Antoine Payment, 27 December 1848; Lafleur, 1004, obligation, heirs of Pascal Persillier to seminary, 8 August 1859; for a bankruptcy syndic, see Lacombe, 855, quittance, seminary to George Weekes, 23 March 1841; for seminary application of article 79 of the *Coutume de Paris* and its right to *lods et ventes*, see Lacombe, 2237, quittance, seminary to Pierre Cousineau, 7 December 1847.

66 ASSM, arm. 2, vol. 20.

67 ANQM, Lacombe, 2273, reconnaissance, Daniel Gorrie to seminary, 30 March 1848; ASSM, arm. 3, vol. 110, Compte des recettes faites par J. Girouard dans la seigneurie des Deux Montagnes, 1842–52; ANQM, Lacombe, 1373, Dépôt pour minute par Joseph Comte, 31 May 1843.

68 Protests made by the seminary, 1773–1838, can be found in ASSM, arm. 2, vol. 66.

69 ANQM, Lacombe, 1951, obligation, John Easton Mills to seminary, 5 December 1845; for another example, see Lacombe, 3536, reconnaissance, F.L. Tassé to seminary, 18 October 1858.

70 ASSM, arm. 2, vol. 20.

71 Canada, Province of, *Journals of the Legislative Assembly*, 1852–3, app. YYY, no. 5.

72 Most transfers were entitled simply *transport* but some were entitled *vente et transport*. See, for example, Lafleur, 2119, vente et transport, Édouard Moreau to N. Beaudry and F. Corbeille, 9 October 1867. It is clear some debts were sold in unnotarized forms. See, for example, Lafleur, 2118, transport ... et dépôt pour minute, seminary of Montreal, 5 October 1867.

73 ANQM, Valotte, 670, transport, seminary to Asprit Chaput, 16 March 1847; Lacombe, 3178, transport, seminary to Joseph Landry, 13 March 1855; Lafleur, 1797, transport, seminary to Benjamin Dorion, 4 May 1864.

74 ANQM, Moreau, 1483, transport, seminary to Eusèbe Proulx, 22 March 1864; Moreau, 1565, transport, seminary to Canfield Dorwin, 15 July 1864; Lacombe, 3300, transport, seminary to Patrick Rice, 8 July 1856.

75 ANQM, Lacombe, 522, transport, seminary to Benjamin Crevier, 10 May 1838; Lafleur, 517, transport, seminary to Arthur Ross, 30 January 1856.

76 ANQM, Lacombe, 2643, transport, seminary to Joseph Dorion, 14 April 1851; examples of "absent" debtors can be found in ANQM, Lacombe, 3178, transport, seminary to Joseph Landry, 13 March 1855; for family transfers, see Lacombe, 810, transport, seminary to Jean-Baptiste Laurin, 21 December 1840, and Lacombe, 2548, transport, seminary to Charles Tate, 24 July 1850.

77 ANQM, Lacombe, 2191, transport, seminary to William C. Meredith, 3 July 1847; Lafleur, 517, transport, seminary to Arthur Ross, 30 January 1856; Lacombe, 2269, transport, seminary to Joseph-A. Berthelot, 21 March 1848; for the transfer of two debts owed by notaries, see Lacombe, 2606, transport, seminary to Laurent Rivard, 14 February 1851, and Valotte, 636, transport, seminary to Pierre Moreau, 2 October 1846.

78 ANQM, Lacombe, 2853, transport, seminary to John Ross, 16 February 1863; Moreau, 1565, transport, seminary to Canfield Dorwin, 15 July 1864.

79 ANQM, Lacombe, 2343, transport, seminary to Dr Joseph Caseneuve, 20 January 1849; Bonin, 1570, transport, seminary to Joseph Renaud, 15 February 1875; Valotte, 589, transport, seminary to Hyacinthe Brunet and Jean-Baptiste Demers, 6 March 1845; Bonin, 1097, transport, seminary to Arsène Charlebois, 6 November 1872.

80 ANQM, Lacombe, 684, transport, seminary to Louis-H. LaFontaine, 11 March 1840; Lacombe, 2269, transport, seminary to Joseph A. Berthelot, 21 March 1848 (Berthelot, later George-Étienne Cartier's partner, took a total of five transfers from the seminary); Lacombe, 2512, transport, seminary to André Jobin, 29 April 1850 (Jobin also took other transfers); Lacombe, 2055, transport, seminary to Henri Valotte, 3 July 1846. A

year later Valotte transferred this debt back to the seminary, Lacombe, 2231, transport, seminary to Valotte, 9 November 1847.

81 ANQM, Lafleur, 2118, transport ... et dépôt pour minute d'un transport *sous seing privé*, Jacques-Victor Arraud, 5 October 1867; Lafleur, 2119, vente et transport, Édouard Moreau to N. Beaudry and F. Corbeille, 9 October 1867; Moreau, 1880, seminary to Ludger Piquette, 14 August 1866.

82 ASSM, tir. 5, no. 43, Mémoire par M. Quiblier à M. Murdoch, Secretary of John Colborne, 7 April 1840. For further examination of the relationship between seigneur and industrial producer, see Baribeau, *La seigneurie de la Petite-Nation*, 151.

83 ASSM, arm. 2, vol. 180; 1864 can be compared to other years in appendix 11; Canada, Province of, *Journals of the Legislative Assembly*, 1852–3, app. YYY, no. 5.

84 Ouellet, "Libéré ou exploité," 351; Robert, "Un seigneur entrepreneur," 381–2; information on Noyan was provided by Françoise Noël (see her thesis, "Gabriel Christie's Seigneuries").

85 Lower Canada, *Journals of the House of Assembly*, 1833, app. NN.

86 Canada, Province of, *Journals of the Legislative Assembly*, 1852–3, app. YYY.

CHAPTER FOUR

1 Quoted in Padover, ed., *Karl Marx on Religion* (New York: McGraw-Hill, 1974), 92.

2 Macpherson, *Property*, 1.

3 Jean-Pierre Wallot emphasizes the link between abolition and anglicization and blends this with the theme that seigneurial abolition was "the wish of the bourgeoisie, not of the people." Wallot, *Un Québec qui bougeait*, 233–4. For other treatments of abolition in Quebec see Lise Pilon-Lê, "Le régime seigneurial au Québec," 132–69; Morin, *Seigneurs et censitaires*; Baillargeon, *La survivance*; Benoît, "La question seigneuriale," Ouellet, "Le régime seigneurial dans le Québec," in Ouellet, *Éléments d'histoire sociale*; see also "L'abolition du régime seigneurial et l'idée de propriété" in the same volume and pp. 225–36 of his *Le Bas Canada*. For commutation in other countries, see Pollard, *Peaceful Conquest*, especially chap. 2; Probyn, ed., *Systems of Land Tenure*; Blum, *Noble Landowners*.

4 This act is published in Doughty and Story, *Documents*, 291–2.

5 Soboul, *Problèmes paysans*, 17.

6 ASSM, Joseph Comte file, Comte to George-Étienne Cartier, 9, 13 November 1854; Comte to Louis Drummond, 20 November 1854.

7 Tassé, *Discours de Sir Georges Cartier*, 8 April 1859; for an interesting example of the collaboration between generations of seminary lawyers on the seigneurial question, see the letter of L.-H. La Fontaine, chairman

of the seigneurial commission, to Attorney General Cartier, 10 April 1860, McCord Museum, Cartier Collection.

8 ASSM, tir. 6, no. 23, Cartier to Comte, 25 March 1859.

9 ASSM, Conseil d'assistants, cahier no. 1, vol. 1, 18 July 1842 – 26 November 1860, meeting of 18 March 1859, 146.

10 BNQM, Biens du Séminaire, no. 193, M.D. Granet to Comte, 3 March 1859. The politics of the passage of the bill and the division between Grits and Rouges can be seen in the Brown Papers, PAC, MG 24, B40, vol. 393, Lewis Drummond to George Brown, 30 April 1859, and C.J. Laberge to Lewis Drummond, 2 May 1859. The importance of Cartier's support to the seminary can be measured by the opposition of important Conservatives to seigneurial reimbursements which were described as "leeching by the priests." PAC, Macdonald Papers, vol. 260, 118, 122, John Ross to John A. Macdonald, 17 September 1855.

11 ANQM, Lafleur, 2479, Rachat de cens et rentes, William Moodie and seminary, 6 August 1871; the interest rate of 6½ per cent apparently reflects rising interest rates of the period; see chapter 5.

12 ANQM, Lacombe, 3402, commutation, seminary to Joseph Martin dit Versailles, 3 July 1857; 3433, commutation, seminary to Simon Valdis, 19 November 1857. A property worth more than £500 and commuted more than fourteen years after 1840 paid a lods commutation representing 6.25 per cent of its evaluation; a property worth less than £100 paid 12.5 per cent in the same circumstances.

13 ANQM, Lacombe, 779, commutation, seminary to William Pawson, 26 October 1840.

14 ANQM, Moreau, 1577, commutation, seminary to Jane Scanlan, 2 August 1864; 1689, commutation, seminary to Joachim Telmesse dit Sans Regret, 11 March 1865; for an interest-free demand loan, see Lacombe, 3669, commutation, seminary to master butcher George Fullum 18 October 1859; delayed interest loans can be seen by comparing notary Joseph Simard's seven-month, delayed-interest obligation to Étienne Dubois's commutation. Lacombe, 3667, commutation, seminary to Joseph Simard, 11 October 1859; 3668, commutation, seminary to Étienne Dubois, 8 October 1859.

15 ANQM, Lacombe, 2611, commutation, seminary to Compagnie du chemin de fer de Montréal à Lachine, 27 February 1851.

16 ANQM, Lacombe, 3100, commutation, seminary to Montreal and Bytown Railway, 4 June 1854.

17 Minutes, 9 February 1875, 16 February 1861, 30 March 1857, 13 May 1870; ANQM, Lacombe, 3904, commutation, seminary to Pères Oblats, 9 March 1861.

18 Minutes, 15 March 1861.

19 Ibid., 30 March 1857, 21 May 1858.

20 ASSM, tir. 37, Canal de Lachine, Estimation des terrains de la commune de Montréal, 25 April 1842.

21 ANQM, Valotte, 645 compromis, seminary and Toussaint Martin, 12 November 1846.

22 ANQM, Valotte, 519, compromis, seminary and John Donegani, 31 October 1845.

23 Notary Édouard Moreau left the seminary business office in 1867 and was not replaced by a full-time notary until 1872. It is not clear if Édouard Lafleur, the seminary's sole known notary for the period, wrote all commutations or if some were written by another notary. Only commutations by Lafleur were discovered, but commutation income figures suggest that others existed. Commutations were examined by Hélène Paré and Peter Gossage.

24 Tulchinsky, *River Barons*, 71; Hamelin and Roby, *Histoire économique*, 75–98; Several attempts made by the author, along with Peter Gossage and members of the Montreal Business History Project, to establish the frequency of commutation demands have led to the conclusion that studies of Montreal land values, of specific neighbourhoods, of credit relations, and of the dynamics of individual classes are necessary preludes to effective analysis of commutation frequency.

25 Only one exception to this rule was found. François Armand *dit* Flamme of Rivière-des-Prairies was permitted to pay £71 in cash and to form the balance of £163 into an obligation. ANQM, 1654, Lacombe, commutation, seminary to François Armand *dit* Flamme, 21 October 1844.

26 ANQM, Lacombe, 1904, commutation, seminary to Romuald Trudeau, 27 October 1845; aside from being a prominent wholesale merchant and municipal politician, Rodier was an important Catholic philanthropist with close ties to the seminary. See Fred Armstrong, "Charles-Séraphin Rodier," *DCB* 10: 625; for other examples of promissory notes given in payment of commutations, see Lacombe, 1778, commutation, seminary to William Burnett, 25 April 1845, and Lacombe, 1781, commutation, seminary to Daniel O'Connor, 3 May 1845.

27 George-Étienne Cartier, for example, arranged a five-year obligation to pay the £83 commutation on his Notre-Dame Street property. ANQM, 2257, Lacombe, commutation, seminary to Cartier, 22 February 1848.

28 McGill Rare Books Room, Manuscript Collection, W. Badgley to D. Giffand, London *Standard* office, 29 April 1840; Rare Books Room, 3979–9, John Fisher, W. Badgley, Copy of instructions to committee, 29 April 1840.

29 ANQM, Lacombe, 808, commutation, seminary to John Redpath, 22 December 1840.

30 ANQM, Lacombe, 1531, commutation, seminary to Stanley Bagg, 9 March 1844.

31 Assigning the term "large" to property holders commuting property evaluated at over £500 seems valid when gauged against the £2 a month paid to the seminary's male cook (1846). House lots for workers in the Saint-Gabriel suburb sold for £60 to £90 in 1861. ASSM, arm. 2, vol. 154; ANQM, Lafleur, notarial acts 1241–1364, 1861.

32 Property evaluations were £22,732 in 1850, £20,983 in 1851, £41,937 in 1852, £75,815 in 1853, and £108,515 in 1854. All calculations were made from the commutation file, a copy of which is deposited in the Montreal Business History Project office at McGill University.

33 Lessors of Lachine Canal water-power rights are listed in Larry McNally's *Water Power on the Lachine Canal*, app. 19.

34 All property evaluations taken from commutation file. For Gibb and tailoring, see Poutanen, "For the Benefit of the Master." For the construction trades, see Lauzon, "Pierre sur pierre," and Lauzon and Stewart, "Stratégies d'accumulation du capital." The three papers are available at the Montreal Business History Project.

35 Paul Craven and Tom Traves note that the Grand Trunk was forced to advertise for copper-smiths; this at least suggests that the "copperworker" in the commutation file may have been skilled. Craven and Traves, "Canadian Railways as Manufacturers," 270.

36 In addition to the commutations noted in table 6, Ransom described himself as a "vendeur de lait" in a commutation on 3 February 1861 and as a "marchand de lait" in his commutation of 6 May 1863 (Lacombe, 4027, 4208).

37 For the difficulty which rural professions present for users of Lower-Canadian census returns, see Courville, "Villages et agriculture," 13.

38 *Cadastre abrégé*, 1861. My own figure from the commutation documents is 253 (appendix 5).

39 ANQM, Lacombe, 1920, "commutation," seminary to John Redpath, 14 November 1845.

40 As well as debts to the seigneur, there may have been heavy indebtedness to local merchants. See Desrosiers, "Un aperçu des habitudes de consommation," and Michel's two articles, "Un marchand rural en Nouvelle-France" and "Le livre de compte."

41 McCallum, *Unequal Beginnings*, 33.

42 For Edward Ellice, see Colthart, "Edward Ellice"; Robert Christie figures in Françoise Noël's thesis, "Gabriel Christie's Seigneuries"; for a list of *patriotes*, see Bernard, *Les rébellions*, 290–315.

43 ANQM, Lafleur, 4135, signification, seminary to F.X. Deladurantaye, 12 December 1879; for the suggestion that the seminary delayed evaluations and commutations, see Georges Baillargeon, *La survivance*, 124.

44 ANQM, Lafleur, 4193, commutation, seminary to André Brunet, 28 March 1880.

45 ANQM, Lacombe, 4089, commutation, seminary to heirs of Hippolyte Guy, 22 June 1862.

46 Tassé, *Discours de Sir Georges Cartier*, 8 April 1859, 198; for similarities between the state's assumption of seigneurial dues and European examples, see Pollard, *Peaceful Conquest*, 55.

CHAPTER FIVE

1 E.J. Hobsbawm, *Age of Capital*, 215.

2 ASSM, vol. 35, F. Glackmeyer to Thomas McKay, 12 March 1842.

3 ASSM, arm. 2, vol. 19, Baux et conventions dans les différentes seigneuries sulpiciennes, 1788–1807.

4 ASSM, arm. 2, unindexed, Baux à loyer.

5 ASSM, arm. 2, vol. 24.

6 Minutes, 14 January, 20 June 1843, 30 April 1851.

7 Minutes, 20 January, 13 February 1857. The telegraph company decided to buy its own building.

8 Minutes, 28 April 1857.

9 ASSM, arm. 2, unindexed volume, Baux à loyer, entry for 1871.

10 Ibid.

11 The Trust and Loan Company paid £5 a year for rental of the safe, other tenants paid an 8 per cent supplement for new windows. ASSM, arm. 2, unindexed volume, Baux à loyer; Minutes, 24 October 1862.

12 ASSM, arm. 2, unindexed volume, Baux à loyer.

13 ASSM, arm. 2, unindexed volume, Baux à loyer; arm. 2, vol. 282.

14 ANQM, Lafleur, 1438, vente, Theodore Hart to seminary, 11 June, 1862; ASSM, arm. 2, unindexed volume, Baux à loyer; arm. 2, vol. 282.

15 ASSM, arm. 2, vol. 217.

16 All capital construction costs are included in ASSM, arm. 2, vol. 237.

17 Minutes, 23 March 1875; ASSM, arm. 2, vol. 282.

18 ANQM, Moreau, 1683, vente, Dame H. Lionais to seminary, 22 March 1865; arm. 2, vol. 282.

19 Lease and tenant information drawn from ASSM, arm. 2, vol. 282; rental income from arm. 2, vol. 157; and arm. 3, vol. 402. A summary is included in appendix 9. Street addresses were used to count seminary commercial properties. On St James Street the seminary owned numbers 116, 124, and 126, on Notre-Dame Street numbers 325 and 329, on Saint-François-Xavier Street numbers 61, 63, 67, 71, 73, 77, 79, 83, 85, 91, 93, 95, 97, 99, 101, 115, 116, 117, 119, 120, 121, 123, 124, 125, and the Bank of Hochelaga. Only buildings in which the seminary rented out space was counted. Most commercial properties included several office tenants.

20 Minutes, 5 June 1841.

21 ASSM, arm. 3, vol. 402.

22 For a detailed description of the relationship of municipal bond issues and railways, see chapter three in the author's *Promoters and Politicians*. There are difficulties in defining the seminary's investment portfolio with certitude. The Chambly and Grand Trunk Railway debentures, for example, were purchased with revenues from government reimbursements for land bought along the Lachine Canal. These sums were included with Saint-Gabriel land-sale revenues and kept in a separate, and as yet unindexed volume in arm. 5, Vente de la ferme St. Gabriel et emploi.

23 Minutes, 15 April 1853; ASSM, arm. 2, vol. 264; arm. 3, vol. 402.

24 Minutes, 2 September 1846.

25 ASSP, doss. 58, Joseph Comte to Joseph Carrière, 17 November 1849.

26 Ibid.

27 Minutes, 10 September 1849.

28 ASSM, arm. 2, vol. 29.

29 For Seminary doubts about its Grand Trunk investment, see ASSP, doss. 58, correspondence of Comte to Carrière, various dates; interest payments are recorded in ASSM, arm. 2, vol. 37.

30 ASSM, arm. 2, vol. 29; PAC, RG 30, vol. 10190, Agreement Grand Trunk Railway and seminary, 13 June 1864; ANQM, Moreau, 1729, notification, seminary to Grand Trunk Railway, 29 August 1865.

31 PAC, RG 30, vol. 10189, Legal Documents ... London office, Grand Trunk Railway, item 98, Jean-Baptiste Larue notarized statement before J.J. Hunter, 13 July 1880; ASSM, arm. 3, vol. 402; arm. 2, vol. 29.

32 Bonner, *Essay on the Registry Laws* 14.

33 Stuart, *Reports of Cases* 264.

34 *Statutes of Canada*, 4 Vict., c. 30, 9 February 1841, "An Ordinance to Prescribe the Registering of Titles to Lands, Tenements and Hereditaments, Real or Immovable Estates."

35 ASSM, arm. 2, vol. 37.

36 ASSM, arm. 2, vol. 251; Doucet and Weaver, "North American Shelter Business," 246.

37 For the growth of the Canadian mortgage business, see E.P. Neufeld, *Financial System of Canada*, 177; Seminary mortgages can be compared to the rural lending of notary Jacques Picard in Wotton, Quebec. Sévigny, "La pratique du prêt hypothécaire."

38 Only 2 of the 103 mortgages written between 1877 and 1900 ended in sheriff sales. The relationship of the seminary and notary is clear from the following letter from procurer J.A. Gaudin to E. Archambault, 10 January 1902, in ASSM, arm. 2, vol. 251; "Cher monsieur, l'avocat de M. Brosseau vient d'écrire à M. Géoffrion, avocat du Séminaire, que, pour régler notre réclamation contre son client il est prêt à remettre $12,000

au lieu de $13,000 demandés par M. Colin [superior] sans nous exposer aux ennuis qu'entrainerait nécessairement avec elle une vente par le shérif. Ce faisant, vous nous obligerez beaucoup."

39 ANQM, Jobin, 7371, power-of-attorney, seminary to cashier of Toronto branch of Bank of Montreal, 20 December 1849; for transfers, see ASSM, arm. 2, vol. 160. It is not clear why government deposits were made at the Toronto branch of the Bank of Montreal rather than in Montreal.

40 ASSM, arm. 2, vol. 37; for the origins of the City and District Savings Bank, see Sweeny, *Guide to the History*, 161–3.

41 ANQM, Lafleur, 365, bail, seminary to Banque d'Épargne, 16 February 1854; arm. 2, vol. 37.

42 ASSM, arm. 2, vol. 180; arm. 2, vol. 235.

43 ANQM, Lafleur, 4126, reconnaissance et hypothèque, Banque Ville Marie to seminary, 12 November 1879; Lafleur, 4308, quittance, seminary to Banque Ville Marie, 4 December 1880.

44 ANQM, Lafleur, 4149, procuration, seminary to Jean-Baptiste Larue, 27 January 1880; Lafleur, 4176, transport, seminary to William Weir, 5 March 1880; for a description of the bank crisis, see Hamelin and Roby, *Histoire économique*, 88–91.

45 ASSM, arm. 2, vol. 219.

46 Minutes, 30 July 1857, 26 April 1858.

47 ASSM, tir. 37, no. 71, obligation, seminary to Joseph Masson estate, 4 December 1850, 18 March 1851, 5 June 1858; ANQM, Lafleur, 1601, 2400, obligations, seminary to Gaspard-Aimé Massue, 22 July 1853, 10 March 1870; ASSM, arm. 2, vol. 250.

48 Minutes, 24 March 1856.

49 For examples of interest demanded in advance, see table 9, loan from City and District Savings Bank.

50 ASSM, arm. 2, vol. 243.

51 Two of the societies received 6 per cent on their deposits, and one 4 per cent; for correspondence concerning the societies and the seminary, see ASSM, Picard correspondence, John Lulen to Picard, 2 December 1857, Benjamin Parent to Picard, 10 April 1858, and L. Beaudry to Picard, 12 October 1857.

CHAPTER SIX

1 Macpherson, *Property*, 10.

2 Bonin, "Le canal Lachine," 271–97; Tulchinsky, "Construction of the First Lachine Canal."

3 ASSM, arm. 2, no. 75.

4 McNally, *Water Power on the Lachine Canal*, 16, 37.

5 *Montreal in 1856*, 39–45; Tulchinsky, *River Barons*, 126, 209, 222.

6 ASSM, tir. 37, Canal de Lachine, Toussaint Pelletier to Joseph Quiblier, February 1844; Opinion of L-H. Lafontaine, 8, 12, 13 November 1844; for Comte's "mémoire" and correspondence with Public Works officials, see ASSM, tir. 37.

7 McNally, *Water Power on the Lachine Canal*, 38, 48, mentions Ostell's bankruptcy and family connection with Bourett, assistant commissioner of public works. His link with the Montreal City Passenger Railway can be traced in Paquin, "L'évolution de l'industrie du tramway à Montréal," 3. For Ostell's subdivision work, see Hanna, "New Town of Montreal," 33, 37; Ostell also directed completion of the western towers on Notre-Dame Church, 1841 and 1843, Toker, *Church of Notre Dame*, 55. For Ostell's accounts, see ASSM, unindexed and unshelved box entitled Gestion: Not. Le Maire (1849–79), Arp. Ostell (1840–8), Arp. Perrault (1862–79); in 1849 the immigrant sheds site was rented for £38. ASSM, arm. 2, vol. 75.

8 "Plan of part of St. Gabriel Farm belonging to the Seminary of Montreal ... showing its distribution into building lots," John Ostell, 19 July 1845 in Archives of the City of Montreal.

9 Montreal *Gazette*, 30 July, 21 August 1845.

10 Ibid., 22 August 1845; ASSM, unindexed and unshelved box, Gestion: Not. LeMaire (1849–79), Arp. Ostell (1840–8), Arp. Perrault (1862–79); ANQM, Valotte, 563, vente, seminary to Charles Austin, 19 December 1845; *significations* are in Valotte, various acts between nos. 499 and 604, various dates, September–December 1845.

11 ASSM, arm. 2, vol. 157.

12 ASSM, unindexed, arm. 5, tir. 46, Vente de la ferme St. Gabriel et emploi des deniers en provenant.

13 ANQM, Lacombe, 2663, vente, syndic of bankrupt Scott Shaw to seminary, 5 June 1851.

14 ANQM, Lafleur, 559, retrocession, heirs of Austin Cuvillier to seminary, 3 June 1856; for other examples of retrocessions, see Lafleur, 561, 562, 7, 11 June 1856, and Lacombe, 2848, 2 February 1853.

15 Tulchinsky, *River Barons*, 224–8; Tulchinsky and Young, "John Young," *DCB* 10: 722–6; ASSM, tir. 37, no. 62, Procès-verbal de bornage ... 1851; ASSM, unindexed, arm. 5, tir. 46, Vente de la ferme St. Gabriel, Lacombe N.P., vente, seminary to Ira Gould and Jacob DeWitt, 12 August 1851.

16 ASSM, unindexed, arm. 5, tir. 46, Vente de la ferme St. Gabriel; ANQM, Lafleur, 350, vente, seminary to John Young, 29 December 1853; Lafleur 1722, transport, John Young to seminary, 13 January 1864.

17 ASSM, unindexed and unshelved box, Gestion, Not. LeMaire (1849–79), Arp. Ostell (1840–48), Arp. Perrault (1862–79).

18 For a discussion of the comprehensive role of the industrial bourgeoisie, see Foster, *Class Struggle and the Industrial Revolution*, especially chaps. 5 and 6.

19 ANQM, Lacombe, 3143, vente, John Ostell to Édouard Lafleur, 15 November 1854; for Lafleur's subsequent sales, see Lacombe, 3195, 3223, 3242; Lacombe's purchase is in Lafleur, 600, vente, seminary to Lacombe, 17 September 1854; ANQM, Valotte, 693, désistement, Robert Begly to seminary, 29 July 1847.

20 ANQM, Lafleur, 320, vente, seminary to Edward Farley, John Taugher, and Nicholas Power, 31 October 1853; Lafleur, 328, vente, seminary to John Flannery, 14 November 1853.

21 Craven and Traves, "Canadian Railways as Manufacturers," 254.

22 For the development of Sainte Cunégonde after 1864, see Massicotte, *La cité de Sainte-Cunégonde*, 11.

23 ANQM, Lafleur, various acts between nos. 283 and 3374.

24 ASSM, arm. 2, vol. 157.

25 ASSM, unindexed and unshelved box, Gestion: Not. Le Maire (1849–79), Arp. Ostell (1840–8), Arp. Perrault (1862–79); ASSM, unindexed, arm. 5, tir. 47, St. Gabriel, livre d'encan, no. 1, no. 2. This tentative professionalization of real-estate sales can be compared to Hamilton, Ontario; see Doucet and Weaver, "North American Shelter Business," 234–62.

26 ANQM, Lafleur, 1168, vente, seminary to Hyacinthe Allard, 27 August 1860; 1318, vente, seminary to Michael Hennessey, 3 July 1861; 1328 vente, seminary to Alexander Henry, 16 July 1861.

27 Minutes, 15 April 1863; ASSM, Lafleur, 1780, vente, seminary to James B. Cowan, 28 March 1864; the first lawyer in the neighbourhood bought a lot in 1872; Lafleur, 3002, vente, seminary to Pierre Poupart, 2 July 1872; Lafleur, 2225, contract and agreement, seminary and Michael Hennessey, 22 August 1868.

28 ANQM, Lafleur, various acts between nos. 283 and 3374; ANQM, Lafleur, 2407, vente, seminary to George Reid and Bernard O'Brien, 26 March 1870; Lafleur, 2021, vente, seminary to Alfred and John Savage, 30 August 1866; *Lovell's Street Directory*, 1876.

29 ANQM, Lafleur, 894, vente, seminary to Patrick Clark, 17 August 1857; see also the retrocessions of train conductor Thomas Phelan and labourer Thomas Courtney, ANQM, Lafleur, 1811, vente, seminary to Thomas Phelan, 6 June 1864; 1837, vente, seminary to Thomas Courtney, 13 August 1864.

30 Paquin, "L'évolution de l'industrie du tramway à Montréal," 3–8; Hopkins, *Atlas of the City and Island of Montreal*, fig. M, 59.

31 ANQM, Lacombe, accord, seminary and Thomas B. Anderson, 26 November 1835.

32 Minutes, 2 September 1846, 4 June 1847; ASSM, arm. 2, vol. 65, last page

inscription, 21 February 1851; ASSM, arm. 2, vol. 250, f. 39. Documents in the latter volume show that the seminary agreed to invest £500 in the Boulevard Company. The Boulevard was in fact not built before 1880.

33 Minutes, 2 September 1846; ASSM, unindexed and unshelved box, Gestion.

34 Hanna, "New Town of Montreal."

35 Minutes, 19 August 1857.

36 Ibid., 4 August 1862; given the anglophone clientele on the Mountain domain and the seminary's practice of writing leases in the language of the tenant, it is unclear why deeds were printed only in French.

37 All Mountain domain sales can be found in ANQM, Lafleur, 1045 to 4164, or in ASSM, tir. 46, 53 contrats de Ed Lafleur sur ferme de la Montagne, 1868–71; the four merchants were William Pratt McLaren, H.B. Smith, James Mullin, and Charles Binmore.

38 For the Boston example, see Warner, *Streetcar Suburbs*, 122; *Lovell's Montreal Directory* gives the strong impression that the two-year construction rule was not kept. Compare, for example, the *Directory* for 1876 to sales contracts written by Lafleur.

39 Paquin, "L'évolution de l'industrie du tramway à Montréal," 5–6.

40 Warner, *Streetcar Suburbs*, 53.

41 Work addresses taken from *Montreal Directory* (1871); sales contracts are in ASSM, arm. 5, tir. 46, 53 contrats de Ed Lafleur sur ferme de la montagne, 1868–71: 2560, vente, seminary to John Foulds, 23 February 1871; 2630, vente, seminary to Nelson Davis, 14 July 1871; 2040, vente, seminary to George Kemp, 20 December 1866; 2160, vente, seminary to John McGauvran, 25 February 1868.

42 Ibid., 1821, vente, seminary to James Alfred Bazin, 1 July 1864; 1903, vente, seminary to James Alfred Bazin, 29 March 1865.

43 Warner, *Streetcar Suburbs*, 119.

44 Doucet and Weaver, "North American Shelter Business," 245–7.

45 For the 1880 rate, see ANQM, Lafleur, 4163, vente, seminary to Ludger Cousineau, 20 February 1880; for farm mortgage rates, see ASSM, arm. 2, vol. 251.

46 ANQM, Lafleur, 1922, vente, seminary to Stephen Mathews, 12 May 1865; 1702, vente, seminary to Peter Redpath, 9 November 1863; for sales of the corner of Sherbrooke and Côte des Neiges, see 1799, 6 May 1864 and 2040, 20 December 1866.

47 ANQM, Lafleur, 1831, vente, seminary to James Alfred Bazin, 1 July 1864; 2014, vente, seminary to David McFarlane, 18 July 1866; 2587, vente, seminary to John Taylor, 23 March 1871; 2578, vente, seminary to John Binmore, 8 March 1871.

48 ANQM, 2618, vente, seminary to Montreal Building Society, 1 June 1872; 2620, vente, seminary to Alexander Robertson, 2 June 1871; 2974, vente, seminary to William Oliver Buchanan, 14 May 1872; 3388, vente, sem-

inary to Montreal Building Association, 30 May 1874; 3915, vente, seminary to Montreal Buiding Association, 1 August 1878; 3381, vente, seminary to Olivier de Guise and Eugène Malo, 4 May 1874; seminary minutes, 23 March 1875; ASSM, arm. 2, vol. 282, Livre de comptes de locataires et maisons, 1875–82.

CHAPTER SEVEN

1 Quoted in Cross, *Workingman of the Nineteenth Century*, 248.
2 Handwritten sermon, 13 May 1871, in ASSM, arm. 3, vol. 37.
3 For popular disturbances in New France, see Crowley's "Thunder Gusts"; Pentland is now easily available in *Labour and Capital*. Palmer's "Discordant Music" is in *Labour* 3 (1978) as is DeLottinville's "Joe Beef of Montreal," 8–9 (1981/2); Heap, "La grève des charretiers à Montréal, 1864," is in *RHAF* 31, no. 3 (December 1977), as is Burgess, "L'industrie de la chaussure à Montréal," 31, no. 2 (September 1977); Filteau's *Histoire des patriotes*, and Rudé, *Protest and Punishment*, both discuss 1837–8. Chapais treats the candle-snuffers' rebellion in "La guerre des éteignoirs." Opposition to local tax collectors in the Bois Franc region, 1848–9, can be found in Little, "Colonization and Municipal Reform," and Senior, *British Regulars in Montreal*, has many examples of civil unrest in Montreal.
4 For the Beauharnois strike, see *Histoire du mouvement ouvrier*, 31. Guardia's "Crime in the Transition: Montreal, 1820–29," examines Montreal judicial records.
5 Rudé, *Protest and Punishment*, 96; the *Gazette* survey was done by Deborah Wells.
6 Le Moine, "Un seigneur éclairé," 321.
7 Little, "Colonization and Municipal Reform," 98–121.
8 DeLottinville, "Joe Beef of Montreal," 29–40; for Allan's insurance activities, see Young, "Hugh Allan," *DCB* 9: 10.
9 For the Grey Nuns, see Gossage, "Abandoned Children," especially chap. 2 and 3; treatment of the medical profession and maternity can be found in Kenneally, "The Montreal Maternity Hospital," chaps. 2, 3, and 4.
10 Ouellet, *Histoire économique*, 467–72; Hamelin and Roby, *Histoire économique*, 53; Bradbury, "Family Economy," 75, 80; ASSP, doss. 120, Report of Patrick Dowd, director of St Brigitte's Refuge, 16 September 1880.
11 Cited in Kerr, "Note sur les relations entre les Hospitalières," 305; ASSP, doss. 120, Report of Patrick Dowd, director of St Brigitte's Refuge, 16 September 1880; Roy, "Paupérisme et assistance sociale"; ASSM, arm. 2, vol. 180, June 1871.
12 Montreal *Gazette*, 11 March 1843.
13 ASSP, doss. 98, Supérior Vincent Quiblier to superior general, 8 January 1831.

14 Minutes, 2 June 1856.

15 ASSM, Baille correspondence, J.A. Baille to Joseph Carrière, 1847.

16 Filteau, *Histoire des patriotes*, 243; Bishop Lartigue did ask that a Te Deum be chanted for the new Queen although many people walked out during the ceremony. Senior, *British Regulars in Montreal*, 47; ASSM, arm. 2, vol. 180.

17 *L'Écho du cabinet de lecture paroissial*, January 1867, 310.

18 L. Colin, Sulpician superior to gathering on fiftieth anniversary of the nuns of Bon Pasteur, 25 June 1894, in *Fêtes jubilaires des religieuses du Bon Pasteur d'Angers à Montréal*, 33.

19 Handwritten Sulpician sermon, 13 May 1871, in ASSM, arm. 3, vol. 37.

20 Gauthier, *Une âme sacerdotale*, 58, 93.

21 BNQM, Grand Séminaire, no. 6, Règlement général du Grand Séminaire, 1840; Collège de Montréal, no. 6, Coutumier à l'usage du portier du Grand Séminaire de Montréal vers 1900.

22 BNQM, Collège de Montréal, no. 109, Procès verbal de la visite du collège ... par E.M. Faillon, 16–24 avril 1850; Minutes, 14 March 1862, 23 April 1866.

23 Hill, "Parliament and People," 120.

24 ASSM, Picard correspondence, Eustache Picard to Sulpician superior, n.d.; Picard to —, 14 January 1874.

25 ASSM, Picard correspondence, Eustache Picard to superior, October 1867; *L'Écho du cabinet de lecture paroissial*, 18 January 1863.

26 ASSP, doss. 68, Antoine Mercier to superior general, 7 February 1865; ASSM, arm. 3, vol. 37.

27 Lacan and Prévost, "An Historical Notice," 17; for other examples of seminary attitudes to Two Mountains Indians, see ASSM, Comte correspondence, Joseph Comte to Claude-Joseph Bardey, curé at Oka, various dates.

28 Rumilly, *Histoire de Montréal* 2: 181; Notice, 78; ANQM, Lacombe, 455, profession, Marie-Luce Coullard, 17 October 1837; for dowries, see Bruno Harel, "François-Auguste Mogon de Terlaye," *DCB* 10: 506–7.

29 Danylewycz, "Taking the Veil in Montreal," 1–2.

30 For examples of the replacement of lay teachers in the Côte-des-Neiges school, see Minutes, 15 April 1863; Faillon, *L'héroïne chrétienne* 16: 53; Gagnon, "Étienne-Michel Faillon," *DCB* 9: 247.

31 ASSP, doss. 120, Report of Patrick Dowd, director of St Brigitte's Refuge, 16 September 1880; Curran, *St. Patrick's Orphan Asylum*, 64.

32 ASSM, Picard correspondence, L. Mealand to Picard, 25 April 1858; Hamelin, "Médéric Lanctot," *DCB* 10: 422.

33 Compare Alan Dawley's rejection of reformers as "moral police for middle-class virtues" and Thomas Dublin's description of boarding-houses to David Rothman's *Discovery of the Asylum*, Dawley's *Class and Community*,

114, and Dublin's *Women at Work*, 75–85. Also useful is Michael Katz, "Origins of the Institutional State."

34 Rousseau, *La prédication à Montréal*, 36, 60.

35 Notice; Maurault, *La paroisse*, 16–25.

36 Maurault, *La paroisse*, 79, 85.

37 ANQM, Lafleur, 3977, reconnaissance, *fabrique* of Notre-Dame Church to seminary, 19 December 1878; ASSM, arm. 2, vol. 225. Among the *fabrique*'s creditors were Peter McGill (£1,500), Dame Catherine Hayes (£1,000), Dame Phoebe Hayes (£1,000), John Redpath (£500), Dame N.F. de Montenbach (£500), Samuel Gerrard (£2,340), Eleazor Hayes (£1,500), and Joseph Eleazor Hayes (£800).

38 ASSM, arm. 2, vol. 237; arm. 2, vol. 225; ANQM, Lafleur, 3977, reconnaissance, *fabrique* of Notre-Dame Church to seminary, 19 December 1878.

39 Notice, 57.

40 ASSM, arm. 2, vol. 250.

41 For the struggle at Notre-Dame-de-Grâce, see ANQM, 2581, Signification et protestation, seminary to Napoléon Marchal, 14 March 1871.

42 In 1862 the seminary paid $230 for insurance on its churches and $256 for taxes on church property. Firewood for its schools and churches cost the seminary $1,264 in 1861. ASSM, arm. 2, vol. 264; for firewood contracts, see ANQM, Lacombe, 237, 405, 513, marché, seminary and Pierre Charlebois, 20 February 1835, 5 January 1837, 14 March 1838.

43 The early nineteenth-century clergy is described in Chabot, *Le curé de campagne*; for the seminary's reluctance to train priests, see Maurault, *Grand Séminaire de Montréal*, 21.

44 In 1857, board at the Grand Séminaire was £10 a year with a supplement if the student stayed during the summer. Minutes, 7 November 1840, 8 June 1857. For examples of promissory notes signed by Grand Séminaire theological students, see BNQM, ASSM file, Grand Séminaire, no. 14, Billets promissoires.

45 D'Antin de Vaillac, "Les constitutions de Saint-Sulpice," 21. Reform of the Quebec clergy and religious communities is described in Danylewycz, "Taking the Veil in Montreal," and Savard, "La vie du clergé québécois."

46 BNQM, ASSM file, Grand Séminaire, no. 6, Règlement général du Grand Séminaire, Joseph Quiblier, 1840.

47 See table 15; Maurault, *Grand Séminaire de Montréal*, 128.

48 Maurault, "Galerie des portraits des supérieurs," 194; *Le diocèse de Montréal*, 75.

49 Debate over the curriculum is described in Lamonde, "L'enseignement de la philosophie au Collège de Montréal"; *Census of 1861*, individual returns, Collège de Montréal; for the history of the college, see Maurault,

Le Petit Séminaire; for biographies of its founder and directors, see Harel, "Jean-Baptiste Currateau," and Maurault, "Galerie des portraits."

50 Atherton, *Montreal* 2: 211; in 1866 part of the old college burned and the remnant was rented as a warehouse.

51 ANQM, Lafleur, 2304, marche, seminary and Ernest Chenteloup, 21 June 1869; Minutes, 8 June 1874.

52 ASSM, arm. 2, vol. 24.

53 ASSM, arm. 2, vol. 294, back pages marked "charbon."

54 ASSM, arm. 2, vol. 157.

55 For example, the accounts for 1821 were marked: "sur l'excédent des recettes on donnera à M. Le Curé £500 comme l'année dernière pour les mêmes fins et 100 aux Soeurs." ASSM, arm. 2, vol. 225.

56 Huguette Roy, "Paupérisme et assistance sociale," 74, 109, 115.

57 Notice, 81.

58 Ibid., 82.

59 Ibid., 80–1; for donations to the Grey Nuns, see appendixes 13 and 14; for the Salle Molin in the Hôpital Général, see *Une fondatrice et son oeuvre*, 3.

60 Notice, 83; Minutes, 26 July 1855, 26 January 1846, 21 April 1862, 12 October 1864, 23 April 1866, 25 January 1862, 13 April 1866.

61 Minutes, 7 October 1853; Notice, 83; Minutes, 22 October 1856, 14 June 1860, 2 November 1868, 12 October 1864.

62 For a description of the congregation's revenues, see Notice, 41.

63 *Lovell's Montreal Directory*, 1891, 63–6.

64 De Lagrave, "Louis Roblot," 681; for an example of Christian Brother ideology, see their history text, *Cours abrégé d'histoire contenant l'histoire sainte, l'histoire du Canada ...* (Québec, 1873).

65 Notice, 48.

66 Appendix 14; 1855–6 and 1872–3 omitted from the averages because of confusion over capital and operating costs. For the history of the Christian Brothers, see François De Lagrave, "Les frères des écoles chrétiennes au Canada (1837–1904)," La société canadienne d'histoire de l'Église catholique, *Sessions d'études*, 1969, 29–47.

CONCLUSION

1 William Blake, "The Marriage of Heaven and Hell," in Alfred Kazin, ed., *The Portable Blake* (Middlesex: Penguin, 1978), 260–1.

2 Montreal *Gazette*, 4, 8, 11, July 1837.

3 Ibid., 22 February 1850, 16 January 1858.

4 For the *voies de passage*, see Marx, *Capital* 3: 334–7; Soboul, *Problèmes paysans*, 12–5; the American example is treated in Post, *American Road*,

45–9; for Redpath's evolution, see Lauzon, "Pierre sur pierre." An interesting example in Gananoque, Ontario, albeit without the *problématique* of the *voies de passage*, is in Akenson, *Irish*, 66–78.

5 As late as 1929 the seminary collected seigneurial rents and capital of $103,219, and seigneurial vestiges were still being tidied up in laws passed in 1935 and 1940. Quebec, *Rapport des seigneuries, 1929; Statutes of Quebec*, 25–6 Geo. v, c. 82, "Seigniorial Rent Abolition Act," 18 May 1935; *Statutes of Quebec*, 4, Geo. vi, c. 25, "An Act to amend the Seigniorial Rent Abolition Act," 17 May 1940.

6 Macpherson, *Property*, 10.

7 Note, for example, rising notarial and office expenses in appendixes 13 and 14.

8 As well, verbal agreements which were difficult to enforce and rents in kind which were usually based on a percentage of produce became increasingly rare. For examples of these verbal agreements, see ASSM, arm. 3, vol. 19; for an example of the debt-recognition contract, see appendix 2.

Bibliography

MANUSCRIPT SOURCES
Archives du Séminaire de Saint-Sulpice de Montréal (ASSM)
This important collection has been divided into *procès-verbaux* (minutes), *correspondance* (correspondence), *tiroirs* (drawers), *armoires* (vault cupboards), miscellaneous, and unclassified. There is a partial subject author index to the *tiroirs* and two unpublished inventories of the *armoires* which are in the possession of archivist Père Bruno Harel. "Inventaire sommaire des cahiers placés dans les armoires 2 et 3 de la voûte numéro 1 du Séminaire," compiled by Bruno Harel and Huguette Lapointe Roy, covers the contents of cupboards two and three of vault one. "Inventaire sommaire des cahiers de l'armoire 3 de la voûte 1 du Séminaire," prepared by Louise Tremblay, Christian Dessureault, and Bruno Harel, lists supplemental volumes in cupboard three of vault one.

Procès-Verbaux
Assemblées des 4 consultateurs, procès-verbaux. 27 August 1840–27 March 1871; 20 October 1873–8 March 1876
Conseils d'assistants, cahier no. 1, vol. 1, 18 July 1842–26 November 1860

Correspondance
Joseph Baille 1834–47
Pierre-Louis Billaudèle various dates to brother and to superior general in Paris
Joseph Comte various dates
Eustache Picard 1857–74

Tiroirs

3, 4, 5 Négociations avec le gouvernement, 1819–40
45 Moulins
63, 64 "Affaire Fleming"
70 Joseph-Vincent Quiblier, "Notice sur le Séminaire de Montréal," unpublished manuscript, 1846
88 Canal de Lachine; fermes, domaines, moulins
90 "Propriétés en valeur du Séminaire de Montréal en 1808"
91 "Notes sur les droits seigneuriaux, 1852–3"

Armoire Two

12 Affaires à régler, 1860–65
13 Partages ... vers 1837
19 Baux, conventions, loyers, 1788 à 1840
20 Cahier des oppositions, 1858–77
21 Liste des oppositions pendant en cour 1799 à 1839
24 Sommaire des recettes et dépenses de l'économe du Séminaire, 1794–1841
27 Journal des arrérages et reconnaissances (de dettes), 1842 à 1898
28 Tableau des échéances de paiement des censitaires de Montréal, 1843
29 Cahier de la dette contractée par The St. Lawrence and Atlantic Railroad, 1850–80
30 Rentes et arrérages, Montréal, 1851
31 Rentes et arrérages, 1852
32 Intérêts sur commutations, reconnaissance de dettes, legs ... 1864–92
34 Cahier des intérêts, 1863–82
35 Livre de comptes livrés, intérêts et rentes annuelles, 1835–42
37 Recettes de rentes constituées, intérêts et obligations, 1839–63
39 Livre des achats chez certains fournisseurs, 1843–63
41 Arrérages, reconnaissances, Faubourg Ste Marie, 1842–78
42 Arrérages, reconnaissances, Faubourg St-Laurent, 1842–64
43 Arrérages et reconnaissances, île de Montréal, 1841–47
44 Arrérages et reconnaissances, île de Montréal, 1842–94
52 Index des reconnaissances, transports dans la ville ...
53 Table générale pour la seigneurie de Montréal
55 Lots non commués dans les faubourgs St-Joseph et St-Laurent, 1867
56 Lods et rentes, villages en l'île de Montréal ... comptes à livrer, 1851–2
63 Comptes de commutation et dettes courantes, 1843–45
64 Registre de commutations demandées, 1841–59
65 Oppositions faites par le Séminaire à la vente de terres et emplacements, 1838–53

66 Oppositions, les 4 traverses de St-Sulpice, 1773–1806

67 Cahier de poursuite par Monsieur L.L. Corbeil (avocat) de 1873 à 1885

73 Loyers dus Vitré et Dorchester, 1877–1904

75 Régie du domaine dit St-Gabriel, 1841–54

77 Journal des recettes et dépenses du domaine de la Montagne, 1864–78

78 Régie de la Montagne, 1841–63

80 Comptes des Moulins, 1839 à 1866

81 Livre de comptes de la ferme du domaine du Sault aux Récollets, 1865–73

85 Sciage du bois ... grains vendus, 1863–67

89 Mémoires, notes et comptes divers 1856 à 1863

102 Casuel du Séminaire 1801 à 1827

127 Cahier de recettes, confrérie de la Bonne Mort, 1835–59

128 Journal de recettes et dépenses de l'économe du Séminaire de Montréal, 1853–57

129 Sommaire mensuel de recette et dépense de l'économe du Séminaire de Montréal, 1853–92

133 Livre des dépenses accidentelles de la maison du Séminaire, 1836–53

134 Dépenses de la maison, 1858–64

144 *Cadastre abrégé de la seigneurie de l'île de Montréal*, 1861

148 Registre des comptes de la Fabrique, 1854–83

149 Registre des bancs dans l'église St-Joseph, 1869–75

153 Dépenses de la Procure, 1840–63

154 Cahier des engagés du Séminaire, 1832–53

155 Comptes du Séminaire, 1863–87

157 Sommaire des comptes de la Procure du Séminaire, 1839–76

158 Le Séminaire de Montréal avec le Procureur de Paris, 1863–79

159 Comptes avec le Procureur du Séminaire de Paris, 1879–1903

160 Dépenses de la Procure depuis 1841

171 Faubourg Ste-Marie, vers 1830 (livre terrier)

173 Livre terrier des Faubourgs St-Antoine et St-Joseph vers 1830

174 Emprunts du Séminaire, 1869–97

180 Livre de caisse, 1865–73

181 Dépenses extraordinaires, 1850–77

192 Comptes donnés à M.L. Guilbault, avocat à l'Assomption

195 Livre de compte tenu par le Procureur du Séminaire de Montréal, 1819–24

196 Livre de compte tenu par le Procureur du Séminaire de Montréal, 1824–32

199 Livre de compte tenu par le Procureur du Séminaire de Montréal dans la chambre où il demeure, 1820–24

203 Sommaire de la recette et dépense de l'Aumônier des pauvres St-Jacques, 1863–95, et inventaire de la succession de Messire Villeneuve et Succession Monsieur Lenoir, et Leclair (PSS)

207 Recettes du Lac des Deux-Montagnes, 1849–94

209 Suite du compte des Messieurs de St-Jacques, 1849–52; Produit du moulin du Lac Oureau, 1849

210 Comptes courants avec diverses personnes, 1848–65

211 Comptes courants, 1843–87

212 Mémoire et comptes divers, 1861–3

217 Comptes divers, 1870–79

219 Dépenses pour construction du Séminaire, Églises en ville, 1848–59

220 Dépenses pour constructions depuis 1874

222 Comptes du Collège de la Montagne, 1869–1928

223 Recettes et dépenses du Procureur, 1820–57

225 Livre de la recette et de la dépense du Séminaire de Montréal, 1789–1839

235 Réserve: Liste des placements de la réserve et remboursements, 1867–1909

237 Dépenses pour constructions, 1859–73

243 Échéance de billets, obligations, reconnaissance de dettes, 1844–81

250 Cahier des emprunts et des intérêts, achat de terrains, 1855–77

251 Cahier des créanciers, 1871–1921

264 Livre de compte du Procureur du Séminaire de Montréal, 1833–1900

267 Debentures et bons, 1882–1909

282 Livre de compte de locataires et maisons, 1875–82

294 Livre d'administration de ventes et de faillites, 1880–1923

296 Dépenses de la Procure et honoraires de notaires, 1860–1907

Armoire Three

37 Sermons en anglais et découpures de journaux, 11 February 1871–12 March 1916

40 Livre des maisons et diverses dépenses de construction, 1876–1908

42 Cahier contenant les permis de coupe de bois, November 1868–October 1903

46 53 contrats de Ed. Lafleur sur ferme de la montagne, 1868–71

69 Journal de notes concernant les gardes forestiers (Oka), 1866–73

80 Droits du Séminaire sur certaines propriétés ... 1800–1909

87 Rachats de rentes dans la seigneurie du lac des Deux-Montagnes, 1882–1917

110 Compte des recettes faites par J. Girouard dans la Seigneurie des Deux-Montagnes, 1842–52

115 Compte de sommes remises à Joseph Comte et autres 1856 vers 1871

118 Terres vendues

180 Recette de la seigneurie de St-Sulpice, 1849–72
187 Rentes constituées, Seigneurie de Saint-Sulpice, 1852–70
195 Mémoire sur le privilège du Seigneur ... par M. Roux, 1822
402 Compte rendu des recettes et dépenses du Séminaire, 1876–1919
403 Livre de caisse du Séminaire, 1857–84

Miscellaneous and Unclassified
Armoire 5, tiroir 45, Baux à loyer
Armoire 5, tiroir 46, unindexed, Vente de la ferme St-Gabriel et emploi
   des deniers en provenant
Armoire 5, tiroir 47, unindexed, St-Gabriel, livre d'encan, no. 1
Armoire 5, tiroir 47, unindexed, St-Gabriel, livre d'encan, no. 2
Unindexed and unshelved box in Vault one, entitled "Gestion: Not. Le Maire
   (Oka), 1849–79; Not. Parent (Québec), 1826–47; Arp. Ostell, 1840–48;
   Arp. Perrault, 1862–79
Vers 1820: Cahier de Jean-Baptiste Bédard, PSS, procureur du Séminaire
   de Saint-Sulpice de Montréal (introduction by Père Harel, PSS)
Carton 133, dossier 4, no. 65b, Bail à ferme entre le Séminaire et Paul
   Deschamps de la ferme Lorette du Sault-au-Récollet, 1886–90

Archives du Séminaire de Saint-Sulpice de Paris (ASSP)
Documents relevant to Canada have been inventoried by Louise Dechêne,
"Inventaire des documents relatifs à l'histoire du Canada conservés dans les
archives de la compagnie de Saint-Sulpice à Paris," *Rapport des archives du
Québec*, 1969, 145–288. Dossiers consulted were 22, 52, 59, 64, 65, 68, 120,
121, 1230, 1269.

Archives of the City of Montreal
Map Department: rolls 30–32, 'Terriers des différentes parties de la ville ... '

Archives nationales du Québec (ANQM)
Notaries
Joseph Bonin January 1872–December 1880
André Jobin April 1836–1853
Patrice Lacombe April 1835–8 June 1863
Edouard Lafleur August 1851–December 1880
Edouard Moreau November 1863–October 1867
Henri Valotte 1842–6 October 1847

Bibliothèque nationale du Québec, Montréal (BNQM)
Microfilm on the Collège de Montréal and the Séminaire de Montréal

McGill University, Manuscript Collection of
Rare Books Room (McLennan Library)

CH302 S262 3960–3968, "Sub-committee report to examine questions at issue between his majesty's government ... and seminary of Montreal, April 1840"

CH302 S262 3978–9, John Fisher and W. Badgley, "Copy of instructions to committee," Montreal, 29 April 1840

CH302 S262 4343, W. Badgley to D. Giffand, London *Standard*, 29 April 1840

Montreal Business History Project
(McGill University)

Nominative File

Miscellaneous notarial contracts

GOVERNMENT DOCUMENTS

Canada

Sessional Papers. Bank and insurance company shareholder records, 1870, 1887, 1890, 1900.

Canada, Province of

Cadastre abrégé de la seigneurie de l'isle de Montréal. Québec, 1861.

Cadastres abrégés des seigneuries du district de Montréal. Vols. 1–3. Québec, 1863.

Census of Canada. 1861. Individual returns.

Edicts, Ordinances ... Relative to the Seigneurial Tenure. Quebec, 1852.

Journals of the Legislative Assembly, 1843. App. F, "State of the Laws Concerning Seigneuries."

Journals of the Legislative Assembly. 1851. App. NNN, "Proceedings of the Committee on Seigneurial Tenure."

Journals of the Legislative Assembly. 1852–3. App. HHH, "Seigneurial Documents."

Journal of the Legislative Assembly. 1852–3, App. YYY, "Statement of the Estate ... of the Seminary ... of Montreal ... to 1852."

Lower Canada

Copy of Ordinances Passed by the Governor and Special Council of Lower Canada in Victoria III and IV. 1841. No. 164: "An Ordinance to incorporate the Ecclesiastics of the Seminary of Saint Sulpice of Montreal; to confirm their Title to the Fief and Seigniory of the Lake of the Two Mountains, and the Fief and Seigniory of Saint Sulpice, in this Province; to provide for the gradual Extinction of Seigniorial Rights and Dues within the Seigniorial Limits of the said Fiefs and Seigniories and for other purposes, 8 June 1840."

Journals of the House of Assembly. 1831–2. App. NN, "Petition of Divers ... Censitaires ... in the Seigneury of Lotbinière."

Journals of the House of Assembly. 1831–2. "Census and Statistical Returns of Lower Canada, 1831."

Journals of the House of Assembly. 1835. App. EE, "First Report of Standing Committee on Grievances."

Journals of the Special Council. Vict. 3, 1840.

Ordinances Made and Passed by his Excellency the Governor General and Special Council for the Affairs of the Province of Lower Canada. Quebec, 1839. "Ordinance to Incorporate the Ecclesiastics of the Seminary of St. Sulpice ... ," 8 April 1839.

Report of a Special Committee on the Imperial Statutes. 1826.

Report of the Commissioners Appointed to Inquire into the Grievances Complained of in Lower Canada. Montreal, 1838.

Statutes. Geo. IV, c. 6, 17 March 1821, "An Act for Making ... Lachine Canal."

Statutes. Will. IV, c. 10, 31 March 1831, "An Act to Invest City of Montreal with the Property of the Commons of Montreal."

Quebec

Rapport des seigneuries, fiefs et arrière-fiefs de la province de Québec, 1929. Québec, 1930.

Sessional Papers. No. 9, 1877–8, "General Report of the Inspectors of Prisons, Asylums ... "

Statutes. 25–6 George V, 1935, "Seigneurial Rent Abolition Act."

Statutes. 4 George VI, 1940, "Act to Amend the Seigneurial Rent Abolition Act."

NEWSPAPERS AND PERIODICALS

Le Bulletin des recherches historiques. Volumes consulted were 32, 39, 45, and 46.

L'Écho du cabinet de lecture paroissial. January 1859–1873.

Montreal *Gazette.* 7 May 1840–16 June 1840; August 1845; other occasional dates, 1836–76.

Montreal *Transcript.* 9 May 1840.

OTHER SOURCES

Adair, E.R. "The French-Canadian Seigneury." *Canadian Historical Review* 26 (September 1945): 187–207.

Akenson, Donald H. *The Church of Ireland: Ecclesiastical Reform and Revolution, 1800–1885*. New Haven & London: Yale University Press, 1971.

– *The Irish in Ontario: A Study in Rural History*. Kingston and Montreal: McGill-Queen's University Press, 1984.

Antin de Vaillac, Henri d'. "Les constitutions de la compagnie de Saint-Sulpice: Étude historique et canonique." Thèse pour le doctorat en droit canonique, Institut catholique de Paris, 1964.

Armstrong, Frederick H. "Charles-Séraphin Rodier." *DCB* 10: 624–6.

Atherton, William H. *Montreal from 1535 to 1914*. 3 vols. Montreal: S.J. Clarke Publishing, 1914.

Baehre, Rainer. "Origins of the Penitentiary System in Upper Canada." *Ontario History*, 69 (September 1977).

Baillargeon, Georges. *La survivance du régime seigneurial à Montréal*. Montréal: Le cercle du livre de France, 1968.

Baillargeon, Noël. *Le Séminaire de Québec de 1685 à 1760*. Québec: Les Presses de l'université Laval, 1977.

– *Le Séminaire de Québec de 1760 à 1800*. Québec: Les Presses de l'université Laval, 1981.

Bairoch, Paul. "Agriculture and the Industrial Revolution." In *The Fontana History of Europe*, edited by Carlo M. Cipolla, vol. 3: 452–506. Glasgow: Fontana, 1973.

Baribeau, Claude. *La seigneurie de la Petite-Nation, 1801–54. Le rôle économique et social du seigneur*. Hull: Asticou, 1983.

Beaubien, Charles P. *Le Sault-au-Récollet*. Montréal, 1898.

Benoît, Jean. "La question seigneuriale du Bas Canada, 1850–67." MA thesis, Université Laval, 1978.

Bernard, Jean-Paul. *Les rébellions de 1837–38*. Montréal: Boréal Express, 1984.

Bernard, Jean-Paul, Paul-André Linteau, and Jean-Claude Robert. "La structure professionnelle de Montréal en 1825." *RHAF* 3 (December 1976): 383–415.

Bernier, Gérard, and Daniel Salée. "Appropriation foncière et bourgeoisie marchande: éléments pour une analyse de l'économie marchande du Bas-Canada avant 1846." *RHAF* 36 (September 1982): 163–94.

Beutler, Corinne. "Le rôle des moulins banaux du Séminaire de Saint-Sulpice à Montréal entre la campagne et la ville, 1790–1840." Unpublished paper presented at the Colloque franco-québecois de Rochefort, 5–8 July 1982.

– "Le rôle du blé à Montréal sous le régime seigneurial." *RHAF* 36 (September 1982): 241–62.

– "Les moulins à farine du Séminaire de Saint-Sulpice à Montréal (1658–1840): Essai d'analyse économique d'une prérogative du régime seigneurial." Canadian Historical Association, *Report*, 1983, 184–207.

Bindon, Kathryn. "Adam Thom." *DCB* 9: 874–6.

– "Hudson's Bay Company Law: Adam Thom and the Institution of Order in Rupert's Land, 1839–54." In *Essays in the History of Canadian Law*, edited by David Flaherty, vol. 1. Toronto: University of Toronto Press, 1981.

Blum, Jerôme. *Noble Landowners and Agriculture in Austria, 1815–48: A Study of the Peasant Emancipation of 1848*. Baltimore: Johns Hopkins, 1948.

Bois, Guy. *Crise du féodalisme*. Paris: École des hautes études en sciences sociales, 1976.

Boisard, Pierre. *Issy, Le Séminaire et la Compagnie de Saint-Sulpice*. Paris: Séminaire d'Issy, 1942.

– *La compagnie de Saint-Sulpice. Trois siècles d'histoire*. Paris, 1941.

Bonin, R. "Le canal Lachine sous le régime français." *Le Bulletin des recherches historiques* 43 (1936): 271–97.

Bonner, John. *An Essay on the Registry Laws of Lower Canada*. Quebec: Lovell, 1852.

Bottomore, T.B., ed. *Karl Marx: Early Writings*. New York: McGraw Hill, 1963.

Boucher, Jacques. "Les aspects économiques de la tenure seigneuriale au Canada (1760–1854)." In Philippe Solomon, Georges Frêche, and Jacques Boucher, *Recherches d'histoire économique*, 149–213. Paris: PUF, 1964.

Bouchette, Joseph. *Description topographique de la province du Bas Canada avec des remarques sur le Haut Canada*. London, 1815.

Boyer, Raymond. *Les crimes et les châtiments au Canada français*. Montréal: Le cercle du livre de France, 1966.

Bradbury, Bettina. "The Family Economy and Work in an Industrializing City: Montreal in the 1870's." Canadian Historical Association, *Historical Papers*, 1979, 71–96.

Brazant, Jan. *Alienation of Church Wealth in Mexico: Social and Economic Aspects of the Liberal Revolution, 1856–75*. London: Cambridge University Press, 1971.

Brown, Richard. *A History of Accounting and Accountants*. Edinburgh, 1905.

Bruneau, Thomas C. *The Political Transformation of the Brazilian Catholic Church*. London: Cambridge University Press, 1974.

Brunet, Michel. "L'église catholique du Bas-Canada et le partage du pouvoir à l'heure d'une nouvelle donne." In *Les idéologies québécoises au 19⁰ siècle (1837–1854)*, edited by J.P. Bernard. Montréal: Boréal Express, 1973.

Burgess, Joanne. "L'industrie de la chaussure à Montréal, 1840–1870: Le passage de l'artisanat à la fabrique." *RHAF* 31 (September 1977): 187–210.

Careless, J.M.S. *Union of the Canadas: The Growth of Canadian Institutions*. Toronto: McClelland and Stewart, 1967.

Chabot, Richard. *Le curé de campagne et la contestation locale au Québec de 1791 aux troubles de 1837–38.* Montréal: HMH, 1975.

Chandaman, C.D. *The English Public Revenue, 1660–1688.* Oxford: Clarendon, 1975.

Chandler, Alfred D. *The Visible Hand: The Managerial Revolution in American Business.* Cambridge: Harvard University Press, 1977.

Chapais, Thomas. "La guerre des éteignoirs," Royal Society of Canada, *Procedures and Transactions,* series 3, XXII (1928).

Chassé, Béatrice. "Le notaire Girouard, patriote et rebelle," PHD thesis, Université Laval, 1974.

Chaussé, Gilles. *Jean-Jacques Lartigue, premier évêque de Montréal.* Montréal: Fides, 1980.

Choquette, C.P. *Histoire du Séminaire de Saint-Hyacinthe depuis sa fondation jusqu'à nos jours.* Montréal, 1911.

Colletti, Lucio. *Marxism and Hegel.* London: NLB, 1969.

Colthart, James, "Edward Ellice," *DCB* 9: 233–9.

Confino, Michael. *Domaines et seigneurs en Russie vers la fin du XVIII' siècle.* Paris: Institut d'études slaves de l'université de Paris, 1963.

Consultation de douze des plus célèbres avocats de Paris touchant les droits de propriété du Séminaire de Montréal en Canada. Paris, 1819.

Consultation de M. Dupin, avocat à la cour royale de Paris pour le Séminaire de Montréal en Canada. Paris, 1826.

Courville, Serge. "La crise agricole du Bas-Canada: Éléments d'une réflexion géographique." *Cahiers de géographie du Québec* 24, no. 62 (September 1980): 193–223.

– "Rente déclarée payée sur la censive de 90 arpents au recensement nominatif de 1831: Méthodologie d'une recherche." *Cahiers de géographie du Québec* 27, no. 70 (April 1983): 43–61.

– "Villages et agriculture dans les seigneuries du Bas-Canada: Éléments pour une réinterprétation du développement rural québécois dans la première moitié du 19ᵉ siècle." Unpublished paper presented at Canadian Historical Association meetings, University of Guelph, 1984.

Craven, Paul and Tom Traves. "Canadian Railways as Manufacturers, 1850–80," Canadian Historical Association, *Historical Papers,* 1983, 254–81.

Creighton, Donald. *The Empire of the St. Lawrence.* Toronto: Macmillan, 1956.

Critchley, J.S. *Feudalism.* London: George Allen and Unwin, 1978.

Cross, Suzanne, "The Neglected Majority: The Changing Role of Women in Nineteenth Century Montreal," *Social History* 16, no. 12 (November 1973): 202–23.

Crowley, Terrence. "Thunder Gusts: Popular Disturbances in Early French Canada." Canadian Historical Association, *Historical Papers,* 1979, 11–31.

Curran, J.J., ed. *St. Patrick's Orphan Asylum.* Montreal: Catholic Institution for Deaf Mutes, 1902.

Dansereau, Antonio. "Antoine Mercier." *DCB* 10: 510–11.
- "Jacques-Victor Arraud." *DCB* 10: 16–17.
- "Michel Barthélemy." *DCB* 2: 45–6.
- "Nicolas Dufresne." *DCB* 9: 227–8.
- "Pierre-Louis Billaudèle." *DCB* 9: 50–2.
Danylewycz, Marta. "Taking the Veil in Montreal, 1850–1920: An Alternative to Migration, Motherhood and Spinsterhood." Unpublished paper presented at Canadian Historical Association meetings, University of Western Ontario, 1978.
Daoust, Gilles, and Roger Viau, eds. *L'île des moulins (Terrebonne)*. Québec: Ministère des affaires culturelles, 1979.
Dawley, Alan. *Class and Community: The Industrial Revolution in Lynn*. Cambridge: Harvard University Press, 1976.
De Chalendar, Xavier. *Les Prêtres*. Paris: Seuil, 1963.
Dechêne, Louise, "L'évolution du régime seigneurial au Canada: Le cas de Montréal aux XVIIᵉ et XVIIIᵉ siècles." *Recherches sociographiques* 12 (1976): 143–83.
- *Habitants et marchands de Montréal au XVIIᵉ siècle*. Paris: Plon, 1974.
- "La rente du faubourg Saint-Roch à Québec, 1750–1850." *RHAF* 34 (March 1981): 569–96.
De Lagrave, François. "Louis Roblot." *DCB* 9: 680–1.
DeLottinville, Peter. "Joe Beef of Montreal: Working Class Culture and the Tavern, 1869–89." *Labour* 8–9 (1981–2): 9–40.
Delumeau, Jean. *Le catholicisme entre Luther et Voltaire*. Paris: PUF, 1971.
Denault, Bernard, and Benoît Lévesque. *Eléments pour une sociologie des communautés religieuses au Québec*. Sherbrooke: Université de Sherbrooke, 1971.
Desrosiers, Claude. "Un aperçu des habitudes de consommation en milieu rural à la fin du XVIIIᵉ siècle." Unpublished paper presented at Canadian Historical Association meetings, University of Guelph, 1984.
Dessureault, Christian. "La colonisation dans la seigneurie du Lac des Deux-Montagnes, 1780–1820." MA thesis, Université de Montréal, 1979.
De Volpi, Charles, and P.S. Winkworth. *Montreal: A Pictorial Record*. Vol. 1. Montreal: Dev-Sco Publications, 1963.
Déziel, Julien. *Histoire de Verdun*. Québec: Comité du centenaire, 1976.
Diamond, Sigmund. "An Experiment in 'Feudalism': French Canada in the Seventeenth Century." *William and Mary Quarterly* 28 (January 1961): 3–34.
Dickinson, John. "La justice seigneuriale en Nouvelle-France: le cas de Notre-Dame-des Anges." *RHAF* 28 (December 1974): 323–46.
Dictionary of Canadian Biography. Edited by George Brown *et al.* In progress. Toronto: University of Toronto Press, 1965– .
Le Diocèse de Montréal à la fin du dix-neuvième siècle. Montréal: Sénécal and Co., 1900.

Dobb, Maurice. *Studies in the Development of Capitalism.* New York: International Publishers, 1963.

Dobb, Maurice and Paul Sweezy. *Du féodalisme au capitalisme: problèmes de la transition.* Paris: Maspero, 1977.

Donnachie, Ian. *A History of the Brewing Industry in Scotland.* Edinburgh: John Donald, 1979.

Doucet, Michael. "Working Class Housing in a Small Nineteenth Century Canadian City: Hamilton, Ontario, 1852–1881." In *Essays in Canadian Working Class History,* edited by Gregory S. Kealey and Peter Warrian. Toronto: McClelland and Stewart, 1979.

Doucet, Michael, and John Weaver. "The North American Shelter Business, 1860–1920: A Study of a Canadian Real Estate and Property Management Agency." *Business History Review* 58 no. 2 (summer 1984): 234–62.

Doughty, Arthur G., and Duncan A. McArthur, eds. *Documents relating to the Constitutional History of Canada, 1791–1818.* Ottawa, 1907.

Doughty, Arthur G., and Norah Story, eds. *Documents relating to the Constitutional History of Canada, 1819–1828.* Ottawa, 1935.

Dublin, Thomas. *Women at Work: The Transformation of Work and Community in Lowell, Massachusetts, 1826–1860.* New York: Columbia, 1979.

Duby, Goerges. *L'économie rurale et la vie des campagnes dans l'occident médiéval.* Vol. 2. Paris: Flammarion, 1977.

Dumont-Johnson, Micheline. "Des garderies au XIXᵉ siècle: Les salles d'asile des Soeurs Grises à Montréal." *RHAF* 34, no. 1 (June 1980): 27–55.

Eid, Nadia F. *Le clergé et le pouvoir politique au Québec: Une analyse de l'idéologie ultramontaine au milieu du XIXᵉ siècle.* Montréal: HMH, 1978.

Ennis, Arthur. "The Conflict between the Regular and Secular Clergy." In *The Roman Catholic Church in Colonial Latin America,* edited by R.E. Greenleaf. New York: Knopf, 1971.

Faillon, Étienne-Michel. *L'héroine chrétienne du Canada, ou vie de Mlle. Le Ber.* Montréal: Les Soeurs de la Congrégation, 1860.

– *Vie de M. Olier, fondateur du Séminaire de Saint-Sulpice.* Paris, 1873.

Faucher, Albert. *Histoire économique et unité canadienne.* Montréal: Fides, 1970.

– *Québec en Amérique au XIXᵉ siècle.* Montréal: Fides, 1973.

Fauteux, Aegidius. *Monsieur Lecoq, souvenirs d'un ancien séminariste.* Montréal: Éditions Édouard Garand, 1927.

Fêtes jubilaires des religieuses de Notre-Dame de Charité du Bon Pasteur. Montréal, 1894.

Filteau, Gérard. *Histoire des patriotes.* Montréal: L'Aurore, 1975.

Une fondatrice et son oeuvre: Mère Mallet. Québec: Action Catholique, 1939.

Foster, John. *Class Struggle and the Industrial Revolution: Early Industrial Capitalism in Three English Towns.* London: Methuen, 1974.

Foucault, Michel. *The Birth of the Clinic: An Archaeology of Medical Perception.* London: Tavistock, 1973.

– *Discipline and Punish: The Birth of the Prison.* New York: Vintage, 1979.

Fournier, Marcel. *Rawdon: 175 ans d'histoire.* Joliette: Société historique de Joliette, 1974.

Francœur, Madame. *Trente ans, rue St. François-Xavier et ailleurs.* Montréal, 1928.

Frégault, Guy. *Le XVIIIᵉ siècle canadien: Études.* Montréal: HMH, 1970.

Les Frères des écoles chrétiennes. *Cours abrégé d'histoire contenant l'histoire sainte, l'histoire du Canada et des autres provinces de l'Amérique britannique.* Québec, 1873.

Gagnon, Serge. "Étienne-Michel Faillon." *DCB* 9: 246–9.

– *Le Québec et ses historiens de 1840 à 1920.* Québec: Les Presses de l'université Laval, 1978.

Gagnon, Serge and Louise-Lebel Gagnon. "Le milieu d'origine du clergé québécois, 1775–1840: Mythes et réalités." *RHAF* 37 (December 1983): 373–97.

Galarneau, Claude. *Les collèges classiques au Canada français.* Montreal: Fides, 1978.

Gauthier, Henri. *Une âme sacerdotale: Charles Lecoq, prêtre de Saint-Sulpice, 1846–1926.* Montréal: Em. A. Deschamps, 1939.

– *La compagnie de Saint-Sulpice au Canada.* Montréal: Séminaire de Saint-Sulpice, 1912.

– *Sulpitiana.* Montréal: Bureau des œuvres paroissiales de Saint-Jacques, 1926.

Genovese, Eugene D. and Elizabeth Fox-Genovese. *Fruits of Merchant Capital: Slavery and Bourgeois Property in the Rise and Expansion of Capitalism.* Oxford: Oxford University Press, 1983.

Gerth, H.H., and C. Wright Mills. *From Max Weber: Essays in Sociology.* New York: Oxford University Press, 1958.

Giroux, H. *Une héroïne du Canada: Madame Gamelin et ses œuvres.* Montréal, 1885.

Goad, Charles E. *City of Montreal ... Showing all Buildings and Names of Owners.* Montreal, 1881.

Gossage, Peter. "Abandoned Children in Nineteenth-Century Montreal." MA thesis, McGill University, 1983.

Gramsci, Antonio. *Selections from the Prison Notebooks.* New York: International Publishers, 1971.

Greenwood, Murray. "L'insurrection appréhendée et l'administration de la justice au Canada: le point de vue d'un historien." *RHAF* 34 (June 1980): 57–91.

Greer, Allan. "Habitants of the Lower Richelieu: Rural Society in Three

Quebec Parishes, 1740–1840." PHD thesis, York University, 1980. Published as *Peasant, Lord, and Merchant: Rural Society in Three Quebec Parishes, 1740–1840.* Toronto: University of Toronto Press, 1985.

Guardia, Raymond. "Crime in the Transition: Montreal, 1820–29, A Preliminary Report." Unpublished undergraduate paper, McGill University, 1984.

Gutelman, Michel. *Structures et réformes agraires*, Paris: Maspero, 1974.

Hamelin, Jean. "Médéric Lanctot." *DCB* 10: 420–6.

– and Yves Roby. *Histoire économique du Québec, 1851–96.* Montréal: Fides, 1971.

Hanna, David. "The New Town of Montreal: Creation of an Upper Middle Class Suburb on the Slope of Mount Royal in the Mid-Nineteenth Century." MA thesis, University of Toronto, 1977.

– and Frank W. Remiggi. *Montreal Neighbourhoods: The Dynamics and Diversity of Montreal Neighbourhoods in Expansion at the End of the Nineteenth Century.* Montreal: Canadian Association of Geographers, 1980.

Hardy, René, Jean Roy and Normand Séguin. "Une recherche en cours: Le monde rural mauricien au 19e siècle." *Cahiers de géographie du Québec* 26, no. 67 (April 1982): 145–54.

Harel, Bruno. "François-Auguste Mogon de Terlaye." *DCB* 4: 506–7.

– "Jean-Baptiste Curatteau." *DCB* 4: 187–9.

– "Jacques Degeay." *DCB* 4: 200–1

– "Pierre-Paul-François de Lagarde." *DCB* 4: 431–2.

– "Saint Sulpice et la conquête du Canada par les Anglais (1760–1764)." *Bulletin de Saint-Sulpice*, no. 4 (1978).

Harris, R. Cole. "Of Poverty and Helplessness in Petite-Nation." In *Canadian History before Confederation*, edited by J. Bumsted. Georgetown: Irwin Dorsey, 1979.

Harrison, Brian. "Religion and Recreation in Nineteenth Century England." *Past and Present* 38 (1967); 98–125

Hay, Douglas, *et al. Albion's Fatal Tree: Crime and Society in Eighteenth Century England.* Middlesex: Penguin, 1975.

Heap, Margaret. "La grève des charretiers à Montréal, 1864." *RHAF* 30, (December 1977): 371–95.

Hill, Christopher. *The English Revolution, 1640: An Essay.* London: Lawrence and Wishart, 1979.

– "Parliament and People in Seventeenth Century England." *Past and Present* 92 (August 1981): 100–24.

– *Reformation to Industrial Revolution.* Middlesex: Penguin, 1967.

Hilton, Rodney, ed. *The Transition from Feudalism to Capitalism.* London: Verso, 1978.

Histoire du mouvement ouvrier au Québec (1825–1976). Montréal: Centrale de l'enseignement du Québec, 1979.

Hobsbawm, E.J. *The Age of Capital, 1848–75.* London: Abacus, 1977.

Hoffman, Philip T. "Le rôle social des curés de l'ancien diocèse de Lyon (XVIᵉ–XVIIIᵉ siècles)." *Bulletin du Centre d'histoire économique et sociale de la région lyonnaise* 4 (1979): 1–20.

Holderness, B.A. "Capital formation in Agriculture." In *Aspects of Capital Investment in Great Britain, 1750–1850*, edited by J.P.P. Higgins and Sidney Pollard, 159–83. London: Methuen, 1971.

Hopkins, Henry W. *Atlas of the City and Island of Montreal ... Montreal.* Montreal, 1879.

Horne, Oliver H. *A History of Savings Banks.* London: Oxford, 1947.

Jean, Marguerite. *Evolution des communautés religieuses de femmes au Canada de 1639 à nos jours.* Montréal: Fides, 1977.

Johnson, J. *Johnson's Complete Map of Montreal and Vicinity: 1872.* Montreal: George Desbarats, 1872.

Jones, Gareth Stedman. "Class Expression versus social control? A critique of recent trends in the social history of 'leisure'." *History Workshop* 4 (autumn 1977): 162–70.

– *Outcast London: A Study in the Relationships between Classes in Victorian Society.* Oxford: Oxford University Press, 1971.

Jones, P.M. "Parish, Seigneurie and the Community of Inhabitants in Southern France." *Past and Present* 91 (May 1981): 74–108.

"Les journaux Emilie Berthelot-Girouard." *Rapport des Archives nationales du Québec* 53 (1975): 105–264.

Kallmann, Helmut. "Jean-Chrysostome Brauneis." *DCB* 10: 88–9.

Katz, Michael. "The Origins of the Institutional State." *Marxist Perspectives*, winter 1978, 6–22.

Kenneally, Rhona Richman. "The Montreal Maternity Hospital, 1843–1926." MA thesis, McGill University, 1983.

Kerr, Corinne. "Notes sur les relations entre les Hospitalières de Montréal et les Irlandais." In *L'Hôtel Dieu, 1642–1973*, 301–8. Montreal: HMH, 1973.

Kesteman, Jean-Pierre. *Le Progrès (1874–78): Étude d'un journal de Sherbrooke:* Sherbrooke: Université de Sherbrooke, 1979.

Kolish, Evelyn. "Changements dans le droit privé au Québec et au Bas Canada, entre 1760 et 1840: attitudes et réactions des contemporains." PHD thesis, Université de Montréal, 1980.

– "Le Conseil législatif et les bureaux d'enregistrement (1836)." *RHAF* 35 (September 1981): 217–30.

La Brèque, Marie-Paule. "La dîme dans Saint-Frédéric de Drummondville au temps des missionnaires." *Les Cahiers nicolétains* 4 (March 1982): 2–11.

Lacan, J., and W. Prévost. *An Historical Notice on the Difficulties Arisen between the Seminary of St. Sulpice of Montreal and Certain Indians at Oka, Lake of Two Mountains. A Mere Case of Right of Property. By No Means a Religious Question.* Montreal: La Minerve, 1876.

Lachance, André. *La justice criminelle du roi au Canada au XVIIIᵉ siècle.* Québec: Les Presses de l'université Laval, 1978.

Lahaise, Robert. *Les édifices conventuels du Vieux Montréal. Aspects ethno-historiques.* Montréal: Hurtubise HMH, 1980.

– "François Picquet." *DCB* 4: 636–7.

Lajeunesse, Marcel. *Les Sulpiciens et la vie culturelle à Montréal au XIXe siècle.* Montréal: Fides, 1982.

Lambert, James H. "Monseigneur, the Catholic Bishop. Joseph-Octave Plessis, Church, State, and Society in Lower Canada: Historiography and Analysis." PHD thesis, Université Laval, 1981.

Lamonde, Yvan. "L'enseignement de la philosophie au Collège de Montréal, 1760–1876." *Culture* 31 (1970): 110–23, 214–24, 312–26.

– "L'enseignement de la philosophie au Québec, 1665–1920." DEL, Université Laval, 1977.

Langlois, Claude. *Le diocèse de Vannes au XIXe siècle, 1800–1830.* Paris: C. Klincksieck, 1974.

Larkin, Emmet. "Economic Growth, Capital Investment, and the Roman Catholic Church in Nineteenth-Century Ireland." *American Historical Review* 62 (April 1967): 852–84.

Lauzon, Gilles. "Pierre sur pierre: L'accumulation dans la maçonnerie, 1820–27." Unpublished paper presented to Canadian Historical Association meetings, University of British Columbia, 1983.

Lauzon, Gilles, and Alan Stewart. "Stratégies d'accumulation du capital: Le cas des métiers de la construction." Unpublished paper, Montreal Business History Project, 1983.

Lebel, Alyne. "Les propriétés foncières des Ursulines et le développement de Québec, 1854–1940." *Cahiers de géographie du Québec* 25, no. 64 (April 1981): 119–32.

Leflon, J. *Monsieur Emery: L'Église d'ancien régime et la Révolution.* Paris: P. Boisard, 1944.

Lemieux, Lucien. *L'établissement de la première province ecclésiastique au Canada, 1783–1844.* Montréal: Fides, 1967.

– "Etienne Montgolfier." *DCB* 4: 542–5.

– "Gabriel-Jean Brassier." *DCB* 4: 89–90.

Lemire, Maurice. "Patrice Lacombe." *DCB* 9: 439–40.

Le Moine, Roger. "Un seigneur éclairé, Louis-Joseph Papineau." *RHAF* 25 (December 1971): 309–36.

Linteau, Paul-André. *Maisonneuve, ou comment des promoteurs fabriquent une ville.* Montréal: Boréal Express, 1981.

Linteau, Paul-André and Jean-Claude Robert. "Land Ownership and Society in Montreal: An Hypothesis." In *The Canadian City: Essays in Urban History*, edited by Gilbert A. Stelter and Alan F.J. Artibise. Toronto: McClelland and Stewart, 1977.

Litalien, Rolland. *Le prêtre québécois à la fin du XIXe siècle.* Montréal: Fides, 1970.

Little, Jack. "Colonization and Municipal Reform in Canada East." *Social History* 14, no. 27 (May 1981): 93–121.

– "Missionary Priests in Quebec's Eastern Townships: The Years of Hardship and Discontent, 1825–53." Canadian Catholic Historical Association, *Study Sessions* 45 (1978): 21–35.

Lovell's Montreal Directory. Montreal: John Lovell, 1876, 1880.

Lucas, C.P., ed. *Lord Durham's Report on the Affairs of British North America*, 3 vols. (Oxford: Clarendon Press, 1912).

McCalla, Douglas. "The 'Loyalist' Economy of Upper Canada, 1784–1806." *Social History* 16, no. 32 (November 1983): 279–304.

– *The Upper Canada Trade, 1834–72: A Study of the Buchanans' Business.* Toronto: University of Toronto Press, 1979.

McCallum, John. *Unequal Beginnings. Agriculture and Economic Development in Quebec and Ontario until 1870.* Toronto: University of Toronto Press, 1980.

McGuigan, G.F. "Land Policy and Land Disposal under Tenure of Free and Common Socage, Quebec and Lower Canada, 1763–1809." Doctoral thesis, Université Laval, 1962.

McInnis, R.M. "A Reconsideration of the State of Agriculture in Lower Canada in the First Half of the Nineteenth Century." In *Canadian Papers in Rural History*, edited by D.H. Akenson, vol. 3: 9–49. Gananoque: Langdale Press, 1982.

McNally, Larry. *Water Power on the Lachine Canal, 1846–1900.* Quebec: Parks Canada, 1978.

Macpherson, C.B., ed. *Property: Mainstream and Critical Positions.* Toronto: University of Toronto Press, 1978.

Marcuse, Herbert. *One Dimensional Man: Studies in the Ideologies of the Advanced Industrial Society.* Boston: Beacon, 1964.

Marx, Karl. *Capital: A Critique of Political Economy.* Vols. 1 and 3. New York: International Publishers, 1967.

– *Grundrisse: Foundations of the Critique of Political Economy.* New York: Vintage, 1973.

Massicotte, É.-Z. *La cité de Sainte-Cunégonde de Montréal, Notes et Souvenirs.* Montréal: Stanley Houde, 1893.

– "Notre-Dame des Neiges." *Cahiers des Dix* 4 (1939): 141–66.

Maurault, Olivier, "Galerie des portraits des supérieurs du Collège de Montréal." *Cahiers des Dix* 25 (1960): 191–217.

– *Grand Séminaire de Montréal.* Montréal: Association des anciens élèves, 1940.

– *La paroisse: Histoire de l'Église Notre-Dame de Montréal.* Montréal: Editions du Mercure, 1929.

– *Le Petit Séminaire de Montréal.* Montréal: Derome, 1918.

- "Une révolution collégiale à Montréal il y a cent ans." *Cahiers des Dix* 2 (1937): 35–44.
- *Saint-Jacques de Montréal. L'église – la paroisse.* Montréal: Saint Jacques, 1923.
- "La seigneurie de Montréal." *Cahiers des Dix* 22 (1957): 69–82.

Mayeur, Françoise. *L'éducation des filles en France au XIXe siècle.* Paris: Hachette, 1979.

Merquior, J.G. *The Veil and the Mask: Essays on Culture and Ideology.* London: Routledge and Kegan Paul, 1979.

Michel, Louis. "Le livre de compte (1784–1792) de Gaspard Massue, marchand à Varennes." *Social History* 13, no. 26 (November 1980): 369–98.
- "Un marchand rural en Nouvelle France – François-Augustin Bailly de Messein, 1709–1771." *RHAF* 33 (September 1979): 215–62.

Miller, Carman. "John Boston." *DCB* 9: 61–2.

Moir, John S. "The Problem of a Double Minority: Some Reflections on the Development of the English-speaking Catholic Church in Canada in the Nineteenth Century." *Social History* 7 (April 1971): 53–67.

Montreal in 1856: A Sketch ... for the opening of the Grand Trunk Railway. Montreal: Lovell, 1856.

Morin, Victor. *Seigneurs et censitaires.* Montréal: Éditions des Dix, 1941.

Munro, W.B. *Documents Relating to the Seigneurial Tenure in Canada.* Toronto: Champlain Society, 1908.
- *The Seigneurial System in Canada: A Study in French Colonial Policy.* New York: Longmans, 1907.

Neale, R.S. *Class and Ideology in the Nineteenth Century.* London: Routledge and Kegan Paul, 1972.

Neream, André. *Vie de la Mère Sainte-Madeleine, supérieure de la Congrégation de Notre-Dame de Montréal.* Montréal: Sénécal, 1876.

Neufeld, E.P. *The Financial System of Canada: Its Growth and Development.* Toronto: Macmillan, 1972.

Noël, François. "Gabriel Christie's Seigneuries: Settlement and Seigneurial Administration in the Upper Richelieu Valley, 1764–1854." PHD thesis, McGill University, 1985.

Objois, Catherine. "Les meuniers dans la seigneurie de l'île de Montréal au XVIIIe siècle." MA thesis, Université de Montréal, 1981.

Ormsby, William, ed. *Crisis in the Canadas, 1838–39: The Grey Journals and Letters.* Toronto: Macmillan 1964.

Ouellet, Fernand, "L'agriculture bas-canadienne vue à travers les dîmes et la rente en nature." *Social History* 8, no. 7 (November 1971): 5–44.
- *Le Bas Canada, 1791–1840: Changements structuraux et crise.* Ottawa: University of Ottawa Press, 1976.
- *Eléments d'histoire sociale du Bas Canada, 1791–1840.* Montréal: HMH, 1972.
- *Histoire économique et sociale du Québec, 1760–1850.* Montréal: Fides, 1966.

- "Libéré ou exploité: Le paysan québécois d'avant 1850." *Social History* 13, no. 26 (November 1980): 339–68.
- *Papineau: Textes choisis*. Québec: Les Presses de l'université Laval, 1970.
- "Propriété seigneuriale et groupes sociaux dans la vallée du Saint-Laurent (1663–1840)." University of Ottawa *Quarterly* 47, no. 1–2 (January–April 1979): 182–213.
- "Simon McTavish." *DCB* 5: 561–7.
Palmer, Bryan. "Discordant Music: Charivaris and Whitecapping in Nineteenth-Century North America." *Labour* 3 (1978): 5–62.
Paquin, Christian. "L'évolution de l'industrie du tramway à Montréal (1861–1911)." Unpublished undergraduate essay, Université du Québec à Montréal, 1981.
Parent, Françoise. "Les cabinets de lecture dans Paris: pratiques culturelles et espace social sous la Restauration." *Annales*, 34ᵉ année, no. 5 (September–October 1979): 1016–38.
Parizeau, Gérard. *La vie studieuse et obstinée de Denis-Benjamin Viger*. Montréal: Fides, 1980.
Pelling, Henry. *Popular Politics and Society in Late Victorian Britain*. London: Macmillan, 1968.
Pentland, H. Clare. *Labour and Capital in Canada, 1650–1860*. Toronto: James Lorimer, 1981.
Perin, Roberto, "Joseph-Alexandre Baile." *DCB* 11: 42–3.
Pilon-Lê, Lise. "Le régime seigneurial au Québec: contribution à une analyse de la transition au capitalisme." *Les Cahiers du socialisme* 6 (autumn 1980): 132–69.
Plongeron, Bernard. *La vie quotidienne du clergé français au XVIIIᵉ siècle*. Paris: Hachette, 1974.
Pollard, Sidney. *The Genesis of Modern Management: A Study of the Industrial Revolution in Great Britain*. Cambridge: Harvard University Press, 1965.
- *Peaceful Conquest: the Industrialization of Europe, 1760–1970*. Oxford: Oxford University Press, 1981.
Pope, Liston. *Millhands and Preachers*. New Haven: Yale University Press, 1942.
Portelli, Hugues, *Gramsci et la question religieuse*. Paris: Éditions Anthropos, 1974.
Post, Charles. "The American Road to Capitalism." *New Left Review* 133 (May-June 1982): 30–51.
Poulantzas, Nicos. *Pouvoir politique et classes sociales*. Paris: Maspero, 1970.
Pouliot, Léon. "La difficile érection du diocèse de Montréal (1836)." *RHAF* 16 (1962): 506–35.
- "Les évêques du Bas Canada et le projet de Union." *RHAF* 8 (1954): 157–70.

- "Il y a cent ans: le démembrement de la paroisse Notre Dame." *RHAF* 19 (1965): 350–83.
- *Monseigneur Bourget et son temps*. Vol. 3. Montréal: Bellarmin. 1972.

Poutanen, Mary Anne. "For the Benefit of the Master: Gender and Apprenticeship in the Montreal Needle Trades during the Transition." Unpublished graduate paper, McGill University, Montreal Business History Project, 1984.

Probyn, John W., ed. *Systems of Land Tenure in Various Countries*. London, 1876.
- *A Remedy for the Evils of Banking*. London, 1839.

Robert, Jean-Claude. "Montréal 1821–1871. Aspects de l'urbanisation." Thèse de doctorat de 3ᵉ cycle, École des hautes études en sciences sociales, Paris, 1977.
- "Un seigneur entrepreneur, Barthélemy Joliette, et la fondation du village d'Industrie (Joliette), 1822–50," *RHAF* 26 (December 1972): 375–95.

Robertson, Roland. *The Sociological Interpretation of Religion*. New York: Schocken Books, 1970.

Rothman, David J. *The Discovery of the Asylum: Social Order and Disorder in the New Republic*. Boston: Little Brown, 1971.

Rousseau, Louis. "Jean-Baptiste Saint-Germain." *DCB* 9: 697–8.
- *La prédication à Montréal de 1800 à 1830: approche religiologique*. Montréal: Fides, 1976.

Roy, Huguette. "Paupérisme et assistance sociale à Montréal, 1832–65." MA thesis, McGill University, 1972.

Roy, Pierre-Georges. *Inventaire des concessions en fief et seigneurie*. Vol. 1. Beauceville: L'Éclaireur, 1927.

Rudé, George. *Protest and Punishment: The Story of the Social and Political Protesters transported to Australia, 1788–1868*. Oxford: Clarendon Press, 1978.

Rumilly, Robert. *Histoire de Montréal*. Vols. 1–3. Montréal: Fides, 1970–72.

Rusche, George, and Otto Kirchheimer. *Punishment and Social Structure*. New York: Columbia University Press, 1939.

Savard, Pierre, "Le catholicisme canadien-français au XIXᵉ siècle." *Social History* 7 (1971), 68–73.
- "La vie du clergé québécois au XIXᵉ siècle." *Recherches sociographiques* 8, no. 3 (September-December 1967): 259–73.

Séguin, Maurice. *La nation "canadienne" et l'agriculture (1760–1850)*. Trois-Rivières: Boréal Express, 1970.

Séguin, Normand. *Agriculture et colonisation au Québec*. Montréal: Boréal Express, 1980.

Senior, Elinor. *British Regulars in Montreal: An Imperial Garrison, 1832–54*. Montreal: McGill-Queen's University Press, 1981.

Sévigny, Daniel. "La pratique du prêt hypothécaire dans le Québec rural au 19ᵉ siècle: Le cas de Jacques Picard à Wotton (1856–1905)." Unpublished paper presented to the meetings of the Institut d'histoire de l'Amérique française, October 1983.

Smith, Donald Eugene. *Religion and Political Development.* Boston: Little Brown, 1970.

Smyth, T. Taggart. *The First Hundred Years: History of the Montreal City and District Savings Bank.* Montreal, 1946.

Soboul, Albert, *Contributions à l'histoire paysanne de la révolution française.* Paris: Éditions Sociales, 1977.

– "Du féodalisme au capitalisme: La révolution française et la problématique des voies de passage." *Pensée* 196 (1977): 61–78.

– *Problèmes paysans de la révolution, 1789–1848: Études d'histoire révolutionnaire.* Paris: Maspero, 1976.

Stedman Jones, Gareth. "Class expression versus social control? A critique of recent trends in the social history of 'leisure'." *History Workshop* 4 (autumn 1977): 162–70.

Stewart, Alan. "Structural Change and the Construction Trades in Montreal: The Carpenters, Joiners and Masons of the St. Laurent Suburb, 1800–30." Unpublished graduate paper, McGill University, 1983.

Stone, Lawrence. *The Causes of the English Revolution, 1529–1642.* London: Routledge and Kegan Paul, 1972.

Stuart, George Okill. *Reports of Cases argued and determined in the Courts of Kings Bench and in the Provincial Court of Appeals of Lower Canada.* Quebec, 1834.

Sur le féodalisme. Paris: Éditions Sociales, 1974.

Sweeny, Robert. *A Guide to the History and Records of Selected Montreal Businesses before 1947.* Montreal: Centre de recherche en histoire économique du Canada français, 1978

– "Internal Dynamics and the International Cycle: Questions of the Transition in Montreal, 1821–28." PHD thesis, McGill University, 1985.

– *Protesting History: Four Papers, 1983–84.* Montreal: Montreal Business History Project, 1985.

Sylvain, Philippe. "Un adversaire irréductible du clergé canadien-français au dix-neuvième siècle: Joseph Doutre." *Cahiers des Dix* 41 (1976): 109–25.

Takahashi, H. Kohachiro. "Place de la révolution de Meiji dans l'histoire agraire du Japon," *Revue historique* 210 (July–September 1983), 229–70.

Tackett, Timothy. *Priest and Parish in Eighteenth-Century France: A Social and Political Study of the Curés in a Diocese of Dauphiné.* Princeton: Princeton University Press, 1977.

Tassé, Joseph, ed. *Discours de Sir Georges Cartier.* Montreal, 1893.

Taylor, William B. *Landlord and Peasant in Colonial Oaxaca.* Stanford: Stanford University Press, 1972.

"La 'Terre paternelle' de Patrice Lacombe." *Le Bulletin des recherches historiques* 32, no. 1: 116–18.

Third Report of the Committee of the Legislative Assembly to whom were referred the Resolutions passed by the Legislative Assembly on the sixteenth day of June, 1850, on the subject of the seigneurial tenure. Toronto: Canadiana House, 1972.

Thompson, Edward P. *William Morris: Romantic to Revolutionary.* New York: Pantheon, 1955.

Toker, Franklin. *The Church of Notre-Dame in Montreal: An Architectural History.* Montreal: McGill-Queen's University Press, 1970.

Tremblay, Louise. "La politique des sulpiciens au XVIIᵉ et début du XVIIIᵉ siècle, 1668–1735." MA thesis, Université de Montréal, 1981.

La troisième centenaire de Saint-Sulpice. Montréal, 1941.

Trudel, Marcel. *L'Église canadienne sous le régime militaire, 1759–64.* Québec: Les Presses de l'université Laval, 1957.

– "Les Églises ont-elles souffert de la conquête?" *RHAF* 8 (1954–5): 25–71.

– *Le terrier du Saint-Laurent en 1663.* Ottawa: Editions de l'Université d'Ottawa, 1973.

Tulchinsky, Gerald J.J. "The Construction of the First Lachine Canal, 1815–26." MA thesis, McGill University, 1960.

– "John Frothingham." *DCB* 9: 288–9.

– "John Redpath." *DCB* 9: 654–5.

– *The River Barons: Montreal Businessmen and the Growth of Industry and Transportation, 1837–53.* Toronto: University of Toronto Press, 1977.

– "William Workman." *DCB* 10: 717–18.

Tulchinsky, Gerald J.J. and Brian Young. "John Young." *DCB* 10: 722–8.

Vallier, Ivan. "Religious Elites: Differentiations and Developments in Roman Catholicism." In *Elites in Latin America*, edited by S.M. Lipset and Aldo Solari. New York: Oxford, 1967.

Valois, Jacques, "François Dollier de Casson." *DCB* 2: 190–7.

Vilar, Pierre. *La Catalogne dans l'Espagne moderne: Recherches sur les fondements économiques des structures nationales.* Paris: Flammarion, 1977.

– *Une histoire en construction. Approche marxiste et problématiques conjoncturelles.* Paris: Le Seuil, 1982.

Vogler, Bernard, ed. *Les actes notariés: Source de l'histoire sociale, XVIᵉ–XIXᵉ siècles.* Strasbourg: Librairie Istra, 1979.

Wallot, Jean-Pierre. "The Lower-Canadian Clergy and the Reign of Terror (1810)." Canadian Catholic Historical Association, *Study Sessions*, 1973, 53–60.

– "La querelle des prisons dans le Bas-Canada, 1805–7." In his *Un Québec qui bougeait: Trame socio-politique du Québec au tournant du XIXᵉ siècle*, 47–105. Montréal: Boréal Express, 1973.

– "Le régime seigneurial et son abolition au Canada." In his *Un Québec qui* *bougeait: trame socio-politique au tournant du XIXe siècle*, 225–51. Montréal: Boréal Express, 1973.

– "Sewell et son projet d'asservir le clergé canadien (1801)." *RHAF* 16 (1962–3): 549–66.

Warner, Sam B. *Streetcar Suburbs: The Process of Growth in Boston, 1870–1900.* New York: Atheneum, 1973.

Watkin, Edward W. *Canada and the United States: Recollections, 1851–96.* London: Ward, Lock, 1887.

Weber, Max. *On Charisma and Institution Building.* Chicago: University of Chicago Press, 1968.

– *The Protestant Ethic and the Spirit of Capitalism.* New York: Charles Scribner's Sons, 1958.

Wrong, George. *A Canadian Manor and Its Seigneurs: The Story of a Hundred Years, 1761–1861.* Toronto: Macmillan, 1926.

Young, Brian. *George-Étienne Cartier: Montreal Bourgeois.* Kingston and Montreal: McGill-Queen's University Press, 1981.

– "John Donegani." *DCB* 9: 207–9.

– "Hugh Allan." *DCB* 11: 5–15.

– *Promoters and Politicians: The North-Shore Railways in the History of Quebec, 1854–85.* Toronto: University of Toronto Press, 1978.

Zoltvany, Yves. "Esquisse de la Coutume de Paris." *RHAF* 25 (1971): 365–84.

Index